Investigating Arthur Upfield

Investigating Arthur Upfield:
A Centenary Collection of Critical Essays

Edited by

Kees de Hoog and Carol Hetherington

**CAMBRIDGE
SCHOLARS**

PUBLISHING

Investigating Arthur Upfield:
A Centenary Collection of Critical Essays,
Edited by Kees de Hoog and Carol Hetherington

This book first published 2012

Cambridge Scholars Publishing

12 Back Chapman Street, Newcastle upon Tyne, NE6 2XX, UK

British Library Cataloguing in Publication Data
A catalogue record for this book is available from the British Library

ISBN (10): 1-4438-3452-1, ISBN (13): 978-1-4438-3452-0

This collection of critical essays on the works of Arthur Upfield was compiled and published to mark and celebrate the centenary of his arrival in Australia from England on 4 November 2011.

Arthur Upfield ca.1930

TABLE OF CONTENTS

LIST OF ILLUSTRATIONS

PREFACE

Arthur William Upfield was born in England on 1 September 1890, and first arrived in Australia at Adelaide on 4 November 1911. Apart from serving with the Australian Imperial Force in Egypt, Gallipoli, England and France during the First World War, he lived and worked in Australia for the rest of his life. He passed away on 14 February 1964.

He created fictional Detective Inspector Napoleon Bonaparte (better known as Bony) of the Queensland Police Force who features in twenty-nine crime detection novels written over forty years from the 1920s to the 1960s. Upfield also wrote another eight published books, and more than two hundred and fifty published short stories and articles. From the early 1930s he was one of the few freelance writers in Australia to make a living from his writing. Initially his books were mainly published and sold in the United Kingdom and Australia, but he struck gold in 1943 when the Bony novels began to be published in the United States. He is now recognised as the first Australian professional writer of crime detection novels.

So far as we, the editors, are aware the centenary of Upfield's birth in 1990 was not marked or celebrated in any way, and we hope to atone for that omission by compiling and publishing this collection of critical essays on his works. They are substantial literary analyses, all written by academics or scholars, and not simply reviews of his books or articles for "glossies" designed to promote his books.

We found a few essays from the 1970s, and some more from the 1980s; the number more than doubled in the 1990s and increased again in the 2000s. Of the twenty-two articles selected, thirteen were written in Australia, eight are from the United States, and one is from the United Kingdom. Two from Australia are extracts from Ph.D. theses, and have not been published previously.

They are presented in chronological order of publication to give readers a sense of the evolution of criticism about Upfield's works. The first, an epitaph to Upfield by Pamela Ruskin written in 1964, is included to provide some background for readers not familiar with his works.

Cambridge Scholars Publishing guidelines for manuscripts required us to convert references and notes for most of the articles to comply with the *Chicago Manual of Style*, and to make some other formatting changes. Some contributors chose to revise their essays before they were reprinted, and we added references to some of the earlier essays. Otherwise we corrected only typing and other obvious errors. To preserve the integrity of the articles, we did not standardise spelling or references.

We are indebted to the authors who wrote the articles in this collection. Without them, of course, this anthology would never have been conceived. Also, we are grateful for the permissions to republish the articles from the copyright owners and previous publishers.

The articles we initially considered for inclusion were identified from many sources that include *AustLit*[1] and bibliographies in various books and essays. Copies were obtained with the help of many sources, but in particular we acknowledge the National Library of Australia, the State Library of Western Australia, the State Library of Victoria, the University of Queensland Library, and the Reid Library at the University of Western Australia.

We thank Cambridge Scholars Publishing for publishing this book, and also the board of Bonaparte Holdings Pty Ltd, the manager of Arthur Upfield's estate, for endorsing this project.

                                                                  Kees de Hoog

---

[1] *Austlit: The Australian Literature Resource*, http://www.austlit.edu.au/.

INTRODUCTION

In her obituary tribute to Arthur Upfield, the first essay in this collection, journalist Pamela Ruskin, Upfield's long-time friend and literary agent, poses the question as to "whether death will bring him the sort of recognition he always hoped would come to him in Australia". This book aims to provide an answer to her question: its intention is to present a selection of responses to Upfield's work that are serious and scholarly, originating both in Australia and overseas. The essays, apart from Ruskin's epitaph, date from 1974, a decade after Upfield's death, and the first Australian contributions are generally later than the American—an implicit comment on the differences between the literary and cultural environments within the two countries at the time.

The absence of serious critical attention to Upfield's work during his life-time, alluded to by Ruskin, is confirmed by the dates of the essays. Upfield was outspoken about his lack of recognition as a writer, which he attributed to the snobbery and pretension of a closed literary elite. There was bad blood between himself and the influential husband and wife duo of critic Nettie Palmer and writer Vance Palmer. Nettie Palmer reviewed Upfield's early novel *The Sands of Windee* dismissively and Upfield never forgave her. In a letter to his friend, fellow author J.K. Ewers, Upfield commented "one day I'll cut her throat".[1] Upfield did resort to violence in this regard but it was fictional. The Palmers are savagely lampooned in one of the Bony mysteries, *An Author Bites the Dust*, although here it is Vance Palmer (thinly disguised as Mervyn Blake) who is murdered by his wife.

Richard Nile ("Pulp Fiction" in this volume) rehearses the plot of this novel as a prelude to his examination of the role of the Palmers and others in their attempts to establish a "national aesthetic".[2] Nile's essay is one of the first to draw attention to the "tensions that exist between the makers of a national literature ... and popularisers such as Upfield who wrote novels

---

[1] Arthur Upfield, Letter to J.K. Ewers, 17 July 1934, Archive of Patricia Kotai-Ewers.
[2] Richard Nile, "Pulp Fiction: Popular Culture and Literary Reputation", 144 in this volume.

as a commercial enterprise;"[3] it contextualises the deliberate eschewing of popular culture by the literary establishment in 1930s and 1940s Australia. This was not personal; it was neither specifically directed at nor confined to Upfield and indeed it was to continue into the 1970s as attempts to establish a national critical culture, and later the study of Australian literature in universities, gained momentum. Stephen Knight in his pioneering work on Australian crime fiction has also commented on the "exclusion of popular culture from the academy". He points to the "academic and critical treatment of the genre" in Australia, observing that "Local literary historians have not made crime fiction, being a popular form, part of their literary history".[4]

We hope that this selection sheds some light on the extent and nature of critical responses to Upfield over time, demonstrates the type of recognition he has received and highlights the way in which different preoccupations and critical trends have dealt with his work. Upfield's fictional detective, the mixed-race Detective Inspector Napoleon Bonaparte, is the principal focus of all the essays. Yet while Bony is always centre stage, the types of critical enquiry vary across time and place. The representation of race and nation preoccupies the Australian critics until quite recently when a new interest in critical reception, readership and publishing history emerges in Australian studies; American popular culture and postcolonial scholars, on the other hand, engage more with the novels as fiction, exploring themes more traditionally the province of literary criticism.

The first Australian essays in this selection approach Upfield not from a literary but from anthropological or sociological standpoints, focusing on his depiction of Aboriginal culture and the attitudes expressed in his work. Heather Parish's 1974 essay discusses prevalent and changing Australian racial attitudes as expressed in Upfield's works; it was published not in a literary journal but in *Issue: South Australian Journal of Social, Political and Cultural Comment*. Similarly, Basil Sansom's semi-playful address to a gathering of academic anthropologists in 1980 was published in *Anthropology News*. However, even from the 1980s, when popular and genre fiction begin to attract academic attention, most Australian writing about Upfield reflects a preoccupation with historical and racial issues. Kay Torney's essay "Terra Nullius: Bony in the Deathspace" (1996) concentrates on those novels which portray Aboriginal life, culture and characters and provide material for discussion of genocide, child-stealing

---

[3] Nile, "Pulp Fiction", 140.
[4] Stephen Knight, "The Case of the Missing Genre: In Search of Australian Crime Fiction," *Southerly* 48.3 (1988): 241.

and "cultural vandalism"; the novels are read primarily as documents of cultural and historical interest. Two other essays presented here have a similar focus—Tamsin Donaldson, in 1991, and more recently Russell West, in 2003, each compare Indigenous author Sally Morgan's *My Place* with Upfield novels as examples of Indigenous detection. Considered together their essays work off each other in interesting ways: the novels they discuss are different, *The Barrakee Mystery* and *Bony and the Black Virgin* respectively, and these are read against different temporal backgrounds, but both essays are concerned with "the capacity of an Indigenous investigator to read Australian history for traces of crimes hidden by the passage of time".[5] West gives more emphasis to fictional conventions and narrative techniques, but both essays essentially read the novels as foils for the social, national and racial issues they expose. Race and nation are also key concerns in Glen Ross's contribution; he examines the Bony series as narratives of nation, particularly the way in which the character of Bony enables Upfield to mediate the gulf in the national psyche between black and white cultures. However, in his consideration of Bony as a cross-cultural mediator Ross moves closer to an assessment of the novels as products of the detective genre, noting that "in the end, however, Bony was simply a textual device used to help sell books, and Upfield's correspondence reveals a readiness to transform the character into whatever the reading public might desire".[6]

While a painful coming-to-terms with an exploitative colonial past has dominated the work of Australian scholars and critics, all eight of the twenty-two essays in this volume which originate from America focus more on Upfield's achievements as a practitioner of the craft of fiction within a particular, well-defined fictional genre and in comparison to similar authors in other literatures. America was much earlier than Australia in recognising popular and genre fiction, including crime fiction, as legitimate subjects for serious discussion and study: two of the earliest of the essays here, John Cawelti's "Murder in the Outback" (1977) and Ray Browne's "The Frontier Heroism of Arthur Upfield" (1986), are both by established scholars of popular literature. The themes addressed in the American essays include many that are traditional in literary studies: the concept of the frontier (Browne), themes of time and nostalgia (Coe), and the portrayal of women (Howe). They also look forward to the widespread and strong interest in Upfield as an early creator of a popular fictional convention—the "ethnic detective"—a favourite subject of study for both

---

[5] Russell West, "Sally Morgan's *My Place* as Australian Indigenous Detective Narrative," 177 in this volume.
[6] Glen Ross, "Bony as Grotesque", 121 in this volume.

anthropologists and literary critics in the crime fiction and postcolonial studies areas: James Pierson's essay is a case in point, as are Murray S. Martin's, Marilyn Rye's and Margaret Lewis's.

Returning to the Australian contributions, the final three essays in the volume can usefully be grouped together and to some extent share Richard's Nile's earlier focus on the political economy of literature: readership, reception and reputation, and publishing history. John and Marie Ramsland offer a re-assessment of Upfield's works for their "historicity of a disappearing culture";[7] my own "In Their Different Ways, Classics" is a plea for their recognition as fine examples of their literary genre. However both these contributions, together with "Bony at Home and Abroad", are also concerned with readership and marketing in both North America and, in translation, in Europe, particularly contemporary France.

Bony has been the key to Upfield's success. An unlikely, even audacious creation in the social climate of 1929, he has continued to exercise an imaginative hold over generations of readers: speculation about the basis for his name and character, both in real life and literature, is seemingly endless. Three pieces in this selection focus particularly on him. Travis Lindsey's thesis chapter "The Genesis of Bony" looks behind some of the popular myths surrounding Upfield's creation, paying careful attention to archival material and possible literary antecedents. The other two, in contrast to the mostly academic discussions in this volume, are responses to Bony from creative writers. One is non-fiction, a personal acknowledgement by American writer Tony Hillerman of Bony as the source of inspiration for his own highly-regarded fiction featuring part-Navajo detectives Joe Leaphorn and Jimmy Chee. The second is a short story, one of a series of several by Australian author Mudrooroo, featuring another fictional Indigenous policeman, Detective Inspector Watson Holmes Jackamara of the Black Cockatoo Dreaming—at once a recognition and a criticism of Upfield's character. Numerous themes and concerns expressed throughout the other pieces in this volume—questions of authority, legitimacy, cultural appropriation—come into play here in contrasting these two pieces. Tony Hillerman, like Upfield, is a non-indigenous creator of an indigenous character; Mudrooroo is a writer who claimed Indigenous heritage but whose own claims of indigeneity have been called into question.

For an author commonly regarded as under-recognised, Upfield has received a surprisingly large amount of attention in academic circles. This

---

[7] John Ramsland and Marie Ramsland, "Re-assessing Arthur W. Upfield's Napoleon Bonaparte Detective Fiction," 222 in this volume.

selection of twenty-two essays from the many published in the forty years since Upfield's death is a testimony to the interest his work continues to provoke from a wide range of view points and across several countries. It was not possible to include some essays written in French and German. And although we have been unable to include anything by Stephen Knight because the broad thematic style of his work does not lend itself to the format of the present collection, we would like to pay tribute to the importance of his contribution to the field. Knight was the first literary academic in Australia to comment on Arthur Upfield's work. His 1988 essay on crime fiction, "The Case of the Missing Genre", revealed a "vigorous area of literary culture" ignored by scholars and literary historians. This work and its sequel, *Continent of Mystery* (1997), paved the way for further discussions of mystery writers by making them academically respectable.

There has never been any question about Arthur Upfield's popularity as a writer; his acclaim is widespread and remarkably long-lived; he still has a significant readership world-wide, as several of the articles here show. Detective Inspector Napoleon Bonaparte will almost certainly retain a permanent place in the gallery of famous fictional detectives. In 1963, Upfield was quoted as asking "What is my place in Australian literature?" and answering "I haven't one. I'm not literary".[8]

But concepts of the literary vary and change across time and place. We hope this volume, published a century after his arrival in Australia, demonstrates that Upfield can be considered "a literary man", with a place not only in the international annals of crime fiction but also in the literary and cultural history of the country he came to love so passionately.

Carol Hetherington
The University of Queensland

---

[8] "He Won't be a Literary Man", *Readers Review: For Members of the Readers Book Club* 10.12 (October 1963): 1.

ARTHUR UPFIELD:
AN EPITAPH

PAMELA RUSKIN

"To be a success in Australia, you must work somewhere else; for Australians are constitutionally unable to appreciate their own creative workers unless they are living abroad or dead. At present, I'm not interested in the former condition and I'm not really in a hurry to achieve the latter one."

Australia's ace mystery writer, Arthur Upfield, wrote that in a letter to me, six years ago. Now he has fulfilled the latter condition too, dying alone at his home in Bowral of a heart disease that had wrecked his health for the last four or five years.[1] It remains to be seen whether death will bring him the sort of recognition he always hoped would come to him in Australia.

During his last years, Upfield did, in fact, acquire a great measure of the fame he had battled for so hard and so long. Consistently good reviews welcomed most of his new books, but, in contrast to the superlatives that were lavished on his work in America and Western Germany, and even in Great Britain, the more restrained praise offered by Australian reviewers, interlaced with a due appraisal of his limitations, seemed to him rather half-hearted. He resented very much the attitude that because he wrote mystery stories, he wasn't to be considered a serious writer.

Yet, above all, Upfield was an honest man; a craftsman who knew his own faults as a writer, admitted them freely and strove hard to correct them. He was human enough to dislike attention being drawn to them in print.

Arthur Upfield's success rested on one main plank. He created a detective whom Anthony Boucher, crime editor of the *New York Times*, called the most original fictional detective of the last twenty years.[2] He

---

[1] Ed.: Upfield died on 14 February 1964.
[2] Anthony Boucher, "Review of *The Bushman Who Came Back*," *New York Times*, 23 June 1957, section 7: 18.

was the suave, urbane half-aboriginal Detective Inspector Napoleon Bonaparte who combined in himself the sensitivity and almost mystic intuition of his aboriginal mother, with the sophistication and educated intelligence of his white father.

It was Upfield's constant delight that his readers all over the world reacted to "Bony" much as a wider reading public had reacted to Sherlock Holmes, and thought of him as a real person. He received hundreds of letters addressed to "Bony", and even newspapermen, much to his amusement, would question him closely to find out more about this blue-eyed, courteous sleuth who bucked authority, never lost a case, and treated women as though they were all princesses.

Bonaparte was, as Upfield told me very often, a real person. He was based on the half-caste son of a station owner, on whose property in the Darling Downs the young Arthur worked. This man was, like Bony, university-trained and wholly civilised, yet he too felt the call of his mother's tribe, and possessed many of its skills. Bony is thus four-fifths fact and only one-fifth fiction.

Whatever the balance, Bony was the kingpin in the structure of Arthur's success. He knew it and was never tempted to write a book in any other form, although he did write four romantic novels in his early days, before Bony was conceived.

What sort of a man was Arthur Upfield?

He was a tough, irascible, wiry man. He had slate-coloured eyes, a thin trap of a mouth and ears like jug handles. He spoke almost through clenched teeth and was thus the despair of radio interviewers. His truculence hid a good deal of shyness. He knew Australia as few know it to-day. His Australia was not the Australia of big cities, which he believed were pretty much the same everywhere and which he loathed anyway. He loved the outback; the hot thirsty plains baking under the sun, the endless quiet of the bush night, the roistering companionship of the small country pub, where weeks of hard-earned wages went down the hatch in one glorious bender, ending in oblivion and a headache.

To meet, he was as dinkum an Aussie as you'd find anywhere; yet he was an Englishman. According to his own account, he was the black sheep of a yeoman Sussex family. He felt smothered by the prospect of the respectable white collar life that awaited him there, and utterly refused to settle down. Armed only with an overweening passion for Dickens and H.G. Wells, implanted in him by a solicitor uncle, and a fierce independence, Upfield was shipped off to Australia with his family's relieved blessing and some letters of introduction which he disdained to use. Immediately he fell hopelessly in love with the outback. "I clung to it till my teeth fell out," he said later.

As the years passed, Upfield's knowledge of Australia grew. He worked a mule team and was a boundary rider on a camel station in Western Australia. He dug opals at Coober Pedy, carried his swag on a bicycle without pedals all over Queensland and New South Wales, picked grapes, sheared sheep and took a job as a shearers' cook while, encouraged by the owner's wife, he wrote his first book, *The House of Cain.*

In those days, every swaggie and station hand knew and loved the poems of Banjo Paterson, Henry Lawson and Adam Lindsay Gordon, and would recite and talk about their favourites round the camp fire at night. This, Upfield was to say very often, was the true voice of Australia, and it showed a pride in the writers who belonged to Australia which is less evident to-day.

After serving in the Australian Imperial Force for more than four years of World War I, Arthur was more than ever in love with his adopted country. It was about this time that he started writing, but his first novel wasn't published until 1928. Just before Christmas, 1963, his thirty-second novel was on the bookstalls. In those thirty-five years, Upfield worked and travelled, and battered his way to success. He wrote about Australia for *World Wide Magazine.* He was a contributor to *Walkabout* from the first issue which came out in November, 1934, at a time when Ernestine Hill, Bill Harney, Donald Thompson and Ion Idriess were also writing for it. Even before this, he had become a "special" writer for the Melbourne *Herald* and even wrote a racing serial for it, aided by the paper's racing staff.

If in his youth he was hard-drinking, hard-swearing and truculent, in his advanced years he mellowed considerably. Underneath his prickly exterior, he was a shy, affectionate and kindly man, who never forgot a kindness and never knew how to hold a grudge. He said of himself: "I'm like a summer fire. I flare up quickly but I never persist with hard feeling." He had a wry, dead-pan sense of humour. Typical of this was a comment in one of the last letters I had from him: "I never use bad language. I only use Australian words!" He could always laugh at himself, uneasily signing autographs in a city store or submitting to radio and T.V. questions with forthright but agonised candour.

He was always rather cagey about his age. In a letter written in the late '50s he refers to an article in which I had said he was in his late sixties. "Hardly the late sixties," he wrote, "not yet!" But as *Who's Who* and other reference books give his birth date as 1888, he was every bit of that. He was sixty when he led a five-thousand-mile expedition through the

Kimberleys, in 1948,[3] for the Australian Geographic Society.[4]

Although his books were being published, early success eluded his grasp, and the bitterness of those first years of failure stayed with him always. When success did come, it came from abroad. America had just entered the Second World War, and thousands of G.I.s were packed off to Australia. There was a tremendous surge of interest in the country "down-under", about which few Americans knew anything at all.

Upfield's agent offered his work to Doubleday and Company, and they snapped up six titles overnight. Mothers, sisters, aunts and cousins of G.I.'s eagerly welcomed Upfield and Bony, and he achieved best-seller status within a very short time. Americans at home saw Australia through Upfield's eyes, and felt they knew the sort of towns where their boys were stationed.

It has been said that Arthur Upfield's descriptive writing is so vivid and alive that it gives a truer picture of Australia and Australians than does that of many of our more literary writers. Although he was a crime writer, his plots were generally weak, but his descriptions of the outback and the odd characters with whom he peopled it were superb. Maybe it was the Australia of yesterday, without the great sprawling cities and the vast population growth caused by post-war migration, but it was the Australia he knew.

It is no coincidence that critics all over the world acclaimed his backgrounds, with their sprinkling of bush lore, aboriginal customs and marvellous revelation of what he liked to call "the book of the bush". For example, his story of a lake, Lake Victoria in fact, which he told in *Death of a Lake*, and of animals and birds desperately trying to get to the last of the water, while dead bodies pile up in their thousands, is masterly. As almost every critic remarked, "The lake is the real hero of this novel". Upfield really saw this lake dry up, when he was working for a Mr. James Hole on a property above Wilcannia, and he never forgot the horror of it. When the book was published, Mr. Hole, to whom it was dedicated, was able to state unequivocally that nothing Upfield wrote about it was exaggerated.

His story of Broome and the death throes of the pearling industry was another outstanding success both here and in the States. It was *The Widows of Broome*, and the first of his books to appear under the

---

[3] Ed.: It had been generally accepted that Upfield was born on 1 September 1888. A check of the records in England made about 25 years after his death revealed he was born in 1890, so he was 57 during the Kimberley expedition.
[4] See "Australian Geographical Society Tour to the North-West (Division) of Western Australia," *Walkabout* 30.5 (October 1948): 29.

Heinemann colophon, after his break with Angus and Robertson. It told readers of a colourful corner of Australia, quite different and virtually unknown to them. This of course was the essential ingredient of Upfield's popularity. Almost every "Bony" adventure took readers to a new part of Australia, where Upfield had lived and worked during some part of his rolling stone existence.

By 1953, the elusive fruits of successful authorship were coming to him, and he was able to say that he was one of a meagre four or five Australian authors living wholly from the proceeds of his books. For this he gave credit to the United States, and he was and still is, as far as I know, the only foreigner to be admitted as a full member of the Mystery Writers' Guild of America. Late in 1962, he showed me proudly a set of cuff-links bearing the M.W.G. insignia, which had just been sent to him as a tribute to his contribution as a mystery writer. He was truly touched by this and he told me again of his ambition to be able to accept their invitation to the annual banquet of the Guild. He was never able to do so.

In the 1950s, the rest of the world interested in Australia became interested in Upfield. Western Germany published almost every title of his, first in hard covers and then in paperbacks and in serial form. Italy, Denmark, Finland, Holland, Argentina, Mexico and even Japan sought translation rights and published many titles. He was almost embarrassed when he received letters from learned German professors who wished to discuss with him details of aboriginal lore and to learn from him more of its *mystique*. Anyway his health was not, at this time, good enough to embark on so serious a correspondence.

About 10 years ago, several of his books were turned into a series of radio plays under the title, *Man of Two Tribes*. Two well-known Australians were concerned in this. One was actor Frank Thring, somewhat miscast as "Bony", and Morris West, then head of the radio production firm that produced the series, who was to become an even more successful author than Upfield.

Upfield used the Kimberleys as the background for another successful novel, *Cake in the Hatbox*. In the last few years he lived in Airey's Inlet, then Bermagui and finally Bowral. All these locations he incorporated into books. His new-found prosperity didn't affect his way of life greatly, for his tastes remained simple. But one extravagance did give him considerable pleasure. Around 1952, when he was living at Airey's Inlet, he bought himself a second-hand but shiningly beautiful Daimler, which he kept in immaculate condition. He didn't drive it a great deal, but when he had to make a trip to Melbourne, he would dress himself up in his best suit and an old-fashioned grey homburg and set off, sitting behind the wheel as proudly as any teenager with his first "bomb". He would park it at a garage on the outskirts of the city and continue the rest of the way in a taxi. He wouldn't risk his precious car in the "traffic inferno". After his first serious heart attack, he sold the Daimler rather sadly.

The swagman who pushed a bike across the dusty tracks of the outback became a much-sought-after author—or storyteller, as he preferred it. But he was a rebel to the last. Like "Bony", he hated authority and never bowed to a boss. He thought writers should belong to a union to prevent their being exploited. Like "Bony", he put women on a pedestal and treated them with old-fashioned courtesy. When he met one that didn't belong on that pedestal, he merely said she was an exception. He was a religious man, but a nonconformist in his beliefs.

When time has blurred to-day's picture of Australian writing, will Upfield survive? His style was often bad and his plots were slow. He despised the literary graces and what he termed the "pretentiousness of the literary snobs". He wrote for the "ordinary people of Australia", and the ordinary people will still read his books for many years. In Upfield's work they will find the empty, undeveloped land which bred the tough, hard-living outback men and women he admired so much and wrote about so well.

Now Detective-Inspector Napoleon Bonaparte has solved his last case and laid away his kurdaitcha boots for ever. He has, I think, joined the immortals of detective fiction. Arthur Upfield would have asked no more of posterity.

First Published in *Walkabout* 31.5 (1 May 1964): 33-38. Every reasonable effort was made to trace the copyright and publishing rights owner(s) of this article without success; they are invited to contact the publisher. The references were added by the editors.

BONY AND THE COLOUR QUESTION

HEATHER PAISH

Arthur Upfield came to Australia from England in 1911, when he was twenty-three.[1] In the eighteen years between his arrival and the publication of the first of his Napoleon Bonaparte books he worked as boundary rider, cattle drover, opal gouger, dog fence patroller and manager of a camel station. He also came to have a wide knowledge of the Australian outback and the Australian Aboriginal.

His books are interesting for their good detective yarns, and also for the reflection of attitudes to Aboriginals in the years between 1929 and the last book, published in 1966 two years after his death.

I've noted which attitudes changed during this period and in which direction, and which ones survived that quarter century unaltered. The light-hearted approach to tribal rioting seen in *The Sands of Windee* (1931) could not be written today: "Stop 'em? Why, I wouldn't 'ave stopped 'em for a hundred quid! It's the best bleedin' dog-fight I seen for years."[2] Nor even the following from *Bony Buys a Woman* (1957):

> "Been hell and low water down the abos' camp. Best riot come ever. You oughta see some of 'em. Rex is dragging an ear over his shoulder. Sarah's lost half her teeth somewhere. Meena got hanks of her hair pulled out ... Bodies lying all over the joint when me and the boss and Arnold got there. Crikey! If only I had a movie camera. Been thinking a long time of getting one."[3]

Less in fashion now is the belief which Upfield seems to share that the actual blackness of the skin is both an inborn cause of inferiority in the white man's world and superiority in the black man's skills. In *The Barrakee Mystery* (1929), Bony speaks about Ralph Thornton:

---

[1] It had been generally accepted that Upfield was born on 1 September 1888. A check of the records in England made about 25 years after his death revealed he was born in 1890, so he was 21 when he arrived in Australia on 4 November 1911.

[2] Arthur Upfield, *The Sands of Windee* (Sydney: Angus & Robertson, 1958), 104.

[3] Arthur Upfield, *Bony Buys a Woman* (London: Heinemann, 1957), 114.

"Like many half-caste children—even like myself—the baby was white of
skin. For years the black strain in his blood was held in abeyance by his
upbringing and education ... I watched the growing change in the lad ... I
saw the growing love of colour in his clothes, I noted how quickly his
college accent dropped from him. ... the young man picked up the art of
tracking with remarkable ease. ... Even during the few months I have been
at Barrakee, I have seen Ralph's skin slowly darkening ..."[4]

Speaking about Bony himself in *The Sands of Windee* Upfield says:

He had been born with white man's blood in him and, as is sometimes the
case, a skin as white as his father's. From an early age he had felt his
superiority over the little boys at the mission station, most of whom were
black, or that dark putty colour there is no mistaking.[5]

At the age of eighteen Bony fell in love with a white girl, and then
"[w]ith the inevitability of fate his long dead black mother claimed him
from the grave, claimed him and held him ... the black strain in him ... the
colour mark" physically crept up from his legs to cover him completely.
He gave up his girl and his projected career as a doctor and took to the
bush, where he married a half caste like himself. "Yet always he was
acutely aware of his inferiority to the full-blood white man": this despite
his becoming a detective-inspector with a record of infallibility.[6] This is a
view that Upfield for all his liberal feelings could not shake off, for even
as late as *The Mystery of Swordfish Reef* (1939) Bony's anger is described
in terms of his mother's blood taking charge of him, making him one with
her and her people. "Bony's face became jet black in colour."[7]

In *The Sands of Windee* are other widely accepted myths about mixed-
blood Aboriginals:

His mother had given him the spirit of nomadism, the eye sight of her race,
the passion for hunting; from his father he had inherited in overwhelming
measure the white man's calm and comprehensive reasoning ...[8]

Or again when Bony's wife Marie says of their eldest son Charles, who's
about to start university: "like you and me and all of us the bush will get

---

[4] Arthur Upfield, *The Barrakee Mystery* (London: Heinemann, 1965), 300-302.

[5] Upfield, *The Sands of Windee*, 227.

[6] Upfield, *The Sands of Windee*, 227.

[7] Arthur Upfield, *The Mystery of Swordfish Reef* (Sydney: Angus & Robertson, 1939), 204.

[8] Upfield, *The Sands of Windee*, 1-2.

him in the end. It's in our blood and can't be resisted."[9]

This particular attitude was easier to hold when Upfield was writing because most Aboriginals were living in country towns and locations. The strong movement to the cities had not begun. Despite Bony's intelligence and competence in the white man's world there is also strong disapproval from all sorts of characters, of any sort of marriage or sexual relationship between black and white. Black must marry black, white white and half-caste half-caste. Although Upfield says there are regional differences in attitude to this (mixed marriages being more accepted in North Queensland and the Northern Territory than in western New South Wales "the home of the blue blood squattocracy"), he himself seems to come down strongly on the side of disapproval. In *The Barrakee Mystery*, the love of Ralph Thornton for the Aboriginal girl Nellie Wanting is regarded with sincere horror by his squatter relatives:

> The very last thing Dugdale had expected of young Thornton was that he should have forgotten his colour. ... The thought, so dreadful to him, was that the boy's lips, which had touched Nellie Wanting's mouth, would likely enough be pressed to those of Kate Flinders, the loveliest and purest girl in Australia, before that day was wholly done. ...
> "Cannot you see for yourself that the terrible part of the affair is that Nellie Wanting is black?"[10]

The material evidence suggests that Upfield does not share the squatters' prejudices but in *The Will of the Tribe* (1962) it is likely that he shared Bony's feelings about Tessa who hurried away from a western education to her tribal lover:

> Bony thrilled, knowing that Tessa had surrendered to the elfin call of her people, and had put from her the slowly built influences of white assimilation, even as she had discarded her white women's clothes.[11]

If the above attitudes have been modified to some degree by the passage of time, there are others that have continued relatively unchanged —paternalism for example. There is the paternalism of the charity-givers: "Mrs. Cotton wouldn't have any old rags in her room. Soon as anything got raggety, off it went to the blacks' camp."[12] There is the paternalism of the adoption system, *The Bone Is Pointed* (1938):

---

[9] Upfield, *The Sands of Windee*, 79.

[10] Upfield, *The Barrakee Mystery*, 171-172.

[11] Arthur Upfield, *The Will of the Tribe* (London: Heinemann, 1962), 215.

[12] Arthur Upfield, *The Widows of Broome* (London: Heinemann, 1967), 97.

Jimmy Partner was a splendid product of "beginning on them young". He was a living example, showing to what degree of civilisation an Australian Aboriginal can reach if given the opportunity. He sat before this table upright and mentally alert. He ate with no less politeness than did the woman who had reared him that he might be companion to her own child ... He spoke better than many a white hand ... He was the crown of achievement set upon the heads of Mary Gordon and her dead husband.[13]

But within a few hundred words of these observations, Upfield has Jimmy Partner speaking in the same obsequious pidgin as the boys who had spent their whole lives in the camp. "Things is getting dry Johnny Boss ... [h]e come along half hour ago to say that big feller black-feller p'liceman come to Opal Town."[14] In 1938 at least Upfield only half believed his own words about the possibilities of Aboriginal equality. It is clear however that Upfield does not share the paternalism of the academic Professor of Anthropology in *Murder Must Wait* (1953). He and his wife, who introduces herself as Mrs. Marlo-Jones, Dip.Ed., treat Bony as some non-human member of a fascinating species. "Good heavens! Where did you get it?" he says of Bony to his wife.[15] Bony observes later:

"Thought I was a new flower I believe. Wanted me to stay for a billy of tea and a slice of brownie ... her idea of a smoko tea suitable for a half caste ... Guess to what I owe my self-respect, the facility with which I thumb my nose at superior people."[16]

Aborigines still experience these attitudes, perhaps not in such a crude form, in Europeans who treat them as objects of research.

The picture of the Law's attitude is of that familiar confusion of discrimination, over zealousness in some things and winking at others. In many areas particularly in the outback these attitudes persist. In *Winds of Evil* (1937) a police sergeant is trying to find a murderer. On seeing Bony for the first time he says: "Hey you! Come here! ... I don't stand no nonsense from nigs and half castes. You're a likely looking bird to have done this last crime."[17] In *The Sands of Windee* a policeman states his policy as "I never interfere with 'em unless they go a-murdering".[18] And later in the same book Bony talks about that still-vexed question of tribal

---

[13] Arthur Upfield, *The Bone Is Pointed* (London: Angus & Robertson, 1966), 71.

[14] Upfield, *The Bone Is Pointed*, 68, 72.

[15] Arthur Upfield, *Murder Must Wait* (London: Heinemann, 1953), 14.

[16] Upfield, *Murder Must Wait*, 26-27.

[17] Arthur Upfield, *Winds of Evil* (London: Hamilton, 1939), 76-77.

[18] Upfield, *The Sands of Windee*, 63.

killings: "The details of tribal battles are lost in the excitement ... which is extreme, and, since it was not deliberately planned murder, the law passed it over."[19] In *The Widows of Broome* (1950) a full blood dies from sniffing petrol fumes. The local policeman says:

> "Should be made a flogging matter for a native to be found drunk on booze or anything else. The old days and the old ways were good. I'd flog more and imprison less."[20]

The Final Solution

Upfield examines several of the alternative "solutions" but seems to hope as Daisy Bates did, that the Aboriginal race would simply disappear from existence and in that way solve the "problem". In *The Bone Is Pointed* Bony goes to an isolated property which is the tribal land of the Kalchut tribe. The first white settlers, the Gordons, had drawn up a charter with the chief (Upfield speaks of chiefs and headmen as if they were African tribes) of the tribe in the late nineteenth century, a charter in which both groups pledged non-interference with the other. But by 1938 this had been eroded by various events and pressures. A white shepherd, for instance, had raped a lubra and been killed by the tribe, the Aboriginals themselves had rejected some of the old ways by wearing clothes and working on other stations, and the Gordons, despite their good intentions did not avoid paternalism. They banked and doled out the money earned by the tribe, and said things like: "some of their customs, of course, we Gordons have had to frown upon, gradually getting them prohibited."[21]

In *Murder Must Wait* Bony visits a mission settlement, an extremely enlightened one even by today's standards, with stores, a school, hospital, church and streets of houses; and Aboriginals in status jobs (nurse, watch maker, teacher, storekeeper) while the council of "headmen" decide internal discipline. The white Reverend Superintendent makes the important decisions. He rules that no children can go on walkabout during term time, that no white men can come on to the settlement without his permission, and that adults are to attend church twice on Sundays. The underlying condescension of it all shows in these words:

> "I roused the headmen from their indifference to exert again their old influence and power ... *of course, under my general supervision.* Thus the

---

[19] Upfield, *The Sands of Windee*, 111.

[20] Upfield, *The Widows of Broome*, 184.

[21] Upfield, *The Bone Is Pointed*, 118.

people were brought under the kind of discipline they understand, and they became keenly interested in the *least obnoxious* of the corroborees and the folk dancing."[22]

Bony is at first impressed by the settlement but later reflects:

> Could that ambition (to give back to the Aborigine his traditions and self-respect) be realised by encouraging the old practices only as far as approved by white law and when the white influence had brought the black fellow to a condition of spiritual chaos?[23]

In *Bushranger of the Skies* (1940) a half caste called Rex McPherson gives a preview of the Black Power approach:

> "I am going to force the whites to respect me. ... I am going to make them acknowledge me as an equal. A dirty half caste, eh? Well I'm going to prove to the world that a half caste is as clever as any white man. ... I am going to get McPherson station and add all this open country to it. After that I'll join the Illprinka to the Wantella people. I'll train the bucks to be soldiers. I'll arm them with rifles. And then if the government sends police or soldiers against me I'll engage in a war. ... And even if I lose in the end I'll go down in history as the man who avenged the Aborigines."[24]

Rex was no more successful in creating a unified Aboriginal movement than de-tribalised Aboriginal leaders are today. Significantly he was killed by a full blood who saw the old ways as the only ways, and Rex as "the dangerous fire".

Upfield also considers the policy that has come to form the basis of the current Australian government approach: that of money and bureaucracy. In *Murder Must Wait* Bony reflects on Frederick Wilmot, a surly lazy part-Aboriginal filled with "subdued anger".[25] "Too much money, and too much spoiling by government and societies interested in Aboriginal welfare produced too many Frederick Wilmots."[26] However, in *Bony and the Black Virgin* (1959) Bony sees the gulf between the new expectations and their realisation:

> Tonto [an educated full-blood] was just the average young Aborigine in

---

[22] Upfield, *Murder Must Wait*, 134. Emphasis added.

[23] Upfield, *Murder Must Wait*, 165.

[24] Arthur Upfield, *Bushranger of the Skies* (London: Angus & Robertson, 1963), 220.

[25] Upfield, *Murder Must Wait*, 66.

[26] Upfield, *Murder Must Wait*, 67.

this era, when much money is spent on their education—and barriers erected to prevent them from using it.[27]

And Rex McPherson, the black power man, says:

> "Money! Money can't make our skins white, can it? Money can't even prevent us being insulted, regarded either as dangerous animals or pet poodles. ... We can't mix on equality with white people. They won't let us."[28]

Upfield tries to answer Rex McPherson's angry questions and assertions with his creation of the romantic character of Napoleon Bonaparte. Here he is reflecting on the colour bar question in *The Bone Is Pointed*:

> "In this country colour is no bar to a keen man's progress providing that he has twice the ability of his rivals. ... That I stand midway between the black man, who makes fire with a stick, and the white men, who kill women and babies with bombs and machine guns, should not be accounted against me."[29]

First Published in *Issue: South Australian Journal of Social, Political and Cultural Comment* 4.15 (December 1974): 33-38. Reprinted with permission of the Worker's Educational Association of South Australia. All the references were added, and some minor changes were made by the editors.

---

[27] Arthur Upfield, *Bony and the Black Virgin* (London: Heinemann, 1959), 166.

[28] Upfield, *Bushranger of the Skies*, 219.

[29] Upfield, *The Bone Is Pointed*, 52.

MURDER IN THE OUTBACK: ARTHUR W. UPFIELD

JOHN G. CAWELTI

Though our stereotypical image of the setting of the classical detective story will no doubt remain what W. H. Auden called "Mayhem Parva"— the English country house and village—the genre has been adapted to a variety of climes and locales. American examples obviously spring to mind—the New York City of S.S. Van Dine, Ellery Queen and Emma Lathen, the California of Hammett, Chandler, and Macdonald—but in actuality one could construct quite a world atlas of crime, passing from country to country under the protection of a remarkable galaxy of international detectives: Nicholas Freeling's Inspector Van der Valk of Holland; Simenon's Maigret of France; Sjövall and Wahlöo's Beck of Sweden; Keating's Ghote of India; Van Gulik's Judge Dee of China; Marquand's Mr. Moto of Japan and Biggers's Charlie Chan of Hawaii, to name just a few, though no doubt enough to jangle the nerves of any international criminal. Significantly, though the settings of these stories are global in variety, most of the writers are of Anglo-American or Northern European cultural backgrounds, predominantly the former. The detective story situation works with many different cultural settings because the investigation of a puzzling crime casts light on the workings of a society by catching it at a moment of anomaly and disruption. By exploring the ramifications of such moments, the skillful writer and observer can reveal to us some of the prevailing terms of the social comedy. However, the angle of vision enforced by the conventions of the classical detective story is inevitably a limited one, because its basic assumptions are bound to the social and ideological patterns of Western bourgeois democracies in the 19th and 20th centuries. The quest for cross-cultural understanding so richly developed in a novel like *A Passage to India* is difficult within the confines of the detective story, for, whatever the setting, the classical formula seems to require the importation of certain presuppositions about society, law, and morality from the Anglo-American tradition. This is why most of the writers who deal with detection in other countries come from a predominantly English cultural tradition.

One of the most interesting writers who has explored the interface between different cultures through the medium of the detective story is the Australian, Arthur W. Upfield. His stories illustrate the power of the detective story formula to bring out distinctive qualities of morals and manners in high relief. But they also show how the formula operates to limit the expression of deeper and more complex cultural perspectives.

In most of his work, Upfield deals with crimes that have taken place in the interior regions of Australia, the "outback" which Upfield himself knew well from the years he spent in cattle-raising before he turned to the writing of detective stories. In this region, which resembles the American frontier of the nineteenth century in many ways, three very different cultures conflict and interact in a complex web: the modern, urban and national culture of the coastal regions, predominantly English in its traditions and represented in the outback by state and national agencies, such as the police; the white culture of the outback itself with its distinctive way of life dominated by the great distances and climatic extremes of the region and by the diverse national backgrounds and cultures of its immigrants; and the completely distinctive aboriginal culture with its age-old tribal ways in various stages of assimilation into the dominant white culture.

To mediate these different cultures as they interact around the crisis posed by a crime, Upfield invented a detective figure who is surely one of the most fascinating in the literature: the half-caste Napoleon Bonaparte. Himself the product of an interracial marriage, "Bony", as he prefers to be called, spans the gulf between cultures. Inheritor of the tribal lore and skill of his aboriginal mother, Bony not only possesses insight into the aboriginal mind, he also has the aboriginal ability of tracking and living off the country. Some of his feats at reading footprints and other signs would put Sherlock Holmes to shame. Upfield's ability to represent the customs, beliefs, and powers of aboriginal culture through the mediating consciousness of Bony is one of the most compelling features of his books. Just as Thomas Berger dramatized the American Plains Indian culture through the experiences of a white boy captured and raised by the Cheyenne Indians in *Little Big Man*, Upfield at his best gives us a rich and complex sense of aboriginal culture through the perceptions of his half-caste protagonist.

Detective Inspector Bonaparte is steeped, as Upfield himself must have been, in aboriginal myth and legend. As a man once "sealed" into a tribe, Bony is powerfully aware of the psychological potency of ceremony. The dreaded ritual of "pointing the bones" and the fear it evokes in a person who has gone through the process of tribal initiation plays a significant role in a number of Upfield's stories, in one of which Bony himself suffers the trauma of being the object of this form of magic.[1] Such episodes show Upfield's ability to evoke the psychological reality of aboriginal culture. While Upfield was certainly not a trained anthropologist, his stories are richly evocative of the aura of tribalism and its age-old way of life.

Yet, as the agent of a national police authority, Bony also represents the thrust of modernization with its emphasis on centralized authority and bureaucratic administration and its hierarchy of educated expertise. Though there is some conflict between the two sides of Bony's nature, his role as a detective requires that he be able to use his aboriginal intuition and his civilized authority in a unified way to penetrate the truth of crime and restore the threatened fabric of society. He becomes, in the end, another avatar of that mythical figure who has played such an important role in the imaginative history of European imperialism: the man who is at once the epitome of the British gentleman and yet can fully penetrate into the mysteries of alien cultures. We find this fantasy represented in the legends which grew up around such historical figures as Chinese Gordon and Lawrence of Arabia, and in such fictional characters as John Buchan's Sandy Arbuthnot, Kipling's Kim, and Edgar Rice Burroughs's Lord Greystoke, otherwise known as Tarzan of the Apes. These figures express the fantasy that the profound cultural conflicts inherent in the relationship between imperial power and colonial peoples, and modernizing Europeans and traditional cultures can be effectively mediated and justly resolved. Upfield's Bony is in this tradition. His function as detective mediator limits the degree to which Upfield can fully dramatize the tragic conflict between the aboriginal Australian tribal cultures and the colonizing Europeans. But it is to Upfield's credit that within the limits of the essentially comic mode of the detective story, he weaves a richly colored tapestry of the conflicting cultural strains that come together in the Australian outback.

The outback itself is both the setting and the subject of Upfield's most striking work. The vast desert and semi-desert landscape of Australia's interior broods in the background of Bony's cases, its strange flora and fauna and mysterious geological features creating an appropriate stage for murder and its exposure:

> What is geographically named the "Lake Eyre basin" roughly comprises two hundred thousand square miles and most of it is below sea level. Save

---

[1] *The Bone Is Pointed* (1938).

along the western edge where run the rare trains northward to Alice
Springs, the white population is less than two hundred, and the aborigines
number but a hundred more. The rivers, when they run every decade or so,
run uphill. Sand dunes float in the air and kangaroos leap from cloud to
cloud. The horizon is never where it ought to be. A tree one moment is a
shrub and the next a radio mast. A reptilian monster sunning itself on a
mountain ridge, is, after all, a frilled lizard sprawled on the dead branch of
a tree partially buried in a sand dune.[2]

This "deceitful landscape" plays a direct role in some of Upfield's best
stories. In *Death of a Lake*, for example, a body is concealed in a periodic
lake. As the body cannot be retrieved until the lake dries up, detective and
suspects wait anxiously on the receding edge of the water. Finally, in a
thunderous climax marked by the panicked flight of rabbits and kangaroos
driven wild by the disappearance of their water source, the lake bed finally
gives up its hidden corpse and Bony is able to reveal the murderer. In such
moments, the landscape takes on a moral and mythical ambience
integrated with the movement of the story.

The people of the outback—the murderers, victims, and suspects who
pose Bony's problems of detection—constitute a thin and fragile layer of
human community struggling to maintain its hold on the vast emptiness of
the landscape. Far from the complex modern society of the cities, and
equally distant in another direction from the aboriginal tribalism of the
native inhabitants, the outback communities have developed their own
distinctive culture, based on intense ties of personal and family loyalty
involving both white ranchers and the semi-civilized aboriginal groups
who work periodically on the ranches and live on the margins of
settlement. These are people outside both traditional tribalism and modern
urban civilization. They have created their own form of community which
is in many ways an admirable mixture of the intense human unity of tribal
culture and the individualism of modern society. Yet the outback
community is deeply vulnerable to the crisis posed by murder, for crimes
of violence not only threaten the texture of loyalties on which such a
subculture depends, but require the intrusion of outside authority into the
community.

Bony, himself divided between his aboriginal heritage and his role as
agent of the modern state, has the complex perceptions and skills
necessary to mediate these cultural tensions, to expose the murderer and to
restore the threatened fabric of the community. In his best works, such as
The Bushman Who Came Back, *The Will of the Tribe* and *The New Shoe*,

---

[2] Arthur Upfield, *Bony Buys a Woman* (London: Heinemann, 1957), 24. Also
published as *The Bushman Who Came Back*.

Upfield develops Bony not so much as ratiocinative deducer from clues, but as penetrator into the complex of local loyalties which shield the murderer from outside authority. One of the recurrent, haunting images of his stories is of the "shuttered eyes" of aboriginal leaders refusing to reveal their knowledge because of their sense of loyalty to some local stockman or family. Bony's character gives him the understanding, compassion and psychological skill to enter fully into the moral and emotional ethos of particular outback communities and, because he has this capacity, he is able to solve the crime without dissolving the community.

At the top of his form, Upfield turned the detective story into a rich fable of the interaction of cultures and their differing systems of authority, justice, morality and community. Set against the extraordinary social and geological landscape of the Australian outback, these fables are set in motion by the social crisis of murder and then mediated by the idealized figure of the half-caste detective, Napoleon Bonaparte. Thus, Upfield's work takes on some of the depth, simplicity, and aboriginal mystery of the native legends which his detective often repeats and which evidently fascinated Upfield himself. In all, Upfield published over two dozen detective novels about Bony. Some of these are fairly routine attempts at mystification based on the usual crowded parade of clues, witnesses, alibis, and red herrings. But those five or six Upfields which fully develop the magical combination of Australian landscape, cultural conflict and the ambiguous relationship of law, loyalty, and justice are among the major achievements of the genre. I am told that Australian television has recently produced a series based on the exploits of Bony. I have not seen any of these episodes and cannot say how successful they are, but I hope that some enterprising American distributor will make them available here. They would give us a wonderfully refreshing contrast to the hard-boiled urban police thrillers which presently dominate our screens.

First Published in *New Republic* 177.530 (July 1977): 39-41. Reprinted with permission of the *New Republic*. The references were added by the editors.

BONY:
A WHITE MAN'S HALF-CASTE HERO

BASIL SANSOM

In many ways, Arthur Upfield writes badly. Somehow, though, in all his long series of books, he conjures more vividly perhaps than any other popular writer the feel of the Australian outback: its heat, dust and rawness; its colours and its features; and the passionate inarticulate love with which it holds people. In addition, Upfield has created a character; the half-caste Detective-Inspector Napoleon Bonaparte, a character who almost steps alive off the page.[1]

Tonight I want to contrast Upfield's outback with Upfield's hero. Like so many of us I think that I first learned about Australia through Upfield's work. My father was an infected reader of thrillers, located either out West or very snobbishly in London. There was also this Australian series, and from this I learned the vocabulary of the Australian outback.

Sometimes we should consider seriously that which we usually consider defined. There are two arguments that are the obvious ones to cite in this context; the first being the fact that Upfield's works have sold over the millions. If they are so widely disseminated there must be a market for them. To understand the nature of that market it is necessary to understand something about our society. There is a case for the study of general literature: it is important and does have an impact on society.

When we come to detective literature, we address a particular variety of general literature. In particular, detective literature is often highly class conscious. Detective literature is distinctively replete with sociological analyses. Have you ever thought just how the snobbish Peter Wimseys came to be, what they are? Since the last century when the "Peelers" started work, there has been a general rule in the Police Force that you have got to come up from the ranks. They have to have access to the Upper Classes. There are all sorts of ways in which the authors of detective novels have commented on the ability of their detectives to cope

---

[1] *Times Literary Supplement*, 11 March 1960, 166.

with such situations.

When we come to Australia and start to consider Upfield's Outback, we find that he immediately starts to talk about the nature and place of class.

> On the majority of Australian sheep and cattle stations, people are divided into three grades or classes; for, even amongst Australia's most democratic portion of her allegedly democratic population, class distinctions are rigidly maintained. Heading this class trilogy on the average station is the owner, or the manager, and his family. They reside in what is termed "government house", the main residence on the property and the centre from which it is directed. On a great number of stations there is another and less pretentious building housing the apprentices or jackaroos and the overseer or boss-stockman. They are provided with a sitting room, and a dining room. The "lower orders," comprising the station men and the tradesmen, inhabit a hut, and their dining room adjoins the kitchen, ruled by their own cook.[2]

And three pages later, we arrive in the Aboriginal camp which constitutes the fourth division. That essay is quite explicit and if that was in a MA thesis I would thoroughly approve of it. The statement is made in precise and pedantic style which is very much Upfield's.

He is also very conscious of the urban-rural contrast, and makes something of it throughout his books. Apart from general statements about the nature of towns and country, the "outback" and the "inside" to use the language of the Thirties, he deals with issues of deference and demeanour. Little scenarios that evidence differences in city versus Outback behaviour.

In *Wings Above the Diamantina* (1936), there is a scene with a young lady in a car. She is wearing white gloves and is with her father, who is the owner of the station. There is a rather handsome head stockman. He says:

> "We're all going to Golden Dawn tomorrow Miss Eliz'beth." The boss stockman called this out while distance still separated them. "Mr Nettleford says we can go. Hope to see you there too. You must command your father to take you."
>
> "I never command my father to do anything," she corrected him, a serious expression belying her laughing eyes.
>
> The big bluff manager of Coolibah regarded her with obvious pride. Everything about her—the grey tailor-made costume, the modish hat which did not conceal the golden sheen of her hair—combined to place his

---

[2] Arthur Upfield, *Wings Above the Diamantina* (Sydney: Angus & Robertson, 1940), 66.

daughter on an equal footing with the smartest city woman.[3]

"The smartest city woman ..." She had been driving in that motor-car for three hours in her white gloves across the paddocks of "Coolibah", neat and tidy, and of course there was the mystery, in what is not the "Mister" country. In many of the books the point is made that the "Mister country" is Inside, not Outback! The rural-urban divide is being expressed time and time again. Another aspect of it all is sexuality: male and female relationships are a continuing and definitive theme for so many things. The young woman, instructed to "command" her father, denies that she commands her father, and then, a few pages later, she does just that and he gives in, as Upfield says, "with the sulkiness betrayed by a woman-defeated man".[4]

In making his contrasts between town and country, Upfield continues to repeatedly tell you what the difference between town and country is. Here comes the first point that he makes.

In the country, the incidence of crime is generally low. Secondly, the crime is committed in small face-to-face communities where people enjoy multiple complex relationships with one another. (He doesn't say multiplex relationships, but spends three paragraphs defining what sociologists mean by that term.)

When crime is committed in the country, you turn not to forensic science (which has to do with enclosed space, with dust in envelopes, with finger-prints), but to something called "the book" of the bush.

For the book of the bush to be read, you need to be a trained reader, a tracker, a person who can see signs, who can tell you not only that a dog has been, but whose dog it was, and that yesterday it had a sore front paw. We know that Napoleon Bonaparte, because of his ancestry, has such talents. Rural crime, then, in Australia, is radically distinguished in structural terms from urban crime.

I must remind you though, that Napoleon Bonaparte has a problem: he is a half-caste, and he has to "make it". He has to "make it" at a difficult time, during the interbellum years when these books started coming out. Napoleon Bonaparte is M.A. (Brisbane)! An M.A. (Brisbane). In fact, Bony is an anachronism in the frontward, not the backward sense. Nobody had yet made it in the way he was alleged to have made it. For Upfield, there is this general problem, as expressed by a third party. "I wonder, if given the same opportunities, how many Australian half-castes could reach the level of Bony's attainments", says Cartwright. He is answered by an

---

[3] Upfield, *Wings Above the Diamantina*, 4-5.
[4] Upfield, *Wings Above the Diamantina*, 53.

aeroplane pilot who frowns, and says:

> "I have dealings with a lot of them ... In answer to your question, I'd
> say that quite a number of them could. Among the many I have met there
> are several really smart fellows. Environment is against them, and so ..."
> "Well?" Cartwright pressed.
> "The bush generally gets 'em in the end. You could take a black or a
> half-caste, and you put him [in] college and teach him a trade, but the time
> surely comes when he leaves it all to bolt back to the bush. They can't long
> resist the urge to go on walkabout."
> "Perhaps they are happier on walkabout."
> "Of course ... they haven't got the curse of Adam laid on 'em, like the
> white man. You can't tell me it's natural for a man to slave in a factory, or
> on a road, or in an office. It is not natural for a man to work. That the white
> man does so is just because he has always been greedy for power over his
> fellows. The blacks never have worked. They never *had* to work, and they
> can't see the *sense* of working. Blessed if I can see the sense of it, either. I
> know well enough that were I a half-caste I wouldn't work when I could go
> on walkabout ..."[5]

So there is always the threat of reversion as far as the educated part-
Aboriginal person is concerned, and this is the situation described in this
extract. Bonaparte explicitly tells the reader how this feels for him. He
experiences a continuing two-way pull: there is his maternal ancestry on
the one side, which is his Aboriginal ancestry, and then there is that casual
event which gave him White paternity which pulls him in another
direction. In every day of his life Napoleon Bonaparte the half-caste
detective, has to resolve these two pulls. He is the classic "man in the
middle", the marginal man, and the detective. Detectives are always
strangers though when they come into the community, and this provides a
structure in which can be elaborated to Bony's participation in society.

The problem for Bony is that he must reconcile in himself these two
contending forces, as he goes on toward the solving of mysteries.

> "You see a half-caste, a detective inspector in a state police department. I
> was given the chance of a good education by a saint, the matron of a
> mission station to which I was taken when abandoned as a baby. I passed
> from a state school to a high school, then to the Brisbane University, where
> I won my Master of Arts degree, and so prove once again, if proof is
> necessary, that the Australian half-caste is not a kind of kangaroo. But I
> had to conquer greater obstacles ... I had to conquer ... the almost

---

[5] Upfield, *Wings Above the Diamantina*, 132-133.

irresistible power of the Australian bush over those who belong to it."[6]

A similar paragraph is in most of the Bony books: it is a rote statement which the character was to make repeatedly. In *Death of a Swagman* having told how he went to Brisbane University, he goes on in more detail.

> "You have been in the bush long enough to have felt the power yourself, and you are a white man. A similar power is exercised over seafaring men by the sea, but it is not so strong as this power of the bush. The only counter-power preventing me from surrendering to it is pride, with a capital P, and faith in myself. Without pride in my scholastic attainments and pride in my success as a crime investigator, the bush would have had its way with me. My record is unblemished by failure, and that is behind the faith in myself. Once I fail to solve a crime mystery ... I lose faith in myself ... and the great Detective Inspector Napoleon Bonaparte becomes Bony the half-caste nomad."[7]

Every time when he goes to solve a case there is a tension in the book: is he or is he not going to cope with the half-caste reversion bit. This is an additional tension: it is a thriller with two plots. He has to maintain an ultimate pride. He has always to succeed. That is the problem.

Let us look for a moment at the difficulty facing Upfield. He has to insert this half-caste man into a society where the participation of an educated M.A. (Brisbane) half-caste Aborigine is unprecedented. He has to put him there, where no Aboriginal man has walked before. This presents a number of problems, one of which I want to take up. This is the matter of sexuality. The relationship between black and white in Australia is associated with asymmetrical sex, as we all know, Here, you have an educated man. In terms of his status background, he is going to be a better than or better qualified than many of the White men with whom he associates. Sexually, that is terribly threatening.

When you look at Bony's personal problem, it is to resolve that tension between the half-caste nomad back in the bush and the man of pride who is still making it. The author of Bony uses the very same terms to solve the problem. There is a moment in one of the books where Bony says, "Until a few days ago, I thought that I knew everything. It is a conceit due, I think to my wife, to whom I really am a hero."[8] Note that his confidence is in his wife. The interesting thing is that Bony says of his, whenever he is in dire bounds and thinks that he is going to fail a case,

---

[6] Arthur Upfield, *Death of a Swagman* (Sydney: Angus & Robertson, 1947), 20.

[7] Upfield, *Death of a Swagman*, 20.

[8] Upfield, *Wings Above the Diamantina*, 134.

"I'll tell her right off and we'll go bush".[9] One thing is sure: she will go bush. That particular relationship is never threatened by the possibility of failure. All that is threatened by the possibility of failure is that "Pride", which is the very same thing that makes him the white man's half-caste hero. There is that stable relationship behind him, with total expectation that it maintained. Her worship of him will decline not at all.

Returning to the earlier quotation, we must consider how Bony can talk with the young lady who was wearing white gloves three hours out from the station homestead. Here he is, this half-caste hero, and he wants to talk with her about knickers! The situation is thus: there is a young woman in another room who is totally paralysed because she has been drugged, though she is wholly conscious. They are very worried to identify this young woman. Miss Nettleford has undertaken to nurse this young woman at the station, and the only suggestion of identity that has so far come forward is that this young woman has a yen for embroidery, and has put a double "M" all over her underclothes. Bony says:

> "A moment Miss Nettleford, before we go to the sick room," ... [S]he turned and calmly looked at him, her hostility towards his colour not yet vanished. "I have one or two questions to ask you concerning this poor young woman. I understand you have closely examined her clothing and have found on several articles the initial M.M. Once we have identified your patient our task of unmasking the person who is conspiring against her life will be partly accomplished. Now tell me please, of what quality is the young woman's underwear?"
>
> He saw the quickly gathered frown, and he knew in Elizabeth Nettleford he was facing the same battle he had during his career so often faced and won.
>
> "Well, really ..." she began haughtily.
>
> "I am forty three years old, Miss Nettleford, and I have been married twenty years," he cut in. "Believe me, the information I seek is for the purpose of establishing the patient's identity. Do her clothes lead you to assume that she is—well, high in social circles? Are they expensive, or are they cheap and of poor quality?"
>
> "I should say that her clothes have been purchased at middle-class shops," she replied steadily.[10]

I want you to notice just how he got her to talk about the knickers. He invokes his wife; this absent presence who never appears once in any of the Bony books. She is always referred to; she is "back there". He is safely married, and has this very beautiful stable relationship. He constantly takes

---

[9] Upfield, *Wings Above the Diamantina*, 223.
[10] Upfield, *Wings Above the Diamantina*, 69.

out the metaphorical warrant of his status by showing people pictures of his wife and children. He is safe, and sexually neutered, as most married men are sexually neutered, by the closeness of his relationship with his spouse.

Bony, then, can move freely in society, and one of the problems is removed: that is this matter of breaking the bounds of asymmetrical sex. It would have been just too terrible for his future career had he not in his early years met that so-nice girl at the mission station who happened to be of the same status as he was, and married her.

Realistic as all this may sound, the Bony books always invoke a moment when the reader's credulity becomes absolutely strained, and this is the moment when you first encounter the Napoleonic bow. Bony bows to ladies constantly, formalising his relationship with women to the extent that he is always paying them those fruitful compliments. He bows as no man has done before; another device that allows Upfield to deal with the relationship of colour and sex. It is often over-formalised, neat and tidy, but from time to time we come to the very nasty bits. These occur not only in one book but in the whole series. When does he make his most crucial and effective bows? In *Death of a Swagman* the moment of the bow is when he addresses the Minister's wife. This is a special Minister. He is a Welshman with a high-pitched whining voice, and he earns the disapprobation of Bony because he went to two funerals with him, and the Minister dealt with them with overzealous dispatch. Bony began to suspect this man. The Minister became seedier and seedier and nastier and nastier, asserting that he had a heart condition, and spending his time on the verandah reading books while his wife works out back on the wood-pile. Bony comes around the back to the wood-pile.

> Soft, grey eyes examined him. Once she had been fresh and pretty; now her complexion was ruined by the hot suns and the hotter kitchen stove. Perspiration dewed her forehead.
>
> "That is unfortunate, and we should be glad that we are strong", Bony said. The smile continued to light his eyes [he has just been told that she has to chop because her husband is weak], and before she realized it his hat had dropped from his hand and he had taken the axe from her hands and wrenched it from the log. "I am considered the best axe-man in my family", he told her. "Charles, my eldest son [notice that he is talking to a woman so now the whole family is there as well] is much too cunning to take any interest in woodcutting, and James, my next boy, makes blind swipes and often splinters the handle."[11]

---

[11] Upfield, *Death of a Swagman*, 137.

Now observe the champion axeman of the Robert Burns family (Bony's current pseudonym), an old chap who could not saw quickly, but he could cut wood for the stove. So he does it.

> "Where would you like the wood, ma'am?" he asked.
> "Oh, I could take it to the kitchen. Thank you for having cut it."
> "Where is the kitchen? Suppose you show me? If I have to drop this load through sheer weariness ..."
> "Over here, thank you so much." ...
> [H]e bowed as no man ever had bowed to Lucy James.[12]

Then Bony goes to the front verandah, and the Minister has the Epistles inverted on his chest and behind it is a book called *Life of a Flirt*. Bony has done it again. What has he done? He has sought out a victim lady, tired, weary, and woebegone, and he has given her one of those great Bony bows in her life. If you are but on the wood-heap with your husband out front with his hypocritical pretensions, and this bloke comes and gives you a sniff of what the other side is really, are you going to remember this starry-eyed and say "Oh that Bony, Oh that Bony", or are you going to get entirely discontented with your lot? He never seems to sow the seeds of discontent in these women but I think he must do this if we are to believe in him at all. So what does he do? He goes into cities and towns and he finds the females who will respond most ardently and avidly to the Bony charm. And he charms them. Having charmed them, he wins allies. Now I think that this is one of the most immoral intersexual approaches I have ever heard described. It is quite unbelievable too when you start thinking about the effect he must have on these poor women if we are to believe in their lacklustre lives.

In one of the books, Bony spends two chapters giving his philosophy of crime. What he says is that for his cases to be resolved all he needs is time. The small-scale communities he enters are involved, where relationships have long histories, and he needs to spend a great deal of time there in order to resolve the problem. He says that it does not matter if he fails to solve the case quickly, since the problems will continue to come in, and with the flux of time he will get the evidence. Bony always chokes off the complaints of his superiors in Brisbane, saying "Give me the time and I will finish the job". Some of these cases quite clearly took six or nine months to complete, and if you start adding them all up there just is not the time between 1914-18 and 1945 to have done most of those things.

---

[12] Upfield, *Death of a Swagman*, 138.

Bony does not rely on the deductive method of the classical Sherlock Holmes. In *A Study in Scarlet*, Conan Doyle makes the prototype statement about the detective novel, where Holmes (talking as usual to Watson) distinguishes between analytic and synthetic thinking. Synthetic thinking is when you put things together and think forwards towards a result. Analytical thinking is when events have occurred and you have a result, and you have to work backwards to find out how it happened.[13] Now, the Sherlock Holmes story is always about thinking backwards to get to the situation. Bony never does this: he goes into a community and waits for the murderer to do something foolish, and the silly thing he does is usually to kill somebody else. By the time Bony comes out at the other end he has had four or six bites at the cherry with people falling down like flies all over the place. He must have this parade of deaths to provide a pattern he says when describing his method. When he works he does not run round questioning everybody. He waits for Providence to show him the way, and while that is being shown, he does not succumb to any humanitarian feeling.[14] So he waits then, until he has enough bodies and he knows he will come out on top in the end. Bony can walk out of that community with his Pride intact, and he will not have to revert to become that other ego the half-caste nomad.

I think that Bony is a terribly expensive detective. For all the outback that Upfield taught me about, all the charm of his descriptions and language, I think he wrote very horrid immoral books.

First published in *Anthropology News* 17.7 (August 1980): 107-113. Reprinted with permission of the Anthropological Society of Western Australia. Some revisions were made by the author. Summary of the Presidential Address to the Annual General Meeting of the Society on 14 July 1980.

---

[13] Arthur Conan Doyle, "A Study in Scarlet," in *The Celebrated Cases of Sherlock Holmes* (London: Octopus Books, 1981), 619.

[14] Upfield, *Death of a Swagman*, 153-154.

UPFIELD:
THE MAN WHO STARTED IT

TONY HILLERMAN

On this cold winter morning in my faculty office at the University of New Mexico, I close my eyes, energize the proper brain cells, and see the Australian Outback. A skinny aborigine squats beside the ashes of a cold fire, staring into the distance at a horizon an infinity away. The smell of drought is in the air, there's the silence of an immense, dry emptiness, and a sense of dread.

I have never been nearer to Australia than Los Angeles. I experienced that scene when I was a school boy at Sacred Heart, Oklahoma, trying to sell magazines to cotton farmers for Curtis Publishing Company. I tried to sell *The Saturday Evening Post, Country Gentleman*, and *Ladies Home Journal*, and if my memory is correct I met Napoleon Bonaparte, the half-white, half-aborigine detective invented by Arthur Upfield. But much more important than introducing me to Bony, Upfield led me into his desert and showed me the strange stone-age culture which still inhabited parts of it. I was about twelve at the time and a voracious reader of everything that I could lay hands on—which, when you live thirty-five unpaved miles from a library, is a mixed bag. I'd read Washington Irving's *Conquest of Granada*, and Prescott's histories of the conquests of Mexico and Peru, and even Plutarch's *Lives of the Famous and Illustrious Men of Greece and Rome*, the memoirs of *Bryan, The Iconoclast*, and even *The Lives of the Saints*. But nothing had excited me as much as Upfield's landscapes and the people who somehow survived upon them.

A lot of time passed before this early exposure to Upfield translated itself into anything concrete. The Depression ended, World War II came and went, college, marriage and children, police reporting, newspaper editing, life in general. I had quite frankly completely forgotten who had written those indelible descriptions when I checked *The Bone Is Pointed* out of the Santa Fe library and—thrilled and excited—found myself not only again in the Outback, but jerked back into my own boyhood. I read what Upfield I could find, which wasn't much then because he was not yet being rediscovered. Once again, Upfield caught me in his spell; the devastating drought which dominates *Bony and the Black Virgin*, the details of tracking in *Sinister Stones*, the insight into aboriginal values of *The Bone Is Pointed*, but most of all the land. The Nullarbor Plain, the Great Victoria Desert, Lake Disappointment, places like West Wyalong, Warrambungle, Mundiwindi, and Thargominda, the dust storms, the rivers which run a thousand miles only to evaporate, the lakes which are dust bins except in rare monsoon years, the feel of a country in which man is tiny, trivial, and not at all in control.

I cannot honestly say that when I set about to write my own version of the mystery novel, Arthur Upfield was consciously in my mind. Subconsciously, he certainly was. Upfield had shown me—and a good many other mystery writers—how both ethnography and geography can be used in a plot and how they can enrich an old, old literary form. When my own Jim Chee of the Navajo Tribal Police unravels a mystery because he understands the ways of his people, when he reads the signs left in the sandy bottom of a reservation arroyo, he is walking in the tracks Bony made fifty years ago.

My taste in Upfield is not standard. Many of the critics seem to prefer *The New Shoe* or others of his books which display Upfield's talent for plotting. But reading Upfield for plot is as bad as reading Shakespeare for plot. That wasn't where his genius lay. He was not above bad writing and bad plotting. But when Upfield captures you in his landscapes—strange as the dark side of the moon—and enchants you with his explorations of aborigine cultures, such considerations become quibbles.

Read *A Royal Abduction* with pleasure. It's neither his best, nor his worst. Then read *The Sands of Windee, Death of a Lake*, or one of the others in which Upfield broke the ground on which Navajo, and Zulu, and Caribbean, and Bombay, and Brazilian, detectives now walk, showing us strange cultures and strange landscapes while they deal with that age old universal we call evil.

First published in *A Royal Abduction*, by Arthur Upfield, v-vii. San Francisco: McMillan, 1984.

THE FRONTIER HEROISM
OF ARTHUR W. UPFIELD

RAY B. BROWNE

The essence of frontier heroic literature commits a hero against evil forces in a setting where nature is powerful and is either indifferent or hostile and therefore presents awesome difficulties for the hero. In this setting, the superperson fights for the good of individuals and of society as a whole. Part of the accomplishment of the hero is in triumphing over or in the presence of powerful nature which if not hostile seems to be purposefully throwing obstacles in the path of the hero in his quest.

Since part of the heroic stature of the individual comes from overcoming the forces raised by nature, he becomes a *natural* hero as opposed to a *social* hero that arises as society becomes more the battleground. The forces of nature extend beyond mere earthly setting, of course, and rise to the supernatural in the shape of evil or indifferent gods who may or may not be interested in the fate of man.

Two classic American writers who perhaps most clearly exemplify these two aspects of the hero are James Fenimore Cooper in the Leatherstocking Tales, in the person of Natty Bumppo (in his various names), and Herman Melville in at least a half dozen characters, the most notable of whom are Ahab in *Moby-Dick* and Billy Budd in the short novel of the same name.

Bumppo combats evil Indians and treacherous whites for the benefit of individuals and through them society. But his battles are waged in the presence of a second powerful force, nature, which although at times benign or indifferent, nevertheless constitutes a force that often becomes hostile and must always be reckoned with.

In Melville the frontier is of a slightly different kind: it is a transcendental nature sometimes imbued with a supernatural spirit which seems to combat the godliness in mankind. When Melville's heroes struggle for themselves and mankind they must fight on at least two levels and sometimes against three foes: man, nature and God. Thus on two levels the battles of these two authors exemplify the essence of the heroic, frontier struggle. The authors are concerned with the hero in epical battles.

Arthur W. Upfield (1888-1964),[1] one of two or three of the major Australian popular authors, resembles Cooper and Melville perhaps more than he does any other authors. His settings are similar. His working area is the whole of the continent of Australia, as Cooper's were the whole frontier and Melville's the entire frontier of Transcendentalism. Upfield's antagonists are nature and man, and in Australia, nature, often more terrible than man, is always heroic. Upfield's protagonist is Detective-Inspector Napoleon Bonaparte—called Bony by himself, his friends in the books, and by his readers. He faces deserts of sand hundreds of miles across, sand spouts fifty miles wide, rabbits in the millions, lakes that dry up in water spouts that blot out the sun, great distances of miles and the loneliness that comes in such a country. "Common to all" says Upfield in *Man of Two Tribes* "is the force of opposition to man." The country, he adds, "will destroy any man who goes out alone".[2] This is perhaps Upfield's reason for trying to discover and instill compassion and communality among his people.

But Upfield's fiction differs somewhat from that of Cooper and Melville. Whereas theirs is epical, and therefore concerned with a nation and a people, Upfield's is crime fiction, therefore concerned with crime and punishment, though against a background of civilization against pre-civilization.

Nearly all detective fiction develops through heroes and heroines as protagonists. Generally these heroes combat crime to set society aright after the intrusion of a convulsion of crime that has knocked it askew, to piece together the elements of a puzzle or to protect society. Such heroes are social heroes. Upfield's hero is different. His books are about frontier offenses and retribution. They are conventional books in that the hero is a superman of sorts, with the classic birth which is mysterious and somewhat unusual. In *Man of Two Tribes* Bony gives perhaps the most succinct description of his origin:

> "I never knew my father ... I never knew my mother either. She was found dead under a sandalwood tree, with me on her breast and three days old ... In spite of my parentage, I am unusual. Or is it because of my parentage?"[3]

---

[1] Ed.: It had been generally accepted that Upfield was born on 1 September 1888. A check of the records in England made about 25 years after his death revealed he was born in 1890.

[2] Arthur Upfield, *Man of Two Tribes* (London: Heinemann, 1956), 7.

[3] Upfield, *Man of Two Tribes*, 20-21.

Bony readily and frequently admits that there is no crime he cannot solve.

In many ways Bony is also "godlike". He prefers crimes that are somewhat old. Time, as he says, is an ally. He does not like to witness violence; and Upfield does not portray much crime on stage. Most of his is done offstage or was committed in the past. Bony does not particularly care whether criminals are punished for their crimes. He likes to solve crimes because they provide him with mental exercise, and in that respect he is a standard cerebral detective, and having solved them he at least once acts as judge and dismisses the criminal, wishing the guilty person a happy future.

The world in which Upfield works is different from that of other detective writers. It is different from America in being a society that is less generally violent though just as down-to-earth and realistic. Upfield is more deeply and more directly concerned with the physical and natural background than other detective fiction authors who write about other continents: any of the English, George Simenon about France, Wahloo and Sjowall and their stories about Sweden, H.F.R. Keating and his stories about India; Robert Van Gulik and his tales about Judge Dee in Classical China; and Elspeth Huxley and James McClure and their probing stories of crime in Africa. These people are more concerned in the conventional way with people and social justice. In other words, these are books about *social* crime. Upfield's are different.

Upfield's books are perhaps the most heroic of Australian popular writings. Whereas other popular writers like Colleen MacCullough in *The Thornbirds* and Nevil Shute in *A Town Like Alice* are epical and therefore heroic in their presentations of life in Australia, Upfield writes of substantially the same kind of subject but with less epical sweep. He is more concerned with the narrowly heroic aspect, though he writes of virtually every aspect of Australian life of the first half of the twentieth century: the outback, cattle and sheep raising, drought, combatting "vermin" (rabbits), crime in small cities, mining, the sea, etc.

Upfield is similar to Cooper and Melville, especially Melville, in that he was not college trained. As Melville declared that the whaleship was his Harvard and Yale (and reacted against his lack of formal education though he was widely read in his own way), Upfield, who was born in England and sent by his father to Australia because there he would be least nuisance to his parents in England, said that the continent of Australia was his Oxford and Cambridge. Like Melville in his own world, Upfield wandered the Continent, doing every kind of manual labor available, thereby gaining firsthand knowledge of the world he would later write about. Like Melville, also, Upfield became a voracious and wide reader.

Unlike Melville, however, Upfield made his hero a college graduate (M.A. Brisbane University) with the social graces that would enable him to ingratiate himself into the most polite society, yet with the naturalness that would allow him to move in the meanest society. In fact, the tension that arises in the conflict between the two societies drives Bony's attitude and action. Bony—Everyman in the sense of Billy Budd and Ishmael—was the great hero-equalizer between the two societies and between the two races, the white and the aborigines.

Bony is like Cooper's Natty Bumppo in being caught between two worlds. He is a half-caste, his mother having been an aborigine, his father an Englishman. This dual nature, which Melville in *Moby-Dick* said is the ideal mixture of races, gave Bony the best of both cultures: the reasoning nature of his father and the warm-hearted intuition of the aborigine which allowed him to follow invisible trails through sand and over rocks that no white and few pure aborigines could follow. The character of Bony (which was based on a man named Tracker Leon whom Upfield met in his travels throughout Australia) allowed Upfield to study the situation of the two cultures in Australia to point out the characteristics and to make his suggestions for a solution to the problems.

On the subject Upfield wrote thirty-three books (Bony is in thirty of them)[4] and numerous short stories (some of which are not available in the United States, though the canon is being republished in two or three places now). Some of the subjects are narrow, almost ordinary detection and conventional accomplishments, though they present little-known and interesting aspects of Australian life. All have moments that could have been created only when the subject is Australian life and the author Arthur Upfield, and the detective the fascinating Bony, whom all readers classify as among the most successful half dozen detectives of all crime fiction. At his best, moreover, Upfield in his concept of Bony and the challenge of detective fiction against nature and man, and the power of his accomplishment in working out the story can be compared with the absolute strongest.

Upfield makes it clear from the beginning of his series that Bony walks between two cultures, at times blessed by his mixed blood, at times cursed:

> He walked with the soft tread of the Australian aboriginal. Of medium height and in his early to middle forties, free from impeding flesh, and hard as nails, there was yet in his carriage more of the white man than of the

---

[4] Ed.: Upfield wrote only 29 Bony novels, but also wrote one Bony short story, "Wisp of Wool and Disk of Silver", first published in *Ellery Queen's Mystery Magazine* 433 (December 1979): 7-19.

> black. By birth he was a composite of the two. His mother had given him
> the spirit of nomadism, the eyesight of her race, the passion for hunting;
> from his father he had inherited in overwhelming measure the white man's
> calm and comprehensive reasoning: but whence came his consuming
> passion for study was a mystery.
>
> Bony, as he insisted on being called, was the citadel within which
> warred the native Australian and the pioneering, thrusting Britisher. He
> could not resist the compelling urge of the *wanderlust* any more than he
> could resist studying a philosophical treatise, a revealing autobiography, or
> a ponderous history. He was a modern product of the limitless bush,
> perhaps a little superior to the general run of men in that in him were
> combined most of the virtues of both races and extraordinarily few of the
> vices.[5]

In almost every book Upfield makes his point clear. In Bony the two
races—the primitive and the civilized, the past and the present—struggle.
Caught in the crossfire of the two civilizations, Bony, led by his heart,
almost has to become a cultural conservative, though he is never quite sure
where he stands. He benefits personally from the mixture, as does his half-
caste wife and half-caste children; he is always proud of his station in life
and invariably leaves the bush and the aborigines to return to his cultured
home. But Bony has not departed far from his upbringing. His civilization
"was but a veneer laid upon the ego of modern man" and he was "often [a]
tragic figure, in whom ever warred the influence of two races".[6] At times
in reaction to some monstrous act by whites he would declare, "It was full
time that the Creator of man wiped out altogether this monster called
civilization and began again with the aborigines as a nucleus."[7]

But generally Upfield is not content with such a conclusion. His books
approach the subject from varying points of view. In the most extremely
folkloristic and anthropological of his books, *The Bone Is Pointed*, Upfield
has Bony tracing out a small group of aborigines who have for their own
purposes committed a murder. Bony, who intellectually is pure white, is
nevertheless caught up in the voodoo of the black rituals, and when the
bone is pointed at him (the curse laid on him), he becomes sick and almost
dies, his nature telling him he cannot resist, his subconscious driving him
to fight the curse.

He overcomes the pointed bone, solves the murder and though there
has obviously been a tug of war in his nature over the importance of the
aboriginal culture and that of the whites, the latter triumphs in Bony's

---

[5] Arthur Upfield, *The Sands of Windee* (London: Hutchinson, 1931), 1-2.

[6] Arthur Upfield, *The Mountains Have a Secret* (London: Pan Books, 1954), 93.

[7] Arthur Upfield, *The Bone Is Pointed* (Sydney: Hinkler, 1994), 121.

nature. At the end of the book he heads for the city in the strongest symbol of white man's progress that he could have used, an airplane, and he heads into the sunset and toward civilization where reason searches for truth in a kind of apotheosis: "The scarlet mist and the scarlet sun painted the machine with glowing colour, and made scarlet searchlights of its windows."[8]

Sometimes Upfield's working out the conflict between the two cultures is Romantic in the historical sense of the word. One book, *Bony and the Black Virgin*, is Hemingwayesque in its starkness, love, use of nature and in its denouement. It is a stark rendition of what happens in Australia when East meets West, that is when white meets aborigine in a setting in which the two are not and cannot be equals: A white man grows up with a beautiful aboriginal child and they mature into a love for each other which comes natural and overrides all other considerations. Yet the white man's family will not accept the black lady as their equal, and the aboriginal society will not accept the white man into their tribe. The situation presents a problem that even Upfield does not quite know how to handle. Bony's heart lies with the aborigines:

> "So many people fail to see these aborigines for what they are. To regard them as uncouth savages is such a boost for the ego, and yet, search as you might, you won't find a moron among them. I know an aboriginal head man who might have skipped four thousand years to come down to this age, for mankind has deteriorated mentally and spiritually."[9]

Yet he felt that for the aborigines

> complete assimilation isn't achieved by the aborigine via swift passage from one State to another, as the foreign national is granted citizen rights at a Town Hall ceremony. Assimilation is gradual, and requires several generations.[10]

At the end, Upfield gives in to his conservatism and pessimism and has the book end in a self-destruction that is worthy of Hemingway—shaded a little perhaps by the O'Henry of such a story as "Gift of the Magi". He has the two lovers sail a boat out into a lake and sink it and themselves.

Of all authors who write about heroes, Upfield at his strongest reminds us of Herman Melville at his most powerful, when he is writing of the essence of the hero. Upfield accomplishes this parallel in at least three ways: 1) in his notion of the brotherhood of all men and women; 2) in his

---

[8] Upfield, *The Bone Is Pointed*, 288.
[9] Arthur Upfield, *Bony and the Black Virgin* (London: Heinemann, 1959), 192.
[10] Upfield, *Bony and the Black Virgin*, 183-184.

rhetoric; and 3) in his symbolism.

Upfield is one of the most humanistic of authors. In writing about the great schism and conflict between the aborigines and the whites, he develops in dozens of places the aspects of life that they have in common and the need for each to respect the rights and culture of the other so that they can come together in the end. Though he realizes that there is a cultural lag in the civilization of the aborigines, he insists that in some ways they are superior to the whites who condescend to them. As Melville insisted in his way, Upfield echoes that all people belong to the great League of Nations, and as such they need to be treated with respect.[11]

In many ways Upfield approaches Melville in his figures of speech. Both authors thought of nature as a symbol, both conceived cosmically and both were powered by great outbursts of rhetorical flourish. Upfield sounds Melvillian, for example, in one passage where he addresses and describes nature:

> Old Man Drought was dead, battered and bludgeoned by the drops of water. The beaten Earth, ravished and scared, bedraggled and weary, conceived, and the womb prepared to give forth its fruit.[12]

To Upfield Nature is a Bible: "The print of the Book of the Bush doesn't quickly vanish."[13] He repeats this concept in one way or another in virtually every book. Sometimes the acts of nature are demonic:

> Like a thousand devils the wind howled among the trees and plucked at their branches to tear them away from the parent trunks and lay them violently on the ground.[14]

Sometimes Australian nature creates sand storms that are virtual solid walls of sand swirling up for a circumference of fifty miles.[15] Upfield personifies inanimate things: "The dominating mountain watched. One could not get away from those grey-and-brown eyes. Even in the dense scrub they sought one out."[16]

Sometimes the books begin with an epical sweep and flourish that echoes the cosmos and eternity. In speaking of a set of mountains, Upfield writes:

---

[11] Upfield, *The Bone Is Pointed*, 166.

[12] Upfield, *Bony and the Black Virgin*, 147.

[13] Upfield, *Bony and the Black Virgin*, 231.

[14] Arthur Upfield, *Winds of Evil* (London: Hamilton, 1939), 147.

[15] Arthur Upfield, *Wings Above the Diamantina* (London: Pan Books, 1972), 105.

[16] Upfield, *The Mountains Have a Secret*, 43.

They rose from the vast plain of golden grass; in the beginning, isolated rocks along the north-west horizon, rising to cut sharply into the cobalt sky, the rocks united and upon that quarter of the plain it could be seen that a cosmic hurricane had lashed the earth and created a sea, a sea of blue-black waves poised to crash forward in geographical suds.[17]

Sometimes the metaphors and similes surge with heroic gusto: "Another week was devoured by the year ..."[18] An observer "watched the night extinguish the furnace colours" of a lake.[19] Bony saw pelicans "gathered in close-packed mobs like crowds about road accidents".[20] Bony hears a conversation of water birds.[21] A man has "a halo of grey hair resting on his ears".[22]

At times Upfield peoples his stories with characters and humor reminiscent of a mixture of Melville and Dickens.

Almost all the books have characters with funny, descriptive names: Bill the Better in *The Bone Is Pointed* is a person who will bet on anything, even against himself. The "Spirit of Australia" is an 80 year old floater who embodies the very essence of the Continent.[23] Old Simpson in the *Mountains Have a Secret* is a *Moby-Dick* character: talkative, oracular, wise and experienced. Mr. Penwarden looks like "Father Time, and the rule he waved in his left hand the scythe".[24] Dead March Harry is a mental defective who thinks he's dead.[25]

The broadest and most effective comes from *The New Shoe* where Mr. Penwarden, an old artisan, builds coffins for the people around him. The purchasers try them out before their final use just to make sure that they are comfortable. Mr. Penwarden philosophizes: "Life is a Forge. Sorrow is the Fire and Pain the Hammer. Comes Death to cool the Vessel." He coaxes Bony to lie down in a coffin to test it and says: "You'd fit nicely. Take off your shoes ... might scratch." Bony replies: "I couldn't be more comfortable in bed."[26] On another occasion, Penwarden tells Bony:

---

[17] Upfield, *The Mountains Have a Secret*, 1.

[18] Arthur Upfield, *Death of a Lake* (London: Heineman, 1954), 64.

[19] Upfield, *Death of a Lake*, 73.

[20] Upfield, *Death of a Lake*, 64.

[21] Upfield, *Bony and the Black Virgin*, 142.

[22] Arthur Upfield, *Mr. Jelly's Business* (Sydney: Angus & Robertson, 1937), 286; also published as *Murder Down Under*.

[23] Arthur Upfield, *Mr. Jelly's Business*, 50.

[24] Arthur Upfield, *The New Shoe* (New York: Doubleday, 1951), 166.

[25] Arthur Upfield, *Madman's Bend* (London: Heinemann, 1963), 76-77.

[26] Upfield, *The New Shoe*, 45.

"I'll tell'e what ... sir ... There be no one now wantin' a first-class coffin, and as you just told me, I must keep me hand in or go sort of stale on the junk. What about one for you, now? A good one to keep out the cold and wet for two or three hundred years?"[27]

On another occasion, Penwarden says to Bony: "We all want a corrector ... sir, and there's nothin' like the sight of a coffin to melt away pride and vanity."[28]

Two of Upfield's strongest novels are *Mr. Jelly's Business* (1937) and *Bony and the White Savage* (1961). The former is an excellent story of a small town that is caught up in a murder mystery and in solving it Bony's language is stark, idiomatic and powerful.

Bony and the White Savage is the more powerful of the two. It concerns the return of a giant man from prison who had been committed for numerous cases of assault, rape and various other crimes. He is a "psychopath as well as a paranoic", a "gorilla"[29] and a "throw-back to a prehistoric monster"[30] yet the people in the small community where he was born and reared looked upon him as an intellectual and good-boy. The point of the novel is the need to educate the naive, to bring them out of their Alice in Wonderland state of mind and get them to recognize evil, which the man is. In doing this, Upfield elevates Marvin, the criminal, into gigantic proportions by frequent references to classical allusions, such as the Trojan horse, to "Bellephon on the back of Pegasus".[31] He illustrates the innocence and naiveté of the town by discussing the books they buy and read, such "good blood-and-gutzers" as *Wuthering Heights! Kidnapped! Peyton Place! Blood on the Sand!*[32] and *Ivanhoe*, "a lovely tale".[33]

The style of writing in this book is unusually hard, stark, harsh, and yet at the same time metaphoric and heroic, as witness this one bit of description:

The eye of the wind, having circled toward the Antarctic, had worked on the sea with spectacular results. The Front Door of Australia was now being savaged by all the white ghosts from the South, tearing at the feet of this monolith, leaping high as though to clutch the hair of a giant and pull

---

[27] Upfield, *The New Shoe*, 88.

[28] Upfield, *The New Shoe*, 166.

[29] Arthur Upfield, *Bony and the White Savage* (London: Heinemann, 1961), 57.

[30] Upfield, *Bony and the White Savage*, 19.

[31] Upfield, *Bony and the White Savage*, 76.

[32] Upfield, *Bony and the White Savage*, 8.

[33] Upfield, *Bony and the White Savage*, 59.

him down for the lesser attackers to devour.[34]

Upfield's strongest books, in fact, have to do with various aspects of the supernatural. In one book, *Bushrangers of the Skies* (1940), the symbol is an airplane, a common aspect of Australian bush life, and widely used in Upfield's books though never before or after as such a supernatural agent. The symbol in this book is strong, the development powerful, though the book is not necessarily one of Upfield's half dozen most effective books.

In this book the airplane is a demonic agent, used by a madman to destroy people on the ground. Its introduction is given as a violation of the sanctity of a natural cathedral on the ground. The opening paragraph of the book unfolds the sacredness of the surroundings:

> One of Nature's oddities was the grove of six cabbage-trees in the dense shade of which Detective-Inspector Bonaparte had made his noonday camp. They grew beside an unmade road winding like a snake's track over a range of low, treeless and semi-barren hills; and, so close were they, and so virile their foliage, that to step in among them was not unlike stepping into an ivy-covered church porch on a brilliant summer morning.[35]

Bonaparte, safely inside the cool of this natural grove looks out at the events transpiring outside through a picture "framed within a leafy arch of Gothic type".[36] While around him two crows, unaware of his existence but fearing him far less than the approaching terror caw and flutter; then as the plane drops a bomb inside the grove the crows "shrieked defiance"[37] as the plane passed low above them, and the crows "left their sanctuary, and fleeing as though pursued by ten thousand hawks"[38] they fled from their sanctuary. Bony, stunned though unhurt by the bombing reacts naturally and animal-like to the attack of the silvery-gray, unmarked plane in which one person sits. His "fine lips were drawn taut, revealing his white teeth in what was almost an animal snarl of fury".[39] Thus, the lines are drawn for developing the story between the human-animal cunning of Bonaparte and the devil in the supernatural airplane. The result, though not one of Upfield's finest books, is a powerful statement of the supernatural aspects of man-made nature.

Upfield's second use of a supernatural symbol is of a different kind,

---

[34] Upfield, Bony and the White Savage, 211.

[35] Arthur Upfield, *Bushranger of the Skies* (Sydney: Angus & Robertson, 1940), 1.

[36] Upfield, *Bushranger of the Skies*, 4.

[37] Upfield, *Bushranger of the Skies*, 3.

[38] Upfield, *Bushranger of the Skies*, 5.

[39] Upfield, *Bushranger of the Skies*, 6.

less Christian but more heroically supernatural. And this book, living up very fully to the promise of the symbol, is perhaps his most powerful. *The Will of the Tribe* turns on Bony's greatest problem, whether as mediator between the two civilizations, white and aboriginal, he should give in to one or the other. In other words, the tug between the two which he and his author, Upfield, read as wrenching the country and the two cultures apart every day. This book is Upfield's most anguished examination of the struggle, and in this one, though not in others, Upfield and Bony come down on the side of the aborigines.

In a crater called Lucifer's Couch, created three hundred years ago by a falling meteor, a dead white man is discovered by a plane load of people flying over. The crater had been fearfully avoided by natives for years. Now, however, the cosmically created cause of tension, or a symbol of tension, between the whites and the aborigines must be studied in order to catch the murderer. The supernatural symbol is subsumed under a more mundane but omnipresent symbol of civilization versus naturalness, and is given social ramifications by virtue of the fact that a group of politicians have descended upon the environs to investigate the murder.

Throughout his series of books, Upfield, like Thomas Carlyle and many others before and after him, especially those prone to see symbols, uses a dominant symbol in depicting freedom vs. restraint, happiness vs. civilization, the aborigine vs. the civilized: clothes. Nakedness is natural, wearing clothes is civilized and unnatural. In one way or another, to one degree or another, in all the books where he is contrasting aborigines against whites, Upfield uses the figures of dressedness and undressedness. Aborigines wear as few clothes as possible, civilized whites wear many clothes. Where the aborigine must wear something to hide his nakedness, he should wear feathers, a natural kind of covering, but not the clothes of the whites. In the powerful study of the power of primitiveness and of tribal customs, *The Bone Is Pointed*, the witch doctor and others of the tribe, when they were casting their spell were "entirely naked save for the masses of feathers about his feet".[40] In *The Mystery of Swordfish Reef* (1939), Upfield, who has admitted that on the sea Bony is outside his element, more vulnerable, is therefore more likely to present his symbols in their starkest strength. Such is his presentation of the clothes metaphor. Mr. Rockaway, a Jekyll-and-Hyde character whose obsession is, significantly, swordfishing, is trying to destroy Bony, who, however, has escaped and is sneaking upon Rockaway from the rear to destroy him for the pain and suffering he has inflicted upon others. Bony's garb is the ultimate in reversing to the natural state:

---

[40] Upfield, *The Bone Is Pointed*, 139.

His general appearance was the antithesis of that of the being known to his colleagues. The veneer of civilization, so thin in the most gently nurtured of us, was entirely absent. He was wearing nothing. A film of oil caused his body to gleam like new bronze. His hair was matted with blood. His eyes were big, and the whites were now blood-shot. His lips were widely parted, revealing his teeth like the fangs of a young dog.[41]

In *The Will of the Tribe* the role clothes play is even more extended and dramatic. The kind and civilized Brentner family with two daughters of their own have taken into their family a beautiful aboriginal girl, Tessa, the age of the daughters. The family plans for Tessa, who is treated like the white people, to go to college, which is unheard of for an aborigine, and then to become a school teacher. Tessa generally dresses in white, like the rest of the family. On the farm there is another aborigine, a young man, two years older than Tessa, who is called Captain, and is treated almost like a member of the family, surely with the same respect that other members of the working crew are accorded. He too dresses in white.

Nakedness and naturalness, or the lack of it, is the dominant theme in the plot. The countryside around the farm is described as "naked" therefore natural though barren. The aborigines are always being reprimanded for walking around naked, even without the customary feathers on their feet.

Tessa and the Captain represent two degrees of nativeness. She is trying to get away from it, the Captain, on the contrary, trying to conform to it and retain it. Yet in her reluctance to be entirely separated from her background, Tessa collects legends of the aborigines. The Captain is writing a history of his people. She is treating the subject nostalgically and romantically; he is treating it realistically. Bony, as the plot unfolds, is torn between the two points of view. He commends Tessa for her accomplishment: "You are a remarkable girl, Tessa," he told her, and she accepted the compliment with natural ease. Bony elaborates his point of view:

> "You know, there have been situations in my career when I've found myself acting as a kind of bridge spanning the gulf between the Aboriginal and the white mind. If you realise your ambitions you might well build a far stronger bridge, because you are thinking as a white woman."

He explains his situation: "I am only half black, and yet I, too, have felt the pull towards my mother's race. It's tremendously powerful ..."[42] The

---

[41] Arthur Upfield, *The Mystery of Swordfish Reef* (Sydney: Angus & Robertson, 1939), 243-244.

[42] Upfield: *The Will of the Tribe*, 68.

Captain has already decided to serve his people; in fact he never toyed with the idea of serving any other.

Bony is torn between these two forces, his head telling him that one serves best by being outside the tradition, his heart telling him that instead one serves best by being within and a part of the system. The solution of the plot of the book and the resolution of this dilemma turns on clothes as a symbol.

Tessa, though the sweetest of individuals and trying hard to be white, cannot wear her two traditions without much personal conflict. She dresses immaculately, yet, like an aboriginal woman, she is likely to swing her hips around men to attract their attention. She admits she is vain and enjoys being stared at. The Captain, loving Tessa, thinks that the clothes keep her too far from him, representing too much civilization for a young aboriginal woman; he resents them.

This particular tension of the book is released in one of the most dramatic and bizarre episodes in literature. The Captain, caught as being guilty of having killed the white man found in Lucifer's Couch, turns a gun on Bony and Tessa, telling her that she is his lubra (his woman). She, not sure she wants to give up civilized life, starts to run from Captain. He follows. Now the role of clothes becomes dominant. Tessa, realizing that she has become soft wearing white woman's clothes and shoes, realizes that if she is to escape from Captain she must discard her clothes. Captain, refusing to allow Tessa to get away, chases after her. During the chase, Tessa, in order to escape, first strips her skirt off, then, not being able to outrun the man, she stops and pulls her slip over her head. Then she pulls off her blouse and her bra. When she is virtually naked, feeling the cool air about her body, she feels free. "She knew she had regained what they said was her second wind, and another glance behind her showed her Captain was losing the race."[43]

But she has not won the race for her life, and is not sure that she wants to. As she runs, she thinks over her past life and realizes that

> the clothes she had worn for so long, the books and the study, the ambition to become a teacher, it hadn't been real after all. It was all a story told her by someone ... She was an Aborigine.[44]

In her ears sings

> her mother's voice, and the voices of all the women in the world.

---

[43] Upfield: *The Will of the Tribe*, 207.
[44] Upfield: *The Will of the Tribe*, 208.

"Now you know what to do if you are caught away from camp by a strange Aborigine", they said.[45]

And Tessa, hearing this admonition, reaches down and pulls off her "beautiful green silk panties" and then collapses upon "the sandy ground and clawed the sand over her breasts and between her thighs".[46]

In her mad chase to achieve what she thought was freedom, Tessa has turned several times toward Lucifer's Couch, feeling that in its confines she can hide and be protected—is calling on demonic assistance. But each time the supernatural assistance she is seeking is denied, and the natural life of the Aborigines pursues and eventually catches up with her. And she is glad. She becomes Captain's lover and his love. It is not a union of unequals, but of equals. The man and woman, now together, ran, not fast, "but together," toward what is obviously the accomplishment of the Aborigines, life in the traditional style.

> [Bony knew that] Tessa had surrendered to the elfin call of her people, had put from her the slowly built influences of white assimilation, even as she had discarded the white-woman's clothes.[47]

But Upfield wants to give Tessa another chance to relinquish the life of the aborigine. He is not sure Tessa has made up her mind, and not sure that he wants her to make that choice. So Bony brings her a new set of clothes which she puts on.

> [He] calculated that now, as she dressed in clothes she had been educated to wear with distinction the primitive woman would be conquered by the sophisticated girl of the homestead.[48]

But with her mind now made up for the return to Aboriginal life, Tessa will not revert from her reversion, for her clothes are now ill-fitting and uncomfortable. These clothes "without the foundations, the smartly-cut skirt and the light-blue blouse made her pathetic", but her reversion is not complete.[49] As they gather around a campfire to boil tea, Tessa at first squatted on her heels, as a lubra does, but then remembered, "correcting herself by sitting on the grounds and tucking her knees under the skirt".[50]

---

[45] Upfield: *The Will of the Tribe*, 208.
[46] Upfield: *The Will of the Tribe*, 209.
[47] Upfield: *The Will of the Tribe*, 215.
[48] Upfield: *The Will of the Tribe*, 228.
[49] Upfield: *The Will of the Tribe*, 228.
[50] Upfield: *The Will of the Tribe*, 229.

But despite the momentary glance back into civilization, Tessa had made the decision she wanted. She tells Bony that she and Captain had had their way with each other: "We ran together into Eden by the back door."[51] That does not mean that she has given up her civilized way of life, just properly proportioned it. After she and Captain are married, she remains at the homestead to help out, in a position hardly changed from that she had held before the great trauma, but not with the plans to become a school teacher and act as an intermediary between her race and the white one.

What does this episode in what is perhaps Upfield's strongest book really mean? This is the next to the last book that he finished, and his concluding statement on the subject, after a lifetime of observing and worrying. Was Upfield, after all, a sexist? Did he believe that a woman's place was on the reservation? This is his most obvious and powerful statement of such an attitude. Surely he is saying that civilization is not beneficial for the Aborigines. In *Man of Two Tribes* he says that "[e]ighty per cent of tribal strife has its origin in white interference".[52] He is certainly interested in advancing the cause of the Aborigines, Bony's great ambition in life, and he may well believe that the cause can best be served by working from within. It would seem that he is denying Tessa the goal in life that she at least at one time thought she would enjoy and deserved. He is not saying that the two races can't mix; Bony was himself a half-caste and knew many others who were exemplary and useful citizens. And he painted many full-blooded aborigines as scoundrels. One thing is clear. Despite a life of wandering the Australian continent, or because of it, Upfield, like Bony, seemed to prefer order to chaos. Bony admired General Napoleon Bonaparte, for whom he was named, since Napoleon "never lost a battle because he planned against the future". Maybe Upfield felt it was easier to plan ahead in one's established role in society, to work from the inside out, evolutionarily rather than revolutionarily. As he had declared earlier, in *Bony and the Black Virgin*,

> complete assimilation isn't achieved by the aborigine via swift passage from one State to another ... Assimilation is gradual and requires several generations.[53]

But there can be no question that Upfield was not antifeminist. Though he had some difficulty picturing real-life women, he was not alone. Most men have this difficulty regardless of their attitude toward liberated

---

[51] Upfield: *The Will of the Tribe*, 231.
[52] Upfield, *Man of Two Tribes*, 16-17.
[53] Upfield, *Bony and the Black Virgin*, 183-184.

women. In one book in particular, *Madman's Bend*, Upfield had pictured the evils of men and the strength of women. In this book, Lush is a drunken beast who abuses his wife and step-daughter. He is shot, and all evidence points to the step-daughter, who had the gun, the desire, and actually fired the gun through a door directly at her step-father. Although Upfield obviously hates Lush, he uses the book to point out the strength of women, especially young women. There can be no doubt where Upfield stands on the question of the strength of women.

Whatever philosophical and sociological conclusion one can draw from Upfield's books on this particular subject, and it surely must be positive, one must recognize that Upfield always wrote first-class heroic novels which turned on some kind of crime. He created one of the most remarkable detectives in crime fiction, a humanist who worked toward the betterment of society. In his half dozen superior books, Upfield created works of such power that they must be ranked with the finest and most respected works of not only crime fiction but of heroic literature of all kinds.

First published in *Clues: A Journal of Detection* 7.1 (Spring/Summer 1986): 127-145. Some minor revisions were made, and most of the references were added by the editors.

MYSTERY LITERATURE AND ETHNOGRAPHY: FICTIONAL DETECTIVES AS ANTHROPOLOGISTS

JAMES C. PIERSON[1]

Mystery and spy literature make extensive use of a variety of geographic and cultural settings. In most novels of this type, however, the settings are primarily background; any cultural information is very general, almost stereotypic, and of little significance to the story's progress. It may therefore seem presumptuous even to suggest a relationship between ethnographic anthropology and some mystery literature. Nevertheless, there are a number of ambitious writers of detective fiction who include considerable cultural information in an attempt to do more than simply entertain the reader.

The activities of detectives, whether fictional or real, may be of interest to many readers because there is something at least vaguely familiar about their methods. Recognizing a problem, analyzing it, and determining and using methods of solving it are part of almost any occupation. Both Robin Winks,[2] a historian, and William B. Sanders,[3] a sociologist, for example, discuss similarities between their professions' research methods and those of detectives. Mystery writer Ross Macdonald makes observations about detectives and the nature of their work that relate directly to anthropology. He contends that one of the most important qualities of good detectives is a

---

[1] Writing this paper involved anthropological research in the sense that it brought me into extensive contact with a "culture" of novels and literary criticism and analysis. The number of secondary sources is particularly impressive; a useful guide for sorting out the more relevant ones has been Walter Albert, *Detective and Mystery Fiction: An International Bibliography of Secondary Sources* (Madison, Indiana: Brownstone, 1985).

[2] Robin Winks, ed., *Colloquium on Crime: Eleven Renowned Mystery Writers Discuss Their Work*, 1-6 (New York: Scribner, c1986), 4, 5.

[3] William Sanders, *The Sociologist as Detective: An Introduction to Research Methods* (New York: Praeger, 1974), xx.

selfless chameleon aspect which allows them to move on various levels of society, ranging from the campus to the slums, and fade in and out of the woodwork on demand. They are able to submerge themselves in the immediate milieu and behave according to its customs and talk the language: a little Spanish in East Los Angeles, a little jive in Watts, a little Levi-Strauss in Westwood.[4]

Although few anthropologists—and likely few detectives—would claim to be selfless in their work, much of the statement is consistent with general goals of ethnographic research. Macdonald also claims that "a good private detective ... likes to move through society both horizontally and vertically, studying people like an anthropologist".[5]

One implication is that fictional detectives who do their jobs well, as almost all do, are successful at least partly because of ethnographic knowledge and abilities. It seems logical, therefore, that the works of fiction in which these detectives appear are potentially useful sources of information about the various groups of people dealt with by the detectives. A number of critics are nevertheless reluctant to consider mystery literature as a source of sociocultural information. The editors of two fifty-volume series of classic crime fiction, for example, selected novels by Tony Hillerman and Arthur Upfield, both of whom use considerable cultural and geographic description. Hillerman's novel is *The Fly on the Wall*, his only non-Navajo mystery; the Upfield novel makes little use of his detective's part-Aboriginal background. The editors' introduction to the former contends that "reading about the American Southwest or the West Indies is pleasant enough, but crime, character, clues, humor, and plot are apt to be swamped in local color and factuality".[6] Their introduction to Upfield's work claims that his most admirable novels are his later ones that "dispense with exotic scenery and native lore and concentrate on character, mystery, and clues".[7] It is not just that ethnographic information is not considered potentially significant; ethnographic references and contextual descriptions seem to be considered distracting at best and incompatible with the important qualities of a good mystery at worst.

Some critics and novelists disagree with such limitations. Margaret J.

[4] Ross Macdonald, *Ross Macdonald's Lew Archer, Private Investigator* (New York: Mysterious, 1977), v.
[5] Macdonald, *Ross Macdonald's Lew Archer*, xii.
[6] Jacques Barzun and Wendell Taylor, "Introduction" in *The Fly on the Wall*, by Tony Hillerman (New York: Garland, 1983), iv-v.
[7] Jacques Barzun and Wendell Taylor, "Preface" in *The Bone Is Pointed*, Arthur Upfield (New York: Garland, 1976), i.

King, for example, contends that whereas considerable attention has been paid to detective stories as a part of Western cultures, there has been little attention to what detective stories can "teach readers about culture". The educational task of the authors is recognized as a difficult one: both the crime and the "foreign way of life" must be carefully described.[8] John G. Cawelti, on the other hand, maintains that although "the detective story situation works with many different cultural settings because the investigation of a puzzling crime casts light on the workings of a society by catching it at a moment of anomaly and disruption", it is a Western cultural product, and its standard form is not adequate to portray most non-Western cultures.[9] Even detective stories featuring cultural mediators or brokers are limited, claims Cawelti, because such characters fall into the Western tradition of mythical figures who perpetuate a fantasy that the inherent cultural conflicts between traditional and modern/colonial cultures can be "mediated and justly resolved".[10] Cawelti considers Arthur Upfield's fictional detective, Napoleon Bonaparte, to be one of the most successful examples of cultural conflict and ambiguity in detective fiction and a "major achievement" in the genre.[11] The Bonaparte character, however, remains a fantasy to Cawelti for the reasons just discussed.

The potential in detective novels for cross-cultural education is obviously open to question. The rest of this paper is therefore concerned with examining the extent and realization of that potential in detective novels set in a variety of cultural and geographic settings. The discussion that follows is selective, emphasizing the work of writers whose books, all in series, are readily available in bookstores and libraries—these are the books likely to attract the general reader's attention. It begins with a very brief consideration of books that, whatever their appearances; tend to rely on quite general sociocultural information. It concludes with an examination of some works by Upfield and Hillerman.

Lew Archer and Other Detectives as Ethnographers

A logical starting place would seem to be Ross Macdonald's novels. Ironically, however, the detective created by the author whose comments inspired this paper rarely gives readers specific ethnographic information.

---

[8] Margaret King, "Binocular Eyes: Cross-Cultural Detectives," *Armchair Detective* 13 (1980): 255.

[9] John Cawelti, "Murder in the Outback: Arthur W. Upfield," *New Republic* 177.5 (1977): 39.

[10] Cawelti, "Murder in the Outback," 40.

[11] Cawelti, "Murder in the Outback," 41.

The problem, if that is what it is, is that Macdonald's novels are set in a complex society and that the characters in each are from quite diverse backgrounds. This not only tries the ethnographic abilities of his detective, Lew Archer, it also means that the reader is exposed to only a bit of the meaning of that diversity. The reader does not always share in the detective's specific knowledge about the people with whom he is dealing. Just as it would be impossible for even a team of ethnographers to provide a thorough overview of such settings and the people in them, it is impossible for Macdonald, through his detective, to do so. Thus Lew Archer may function like an anthropologist, but the nature of the society in which he works tends to keep his exploits from providing solid ethnographic examples.

The ethnographic potential of other detective novelists is similarly limited by the authors' broad perspectives. Some detective novels that initially seem to include numerous cultural details prove on further examination to provide only a bit of local color. A series of novels by Eric Wright featuring a Toronto police inspector and a series by Peter Corris about a private investigator in Sydney offer similarly impressionistic portraits of their specific urban, national, and cultural settings. There are few details that give a reader insight into the cultural traits of Canadians or Australians. The settings are used to make the novels appear different from other mystery novels, but are not utilized to make the stories themselves much different.

A series of novels by James Melville featuring Superintendent Tetsuo Otani and other detectives of the Hyogo Prefectural Police in Japan makes somewhat better use of its cultural settings. A few details of Japanese etiquette, religious practices, and other cultural traits appear in each book. A type of Japanese puppet plays a crucial role in *A Sort of Samurai*; ivory *netsuke* figures are central to *The Ninth Netsuke*, and traditional Japanese housing and living styles are important topics in *The Chrysanthemum Chain*. Although most elements of Japanese culture are discussed only generally, the detectives' tendencies to learn about both foreign and Japanese cultural traits as they work make them nevertheless similar to ethnographers attempting to piece together cultural information. The ethnographic picture is simply a fragmentary one that portrays only a small part of an immense national character and some of the changes and conflicts between that character and elements of Western life.

Irish Police Chief Inspector of Detectives Peter McGarr, the central character in a series of mysteries by Bartholomew Gill, encounters a variety of people and situations while solving crimes that take him to both rural and urban (especially Dublin) settings. There are generalized glimpses and insights into rural Irish life, sporting and leisure activities, and family and pub life. Considerable attention is also given to the Irish Republican Army. The novels are not ethnographic, but they do provide some of the flavor of selected aspects of Irish culture.

Detective novels by Dutch author Janwillem van de Wetering have been praised for both their descriptions of Amsterdam and their originality, the result of the author's Zen-influenced orientation. Van de Wetering's novels and detectives deal with several topics that are of ethnographic interest. Most relevant here are Amsterdam's social and geographical components and cultural diversity.

Each novel contains characters and situations that take the detectives to different sections of Amsterdam or other parts of Holland. As a result the series has been noted as a useful introduction to Amsterdam.[12] Non-Dutch visitors to or residents of Amsterdam provide van de Wetering's readers with general information about a number of different cultures. Although van de Wetering's first detective novel was titled *Outsider in Amsterdam*, each of his novels includes at least one character fitting that description. That first outsider is a Papuan with colonial ties to Holland; others are from Japan, Surinam, and Curacao. Cultural diversity is further demonstrated through characters from a religious commune, or from a distant Dutch province, as well as others who are Jewish, Italian, American, and Arabic. Obviously, van de Wetering casts a broad net in all of his novels. This broad net does not allow extensive examination of Amsterdam or the cultural groups, but it does provide the basis for a generally informative and appealing series of books.

Another relevant series of detective stories, or "police procedurals", is by James McClure, a former South African journalist. The series features a white South African detective and his Zulu partner, who together are able to work in almost any cultural setting. The novels involve both black and white victims and/or suspects and illustrate a number of characteristics of apartheid, including white attitudes towards blacks and towards each other. Black adaptations to the South African situation surface frequently as the cases are investigated. In *Snake*, for example, the reader learns about black living conditions, such as the absence of electricity,[13] and the scarcity of meat in blacks' diets.[14] He learns also about whites' stereotyping of blacks as being a mixture of the worst characteristics of all races[15] and

---

[12] Derek Shearer, "Books Offer Clues to Solving the Mystery of a City," *Los Angeles Times,* Travel Section, 5 October 1986.

[13] James McClure, *Snake* (New York: Pantheon, 1975), 46.

[14] McClure, *Snake,* 54.

[15] McClure, *Snake,* 116.

as believing that all whites are rich.[16] Finally, he is presented with some alleged black superstitions or beliefs about certain people being witch doctors or wizards.[17] Subtle details and local terms and ideas are scattered throughout the novels, but most noticeable is a general sense of tensions and prejudice.

McClure is quite conscious of his presentation of South Africa to outsiders. He notes that defining the fictional city of Trekkersburg, based on his former home, was difficult. "It was, I felt, not unlike writing science fiction, in that I had to get across what amounted to a totally alien world, with its strange languages, customs, scenery, and laws."[18] This statement is as applicable to anthropological ethnography as it is to science fiction. It is therefore interesting that McClure has written detailed nonfiction books about police departments in Liverpool and San Diego on the basis of long-term first-hand research. It is apparent that McClure's journalistic experiences give him information and insights that are similar to those of more formal, methodologically oriented researchers; he uses these data in works of fiction as well as nonfiction.

Ethnographic Mystery Novels?

The authors of the works just discussed place their detectives in complex sociocultural settings. Arthur Upfield and Tony Hillerman place their detectives, however, in much more specific cultural units and settings, an Australian Aboriginal culture and Navajo culture, respectively. The detectives are also at least partially educated in the white cultures of their respective settings and thus have the ability to interpret relatively subtle aspects of at least two cultures. In fact, this ability is usually necessary for the solution of their cases. The detectives subsequently provide the reader with cultural information throughout a case rather than only in isolated places. Because their socialization took place in cultures that interact closely with the natural environment, descriptions of the physical settings are also important and detailed.

Despite the similarities just discussed, however, there are some important contrasts between the two authors' detectives and novels. Some of these are examined below.

---

[16] McClure, *Snake,* 126.

[17] McClure, *Snake,* 74.

[18] James McClure, "A Bright Grey," in *Colloquium on Crime: Eleven Renowned Mystery Writers Discuss Their Work,* ed. Robin Spinks (New York: Scribner, 1986), 167-188.

Arthur W. Upfield and Napoleon Bonaparte

Arthur Upfield's novels featuring part-Aboriginal, part-white Detective Inspector Napoleon Bonaparte may be even better known now, more than twenty years after Upfield's death, than they were when they were written. They are regularly available in reprint, and it is almost certain that a knowledgeable librarian or bookstore clerk will suggest them if asked for mystery or detective novels with anthropological themes.

Napoleon Bonaparte is the main character in twenty-nine of Upfield's books, almost all of which take place in isolated areas of Australia. The detective's mixed ancestry directs at least some attention in each book to cultural and sometimes implied biological contrasts between Aboriginal and white Australians, especially as they affect Bonaparte's behavior or thinking. Bonaparte is an initiated Aboriginal male as a result of experiences and knowledge acquired late in life, which include tracking skills and religion; he was first formally educated in the "white world" (he even went through the university) after being found with his dead Aboriginal mother by whites when he was an infant. He is acquainted with both Aborigines who have been influenced by white cultural patterns, and with whites who have little formal education. Although some of his physical features demonstrate his part-Aboriginal ancestry, Bonaparte rarely fails to gain the respect of whites quickly when he chooses; when he does not choose to, he is able to play the subordinate role that most whites expect of persons of Aboriginal ancestry. As a Detective Inspector, Bonaparte is a representative of the government, but he has the freedom and the sometimes vague charge to stay with a case until it has been solved. These cases can apparently take him anywhere in Australia and do not always involve interaction with other Aborigines.

Upfield's accounts of outback cultures examine more than differences between Aborigines and whites. As has been discussed effectively by others, for example Cawelti[19] and King,[20] both groups have subdivisions. Bonaparte regularly contrasts the "wild" or traditional Aborigines and the less traditional ones who live near white stations and settlements. Another very small subgroup is represented by Bonaparte, the bicultural part-Aborigine. There are several subdivisions among whites as well, including outback station owners and other people of property; station hands and other workers; and representatives of the government and other components of the distant, more "modern" national culture. Missionaries are noticeably absent from most Upfield books. Although it would be

---

[19] Cawelti, "Murder in the Outback," 39-40.
[20] King, "Binocular Eyes," 258.

instructive to examine each of these groups, attention herein is limited to Aborigines.

A problem arises, immediately, however. It may seem that the multicultural Bonaparte presents an objective perspective of each group and a particularly instructive insider's view of the Aborigine cultures. Yet Upfield tends to send mixed ethnographic messages about Aborigines through Bonaparte, who makes some unfavorable observations about Aborigines despite the great pride that he seems to take in his part-Aboriginal ancestry. It is one thing to have white characters state derogatory attitudes about Aborigines, if that is part of the white world view, but it is quite another to have the hero, an apparently proud and well-adjusted part-Aborigine, do the same. Upfield's novels are consequently sometimes confusing or misleading in an ethnographic sense because it is not always clear whether the perspective that is afforded is Upfield's or that of an "assimilated part-Aborigine," as interpreted by Upfield. In addition, readers can get conflicting messages about Aborigines from different Upfield books. Some specific examples help illustrate these points and the other types of ethnographic information the books contain.

Some of Upfield's plots center around elements of traditional Aboriginal cultures such as the importance of sacred stones and other objects and places (*The Will of the Tribe*), and the practice of causing the death of others through "pointing the bone". The tracking skills of many Aboriginal males, including Bonaparte, the knowledge and ability to influence events far beyond their own travels, the threats of punishment for breaking taboos, and the various spiritual beliefs are frequently part of Aboriginal behavior in Upfield's books. Upfield includes subtle but effective references to cultural traits such as the sitting postures of Aboriginal males, the etiquette of conversation that requires several casual topics to be discussed before getting to the reason for the conversation, and the "shutters" that are said to close in the eyes of an Aborigine when proper etiquette has not been followed or an inappropriate subject is pursued. If there is an ethnographic shortcoming in these and some other cultural references, it is that Upfield, through Bonaparte, tends to imply that there was much more uniformity among Aboriginal cultures than ethnographic records indicate.

A more serious shortcoming is that Upfield's Bonaparte often struggles to limit the influence of his Aboriginal heritage on his behavior as a detective. In one sense, such situations are ethnographically significant because they show the reader a conflict likely experienced by many people caught between two cultures. In another sense, they tend to demean the traditional culture because Bonaparte's "civilized" self eventually takes control. The struggle is not just implied but is one that Bonaparte recognizes. For example:

> Ever the inherited influences of the two races warred for the soul of Napoleon Bonaparte, and it was the very continuity of this warfare which had created Detective Inspector Bonaparte, and which time and again prevented him from sinking back into the more primitive of the two races.[21]

Although Upfield intends this passage to carry the idea that Bonaparte is a successful detective because he possesses knowledge and skills from two cultures, perhaps combining the best from both, it is phrased in a way that makes one culture appear quite inferior to the other.

In *Bony and the Black Virgin*, Upfield sympathetically portrays a relationship between a white man and an Aboriginal woman, and Bonaparte notes the power of the woman's spirituality. These objective passages are undermined to some extent, however, by Bonaparte's thoughts about Aboriginal workers on white settlements as people who "invariably underdo it or overdo it"[22] and numerous "compliments" about the Aboriginal woman's appearance. These descriptions include "for an aborigine, she was pleasing to behold",[23] and Bonaparte's thoughts that "for an aborigine, she was good-looking".[24] The descriptions appear to be devices to convince readers why a white man would be attracted to an Aboriginal woman (that is, she was not typical in appearance). The reader's ethnographic detective in this case provides distressingly subjective descriptions in the context of what appears to be an objective examination of a cross-cultural relationship.

In *The Bone Is Pointed*, however, Upfield not only examines the potential influence of traditional cultures on a "man of two tribes" like Bonaparte but also has the character make numerous observations that stress the strength and importance of Aboriginal cultures and the negative influence of white society on many Aborigines. Bonaparte, for example, explains that Aboriginal superiority in the bush is owing to the "apprenticeship" served by Aborigines while young rather than to natural abilities.[25] He is described as "the man who had so often proved that aboriginal blood and brains were equal to those of the white man".[26] He

---

[21] Arthur Upfield, *Man of Two Tribes* (London: Heinemann, 1956), 57.

[22] Arthur Upfield, *Bony and the Black Virgin* (Sydney: Pan, 1959), 117.

[23] Upfield, *Bony and the Black Virgin*, 57.

[24] Upfield, *Bony and the Black Virgin*, 123.

[25] Arthur Upfield, *The Bone Is Pointed* (New York: Garland, 1947), 105.

[26] Upfield, *The Bone Is Pointed*, 31.

points out that "in many things it is the aboriginal who is the highly developed civilized being and the white man who is the savage",[27] and he suggests that "in this country colour is no bar to a man's progress providing that he has twice the ability of his rivals".[28]

Bonaparte's attempts to solve a missing person case that becomes a murder case lead to his being "boned" (a form of sorcery) by local Aborigines. Although the murderer is white, his close relationships with the local Aborigines cause them, unsolicited, to try to help him. The Aborigines are aware that he killed the missing man, who was consistently cruel to them. Bonaparte recognizes that he is being followed and boned. He nearly dies, and he experiences another struggle between his Aboriginal and white selves. In this case, however, readers get a sense of the power of the Aboriginal beliefs. Most importantly, when Bonaparte does survive, it is because the boning is stopped, not because his white will triumphs. From the beginning, Bonaparte anticipates his struggle with the local Aborigines as a potentially difficult one because the Aborigines will not make the "stupid mistakes" whites usually do.[29]

In general, *The Bone Is Pointed* contains an objective and understanding picture of Aboriginal people and cultures and the potential problems of culture change. Many subsequent Upfield books offer less objective descriptions of Aboriginal cultures. Overall, however, Upfield's use of a part-Aboriginal hero and other Aboriginal characters at all is unusual for the time period during which his books were originally published (the twenties through the mid-sixties). At the same time, some of the situations Bonaparte encounters and his reactions to them may perpetuate stereotypes of Aborigines. Upfield's descriptions of Australian landscapes and the relationships of various cultural groups with the land and with each other are often vivid, but the perspective is that of a white with extensive outback experience, even though the protagonist is part-Aboriginal. Upfield does not often try to present an Aboriginal perspective, although Bonaparte's background makes him seem to be doing so. Bonaparte's main influences are white rather than Aboriginal, and these influences affect the ethnographic perspective.

Tony Hillerman, Joe Leaphorn and Jim Chee

Tony Hillerman's mysteries featuring Navajo policemen share several features with Upfield's novels. The mechanisms used by Hillerman to

---

[27] Upfield, *The Bone Is Pointed*, 45.
[28] Upfield, *The Bone Is Pointed*, 53-54.
[29] Upfield, *The Bone Is Pointed*, 92.

introduce cultural elements, however, contrast more with Upfield's than is initially apparent. For example, Hillerman consistently presents a Navajo perspective. His presentation of Navajo culture is a much more contextual, humanistic one than is Upfield's presentation of Aboriginal cultures, at least partly because of the differences in their detectives.

The first three of Hillerman's seven "Navajo" novels feature Navajo Tribal Police Lieutenant Joe Leaphorn, the next three feature Officer Jim Chee, and the latest features both. Certain characteristics that are the result of growing up in Navajo culture help make Chee and Leaphorn effective police detectives. Their familiarity with Navajo culture is obviously important, but their Navajo emphases on harmony and the interconnections of things and events make them discount coincidences and carefully consider all clues, including irregularities and inconsistencies. Both possess tracking skills and excellent memories that were developed through long, careful training. Chee at various times reflects on how these skills were developed, helping the reader see their significance in traditional settings and their cultural rather than biological basis.

Leaphorn is older and somewhat more comfortable (or familiar) with the ways of whites. Chee's connections to Navajo traditions, especially through his training to be a singer, or ritual leader, are strong. He finds certain Navajo beliefs, such as those in "skinwalkers" or practitioners of witchcraft, more credible and less harmful than does Leaphorn. Neither Chee nor Leaphorn has a thorough understanding of *both* white and Navajo cultures. Subsequently, neither is a so-called fantasy figure like Bonaparte, who is able to resolve cultural differences and misunderstandings. Chee, in fact, is sometimes surprised by whites' behavior and beliefs, which makes his character useful for illustrating Navajo culture and comparing it to that of non-Navajos. In some situations, the differences are subtle yet significant. Since revenge is not a motive for action among Navajos, for example, Chee is slow to realize in *The Dark Wind* that revenge is the cause of what seems to him to be unpredictable behavior. Both Chee and Leaphorn deal with whites in their jobs and often feel obliged to talk when it seems not only unnecessary but rude:

> Chee was conscious that Bales was waiting for him to say something. This white man's custom of expecting a listener to do more than listen was contrary to Chee's courteous Navajo conditioning.[30]

Chee has more of these thoughts not only because he is still learning about whites but also because he spends considerable time with or thinking

---

[30] Tony Hillerman, *The Ghostway* (New York: Avon, 1984), 5.

about his white girlfriend. In one passage, Chee ponders her noticing his drinking the water with which he had just rinsed his coffee cup. To him, his behavior was so automatic that initially he couldn't understand her remark; hauling water most of his life made him so careful of using water that "it had seemed odd to Chee that not wasting water had seemed odd" to her.[31]

In other situations, the cultural differences are less subtle. In *People of Darkness*, for example, Chee reflects on what seems to him to be a strange inscription on a white woman's tombstone:

> Everything about the white man's burial customs seemed odd to Chee. The Navajo lacked this sentimentality about corpses. Death robbed the body of its value. Even its identity was lost with the departing *chindi*. What the ghost left behind was something to be disposed of with a minimum of risk of contamination to the living. The names of the dead were left unspoken, certainly not carved in stone.[32]

Some whites' stereotypes about Indians occasionally trouble Chee, and his reactions can also provide useful contexts for ethnographic information. In one situation, a white who generalized about Indians being good trackers receives an informative lesson from Chee about how and why some Navajos are good trackers while others aren't. The fact that the tracking of people, animals, and vehicles is important in Chee's (and Leaphorn's) work makes this explanation an important one; Chee's tracking abilities are subsequently considered by readers to be highly trained skills. Bonaparte's tracking abilities in Upfield's novels seem to be the result of a much more vague and consequently somewhat mysterious "apprenticeship".

In another case, the common conception among white visitors that many Indians look alike causes Chee to think about the obvious differences he sees not only among Navajo, Hopi, and Zuni individuals but also among Navajos from different areas. These differences, based not only on cultural and kinship differences but also on physical features, are often important to understanding the elements of a crime and its aftermath. It is a lesson on diversity among the Navajos, not just between them and their neighbors.

Chee, in *The Ghostway*, acquaints the reader with the Navajo death practices of preparing the body so the journey of the *chindi* will be completed. When death occurs in a hogan, Chee also describes the proper

---

[31] Tony Hillerman, *Skinwalkers* (New York: Harper, 1986), 146.
[32] Tony Hillerman, *People of Darkness* (New York: Avon, 1980), 11-12.

steps in removing the corpse, plugging the smoke hole, and abandoning the dwelling to the ghost. Knowledge of these procedures is important because their presence or absence can tell the policeman and reader a great deal about what has happened if other evidence is not available. In fact, knowing the importance of belongings or of behavior is often crucial to the Navajo policeman. Chee, for example, risks ghost contamination by entering a hogan with a corpse hole in it and finds a missing man's medicine bundle. This discovery immediately informs Chee that the man is dead because the bundle would have been "his most treasured belonging" and he would not have willingly left it.[33] The significance of the bundle and the discovery is demonstrated in a passage in which Chee recalls collecting the contents for his own Four Mountains Bundle and considers the even greater difficulty the man would have had years earlier in getting to the four distant areas. It is an important clue for Chee and gives the reader information about several elements of Navajo culture.

Hillerman's detectives acquaint readers with such topics as the Navajo-Hopi land dispute, Navajo beliefs in ghosts and witchcraft (and those who oppose such beliefs and their consequences), Zuni Shalako ceremonies and preparations for them, and Hopi ceremonials. Readers learn also about the roles on the reservation of outsiders such as anthropologists, FBI and other federal agents, drug dealers, and trading post operators. There is considerable attention to Navajo rituals and those who lead or need them. Kin and clan relations are shown to be all-important in meeting and interviewing people and anticipating their behavior in a given situation. The detectives' actions, thoughts, and observations also bring out much more subtle elements of Navajo culture such as the etiquette of approaching another's dwelling, the rudeness of looking directly into someone else's eyes or pointing at them, and the actions that characterize a culture in which water is a scarce, valuable commodity.

It is difficult to separate the ethnographic information in Hillerman's novels from the rest of the text, not only because there is so much of it but also because it is well integrated. Hillerman's novels focus on Navajo culture much more than Upfield's focus on Aboriginal cultures largely because Hillerman's detectives are Navajos working for the Navajo Tribal Police. Despite the feelings of some Navajos, they are working for the Navajo; Bonaparte, whatever his own background and attitudes toward the local Aborigines in any given case, is a representative of the larger society. The Navajo police have been trained off the reservation and have been formally educated among whites in other contexts, such as the university, but their identities are those of Navajos with ties to specific regions and

---

[33] Hillerman, *The Ghostway*, 155.

clans. When there is the possibility of a divided loyalty, as when Chee has an opportunity to join the FBI and is romantically involved with a white teacher who does not want to remain forever on the reservation, his struggle does not involve the conflicting parts of his identity; instead, he must simply determine what will be the most appropriate decision. It is significant that Chee chooses to stay on the reservation for at least the time being. The decision is difficult, but Chee's Navajo enculturation and interest in continuing his training to be a singer give a meaning to his life that never really surfaces in Upfield's presentation of Aboriginal cultures.

Hillerman's novels are not ethnographic texts in disguise, but his detectives fulfill Ross Macdonald's aforementioned suggestions much better than do those of other writers largely because of the contexts in which he has them operating. Hillerman is commendably cautious about the use of ethnographic details, which he says must be "germane to the plot".[34] His concern for presenting the cultural traits and situations as objectively and realistically as possible is evident throughout the novels. It also is implied by the fact that the books are read with interest and pleasure by at least some Navajos.[35] It is unlikely that there has been similar interest in Upfield's books among any Australian Aborigines.

Ethnography is Where You Find It

Detective literature has an apparent potential for extensive ethnographic content because of protagonists who regularly interact with representatives of different cultural settings. The potential is, however, rarely realized. Despite the apparent disapproval of some critics and a lack of interest or ambition among most mystery writers, a few authors of detective fiction do carefully integrate considerable ethnographic detail into their novels. Their detectives inform accurately as well as entertain.

Ross Macdonald's statement about detectives as anthropologists, quoted earlier, refers to detectives who provide ethnographic information about "other" groups. Yet, the most successful detective-ethnographers seem to be those who work primarily in their own cultures and provide ethnographic information to outsiders (readers). Their own and other cultures are clarified through comparisons and contrasts. The most successful integration of ethnographic materials into police or detective novels is found in novels by Tony Hillerman. Hillerman's policemen are

---

[34] Tony Hillerman, "Mystery, Country Boys, and the Big Reservation," in *Colloquium on Crime: Eleven Renowned Mystery Writers Discuss Their Work,* ed. Robin Winks (New York: Scribner, 1986), 142.
[35] Hillerman, "Mystery, Country Boys, and the Big Reservation," 147.

credible, somewhat fallible, and, as participants in Navajo culture, unlikely to create or perpetuate ethnic stereotypes in readers' minds. Their behavior is consistent with their experiences and professional and cultural training. They do not become fantasy figures, as other ethnic detectives have been labeled, because their emphasis is on being Navajo within the larger society rather than on seeming to resolve conflicts between different ways of life. Most important in my opinion is the fact that the police detectives regularly provide information about Navajos, whites, Hopis, Zunis, FBI agents, anthropologists, and other groups of people. The information not only does not interfere with plot and characterization, as some commentators seem to fear, but is part of them. The novels can therefore increase cultural understanding, a worthwhile goal for ethnography in any format.

First Published in *Mystery Literature and Anthropology*, edited by Philip A. Dennis and Wendell Aycock, 15-30. Lubbock, TX: Texas Tech University Press, 1989.

AUSTRALIAN TALES
OF MYSTERY AND MISCEGENATION

TAMSIN DONALDSON

In 1988 the Australian government dedicated huge sums of money to celebrating the bicentenary of the "foundation of a nation". The year began with banners proclaiming the moment of origin, the arrival of Captain Phillip and his first fleet in Sydney Cove on 26 January 1788: "Happy Birthday Australia!" From the perspective of an Aboriginal Australia with its own foundation myths traced to an "absolute past" or a metaphysical "everywhen", the bicentenary was an irrelevance or an insult.[1] Nevertheless, 1788 *was* originary. For the first time, outsiders from Europe were intent on staying—or, in the case of the convicts, forced to stay. "Living together" was another of the Bicentennial Authority's provocatively cosy slogans. What sorts of cohabitation did competition for the land make possible?

The branch of history known as "contact history" has a particularly euphemistic ring when it comes to the two extreme transactions possible. One of the extremes, killing, was explicitly part of the imposition of colonial rule. Recent contact history in Australia has been very much concerned with reassessing the extent and intent of mutual violence and killing. The other extreme has been treated more coyly. There are no self-declared historians of sexual contact. Though there is a growing interest in the sexual aspects of colonization, for instance in the work of Ann McGrath, Raymond Evans, Dawn May and Lyndall Ryan (not to mention fictional approaches such as Xavier Herbert's), the attempt to understand has barely begun. By contrast with killing, the demographic consequences

---

[1] "Everywhen" is W.E.H. Stanner's translation for the concept popularized in English as "Dreaming", which is etymologically connected with dreams in some languages, as in Warlpiri *jukurrpa* in Central Australia. Foundation myths about "when people were animals" can also be located in an "absolute past", as in Ngiyampaa *marrathal-pu* from the south-east, where an "absolutizing" suffix is added to the word for "long ago" (Tamsin Donaldson, *Ngiyambaa, the Language of the Wangaaybuwan* (Cambridge: Cambridge University Press, 1980), 78).

of sexual contact are productive rather than reductive. And miscegenation,[2] the birth of new individuals descended from both locals and invaders, not only increases the population but produces people who are a potential challenge to the very terms, and terminology, of the colonial encounter.

Governor Arthur's "Message to the Tasmanian Aborigines in 1829" welcomed the prospect of locals and invaders amicably holding one another's babies. But there is no room in this pseudo-egalitarian scheme for local men and invading women, or vice versa, to stand amicably in couples with babies they have produced together. Neither is there room for recognition that such sexual encounters may be rapes and still produce children. The descendants of these kinds of unions may eventually constitute the entire population, so that no-one is of wholly local or wholly newcomer descent. Continual fresh immigration has ruled out the latter possibility in Australia, but the former has been achieved in many parts of the country.[3]

In 1978 Tom Haydon and Rhys Jones made a film entitled *The Last Tasmanian*, which dealt with the notorious genocide of Tasmanians of fully Aboriginal descent.[4] The surviving mixed population, who identify as Aboriginal Tasmanians, challenged the film's title on the grounds that it constituted a further act of verbal genocide. Whatever the range of disputes of this kind in recent years, it is remarkable that today's Australians are largely intent on debating, publicly at least, in terms of variants on the old binary categories. Various terms have been employed in English, with differences in sticking power: British versus Australians, Australians versus natives, non-Aborigines versus Aborigines, and white versus black. In Aboriginal languages there have been numerous other pairings, with etymologies that often go back to a contrast between ghosts versus persons, or spirits of the dead versus the living. And there are also

---

[2] Despite Ashley Montagu's well-argued rejection long ago of this originally satirical coinage (see *Man's Most Dangerous Myth: The Fallacy of Race* (New York: Oxford University Press, 1974), Appendix B), the word is useful here. Gillian Cowlishaw, in her substantial recent study, explains at the beginning of her three pages of sexual contact history that in the nineteenth century and now, "miscegenation is a subject of great secrecy, more even than violence". See *Black, White or Brindle: Race in Rural Australia* (Cambridge and Melbourne: Cambridge University Press, 1988), 38.

[3] Kevin Gilbert writes: "Within my tribe, the Wiradjuri, the biggest landowner group and biggest tribe in New South Wales, only approximately fifteen full-bloods were surviving in the 1940s. Today there are none." See "Black Policies" in *Aboriginal Writing Today*, ed. Jack Davis and Bob Hodge (Canberra: Australian Institute of Aboriginal Studies, 1985), 38.

[4] Tom Haydon, "The Last Tasmanian," Artis Films, Sydney, 1978.

Governor Arthur's Proclamation to the Aboriginal People.

all the paired terms in the pidgins and creoles, often contrasting "whitefellers" with "blackfellers" or local words for "people". Is the public downplaying of mixture a coincidence? A collusion? A symbiotic runaround? Or is it the beginnings of a new struggle with the colonial aftermath?

The catch-all phrase "black, white and brindle", with its novel twentieth-century use of a word once reserved for streaked animals, is one of the few common locutions in which people of mixed descent are independently identified by a third term without overt reference to degrees of mixture, like the now shunned "half-caste" (though forms of the latter term have been borrowed into Aboriginal languages—an example is the Waramungu term *apukaji*—and are used more unselfconsciously by Aboriginal people talking internal politics among themselves). Perhaps the best place to start trying to understand colonialism and the racialized politics of identity in Australia is to look at constructions of what I shall conveniently call brindlehood. How do each and all of us cope with sexual contact history?

By way of a first foray, I want to go way back, outback, and introduce two outback tales of mystery and miscegenation. Both refer to events in the first decade of the century, though neither begins its narrative there. The first is set on a pastoral station in the far west of New South Wales. The second has its beginnings on a pastoral station in the rural north of Western Australia. Despite the ragged conquest of Australia, it so happens that pastoral stations were set up on Aboriginal land in both areas along roughly the same lines during roughly the same period, the late nineteenth century. New South Wales and Western Australia have also had somewhat similar "protection" policies towards Aborigines, although Western Australia's was often more explicitly concerned with differential treatment of people of mixed and wholly Aboriginal descent.[5]

The two stories, however, are fundamentally different. The first is fictitious, the second biographical. The first is full of secrets in the service of racism and the maintenance of a wilfully unreflective, static fantasy. In the second, secrets develop as resistance to racism, eventually bringing about a new and contagious kind of resistance in the generation from which they have been kept hidden.

In the words of the blurb to the 1965 edition, *The Barrakee Mystery* is Arthur Upfield's first detective novel, and the "first to feature 'Bony', Detective-Inspector Napoleon Bonaparte, the suave, blue-eyed, black-

---

[5] See for instance Patricia Jacobs, "Science and Veiled Assumptions: Miscegenation in W.A. 1930-1937," *Australian Aboriginal Studies* 1986: 15-23.

haired half-Aboriginal sleuth known to all discriminating readers of detective stories".[6] The story takes place in outback pastoral country on the Darling River, starting in 1908 and culminating in a murder and its solution in 1928. By way of background, 1909 was the year in which the New South Wales Aborigines Protection Board first acquired some statutory powers to back up its policies of regulating who should and should not be allowed to live on reserves and removing children from their families to single-sex institutions to be trained domestic servants.

This sixty-year-old detective story might be expected to have little appeal today. Yet the Bony novels appear to have a firm position in Australian popular culture. The Bony books have also sold well in the United States, and were crucial in enabling Upfield to make a living from his writing until his death in 1964. They are still being reprinted—*Bony and the Kelly Gang* in 1988, for example. They were made into a couple of very popular TV series, which were shown in Australia and overseas from 1972. At that time it seems the producers at Channel 7 were unable to find (or look for?) someone of Aboriginal descent to play the "half-Aboriginal sleuth", but chose instead a New Zealander of Maori descent, James Laurenson. Grundy Productions were still suffering from a similar incapacity in their telemovie about the detective's descendants, *Bony*, starring Cameron Daddo, though they were able to find Burnum Burnum to play another role. When I began my linguistic field work in the area of western New South Wales where Bony did his first sleuthing, a professor at the Australian National University insisted on lending me a Bony book each week, library fashion, to help me, as a British newcomer to Australia, to understand the Aborigines.

The plot of *The Barrakee Mystery* covers the first part of the lifetimes of the oldest Aboriginal people alive today, and its paradigmatic popularity has persisted, in certain quarters at least, for most of the remaining part. Ray Browne's *The Spirit of Australia* engages only superficially with the texts' ideology.[7] Apart from the odd squib (for example Basil Sansom's discussion of Bony as "a white man's half-caste hero"[8]) the most lively critical response has been Mudrooroo Narogin's creation of a counter-sleuth, Captain Watson Holmes Jackamara of the

---

[6] Arthur Upfield, *The Barrakee Mystery* (London: Heinemann, 1965), jacket front flap. First published in London in 1929.

[7] Ray Browne, *The Spirit of Australia: The Crime Fiction of Arthur W. Upfield* (Bowling Green, OH: Bowling Green State University Popular Press, 1988).

[8] Basil Sansom, "Boney: A White Man's Half-Caste Hero," *Anthropology News* 17.7 (August 1980) 107-113.

Black Cockatoo Dreaming.[9]

The *dramatis personae* of *The Barrakee Mystery*, introduced to us in 1928, are as follows: Mr Thornton, the owner of Barrakee sheep station; Mrs Thornton, the Little Lady; Kate, her orphan niece, the darling of the Darling, who is engaged to be married to the Thorntons' adored adopted son Ralph, who is conventionally tall, dark and handsome, and is described as a perfect collegiate product.[10] Then there is Frank Dugdale, the overseer, who is desperately but secretly in love with Kate. Other more or less picturesque characters include the people working on the station, such as the newly arrived white stockman, Clair, and sundry Aborigines from the camp on the riverbank with names as reverberant as the detective's, if to different effect—Pontius Pilot, Nellie Wanting and King Henry, "the very finest specimen of an aboriginal",[11] who had worked on the station twenty years earlier.

The world of the novel is starkly black versus white. Mr Thornton is more candid than the governor of Tasmania on the question of killing.

> "We old people and our people before us regard and regarded the lives of black [sic] very cheaply. They regarded our lives and our stock equally as cheap."[12]

The blackness of Aborigines collects about it the usual stereotypes of inferiority, plus a few locally idiosyncratic ones. No waves of horrified concern go through the household when King Henry is discovered murdered near the homestead. But the local policeman is conscientious enough to have a problem, as he writes to Mr Thornton:

> "Murders of, or by, aboriginals generally are difficult to investigate, for as you well know the mind of the aboriginal baffles the intelligence of the white."[13]

Enter the detective Bony "who has, by contrast, a mind high above the average human standard".[14] He also has a university degree, which in real life no-one of Aboriginal descent was to be awarded for another forty

---

[9] "Westralian Lead," in *Crimes for a Summer Christmas*, ed. Stephen Knight (Sydney: Allen & Unwin, 1990), 25-47.

[10] Arthur Upfield, *The Barrakee Mystery*, 17.

[11] Arthur Upfield, *The Barrakee Mystery*, 24.

[12] Arthur Upfield, *The Barrakee Mystery*, 205.

[13] Arthur Upfield, *The Barrakee Mystery*, 11.

[14] Arthur Upfield, *The Barrakee Mystery*, 104.

years.[15] He is the exceptional half-caste who proves the rule of the book's theory of miscegenation, as well as being its chief exponent. The rule has two parts. His parents subscribed to the first part. "My mother was black, my father white. They were below the animals. A fox does not mate with a dingo, or a cat with a rabbit."[16] Bony is an exception to the second part of the rule, as stated by himself: "In no case does a half-caste rise to the status of his superior parent."[17] With his combination of Aboriginal bushcraft and superior intellect, Bony is soon able to implicate Clair in the murder and turn the task of capturing him over to the policeman. But Bony, as a "professor rather than student of human nature",[18] is concerned to discover the motive. Ralph, he notices, is undergoing a "progressive deterioration".[19] Recently, while diving to trap a huge fish in the Darling River, Ralph had drowned, as he thought, and had come to in the embrace of his Aboriginal rescuer, Nellie Wanting. Eventually he disappears to join her, despite her attempts to leave him (at Bony's urging) so as not to drag him "down to our level".[20]

Bony's move to separate Ralph and Nellie is only an attempt to play for time for the sake of sparing the feelings of the older Thorntons. Bony has also seen Ralph's skin slowly darkening during the few months he has been at Barrakee, "as my skin slowly darkened when I was his age". Five or six years more and Ralph would be as obviously a half-caste as Bony.[21] And equally surely "that call to the blood" would become irresistible.[22]

Bony calls a meeting of the Thorntons and Dugdale, and reveals all to them. King Henry, as you may have guessed, was Ralph's father. As she lay dying in childbirth, Ralph's mother, the cook, had confided to Mrs Thornton that "He was so magnificent a man that I became as putty in his hands".[23] Mrs Thornton had promised not to reveal the secret. Forty-eight hours earlier she herself had given birth to a son who had instantly died. She suckled the cook's baby and was overwhelmed by her need to

---

[15] In 1966 Margaret Valadian graduated as Bachelor of Social Studies, University of Queensland, and Charles Perkins as Bachelor of Arts, University of Sydney. Queensland Police Tracker Leon Wood, Upfield's inspiration for Bony, certainly had a high-school education. See Jessica Hawke, *Follow My Dust!* (Melbourne: Heinemann, 1957), 129, 168-9.

[16] Arthur Upfield, *The Barrakee Mystery*, 104.

[17] Arthur Upfield, *The Barrakee Mystery*, 301.

[18] Arthur Upfield, *The Barrakee Mystery*, 199.

[19] Arthur Upfield, *The Barrakee Mystery*, 193.

[20] Arthur Upfield, *The Barrakee Mystery*, 189.

[21] Arthur Upfield, *The Barrakee Mystery*, 302.

[22] Arthur Upfield, *The Barrakee Mystery*, 197.

[23] Arthur Upfield, *The Barrakee Mystery*, 308.

substitute him for her own son. "Seeing his tender flesh was as white as my own", she could not believe that King Henry was his father.[24] Later, King Henry had tried to claim his son. On being refused, he had blackmailed Mrs Thornton. This was why she had asked Clair, the cook's brother, to kill him. "It would be no crime to slay a black, would it?"[25]

On thus meeting her Waterloo (the Napoleonic joke is Upfield's, not mine), Mrs Thornton collapses and asks to see Ralph. When he learns of his Aboriginal ancestry, Ralph is too ashamed to come except under cover of darkness. He feels he can no longer face the darling of the Darling, whose lips he has polluted, or Mr Thornton, who has been a father to him. Delaying his arrival until nightfall, he comes tragically, but decorously, too late. He finds Mrs Thornton already dead, makes his farewell, and leaves again forever.

> She had given him a great maternal love ... yet a love not potent enough to keep him safe from, the power, the unseen power, of his ancestors of the bush. No power was adequate to deal with that inherent, compelling impulse.[26]

Meanwhile, Clair has died a man's death while being pursued, leaving a confession and so no obvious tasks for the law.[27] In fact, Mrs Thornton had been present when Clair attempted to kill King Henry. She had herself delivered the fatal blow with a boomerang, whose trajectory only Bony had been competent to detect. Clair had lost his life protecting her secret, sending her a message to parallel his confession to the crime: "You are safe, Little Lady."[28]

Bony, supporting such values to the last, concludes that the world need know nothing. The Little Lady's only sin was not to have shared the secret of Ralph's paternity with her husband. That promise to secrecy had however been made under the pressure of maternal feeling, as irresistible as—if ultimately less potent than—the call of black blood. In short, "I would find it utterly impossible to tarnish the character of so great a woman as was the Little Lady."[29] Mr Thornton then gains a true adoptive son and heir in the overseer Dugdale, who marries Kate.

I have lingered over some of the self-serving concealments, evasions and exonerations in this tale because *The Barrakee Mystery* idealizes a

---

[24] Arthur Upfield, *The Barrakee Mystery*, 308.

[25] Arthur Upfield, *The Barrakee Mystery*, 299.

[26] Arthur Upfield, *The Barrakee Mystery*, 318.

[27] Arthur Upfield, *The Barrakee Mystery*, 295, 303.

[28] Arthur Upfield, *The Barrakee Mystery*, 203.

[29] Arthur Upfield, *The Barrakee Mystery*, 319-320.

contemporary world of real pastoralist supremacy and subterfuge, some of whose intricacies are purposely made public in the second book that I am going to consider. *The Barrakee Mystery* moves towards fictional closure, a strategic "happy ending" in which the secrets that have been uncovered for the reader are reburied from the world within the book. Sally Morgan's *My Place* is, by contrast, open-ended and dynamic. None of the secrets revealed in it, however painful to those who once kept them, can be reburied to re-create even a partial *status quo ante*.

Let us move now to Corunna Downs in outback Western Australia. Owned by Howden Drake-Brockman, member of a widely known and influential family, Corunna Downs is the location of a story within the story of Morgan's autobiographical *My Place*, published in 1987. Sally, born in 1951, is living in Perth with her mother Gladys, her grandmother Daisy, and her four brothers and sisters. Sally herself turns detective in quest of her own identity. She is the Bony of this book. But there are crucial differences between this autobiographical detective and Upfield's fictional creation. In Upfield's world, where black and white theoretically lead mutually exclusive and unintelligible lives, the only way to articulate any relation of the two is to invent an omniscient person with access to both. The convention is a familiar one in cross-cultural crime fiction. Bony's omniscience is a product of his identity—as so many people of mixed descent in real life have been, he is seen as belonging by birth to two worlds. But his status as a Detective-Inspector allows him to move freely and authoritatively between both.

Sally Morgan, by contrast, is asking questions from an initial position of total ignorance of who she is, of how many worlds there might be and of how they might relate to one another. It is partly this ignorance that makes her confident enough to pursue "her place". This is how Sally first tackles her mother:

> "The kids at school want to know what country we come from. They reckon we're not Aussies. Are we Aussies, Mum?"
> Mum was silent. Nan grunted in a cross sort of way, then got up from the table and walked outside.
> "Come on, Mum, what are we?"
> "What do the kids at school say?"
> "Anything. Italian, Greek, Indian."
> "Tell them you're Indian."
> I got real excited, then. ... It sounded so exotic. "When did we come here?" I added.
> "A long time ago," Mum replied. "Now, no more questions. You just

tell them you're Indian."[30]

Later on, Sally asks Nan why she butters up the rent collectors, laying out scones and tea and treating them like royalty. By way of reply, Nan bursts out, "We're like those Jews ... people like us'd all be dead and gone now if it was up to this country." So Sally tries another detective question:

> "Nan," I said carefully, "what people are we?"
> "I'm not talking, I'm not talking," she muttered ... and put her hands over her ears.[31]

Later Sally marries a white man who grew up among Aborigines as a missionary's son and who takes it for granted that Nan is Aboriginal. It is not until after Sally's marriage that she finally catches her mother in an absent-minded moment and says, very casually:

> "We're Aboriginal, aren't we, Mum?"
> "Yes, dear," she replied without thinking.
> "All those years, Mum," I said, "how could you have lied to us those years?"
> "It was only a little white lie," she replied sadly.
> In no time at all we were giggling uncontrollably.[32]

Now that she has this crucial confirmation, Sally asserts her new identity publicly, on her mother's and grandmother's behalf as well as her own. She gets a special scholarship for Aborigines, leading to a university degree.[33] (It is significant that government policy now positively encourages what was an unprecedented and purely fictional exception for Bony in the 1920s.)

The rest of the book is dedicated to describing the extraordinary piece-by-piece revelation of the secrets between generations and the reasons for their genesis. Each new revelation starts new questions, sometimes for one person in the family, sometimes for another. All sorts of new family connections are discovered. The book shows the emotional struggles and gathering confidence that accompany the process, as well as the sadness and bewilderment that have been suppressed along the way. The hardest of the revelations to make, and by the same token the one ultimately judged

---

[30] Sally Morgan, *My Place* (Fremantle, W.Aust.: Fremantle Arts Centre Press, 1987), 38.

[31] Sally Morgan, *My Place*, 105.

[32] Sally Morgan, *My Place*, 135.

[33] Sally Morgan, *My Place*, 237

least relevant to the reworking of identities, is that Howden Drake-Brockman may be the father of both Nan and Mum. Having established that he is Nan's father, and after pursuing various false trails in search of Mum's father, Mum and Sally look at photos of Howden Drake-Brockman and realize that Mum is the spitting image of him. "You don't think it's possible he was my father?" says Mum, to which Sally replies: "Anything's possible. But he couldn't be yours as well as Nan's."[34] Whatever the reasons for adding the negative conclusion (they may well be legal as well as tactful), once the possibility is discovered, its appalling force is neutralized so that it hardly seems to matter. By this time all the family except Nan have been back to Corunna Downs and met up with various relations there. As Mum says:

> "For nearly all my life, I've desperately wanted to know who my father was, now, I couldn't care less. Why should I bother with whoever it was, they never bothered with me ... All those wonderful people up North, they all claimed me ... I don't want to belong to anyone else."[35]

Nan still has secrets so painful that she dies with them—but not before recording for the world her conversion to being, as Sally puts it, a "proud blackfella", and recording her own story. This is what Daisy Corunna, a contemporary of the fictional Ralph Thornton, is quoted as saying about her shame in her old age.

> "I'm ashamed of myself, now ... I wanted to be white ... Then I could get on in the world ... Fancy, me thinkin' that. What was wrong with my own people?"[36]

Young Ralph Thornton's creator made him so ashamed of his Aboriginal paternity that he voluntarily renounced his future as heir to Barrakee. By the time Daisy Corunna was the age at which Ralph made his fictional renunciation, she had been turned into a Drake-Brockman family servant. First she was removed from camp life with her mother to the station, then she was taken away from her country to the second Drake-Brockman home in Perth. She also has much to say about the racist sexual ethos in practice at the time.

In those days, it was considered a privilege for a white man to want

---

[34] Sally Morgan, *My Place*, 237.

[35] Sally Morgan, *My Place*, 237.

[36] Sally Morgan, *My Place*, 336.

you, but if you had children, you weren't allowed to keep them. You was only allowed to keep the black ones. They took the white ones off you 'cause you weren't considered fit to raise a child with white blood.

I tell you, it made a wedge between the people. Some of the black men felt real low, and some of the native girls with a bit of white in them wouldn't look at a black man. There I was, stuck in the middle. Too black for the whites and too white for the blacks ...

It was a big thing if you could get a white man to marry you. A lot of native people who were light passed themselves off as white, then ... One of my friends married a Slav ... She came to say goodbye ... She'd promised her husband never to talk or mix with any native again. We didn't blame her, we understood ...

I 'member the minister ... tellin' us how we must save ourselves for marriage ... we couldn't look at him. Most of us had already been taken by white men. We felt really 'shamed ...

We had no protection when we was in service. I know a lot of native servants had kids to white men because they was forced ...[37]

I was owned by the Drake-Brockmans and the government and anyone who wanted to pay five shillings a year to Mr Neville to have me ... I been scared all my life, too scared to speak out. Maybe if you'd have had my life, you'd be scared, too.[38]

Sally's conclusion, which also forms the dedication of the book, is as follows: "How deprived we would have been if we had been willing to let things stay as they were. We would have survived, but not as whole people." (Note that she does not say "as a whole people"; I have taken it that the dedication, which does have the indefinite article, misquotes this passage.) "We would never have known our place." But perhaps the most significant point is made by Nan's brother, who also records his story. This comes as part of a conversational battle with Nan, who is insisting on keeping her secrets. He counters that they are history, and that in revealing his to the younger generations "We're talkin' history".[39] "I'm part of history, that's how I look on it. Some people read history, don't they?"[40]

Indeed they do. *My Place* has moved a huge readership, many of whom were previously ignorant or incurious about the social conditions it describes. Sally Morgan's detective enterprise has set in motion an empowering reinterpretation of the past for herself, her family and others similarly placed within the living world, which the publication of the book has actually politically altered. This empowerment limited though it may

---

[37] Sally Morgan, *My Place*, 336.
[38] Sally Morgan, *My Place*, 360.
[39] Sally Morgan, *My Place*, 163.
[40] Sally Morgan, *My Place*, 213.

turn out to be, makes Sally Morgan's work a significant act of intercultural brokerage.

In the end, the difference that informs all the other differences between these two tales of mystery and miscegenation is one of personal purpose and position. The two authors deal with sexual contact history so differently because their own personal histories are so different. Though so many of the characters in both books are contemporaries of one another, located in comparable parts of outback Australia and in comparable social positions, the writers themselves are quite differently located in relation to the worlds they write about. It is not Upfield's place to describe Morgan's place. It is, after all, her place.

Upfield arrived in Australia as a young immigrant from England to try his luck at a more adventurous outback life, and worked on stations in the region where he sets his Barrakee. He turned to spinning yarns to introduce the "spirit of Australia" to a wider audience and to earn his living by writing. He wrote with serene confidence in his use of local colour, as an observer, albeit an enthusiastic participating observer. Twenty years after Upfield's death, when Morgan began writing, she was neither observing nor participating, but learning from the passionate memories of relatives.

As a writer Upfield was equipped with all the inherited plots and readers' expectations of British Australia. The plot of *The Barrakee Mystery* is as old as changeling stories in the culture of Europe, its racial attitudes as old as empire. The genre he wrote in, crime fiction, is far newer, but quite as conventional. The tension in the Bony books that makes them revealing about what I have called sexual contact history is precisely the contradictory presence of Bony, with his unexpected authority, which can be read as fib, token or precedent. He is the larger-than-life, world-upside-down detective hero demanded by the conventions of the genre. Morgan, by contrast, writes *My Place* because she has to. Sexual contact history—in her case, the story of her own becoming—is what she has to write into shape. There is no conventional genre to hand.

I introduced my comparison of these two books on the back of a conceit—that both are in some sense detective stories. The structure of *My Place* actually owes nothing to the conventions of crime fiction except a narrative built on accumulating clues rather than chronology. If we agree with Arthur Corunna that the book is "history", it is certainly not the sort of Australian history people are used to reading. It moves outside the conventions of continuous narrative that have governed most Australian historical writing. The ABC has happily renamed and reconstituted "oral history" as "talking history" for the airwaves. So far Aboriginal talking history in book form has typically involved transcribed and edited personal reminiscences edited into a familiar type of narrative or thematic framework, though some writers, such as Stephen Muecke in *Reading the Country*, have deliberately used oral material to raise questions about the implications of genre. There are also increasing numbers of Aboriginal autobiographies, both written and tape-recorded for transcription and editing. Genealogy and family history projects are outstandingly popular as research topics in Aboriginal studies. But *My Place* is unlike any other work of Aboriginal historical recuperation yet written, in that it pays as much attention to the process of recuperation as to what is retrieved. It is like a collective autobiography, except that Sally Morgan's own story has a different status from the others'. It is novel, but not a novel. Its rhetorical effectiveness derives from the unconventional mixture of means that Morgan has employed to deal with a topic that is conventionally ignored. Eric Michaels has called it "auto-bio-historical".[41] My label "sexual contact history" is a joke, because it is potentially embarrassing. The joke, however, is on objective taxonomies of "proper" historical subject matter. In attempting to speak of the unspeakable, Sally Morgan has removed at least part of the public embarrassment and private shame from the part of Australian colonial history in which the personal is most obviously and insistently political.

First published in *Meanjin* 50.2-3 (Winter/Spring 1991): 341-352. Minor edits were made by the author. The copy of Governor Arthur's proclamation is used with permission of the National Library of Australia.

---

[41] Eric Michaels, "Para-Ethnography," *Art and Text*, 30 (September-November 1988), 42-51.

WHODUNIT? AND WHERE?
CRIME FICTION DOWN UNDER

MARGARET LEWIS

Let us imagine that we are on a train, on a fairly long journey. Ambling down the aisle in a casual fashion, we can make a brisk survey of what people are reading to pass the time. With the exception of a student reading Hardy, and a few businessmen playing power games with computers and portable telephones, everyone in the carriage is reading what we might loosely call popular fiction. Furthermore, everyone is reading fiction with a strong narrative line. As E.M. Forster concluded with a sigh, the novel does tell a story; and the desire for narrative is basic to the enjoyment of reading novels. People like to be told a story; they like to know what is going to happen next. Even the finest works of twentieth-century fiction do not neglect this fundamental duty to the reader: we want to know what happens to Ulrich Voss, although we already know his fate. We want to know how Leopold Bloom's day will develop. We want to know if William Golding's ship, in his brilliant, recently published trilogy, is going to burst into flames before it finally reaches Australia.

You will have noticed, of course, that in this railway carriage there is a very unhealthy interest in crime and violence. Worse still, those blood-bedecked covers are being clutched by the age-spotted hands of ladies who look as though they should be more concerned with pouring tea than with death by blunt instrument. Which brings us to a question that is quite often asked: why do people like to read crime fiction? Even worse, why do they like to write it? And finally, moving with a substantial lurch towards my professed topic in the area of cross-cultural perspectives: what made Ngaio Marsh and Arthur Upfield use the 1930s detective-fiction formula in strange and exotic settings in New Zealand and Australia? Whodunit, all right—but WHERE? Mildura? Wai-atatapu? It is a long way from the world of Mayhem Parva to the thermal, pools of the North Island of New Zealand, or to the bizarre wind-sculpted sweep of the white sand cliffs known as the Walls of China in western New South Wales.

If we were to ask some of the passengers in that train what they find to their taste in crime fiction, we are quite likely to be told that they like a good, well-plotted mystery, and they like a story that takes their minds off everyday worries, providing a sense of escape. Or, as John Cawelti suggests in a more sophisticated way: "the classical detective formula is perhaps the most effective fictional structure yet devised for creating the illusion of rational control over the mysteries of life."[1]

A well-plotted mystery is fundamental to crime fiction. A crime novel must have shape; and, indeed, this is one of the aspects of the genre that appeals to many writers. Agatha Christie was particularly admired for the ingenuity of her plots and criticized for her characterization. Perhaps; but thanks to a series of films and a very successful television series, her crime-solving spinster Miss Marple is well on the way to becoming the kind of literary creation who calmly steps out of the pages of fiction and becomes almost a real person—like Sherlock Holmes, who had to be brought back from the grave by popular demand. He still receives over two hundred letters a week at his address in Baker Street.

Ngaio Marsh, who was born in Christchurch, New Zealand, in 1895 and lived there until her death in 1982, liked shapely novels and compared the best detective fiction to metaphysical poetry. She always began writing with a group of characters, and would then try to imagine what circumstances would lead one of them to commit murder. Characterization was easier than plot, and her letters reveal that she struggled furiously with the second half of many novels to bring them to a satisfactory conclusion. Ngaio divided her readers into two camps, the combatant and the acquiescent. In her view, the acquiescent "take their detective fiction in much the same way as they take their sleeping pills, their crossword puzzles or their aperitifs. For them, the story really is a means of escape." The combatant is harder to please: "his great object is to catch the reader out, and to guess who-done-it as long as possible before he is meant to do so."[2]

The author allows a few clues to drop, and a few red herrings to swim past, in order to keep the reader actively engaged, but like all good storytellers keeps a few surprises to the end. The element of reader-participation is a crucial part of such fiction's appeal, and should never be under-estimated. In classic detective fiction, there is a duel between the writer and the reader, and a great deal of the reader's pleasure derives from this. Avant-garde American writer William Burroughs once provided

---

[1] John Cawelti, *Adventure, Mystery, and Romance: Formula Stories as Art and Popular Culture* (Chicago: University of Chicago Press, 1976), 137.

[2] Margaret Lewis, *Ngaio Marsh: A Life* (London: Chatto & Windus; New Zealand: Bridget Williams Books, 1991), 60.

readers with cut-up sections of the end of a novel so they could finish it as they liked. The readers of a detective novel do this all the time. They do not regard themselves as avant-garde, but they know that trying to work out the solution in different ways is a main clause in the reading-contract.

Although the four "Queens of Crime" in the 1930s (Agatha Christie, Ngaio Marsh, Margery Allingham and Dorothy Sayers) set most of their fiction in England, Ngaio Marsh moved very far from the Home Counties for four of her thirty-two novels. Unable to visit Europe because of the Second World War and its aftermath, she started to situate her novels in recognizable local landscapes. *Colour Scheme* (1943) is set in a region of thermal springs and steaming pools, but all the necessary ingredients of a Golden Age detective novel are transplanted to this extraordinary place. We have the necessary small group of characters, all living in close proximity; but instead of a stately mansion, their residence is a ramshackle wooden guest-house. The rolling acres of the south of England are transmuted into sulphurous pools and hissing jets of steam, and obedient, feudally regulated villagers are replaced by a Maori settlement, whose evening singing drifts hauntingly over the lunar landscape. The victim is led to his death in a boiling mud-pool, a fate that does not surprise the Maori, who discover that he has been plundering their sacred mountain, and deem him justly punished. The landscape itself becomes the murder weapon.

The ingredients are used just as they would be in an English country house mystery, even to the initial suspicion of the native settlement. (In country house murders, the servants or villagers are always the first suspects, but it is nearly always one of the social elite whodunits.) In *Colour Scheme* the murderer is not Maori, but a traitor who is signalling to Japanese shipping and endangering ship movements from the nearby harbour.

Colour Scheme was followed in 1945 by *Died in the Wool*, which is set on an isolated sheep station high in the Southern Alps. The murder weapon is particularly antipodean: the victim is struck on the head with a branding iron and then pressed to death in the middle of a wool bale. She may not have been popular, but it is still a tough way to get rid of your local M.P. In both novels, Ngaio Marsh continues to use her created detective, Roderick Alleyne, who luckily got sent out to New Zealand at the beginning, of the war, following a brief visit in 1937 which led to the solution of the theatre mystery, *Vintage Murder* (1937).

In these three novels, characters interact with landscape in a way that had not happened in previous fiction by Marsh. The author had in her youth trained as an artist and had made several painting trips to the

Southern Alps. Her love of the bleak, high plateaux, the soaring peaks and the sparkling air of New Zealand is easily discerned. Against this background, the conventional closed society at the heart of her investigations is thrown into sharp relief. This landscape operates its own, unique spiritual and psychological pressures.

During the next thirty years, Ngaio Marsh made a number of lengthy visits to England and the Continent, with novels appearing almost annually. Growing sophistication in narrative and characterization added to her high reputation internationally. Her brilliant ear for comic dialogue and social repartee was stimulated by her travels overseas, and enhanced by her work at home in New Zealand as a theatre director. Not until *Photo-Finish*, her penultimate book (1980), did she return to a New Zealand setting. Now aged eighty-five, the author created a complex and unusual detective story, using still-vivid memories of her early response to the landscape of Westland and the Alps. Murder in a luxurious mountain lodge which has been built on an island in the middle of a lake would seem to be the ideal example of a stereotyped setting. What makes the novel fresh and unusual is the response to landscape. Again there are suggestions of the spiritual power connected with Maori beliefs; the island is *tapu* (sacred and forbidden), and this brings a vague sense of unease which is soon focused on the corpse of a famous opera singer who is found with a photograph impaled on the knife embedded in her ample bosom. But every detail of a country house murder is adhered to, with the additional resonance of an Italian revenge plot in an exotic setting.

While Ngaio Marsh used New Zealand settings and characters but kept her English detective, Arthur Upfield (1888-1964)[3] went one better. He invented an Australian detective, and not only Australian, but a half-caste Aboriginal called Napoleon Bonaparte or "Bony" for short, who first appears in *The Barrakee Mystery* (1929). Upfield was English, and came to Australia as a family black sheep. He worked at a variety of manual jobs in the outback and was very familiar with the territory he wrote about. Bony was based on a part-Aboriginal friend of Upfield's (the Queenslander Leon Wood), and in his portrayal of this unusual detective he blends a good university background (Bony has a Masters degree) with instinctive skills in tracking and observation, and an intuitive sense of danger inherited from his mother. But for Detective Napoleon Bonaparte the bush has no terrors; in fact, he refers often to the "Book of the Bush" that is open for him to read. And, although Upfield's detailed knowledge

---

[3] Ed.: It had been generally accepted that Upfield was born on 1 September 1888. A check of the records in England made about 25 years after his death revealed he was born in 1890.

of Australian rural life gives unusual and vividly realized settings to more than thirty novels, the characters and the townships themselves remain recognizably those of 1930s detective fiction.

In *Death of a Swagman* (1945), for instance, the little settlement of Merino has a suspect parson, a doctor, a squatter with a beautiful daughter who wears silk shirts and rides well, and a cook called Sam the Blackmailer who terrorizes his employers. These may be familiar characters in classic detective fiction, but what is not familiar to most European readers is the special quality of the Australian outback, where solitary individuals find themselves shrunk to insignificance against immense and indifferent space. The strange white-sand cliff known as the Great Walls of China in *Death of a Swagman*, the huge meteorite crater which contains a body at its centre in *The Will of the Tribe* (1962) or the white-rimmed, cement-hard depression which is all that remains of Emu Lake in *Wings Above the Diamantina* (1936) provide unsettling contexts for crime, and emphasize the fragile nature of the interaction between scattered communities in an alien but weirdly beautiful landscape.

Small communities where people perform recognized functions are ideal settings for crime novels. Recently, the novelist P.D. James remarked:

> Murder is essentially a domestic crime, in which we explore the effect of the extraordinary upon the ordinary. That's why many of us prefer to write about small towns or small communities. We don't deal with violence in the same way that the sharp-shooting private eye does. We are interested in the details of living.[4]

Bony enjoys solving a crime in a small community because it is more of a challenge: the smaller the community, the better the killer will be concealed. He takes this to extremes in *Man of Two Tribes* (1956) when searching for a missing person in the vast desolation of the Nullarbor Plain in South Australia, where he solves the case with the help of two camels and a dog.

Upfield's use of landscape continued to add a unique dimension to his novels, and similar elements have been incorporated by the more recent writer S.H. Courtier, who develops a frightening, supernatural aspect of Aboriginal culture in *Death in Dreamtime* (1959). But it is a fact universally to be acknowledged that no crime fiction writer can ever produce events that are as strange as real life: few crime writers would have attempted to use all the ingredients of the "dingo baby" case, where

---

[4] Elaine Budd, "P.D. James: Ordinary Lives, Extraordinary Deaths," in *Thirteen Mistresses of Murder* (New York: Ungar, 1986), 68.

Lindy Chamberlain was accused of murdering her baby daughter while the family was camping in the shadow of Ayers Rock.

Uneasiness at the relationship between fact and fiction brings us to a final point about these two writers, Upfield and Marsh, who chose to import an essentially alien literary formula to New Zealand and Australia and to use it to organize their own experience. The greatest writers can provide an insight into the complexities of life and illuminate our own responses. But a writer of detective fiction can also provide a picture of life, and offers us a rather tidier view than we normally hope for. As well as amusing us, puzzling us, gripping us and surprising us, the crime novel can, in the view of writer and critic H.R.F. Keating, tell us something about the world we live in: "it can make a temporary map for its readers out of the chaos of their surroundings. Only it should never let them know."[5]

John Cawelti puts it rather more formally:

> In reading or viewing a formulaic work, we confront the ultimate excitements of love and death, but in such a way that our basic sense of security and order is intensified rather than disrupted, because, first of all, we know that this is an imaginary rather than a real experience, and, second, because the excitement and uncertainty are ultimately controlled and limited by the familiar world of the formulaic structure.[6]

So I am arguing that the formula of detective fiction, far from being an arid and limiting import from Europe to the Antipodes, provided a useful and positive structure for dealing with the conflicting pressures experienced by everyone at some time or other—the need for adventure, uncertainty and freedom as opposed to our basic need for security, love and a place in society. It is a structure that expands to give significance to unusual settings.

And there is nothing new here, either. In 1886 Fergus Hume published what was probably one of the greatest best-sellers in the history of detective fiction, *The Mystery of a Hansom Cab: A Story of Melbourne Social Life.* One of the earliest novels in the genre, it was based on a French formula, set in Melbourne, Australia, and written by a New Zealander who was born in England. Crime fiction is nothing if not international. But then, so is crime itself. Have a good read.

---

[5] H.R.F Keating, *Writing Crime Fiction* (London: Black, 1986), 2.
[6] Cawelti, *Adventure, Mystery, and Romance*, 6.

First Published in *Us/Them: Translation, Transcription and Identity in Post-Colonial Literary Cultures*, edited by Gordon Collier, 385-390. Amsterdam: Rodopi, 1992. Reprinted with permission of Editions Rodopi BV.

HOME ON THE RANGE

MUDROOROO

"Where'd that black bastard get ta?" the mounted constable curses, swinging off his horse and pulling out his rifle. He quickly jerks the bolt forward and down. The resulting clack springs across the gully.

"Don't worry boss about that one, me get him," his companion, the black policeman, Jackamara replies in a level voice. "Just let me go along a little ways into that scrub and I'll bring him out quick smart."

Of course, this is not Watson Holmes Jackamara's natural speech pattern. He has not only lived as a child with a missionary in an almost son—father relationship; but been educated in the white man's school and then gone on to be trained to become Queensland's first token black constable. It is then that his problems begin, for although his smiling face has appeared in the *Courier* above the caption "A Black Opal in the Force", few white policemen feel easy working alongside him, especially as he quickly establishes that he has an ability (perhaps gained from his missionary mentor, a devotee of the fictional detective Sherlock Holmes) to solve cases. It happens too often to be put down to luck and to solve the problem he has become, his fellow white members of the force give him the cold shoulder. His superiors see him as a threat to police morale and solve *their* problem by placing him on special duties or seconding him to other police forces. As a token he is acceptable; but as a policeman ... and so early on in his career Constable Watson Holmes Jackamara finds himself in the Northern Territory supposedly as an example of an Aboriginal policeman; but in the Territory racism is even worse than in Queensland, and so Police Constable Watson Holmes Jackamara becomes simply Jacky, or Wot's Up Jacky and is treated as a black tracker. Unable to even dint the prejudice Wot's Up Jacky grins and bears it. He knows, after all, that he is much better than the above average white police trooper ... and so he finds himself accompanying the white constable as a black tracker hard on the heels of an alleged cattle spearer, that is to him the crime has yet to be proved, but to the trooper the black is a notorious myall to be shot out of hand on the slightest provocation.

Now, they have run the alleged culprit to earth, somewhere in the deep gully into which the waters of a spring tumble over a rock lip to fill a long billabong edged with the rasping downhanging leaves of pandanus palms. The scene is idyllic and peaceful; but this makes the white constable jumpy. He senses an ambush. Wot's Up Jacky knows that this is not the case, that the alleged culprit is lying hidden close waiting for them to pass by. With another man this ploy might have worked. It has worked time after time; but, even then, Jackamara has established a reputation of always getting his man, black or white. He knows that left to his own modus operandi, he will have the handcuffs on the alleged culprit in a short time.

The white constable stares down into the matted pandanus. It is too thick for horses to penetrate and definitely no place for a white man and so he turns to his trusty tracker: "Go and get in there Jacky. Flush 'im out and into my sights."

Jackamara nods and removes his hat and boots, before gliding away and disappearing between the rustling fronds. The white constable stares after him, then curses. One black fellow looks much like another and he can't afford to shoot the black opal of the Queensland police. He slams the safety on his rifle, then finds a shady spot against a boulder in which to squat and roll a smoke as he lets events take their course.

Jackamara silently approaches the bank of the long pool. It is a jungle of pandanus. Impossible to push through without a sound. A path would need to be slashed, and so he slips into the water and paddles his way towards the spring with his head just above the surface of the water. His eyes, though not his head, move from side to side in an effort to catch a movement, or a human shape amid the palms. He waits for a feeling to arise of something not quite right. It comes as he approaches the rush of water into the pool. He slows and carefully, so as not to make the slightest sound, takes the handcuffs from his belt. Suddenly, he ducks and lunges under the downpouring water. There is a hollow beneath. He feels the damp warm body of a man. Quickly, he snaps the cuffs about the wrists. Constable Watson Holmes Jackamara has got his man. He crouches beside him while catching his breath. His hands flicker in sign language, telling his prisoner about the white constable and his gun, then very carefully they go to him.

Jackamara in capturing his man has also more than probably saved his life. On the long ride back to Darwin, he gets to know the black man oddly named Riley and, whenever possible, he passes a word through the guard of the white constable and then others so that Riley instead of finding himself locked away in Fanny Bay Prison becomes a black tracker. Jackamara is ordered to train the new recruit and during this time, he establishes a strong friendship, cemented in a skin or kinship relationship which endures over the years as the black constable rises by sheer ability to do what no other black has done since, that is to become a Detective Inspector in the Queensland police force. It is when the accommodations necessary in his career become too much for him that he thinks of his old mate and kin brother and visits him.

Riley does not last long as a black tracker; he resents being sent after his own people, and eventually ends up in an Aboriginal village or settlement far from the thrust and pull of the white man's world. It is here that Jackamara driving his 1979 Land Cruiser all the way from Queensland comes to visit him. The village might have problems with alcohol and gambling; but it is set next to a sacred cave and Jackamara feels a conduit open between him and the ancient wisdom he often feels that he is losing. Now happy to be away from all that harms his Aboriginality, he sits on the verandah of Riley's house, thinking over the past and how many things have changed, though not his relationship with Riley.

To the right of him is a row of galvanised iron humpies; but on his left are the new stone houses which are slowly replacing them. Riley, as an important man of his community, has received the first of them. In front of him is a resource centre and the school from which an increasing number of youngsters are being turned out to go on to more education at Batchelor College and from there to the University of the Northern Territory. Of course, the white man's education brings problems. Those educated far beyond their parents and grandparents often feel that their elders are holding them back. Perhaps they are. Still, it is a new world which Jackamara thought he would never see, and for all the squabbling, the faction fighting and even downright embezzlement of community funds, it makes him feel good to see black people standing up straight and proud. Jackamara feels that he is of the past, just as is his old mate. As he is glancing toward Riley sitting beside him on the verandah, there arises a long piercing wail.

Instantly, the village comes alive. People spill out from here, there and elsewhere to gather in the dusty main street. One of Riley's grandsons runs up to tell them: "Young fella, buffalo git him, finish him off real good."

This is unusual. It is the first time that he has heard of anyone being attacked by a buffalo, although the village circulates with stories of them being dangerous. This, Jackamara has decided, is a form of social control. The surrounding country holds numerous sacred sites forbidden to children, women, and in regard to women's sites, men. People wandering haphazardly about might inadvertently trespass on one of these sites and so to keep them to well-defined areas and tracks, dangerous buffalo stories were circulated. The educated young man who had met his death supposedly at the horns of one of these beasts and whose name is not allowed to be mentioned, was the son of a prominent law man of the village. Still, he had returned home from Batchelor College in the last few months and may have felt derision for the stories.

Jackamara takes in the scene of the alleged accident in a glance. Beside the young man lies a 303 rifle, obviously fired, for a short distance from the corpse sprawls the buffalo. Blood speckles its forehead and right horn. The young man lies as if he has been tossed. His rifle going one way and his body the other. Still, it is puzzling, how the rifle has discharged. Jackamara surmises that when it struck the ground, it discharged and the bullet struck the animal, when it was in the very act of goring its victim.

He squats beside the body. The head is bloody, the shirt ripped and a gaping hole in the chest has spouted blood over the ground around the corpse. There is also a trail of blood from the body to the head of the animal. He gets up, feeling the stiffness in his bones that has come with advancing age, and goes to the buffalo. He squats again, hearing his bones creak, at the head of the beast. The blood is heavily smeared. Without tests it is impossible to determine whether part of it is human; but it must be a mixture of both. The bullet has smashed its way through an eye and then out of the back of the head. An angle which shows that the buffalo has been shot from below. Jackamara gets to his feet, glancing along the blood trail from body to body, from buffalo to human. As the relations of the young man claim the body, he looks across at Riley who has been watching him all the while. "Bloody strange," he states.

"Bloody strange," his skin brother repeats. He holds out a soft feather, then points down at a blurred footprint. "In other places, black fellas would run a mile if they see one of these; but not here. Not our culture."

"Featherfoot," Jackarnara grunts.

"Yeah, featherfoot, Kaditch. He was away for a while, at that college. All sorts there. Maybe he did something wrong and they come after him on payback. Dunno though. No strangers around."

"Well, maybe, buffalo done it."

"Maybe, maybe not ... You know this young fella, he all the time talking out, talking 'bout things ..."

"And?"

"Maybe, some fella or other not like it."

"You mean, he skitched the buffalo onto him?"

"Buffalo easy to kill; buffalo easy to blame; but why this track?"

"Yeah, why muddy up the waters, when it seems so clear? ..."

"Well, you still big boss policeman. Get on and catch'im that fella just like you catch'im me that time. Quick too, or payback might come. Funny accident this. Every fella can see it. Still, not like work of black fella. Not his work at all."

"No?"

"No, black fella, he make clean kill. Go wild and hit out. This is what you call ..."

"Premeditated?"

"Yeah."

"Maybe, he had a big win in the card game?"

"Naw—never played."

"Maybe, a relation?"

"They bloody lose their shirts last night. Anyway, no relations in card game. One against everyone, you know."

"Well, this track, this print?"

"Maybe, you follow him, see where he goes, where he comes from."

"Me! Can't follow a roo across a muddy field now. Been in that city too long."

"See that bit of grass there?"

"Yeah."

"It bend this way. Along side, 'nother bend the other way. One bin come, other bin go. Further behind another and another. That featherfoot got heavy foot. Carry something here too. Not away though."

"Like what?"

"Dunno 'bout that."

Jackamara goes and squats over the bent grass. He stares down at it and as he stares his old skill returns. He gets to his feet and can see two lines of blurred footprints spotting the land, leading out from and towards the village.

"One fella," he grunts.

"Not black fella though," Riley replies. "You make that out?"

"Now that you say so. Reason why he had to disguise his tracks, and not to scare us poor fellas at all. But why, a white fella? You only got three here: that storekeeper; schoolteacher; the pilot and he's away."

"One of them two fellas."

"Yeah, but no chalk dust, or lolly wrappers to tell us which one, or how or why he did it."

They walk along the tracks, then Jackamara squats and examines a spot of blood. He looks along the tracks and sees that there are more for a few metres. Riley stands looking down and declares: "Can smell that, human blood."

Jackamara pokes out a finger, lifts it and stares at the tip. "Dried."

"Yeah, but still can smell it. Two, four hours old."

"So that fixes the time of death. Near dawn, no one about then; but, dunno, he bled a lot."

"Yeah, them tiny drops. That was a big hole in chest, not much about the head though."

They continue to follow the tracks until the dusty main street where they lose them. They cast around, but find not a trace. Riley shrugs, says, "Teatime," and goes off. Jackamara begins to follow him, then suddenly stops and changes direction. He walks to the school building. It is padlocked up and deserted. He walks around the building with his eyes on the ground, then moves off to the schoolteacher's house which is about a hundred metres from the perimeter of the school. With his gaze on the ground, he ambles around the house before stepping onto the verandah. As he moves towards the front door, a ginger-haired and bearded white man in a grey shirt, dark blue shorts and knee length white socks stained pink from the red dust and shiny black shoes comes out with a scowl on his face.

"You're the Queensland police inspector. It is appropriate that you are on the scene of the, the terrible accident. It was quite a shock. I taught him, you know. Such a shame, but ..."

"Ah, so you knew the deceased, the unfortunate victim of the alleged accident."

"Alleged? What might it have been, but an accident. He was always careless, even thoughtless at times, and worse, the college made him a stirrer."

"And did he stir you?"

"We had our moments. He had become somewhat of a radical."

"And how did he stir you?"

"Look, I saw you at the school building. Don't you think it's a disgrace. I can't even get a teacher to stay on here for more than a few terms. It needs a complete renovation. Well, I applied for funding, on my own bat, you understand, the council would have argued over it for months, and now I intend to make it one of the best and cleanest school buildings in the territory. Naturally, I had to place my plans before the community council and it was then that he came against the whole idea. He came out with some fanciful ideas he called, believe it or not, "black fella education", and wanted the funding diverted to research a different curriculum. Atrocious; but I managed to get the idea defeated, then he decided that the local people should be employed to renovate the building and that no outside workmen should be brought in. Well, I set them straight. I told them that I was here to educate their kids according to the directives of the Education Department which had an Aboriginal advisory board to help them, and also I said that the money had been specifically earmarked for the building and that the work had to be contracted out. It is the way things are done."

"And?"

"And that if he wanted funding for his concerns he should apply to the Education Department himself."

"And?"

"Well, that was the end of it. What could he do about it, especially when I had the support of the council?"

"These contracts and the employment of outside workmen?"

"Department policy, and all above board I assure you. He was just a stirrer ... too much education ..."

Jackamara nods his head. It seemed that it took time for things to change. He makes his way to the store, employing a circular route which takes him all around the building. He stops for a moment at the back door, bends over a tap, has a drink of water, then continues on around to the front of the store where he finds the storekeeper, a slovenly man with peeling red skin and shaking hands, trying to insert the key in the lock. Jackamara stops beside him and the man jerks up.

"Hope you got the time. Just want a tin of Log Cabin tobacco."

"You know, begin to lock up, yer stomach aching for a bit of tucker and someone'll sure to be along for something or other. Well, I'm the white man at your service. What else can I say, but come and get yer baccy."

Detective Inspector Watson Holmes Jackamara enters the store which is as ill-kept and as shabby and dusty as its owner. He looks over the place as the man goes behind the counter. Above the refrigerator is the mounted horns of a buffalo. Jackamara stares at them as he opens the refrigerator and takes out a can of coke. He turns to the counter and finds that the tobacco and coke are way above city prices. He says nothing. The man goes to pick up an account book, then shrugs.

"Forgot that yer a visitor, so it'll have to be cash."

Jackamara pays and leaves. He sits on the edge of the verandah and drinks the coke. The storeman locks up and goes away towards his house which is near, but not too near the schoolteacher's. The detective inspector watches him walk away, then gets to his feet and goes to where the young man lived.

The young man's family have taken his body to the village church, leaving the house open. It is one of the newer stone dwellings with two large interior rooms surrounded by a wide verandah, one side of which holds the kitchen and bathroom. Jackamara gazes around the first room, then goes into the second. It is where the young man has lived. He has a desk in the corner piled with books and papers. A briefcase leans against the leg of the chair. Jackamara glances at the desk, before picking up the case and opening it. It is filled with papers arranged neatly in brown folders. He looks through these and stops and checks the papers in one of them. Lists of figures and names in columns. He nods and shuts the case. He leaves with the folder.

Beside the road passing the village is the airstrip. Detective Inspector Jackamara stands and watches as a light plane makes its approach and lands in a swirl of dust. Two policemen in khakis jump out and come towards him.

"Got your message. Some trouble, eh? Buffalo got some bloke or other. Can be dangerous. Guess it'll be a routine matter, eh?"

"Not exactly."

"What do ya mean? Accidents happen all the time. Usually when they're pissed."

"I have investigated the matter and know that it was murder."

"I know you're a smart city detective; but, well, do we arrest the buffalo?"

"No, the storeman!"

"What? You're having me on. He's been here for years. Gets on well with the people. Maybe likes his booze a bit, but that doesn't stop him from doing his job, what there is of it ..."

"Or in stealing the people blind."

"You got any evidence to back up this, this allegation?"

"It's all in this folder, facts and figures, dates and names. The bloke who was murdered was collecting the evidence against him. Seems he got wind of it and decided to do him in."

"Well, making a few bob on the side is one thing, but murder ... I don't believe it. You city cops see crime where there isn't crime. We ain't like that up here. If there's reasonable doubt? ..."

"I suggest that you impound the murder weapon immediately. He might get rid of it, or even give it a good scouring. He's a sloppy one and thinks that a quick wash and wipe will do the job. There'll be traces of blood on it. If you need more evidence, scoop up some of the mud under the tap at the back of the store. There'll be traces there too and a few tests'll bring them out."

"What murder weapon?"

"You'll find a pair of buffalo horns over the refrigerator. Good thing that they were there in plain sight and easily missed, else he might have gotten rid of them. They're the weapon. He must have shot the buffalo, got the young bloke in the store, struck him on the head with the horns or with the wood they're mounted on, carried his body out where he had previously shot the buffalo and arranged the accident. Doesn't matter if a few of the details are incorrect, a few days without grog and you'll get his statement. Here's the file on his embezzlement. My report is on top. You'd better impound his books too. Okay?"

"You know, you're a bloody wonder."

"I am! ..."

Jackamara and Riley sit on the verandah with large mugs of tea beside them. Riley stares at the plane taking off and says: "That storeman bloke was no good anyways. Knew he was ripping us off ..."

"Why didn't you do something about it?"

"Us old'uns can't read, or write. What to do, but just sit and wait till he comes a cropper."

"It led to murder."

"Yeah, shame; but that young'un had no respect for us elders. No respect. No respect at all. How'd you guess it was that storeman fella?"

"Smelt the blood on that pair of horns he had in his store. New human blood. The horns were wiped clean too, everything else was dusty. Stood out a mile. You know, that's how I found you long ago. Had a scratch on your arm. Smelt it through the water. Seems that water heightens the blood smell. Lucky I got you that time, that trooper was all ready to put a bullet in you."

"Naw, would never have found me, 'cepting for you."

"Well, maybe that time, but another time you finished."

"Just like that store fella. You get everyone you after."

"Well, but you helped, you know. The tracks ..."

"The tracks?"

"Yeah, way he walk, right foot straight, left foot a little out. Featherfoot shoes can't disguise that. Dead give away."

"Yeah, knew who it was as soon as I saw that track."

"Whyn't you tell me straight out. Saved me a bit of walking and thinking."

"Payback. You caught me that time, you know."

"So all that business finish now?"

"Just a little bit to finish. Bin all finish now. All that black fella business bin finish now."

For a long moment, Jackamara stares into the face of his old mate, Riley. Grudges take a long time to die. They build up and up. He begins to go over the evidence, he has quickly, perhaps too quickly found, then pushes it away. "All that business finish now," he says and together the old men stare out over the settlement. Now made a more secure place.

First Published in *Murder at Home*, edited by Stephen Knight, 3-12. St. Leonards, NSW: Allen & Unwin, 1993.

FILLING "TERRA NULLIUS": BONY IN THE DEATHSPACE

KAY TORNEY

The vicious legal fiction of *terra nullius*, so recently laid to rest by what we call Mabo, fitted well with European Australia's vision of what it ambiguously knew as the Dead Heart at its centre. Today, I want to consider one writer's representation of life in a landscape imaged as, on the one hand, rich with the raw materials needed for Western culture and industry (pearls, livestock, uranium), but, on the other, as violently emptied of psychological resources, and containing terrifying spaces into which people and whole cultures disappear. The fantasy of the Dead Heart with a powerful gravity which sucks out human spirit is, I shall argue, a specific product of the history that shaped the contemporary Australian landscape, best understood as a guilty response to living on the site of innumerable massacres. Deborah Bird Rose has named the world produced by mass murder and theft in Far North Queensland a Deathscape, and in this paper, in order to emphasise the psychic rather than the physical-geographical implications, I have adapted her word for the post-massacre emptiness to "the Deathspace". A space made available for use by the obliteration of the original owners may be a wealthy and spacious one, but such places are so marked by the circumstances of their production that they affect the inheritors profoundly. How can the Deathspace be written about, its history of liveliness, intelligence and generativity as well as of atrocity?

The detective novels of Arthur Upfield are useful for my purpose in thinking about the representation of *terra nullius* and the Dead Heart because they provide a sort of mythological envisioning of the effects of the creation of a Deathspace, one which involves dizzying shifts of perspective as received ideas are inverted and reversed. Upfield migrated to Australia from England as a young man in 1911, and led a lively life as a novelist and Outback worker thereafter. His still popular "Bony" novels, which concern the amazing successes of a so-called "half-caste", the educated and elegant Detective-Inspector Napoleon Bonaparte, fight what might be thought of as the deadly "Maralinga syndrome" (currently being evidenced by France in its activities in the South Pacific), which represents a region as more or less empty—at least of any intelligent life, as they used to say on *Star Trek*—and thus available for nuking, or any other destructive act that seems a good idea to the imperial power. Upfield's novels (there are about 20) assert that the fantasised emptiness of *terra nullius* is in fact full of things: love affairs, murder victims, food, shelter, tribal learning, human and animal intelligence, and especially babies, lots and lots of them. The very name of Upfield's hero, who insists that everybody call him "Bony" (which Upfield spells without the "e" usual in the contraction of Bonaparte) links him with the conflicts and contradictions of the Deathspace: his name embodies the deathly translation of European imperialism in the person of the Aboriginal.[1] Bony's mixed-race reading of the Deathspace re-inserts murder, massacre, theft and cross-race passion back into the story of the landscape.

Upfield's novels are concerned with a landscape in which crimes have been made in some way difficult to read, often by the freaks of the landscape itself (its windstorms or floods or simple hugeness), and usually also with the co-operation of two or more ethnicities. In short, the usual whodunnit problem posed by a mysterious corpse in Detective Fiction becomes a problem involving both ethnicity and landscape—strikingly removed from the class preoccupations of British crime fiction, where it might very well be the butler or some horrid social climber who dunnit.[2] Moreover, the conventional racial tables are inverted: whiteness, though generally perceived as racially superior by the characters themselves, is broadly represented as a handicap by the novels as wholes. Take this account of a citizen of Broome, for example:

> "To appreciate [Broome] you must stay at least a year. There is none other like it in the world. ... Should you have an interest in such matters,

---

[1] The name of Napoleon Bonaparte is heavily burdened with signification for the early and mid-twentieth century reader. "Boney", the English contraction of the first Napoleon's name, was the emblem of xenophobic anxiety used to frighten nineteenth-century children into good behaviour. Also, nineteenth- and early twentieth-century madmen would stereotypically insist that they were Napoleon Bonaparte, complete with one hand in waistcoat. The name of Upfield's Bony, then, brings together a range of psychological and colonial questions which are given frightening emphasis in the character's status as mixed-race offspring of a dead black mother. They could be summarised as: can the individual survive colonial construction without himself becoming brutally destructive or mad?

[2] See, for example, P.D. James, *Innocent Blood*, where the problems of child reconsignment are class issues, not Deathspace ones.

you will find the white section of the community of exceptional psychological interest. The whites are entirely lacking in the spiritual attributes making for personality. Observe this person approaching" [says the town eccentric].

The person was arrayed in white duck and wore a white sun-helmet. He was well nourished. His gaze did not deviate from a point exactly to his front and distant probably a thousand miles. His facial expression was that of a Yogi meditating in a blizzard ...

"Ninety per cent of them are like that, atrophied from the frontal bone upward."[3]

This exchange shows the white section of the Outback town cast as the focus of ethnographic interest, with an interesting reversal of the usual terms. Instead of the expected formulation: "the blacks are entirely lacking in the intellectual attributes making for civilization" (for instance), it is the whites who are entirely lacking in the *spiritual* attributes making for personality. As well as these character defects, the white man is seen as physically deficient: his clothes are blankly white, his face is white, and his mind is white too, a quality here which signifies not Blakean innocence, but chilly vacuity, "a Yogi meditating in a blizzard". Neither the man's eyes nor his emotions work properly either, unlike the brilliant darting eyes, warm spontaneity and sparky intelligence of the trackers. Upfield thus typically shows the white settler as absolutely spiritually and physically lost in the bush, as the tribalised Aborigine is at a loss in the European-style culture.

But although he celebrates the skills of the initiated Aborigine as miraculous and integrative compared to the dull administrative competence of the bush copper, Upfield insists that neither the whitefella policeman nor the blacktracker alone can crack the crimes of the Outback, or at least those which have attracted the attention of Bony's big-city superiors. This is because of the nature of these crimes, which is related to the strains of life in the Deathspace. Firstly, in Upfield's work, the prototypical Outback crime is a mixed-race one: both races are in some way involved in it, either as aggressor, victim or as joint perpetrator, or in some bizarre combination of these; and both races are therefore needed to solve the crime. Upfield represents the archetypal victim of this cross-race violence as, logically enough, an abused mixed-race child, or a child abused by two races or ethnicities. Secondly, Upfield argues that Aboriginal life—though often materially impoverished—is intelligent, rich and full in the Outback, and that white life in the bush is stupid, bleak, and spiritually impoverished. Thirdly, he represents the landscape itself as a vital force in

---

[3] Arthur Upfield, *The Widows of Broome* (London: Heinemann, 1967), 40.

the process of crime and mystery, tending to hide and reveal crimes unpredictably, with its winds, shifting sands, and caves.

Upfield's first novel, *The Barrakee Mystery* (1929) shows his initial engagement with these ideas about what happened to the original owners of Australia, and how it affected the white settlers and the surviving black population.[4] The novel's mysteries come thick and fast. Why is the magnificent full-blood, King Henry, murdered? And by whom? Why does the public-school-educated young squatter, Ralph, begin to show such lapses of good taste as the wearing of loud socks when he comes home from college? Why does he even more tastelessly fall in love with the full-blood Aboriginal beauty, Nellie, and slight the Darling of the Darling, his cousin Kate? What is the mystery of Ralph's birth? The answer to all these questions turn on the twin mysteries of maternal passion and racial mixture, each represented as so powerful as to overthrow the strongest rational intentions. The story turns out to be that Ralph was exchanged at birth for the still-born son of the squatter, given freely by his dying mother, Mary Sinclair. His adoptive mother falls in love for ever with the baby when she suckles it, and is then told with the biological mother's last breath, that the infant's father is—King Henry! whom she describes as "so magnificent a man that I became as putty in his hands".[5] Mrs Thornton takes comfort in the baby's fair skin and tells no one, including her husband, about the baby's paternity; but when King Henry comes back to

---

[4] In the light of these ideas, such works as *The Barrakee Mystery*, which Tamsin Donaldson describes merely as part of the "sexual contact history" of Australia, look rather different. See Tamsin Donaldson, "Australian Tales of Mystery and Miscegenation," *Meanjin* 50.2-3 (1991): 342. In one of the rather few analyses of Upfield's work, Donaldson contrasts *The Barrakee Mystery* with Sally Morgan's autobiographical detective story *My Place*, where young Sally persuades her mystifying relatives to tell her where they all came from, and Upfield comes off the worse: Donaldson considers Morgan's account to be more authentic and driven. At a political level, I have no argument with this assessment. But Upfield's work provides a much more dispassionate envisioning and analysis of the cultural effects of murder and miscegenation than Morgan could possibly be expected to do, precisely because the trials and insights of the fictional Bony can be approached with a sort of analytical callousness which is not available to Morgan's representation of her family. Upfield's treatment of the landscape, for instance, concentrates on its frightening capacity to swallow up huge numbers of murdered bodies, generally black, rather than on its religious or personal significance. His protected, distanced and analytical point of view allows the fantasies of engulfment and destruction which underpin the image of the Dead Heart to be teased out, an unimaginable result for writers who are concerned with grief and loss.

[5] Arthur Upfield, *The Barrakee Mystery* (London: Pan Books, 1969), 235-236.

claim the child, she pays him £10 and sends him packing. King Henry keeps returning, and is thought to be blackmailing (though there is very little curiosity about his motives). So Mrs Thornton organises Mary Sinclair's brother to avenge the family shame and simultaneously allow the adopted child to live a happily reconsigned life. Twenty years later, Mrs Thornton and Sinclair jointly murder King Henry, and Bony comes to sort it out. But the wisdom of this novel is that puberty causes the skin to darken and racial yearnings which are figured as regressive to appear. Bony in fact asserts that that was his own experience, and argues that Ralph's Aboriginality will always re-appear. Mrs Thornton dies of grief when the truth comes to light, and the squatter, who now knows the truth, adopts a more appropriate heir who obligingly marries cousin Kate.

The plot here is often distasteful, bordering on eugenics at times in a way that is more than characteristic of the period, particularly in its account of the appearance and behaviour of mixed-race individuals.[6] It does, however, display a number of the powerful motifs which will be refined in Upfield's later work. First, there are primal acts of what Upfield, particularly in his early work, represents as genetic defiance: the racially joint crimes of miscegenation and adoption, which are then covered up jointly by both races. In three Bony novels written three decades on, the issues are clarified somewhat, and, crucially, a sort of compliance is located in the landscape itself. *Bony and the Black Virgin* (1959) involves the murder by another beautiful full-blood girl, Lottee, of two white men who rape her. She and the squatter's son Eric, a former medical student, gone as it were native because of the pull of the bush, are *in love*.[7] Lottee's assaulted virginity is magically restored with the ceremony of tribal fire, and she and Eric attempt to cover their crimes by staging the murder of one of the rapists by the other. When the body of the second man is unexpectedly uncovered in a sandstorm, Lottee and Eric commit a triumphant ritual suicide by ceremonial drowning in the duck lake. Capulets and Montagues of race, they look forward to being tribally united after death, in the spirit of a tree. The crimes of rape and murder are all racially mixed, the love is racially mixed, and murder, rape and love can all be buried in the land itself. The problem is that the emptied landscape

---

[6] See, for example, Susan Squier, *Babies in Bottles*, for an account of the fictional representation of eugenic fantasy in the 1920s and 1930s.

[7] "Love" is always a plot solver for Upfield: he shows little sense of the shadings of the idea, so that whenever Bony asks a young couple who have been behaving oddly, "Are you two in love?" they simply say "Yes." Being in love seems to act as a container for generational misunderstandings, and indicates Upfield's utter lack of interest in purely interpersonal ways of relating.

itself reveals and conceals unpredictably, foiling black and white together. Similar themes appear in *The Man of Two Tribes* (1956), where Bony finds himself imprisoned in subterranean caves under the Nullarbor Plain, for snooping about after a disappearance. A group of vigilantes have used the brilliant tracking and telepathic skills of the "wild" blacks of the Nullarbor to punish murderers who have had their sentences commuted. The scheme was hatched by the mother of a child killed by one of the prisoners, a Polish Holocaust survivor weirdly named Igor Mitski, but it is made clear that Mitski was unlucky, and did not mean to kill the little girl, equally oddly called Mayflower. The conflict, between the traumatised Mitski and the flower of Puritan civilisation, the apparently obnoxious little Mayflower, means death, and the killing of the child by another Deathspace survivor means that the resources of black and white co-operatively mobilise the literal spaces of the land to hide the bodies of killers. These plots are characteristic of Upfield's work. The primal crime involves racial mixture, suffering and cruelty, and the land, emptied by countless such incidents, is now spacious enough to hide numberless dead in its emptiness. Bodies are hidden in caves, burnt, mummified, re-buried; even the living can be swallowed up by these huge emptied spaces which the tribal remnants still control. The spaces of massacre allow the land itself to avenge murder.

The novel of Upfield's that most strikingly embodies the motifs of racially joint crimes in the Deathspace is *Murder Must Wait* (1953). What the solving of the murder must wait for, in this case, is the solving of the crime of childstealing. Five tiny white male babies have been taken from their mothers in the Victorian town of Mitford, and public feeling is running high. When Bony is called in, he realises he cannot solve the mystery without a good woman, and recruits policewoman Alice McGorr, the daughter of a (deceased) master safe-cracker, and whose maternal instincts are described as very intense. What Alice and Bony discover is a plot hatched by a cold-blooded psychiatrist, Dr Nonning, to transfer unwanted infants to desperate women who are "figuratively dying for want of one".[8] Nonning chooses Mitford for his activities, because his equally cold-blooded sister who lives there, married to the local doctor, has just such a child, and is very keen to get rid of it. Dr Nonning believes that it won't help matters much for an infertile woman to select "a child from an orphanage as one might choose an appealing object".[9] No, he wants them to believe that the child is spiritually theirs by right. So, with the help of the loopy anthropologist, Professor Marlo-Jones, and his overbearing wife,

---

[8] Arthur Upfield, *Murder Must Wait* (London: Heinemann, 1953), 244.
[9] Upfield, *Murder Must Wait*, 243.

an intrusive blue-stocking type, he stages an Aboriginal legend, whereby Altjerra, the creator of all things, allows spirit babies to fly from a tree to a woman, by a mixture of 1950s style deep sleep therapy and Aboriginal co-operation. The extraordinary thing is that Nonning organises neglected infants to be taken by the Aborigines and given "to people who wanted them, and would give them wise attention and affection".[10] This idea mixes the ideology of stealing "neglected" infants with the ideology of providing wise (though neurotic) people with them. The first two women actively surrender their children: they are vile sherry-drinking upper-class types whose socialising is inconvenienced by the babes. The next three women, however, are simply deemed to be unfit mothers; one leaves her baby outside the pub while she knocks back gin squashes, one has the temerity to neglect her maternal duties to write novels, and a third leaves baby alone while she slopes off to meet with the child's father (who subsequently murders her). The plot mechanism here is the loving Aboriginal mother, who provides care in the black settlement near the river. This novel represents a startling reimagining of Australian social history, where white officials deemed black babies "neglected" and took them away, combined with the fiction that neurosis in respectable infertile women could be helped by rearing another woman's baby. The extra detail of the deep-sleep charade is a sort of mythological version of present-day I.V.F. pregnancy with donor ova. In *Murder Must Wait*, the issues of cross-cultural child-stealing in Upfield's work are put with appalling clarity: the death of an adult is a small thing, epistemologically speaking; the abduction of children is an atrocity, however it may be rationalised. Professor and Mrs Marlo-Jones, like Macbeth, have no children, so they cannot really understand what forces they are interfering with, and Nonning is represented as the worst sort of manipulative psychiatrist. The image of the sane and loving Aboriginal people rescuing neglected white infants from their drunken and irresponsible mothers, taking them to the warmth and safety of the Black Camp, and then accessing their own mythological "administration" to send the babies to a safer future reads like a return of the repressed. Well- and ill-intentioned blacks and whites make the trouble; Bony sorts it out, a human "Bridge", as he calls himself, between the two cultural imperatives.[11] And the trouble is always caused by a diabolical mixture of ancient tribal realities, contemporary needs, and the wish to believe that babies, black and white, are *tabula rasa*, mere cultural fodder.

In Upfield's work, the primal crime is a form of ethnic cleansing, that

---

[10] Upfield, *Murder Must Wait*, 245.
[11] Upfield, *Murder Must Wait*, 232.

is, forced cultural vandalism, racial mixture, child-stealing and murder. The novels' representation of attempted genocide is insistent: each one involves a fully initiated Aboriginal who clearly remembers the European invasion and knows himself to be "robbed of his birthright by the white man, and shackled by the white man's laws and taboos".[12] The mixed-race detective, like the patriarchal father of psychoanalysis, is both a symptom and a decoder of the illness he comes to read: Bony's endless labours to understand and expose the meanings of the stolen children, raped women and concealed corpses of Australia—meanings inscribed on his own body, as well as in the bush—help to return the repressions of the Deathspace to the fullness of completed narrative.

First Published in *Crossing Lines: Formations of Australian Culture*, edited by Caroline Guerin, Philip Butterss and Amanda Nettelbeck, 108-112. Adelaide: Association for the Study of Australian Literature, 1996. Reprinted with permission of the Association.

---

[12] Upfield, *Murder Must Wait*, 221.

DETECTIVE AS OUTSIDER— OUTSIDER AS DETECTIVE: NAPOLEON BONAPARTE AND ARTHUR UPFIELD

MURRAY S. MARTIN

Most modern detective stories offer far more than the solution to a crime. In fact their settings, and their examinations of motives and personalities, offer a view of the societies in which the detectives work. As Ross Macdonald says in writing of his own work "a good private detective ... likes to move through society both horizontally and vertically, studying people like an anthropologist".[1] This is true also of the regular detective, at least in recent writing, and is particularly true of those who are working in exotic settings. As John Cawelti says in writing of Australian Arthur Upfield,

> The detective story situation works with many different cultural settings because the investigation of a puzzling crime casts light on the workings of a society by catching it at a moment of anomaly and disruption.[2]

This point has been further elaborated by Margaret King in her study of cross-cultural detectives, where she states that the "local color" interest in many of these works is something like a second puzzle as the reader sets out to decipher the clues from an unfamiliar culture.[3]

This is especially true of Upfield's works, which, taken as a whole, provide an outstanding picture of the Australian outback. It is instructive to contrast, briefly, a recent police procedural story, *Count Down for*

---

[1] Ross Macdonald, *Ross Macdonald's Lew Archer, Private Investigator* (New York: Mysterious, 1977), xii.

[2] John Cawelti, "Murder in the Outback: Arthur W. Upfield," *New Republic* 177.5 (1977): 39.

[3] Margaret King, "Binocular Eyes: Cross-Cultural Detectives," *Armchair Detective* 13 (1980): 255.

Murder, by Max Gill, which is also set in the outback. In this instance it is a transformed outback, on the Nullarbor Plain in South Australia, transformed by the activities on the rocket range at Woomera and the opal fields of Coober Pedy.[4] The outback has been invaded by those who are exploiting it for commercial and political reasons. Their only relationship to place is "what's in it for me". Some of the grandeur remains, in brief descriptions of dawn and sunset, but, by and large, the mystery and reverence, so clear in Upfield, have gone. They have been replaced by a kind of modern cynicism.

In a sense, Upfield upholds the values behind the Australian myth, finding health in the lonely places, and beauty in the stubborn countryside. His personal travels, pushing a bicycle, enabled him to gain intimate knowledge of the outback and its inhabitants. He celebrates the dour farmer eking a living from an unforgiving land, even while enchanted by it. Droughts and floods figure in his plots, as do the complex relationships between the rich station-owners, the marginal small farmers, the often itinerant workforce, including that quintessential Australian figure—the sundowner. Of course, Upfield himself was an itinerant and might be expected to show such understanding, but it is clear-eyed. There are few angels in his outback.

Paradoxically, his books concern crime, a kind of desecration of Eden. In the one full-scale study of Upfield, *The Spirit of Australia*, Ray Browne pays great attention to the physical settings, which are indeed detailed enough that maps and locations can be provided, and he distinguishes those which are actual from those which are fictional. They demonstrate the depth of Upfield's knowledge of his adopted country. But they also raise a delicate critical issue. The books themselves are written as from the perspective of an Aborigine, yet the views expressed are, as James Pierson says, those of a European.

> "Upfield's descriptions of Australian landscapes and the relationships of various cultural groups with the land and with each other are often vivid, but the perspective is that of a white man with extensive outback experience."[5]

---

[4] There is perhaps a tendentious link between this term – a combination of *nulla* and *arbor*, with the legal term for the Australia discovered by white men – *Terra nullius* – literally land belonging to no one, which enabled the invading settlers to take over land without compensation.

[5] James Pierson, "Mystery Literature and Ethnography: Fictional Detectives as Anthropologists," in *Literature and Anthropology*, ed. Philip Dennis and Wendell Aycock, (Lubbock: Texas Tech University Press, 1989), 24.

This conflict is scarcely surprising, given the status of the Aborigine at the time Upfield was writing. What is actually most surprising is that he chose to place even a part-Aborigine at the center of the action. The problem is that he appears to be offering the views of an Aborigine, although full understanding of those views was beyond his powers. He does, however, go far beyond the descriptions and ideas offered by most other contemporary writers.

In a way the character Napoleon Bonaparte, called Bony, has joined the others, in that he is a detective inspector with the Queensland police (and apparently has a license to cover the whole country) which is a very different status from that of the Aboriginal tracker so often found in other writing. Bony is said to have been based on one such tracker, Leon Wood, who also had a higher than usual education. Yet he is caught in a world of his own, able apparently to function in both cultures, but uneasily aware that his background, education, and achievements set him apart.

Standing as he does in the middle, he mediates between cultures that cannot understand one another. In a way this is the major achievement of the whole series. As Browne says, Bony is the "hero-equalizer between the two societies and the two cultures".[6] This is the classic role for the Western lawman, and Pierson makes some telling contrasts with Hillerman's Navajo detectives, whose sympathies are clearly with their fellow Navajos. He makes the point that such detectives, or heroes, are "socialized" and "acculturated" by different groups, the first being "native" with their own peoples, the second "colonial" through education. The latter identification endows them with the interpretative ability to explicate the former. Thus, "the detectives subsequently provide the reader with cultural information throughout a case rather than only in isolated pieces".[7] This enhances the teaching function identified by King, though it may occasionally make for heavy going. Through Bonaparte, Upfield examines more than the differences between Aborigines and whites; he also provides subtler distinctions between the many sub-groups within each culture. There are the rich settlers who form the establishment, the many working-class whites, the pure blood Aborigines in rustic seclusion, those degraded by white contact, and those who are of mixed descent. The patterns of contact between these groups are delicate and shifting. Clearly his own hard-earned personal knowledge allows him to differentiate between the rich and successful, those down on their luck, the drifter, and the hard-working station hand. Even the rural postman (these books were written in the days

---

[6] Ray Browne, *Heroes and Humanities: Detective Fiction and Culture* (Bowling Green, OH: Bowling Green State University Popular Press, 1986), 12.
[7] Pierson, "Mystery Literature and Ethnography," 20.

before the widespread use of the radio for communication) can play an important role in the plot.

Despite Upfield's evident intent to praise Bony and his accomplishments, and to pay tribute to Aboriginal culture, there are mixed messages. Derogatory statements about "Abos" from a part-Aboriginal are hard to decode. Are they from the author's own perspective and authorial, or they are from Bony's perspective, in which case are they suspect as mediated? Bony often "struggles to limit the influence of his aboriginal heritage on his behavior as a detective"[8] which is a likely conflict, but often so stated that it seems to make one culture appear automatically inferior. That may be a limitation of the writer rather than an intention. It probably also reflects Upfield's own view that he was regarded as a nobody by other Australian writers. It is almost as if two outsiders merge into one without having their differences reconciled.

Nevertheless these conflicts provide an underlying structure to the novels. To King they are central:

> The loyalties and tensions between the two groups structure the plot and action, and their delicate interactions must be understood and plumbed by Bonaparte amidst the complex encounters of primitive and modern sensibilities—colonial and imperial, traditional and "developed".[9]

Part of the problem in interpreting the cultural message may derive from the genre itself—the police procedural—which is a distinctively European genre, and inadequate in dealing with other cultures. Interest in the "other" culture can often take precedence over interest in the crime and its solution, a conflict common to other writers who have used cross-cultural detectives and settings.

Upfield appears to have taken to heart the doctrines of the Jindyworobaks[10] who felt that Australian writing had to be freed from external influences and should concentrate on Australia and things Australian. Absurd as some of its pretensions were the movement did clear away much of the derivative color that had marred Australian literature. His search to write the "great Australian novel" continued to the end, though he was realist enough to know that he had not done so. His ear for country speech was finely tuned, and his dialog is superb. He undoubtedly was able to portray the ordinary bloke, and to give written expression to

---

[8] Browne, *Heroes and Humanities*, 22.
[9] King, "Binocular Eyes," 255.
[10] William Wilde, Joy Hooton, and Barry Andrews, *Oxford Companion to Australian Literature* (Melbourne: Oxford University Press, 1985), 371-372.

the country that he loved. In this he resembles other antipodean writers who were seeking to form a local identity, but none of these achievements enabled him to break into the inner literary circle. His novels are full of literary references,[11] and in two he pilloried the Australian establishment, using as an alter ego Clarence B. Bagshott, a popular author who liked a good story. His rancor against the literary snobs can best be shown by two quotations:

> Educated people don't read Bagshott's stuff ... No one knows him outside the readers of newspaper serials. Our glorious Australian literature has had too many obstacles to surmount in order to become established without having Bagshott's tripe added to them. They call his books Australian, and people unfortunately read them and judge Australian literature by them.[12]

> In this country literature is a piece of writing executed in school-masterly fashion and yet so lacking in entertainment values that the general public won't buy it. Commercial fiction—and this is a term employed by the highbrows—is imaginative writing that easily satisfied publishers and editors because the public will buy it.[13]

The first is the establishment viewpoint, the second is Upfield's own. In one way he was justified. His novels were and are read widely outside Australia, and have been received into the canon of the best detective fiction. Others may have produced more "literary" works, and there are undoubtedly many great novels which concern the Aborigine, but Upfield's corpus is the single most sustained effort to portray the cultures of the great outback.

They can be read simply as good stories, but the reader must inevitably be drawn into the country and the society so lovingly portrayed. As King has noted, "Upfield's image of the Western Australian landscape, softly lit by the glow of meteors, is of an eerie, other-worldly beauty",[14] and his descriptions of the Nullarbor Plains, or the hills of the Queensland outback are equally memorable. Despite his lapses (of taste or understanding), his regard for the Aborigines is clear. He sympathizes with them in their problems with white development, and hopes for better days. On a comparative note one might cite the treatment of the Maori by down

---

[11] Ray Browne, *The Spirit of Australia: The Crime Fiction of Arthur W. Upfield* (Bowling Green, OH: Bowling Green State University Popular Press, 1988), 132-151.

[12] Arthur Upfield, *The Devil's Steps* (New York: Macmillan, 1948), 155.

[13] Arthur Upfield, *An Author Bites the Dust* (New York: Collier Books, 1987), 73.

[14] King, "Binocular Eyes," 256.

under's other international detective story writer, Ngaio Marsh, who always seems to feel ambivalent about the Maori, stressing their otherness and their fey sensitivity. This may have come from the fact that in Christchurch society, where she grew up, the Maori were not much in evidence, but it is strange that she should be so much less receptive than Upfield, who was, after all, a British immigrant to Australia. Her novels are for the most part set in England, and those set in New Zealand use Maori characters only as grace notes. This ambivalence has been explored by Carole Acheson, who recognizes that she wrote of New Zealand as a visitor might write, in contrast to Upfield who clearly wrote as an Australian who loved Australia. And for him the Aborigine was an Australian whose life and problems were inadequately understood.

Perhaps Upfield's most extensive treatment of the problem of living between two cultures (other than Bony himself) is that of Tessa in *The Will of the Tribe*, where her reversion to and acceptance of her Aboriginal roots is applauded, in an extensive examination of the graduations in Aboriginal society. Here even Bony has to stand back lest his own double sensitivities lead him to interfere and diminish her own decision. Whatever their standing as literature may come to be, Upfield's novels about Bony remain outstanding examples of the ability of the detective novel to convey a sense of other cultures. Bony himself is one of literature's great detectives, evidently with international appeal, since the books have been translated into many languages, and remain in print, not true of the purists who derided Upfield.

First Published in *Clues: A Journal of Detection* 17.1 (Spring/Summer 1996): 33-42.

BONY AS GROTESQUE:
ARTHUR UPFIELD'S "BONY" SERIES
1930-1950

GLEN ROSS

> When we use the word "grotesque" we record, among other things, the sense that though our attention has been arrested, our understanding is unsatisfied. Grotesqueries both require and defeat definition ... They stand at a margin of consciousness between the known and unknown, the perceived and the unperceived, calling into question the adequacy of our ways of organizing the world.[1]

In a 1932 letter to John Keith Ewers, Arthur Upfield suggested that novels such as William Hatfield's *Sheepmates* (1931), Velia Ercole's *No Escape* (1932), and his own *Beach of Atonement* (1930), were going to become *"the real foundations of Australian literature* because they are unaffected and sincere and informative".[2] Upfield is better known, however, for the detective series that features the halfcaste character, "Bony". The books in Upfield's Bony series are still among the most popular in municipal libraries and book exchanges in Australia, and are also well known in Britain and the United States of America.[3] In a letter to a friend, Upfield boasted that his books had also been published in Germany, Mexico, Italy, Japan, Holland and Argentina.[4] It was in the United States, however, that his work appears to have made the greatest impact, with the development of a network of Bony enthusiasts and the

---

[1] Geoffrey Harpman, *On the Grotesque: Strategies of Contradiction in Art and Literature* (Princeton, NJ: Princeton University Press, 1982), 3.
[2] Arthur Upfield, Letter to John Ewers, 1 March 1932, held in a private collection. Emphasis added.
[3] This assertion is based upon discussions with librarians and booksellers during my own searches for a complete collection of Upfield's books.
[4] Arthur Upfield, Letter to Charles Lemon, 2 May 1957, Battye Library W.A. Accession 2138A.

publication of a "newsletter", *The Bony Bulletin*.[5]

What is of particular interest in Upfield's Bony books is the depiction in them of a halfcaste character at a time when the rising halfcaste population was causing concern in White Australia. My argument in this chapter is that the halfcaste presence was neutralised for white Australian readers in the 1930s and 40s Bony series through recourse to ideas associated with the emerging policies of assimilation. Like A.P. Elkin during the same period, Upfield's representations of Aboriginal people both established their difference as inferior others and sought to extinguish this difference through depicting the process of their absorption into the white population. The detective genre proved to be the ideal medium for this ideological elision of the halfcaste presence because of its traditional function in the construction of a national identity. A part of the appeal of detective books is their ability to offer fictional resolutions to real crimes through the efforts of extraordinary characters. Arthur Conan Doyle's famous detective hero "Sherlock Holmes", for instance, was able consistently to succeed where the police had failed.

The formal properties that allowed the success of the Holmes series were open to adaptation in other nations and social periods. In the Australian context, Upfield employed such conventions in the development of his Bony series. Drawing upon populist anthropological and psychoanalytical ideas, Upfield portrayed Bony as a person "split" between the white people and the black. This portrayal of Bony's ambivalent position as neither white nor Aboriginal allowed white readers simultaneously to accept him as an extraordinary detective and to disavow his presence as a halfcaste.

Criticism and the Detective Genre

The development of the detective genre has been a subject of debate among critics. H.B. Pierce points out in "From Poe to the Scientific Detective" (1983) that histories of the genre tend either to locate its origins well before the birth of Christ, or with the work of Francois Eugene Vidocq (1775-1857), and Edgar Allan Poe's "The Murder in the Rue Morgue" (1841).[6] Using Michel Foucault's *Discipline and Punish* (1977), Christopher Lee argues that it was a shift in the exercise of controlling power at the turn of the nineteenth century which laid the foundation for the emergence of the modern detective form. Public exhibitions of "torture

---

[5] Edited and published by Phillip Asdell in Maryland, USA.

[6] Hazel Pierce, "From Poe to the Scientific Detective," in *A Literary Symbiosis: Science Fiction/Fantasy Mystery* (Westport, CT: Greenwood Press, 1983), 16.

and/or execution", which functioned both as pronouncement of the power of the King and as a prohibition of resistance, were transformed with "the development of a sophisticated state bureaucracy and its associated differentiation of the social mass in the interests of its government".[7] Concomitant with this gradual change was the emergence of the police force and the penal system, with the development of the Metropolitan police force to London in 1829 and the formation of its first detective branch in 1842:

> Power thus came to be exercised in a capillary form throughout the social formation. The Police force and its specialist arm in the form of the Detective emerged in conjunction with the formation of an epistemology of surveillance and detection. The role of detection was to expose the abnormal for the purposes of punishment. This act of exposure and rejection then purifies the social body and expresses its normalcy.[8]

In the case of Arthur Conan Doyle's famous detective hero, Sherlock Holmes, this ability to expose the abnormal was facilitated by Holmes' training in science. Pierce outlines the development of Holmes as a scientist/detective from the formation of the character based upon one of Conan Doyle's medical lecturers through to his position as the "Master of both the analytical process and the moral activity which disentangles".[9] Contemporary examinations of the genre have often focussed on its social function as "mythology", as a "set of questions shaped to provide a consoling result for the anxieties of those who share in the cultural activity—the audience".[10]

A part of the pleasure readers gain from the detective genre is through a vicarious identification with the hero's power to succeed where the official law enforcement agencies have failed. Crime may persist, but through extraordinary ability the detective hero *is* able to effect change where the official organisations are ineffectual. Complex crimes beyond the comprehension of the police force need no more than time for them to be unravelled and exposed for the contemplation of the reader. Criticism has identified Holmes in particular as a character embodying this ability to demystify threats to social disorder. In *Critical Practice* (1980) Catherine Belsey argues that

---

[7] Christopher Lee, *Popular Literature: Study Book* (Toowoomba, Qld.: University of Southern Queensland, 1995), 3.3.

[8] Lee, *Popular Literature*, 3.2-3.3.

[9] Pierce, "From Poe to the Scientific Detective," 31; 24.

[10] Stephen Knight, *Form and Ideology in Crime Fiction* (London: Macmillan, 1980), 4.

[t]he project of the Sherlock Holmes stories [wa]s to dispel magic and mystery, to make everything explicit, accountable, subject to scientific analysis ... the stories begin in enigma, mystery, the impossible, and conclude with an explanation which makes it clear that logical deduction and scientific method render all mysteries accountable to reason.[11]

A substantial component of the pleasure of reading detective fiction arises from its ability to represent the expulsion of a criminal threat through knowledges generally available to the public. Extraordinary types such as Sherlock Holmes are able to draw together disparate ideas in order that the criminal threat is demystified and thereby neutralised. As Lee writes, "The detective provides us with a vehicle through which we can enact and experience an empowered sense of personal subjectivity".[12]

Investigations of the genre such as Belsey's have also shown that the fictitious enactment of solutions to crimes is always fraught with the danger of replicating its inconsistencies. Drawing, as they do, upon a range of ideas in the fictitious rendition of the society of which they are a part, the writers of crime fiction also reproduce ideological inconsistencies. Following on from Pierre Macherey, critics have focused on what Peter Hulme called "key locations in a text—*cruces*".[13]

These are sites where hegemony is contested, and which "reveal the areas of central anxiety, the space where ideology works at its hardest to assert that all is normal, that change need not be feared".[14] It is in seeking to fill these spaces, critics argue, that the most contemporary ideological developments are called upon to represent a stable society. This is achieved through the potential of fiction to maintain the illusion of distance from the ideologies it reproduces. As Belsey puts it:

The classic realist text installs itself in the space between fact and illusion through the presentation of a simulated reality which is plausible but not real. In this lies its power as myth. It is because fiction does not normally deal with "politics" directly ... that it is ostensibly innocent and therefore ideologically effective.[15]

---

[11] Catherine Belsey, quoted in "Marxism and Popular Fiction: Problems and Prospects," Tony Bennett, *Southern Review* 15.2 (1982): 279.

[12] Lee, *Popular Literature*, 3.10.

[13] Peter Hulme, *Colonial Encounters: Europe and the Native Caribbean, 1492-1797* (London; New York: Routledge, 1986), 12.

[14] Knight, *Form and Ideology in Crime Fiction*, 5.

[15] "Deconstructing the Text: Sherlock Holmes," in *Popular Fiction: Technology, Ideology, Production, Reading*, ed. Tony Bennett (London; New York: Routledge, 1990), 284.

For Belsey, this ability of classic realist texts to appear "innocent" of an association with the "real" world enables them to present in illusory form both the acceptable and unacceptable ideological changes of a socio-historical period. They provide a location for the ambivalent rendering of contentious ideas in such a way that they can either be dismissed as myth, or accepted as reality.

The critical identification of detective (or popular) fiction as a location disclosing ideological struggle has allowed critics to read such texts as a performance of sociocultural change. To draw again upon Macherey's work, if detective fiction reproduces contemporary ideas in order to conceal inconsistencies between discourses called upon to represent order, then it does so *repeatedly*. The fact that Conan Doyle produced the Holmes stories in serial form is not incidental. If the closure of ideological disruptions salved the anxieties of the readers of the Holmes books, then it only did so temporarily. In investigating this double function of the detective genre as one offering both a sense of stability to its readers while constantly adjusting to socio-historical change, critics of the genre have often discriminated between form and content. A useful development in this area was provided by John Cawelti in "The Concept of Formula in the Study of Popular Literature" (1969). In this article Cawelti built upon the distinction between form and content to develop the complementary terms "convention" and "invention", arguing that:

> Conventions represent familiar shared images and meanings and they assert an ongoing continuity of values; inventions confront us with a new perception or meaning which we have not realized before. Both these functions are important to culture. Conventions help maintain a culture's stability while inventions help it respond to changing circumstances and provide new information about the world.[16]

The critical adaptation of these terms facilitated investigations of historical alterations in the detective genre (and others), from both its gradually changing formal structures through to more rapid "inventions" in response to immediate socio-ideological "needs". As Knight argues:

> The figure of Holmes was so well created and attuned to its time and audience that it has survived to the present. But as different realities have emerged, new ideologies have been required to contain and conceal them. New formations of the detective and ways of presenting and controlling crime have been necessary to appease disquiet. And new detectives, often

---

[16] John Cawelti, quoted in *The Study of Popular Fiction: A Source Book*, Bob Ashley (London: Pinter Publishers, 1989), 87.

owing much to Conan Doyle's inventive and imaginative creation, have appeared, to be read as new encapsulations of socio-cultural responses to the ambient world.[17]

The identification of detective (and other) fiction as an important site for ideological work allows critics to map political as well as historical change.

As is the case with many other critics, however, Knight's words reveal a tendency to read popular fiction as a *product* determined by social change rather than one inextricably imbricated in its *processes*. There has been, in effect, a sense of a "time lag" between the social production of ideas and their fictitious re-enactment in literature. In "Marxism and Popular Fiction: Problems and Prospects" (1982), Tony Bennett calls into question traditional distinctions between fiction and ideology. For Bennett, the connection between them ought to be regarded as

> concerning the diverse and specific forms of the play and interaction between two spheres of the ideological: the discursive (consisting of those discourses which produce imaginary orderings of the relations of men and women to one another, to the conditions of their social existence, and to their history) and the fictional (a specific region of ideology which alludes to the discursive and recombines its elements by means of specific formal devices).[18]

By making a connection between literary practices and the discursive field in a given socio-cultural context, Bennett provides a framework for investigating the way the "articulation of the ideological elements in the text connects with those in the social formation at large".[19] This connection provides a more satisfactory approach to the study of fiction because it takes into account that literature is imbricated "with other regions of ideological struggle"[20] and therefore has an overdetermining effect on the social formation as part of that articulation—"the differing and specific ways in which [literary genres] recombine elements of the ideological by means of formal strategies peculiar to them"[21]—and the way texts may engage with particular discourses as a part of that process of recombination.

---

[17] Knight, *Form and Ideology in Crime Fiction*, 105.
[18] Bennett, "Marxism and Popular Fiction," 229.
[19] Bennett, "Marxism and Popular Fiction," 229.
[20] Bennett, "Marxism and Popular Fiction," 230
[21] Bennett, "Marxism and Popular Fiction," 229.

Upfield and the Detective Genre

As an author who invented a new detective hero by building upon generic conventions, Arthur Upfield's work provides an instance of adaptability to social change and context. Moreover, at a time when whites in the Australian space felt threatened by the increase in the Aboriginal population, it is remarkable that Upfield enjoyed a steady increase in the sales of his "Bony" books despite building the series around a halfcaste detective hero. The acceptance of such a character in Upfield's books problematises the critical understanding of the function of detective fiction in the construction of national identity outlined here. Moreover, it calls into question the notion of pleasure to be gained from a vicarious identification with the detective hero. If the increase in the Aboriginal population can be seen as a threat to the national identity at this time, how was it that the white people of the nation *accepted* and *enjoyed* reading about a university educated "halfcaste" successfully negotiating a position in white society? And how did Upfield represent the halfcaste in such a way that this threat was undermined and neutralised?

So far, criticism of Upfield's texts has failed to answer these questions satisfactorily. Upfield has been described as "One of the giants of Australian crime fiction",[22] and yet his Bony series has so far proven to be of more interest to American scholars than to those in Australia. In 1977 John Cawelti produced an article entitled "Murder in the Outback: Arthur W. Upfield", which was followed by an article by Ray Browne in 1986, entitled: "The Frontier Heroism of Arthur W. Upfield". Browne extended this interest to explore Upfield's work in the most significant monograph on the subject, *The Spirit of Australia: The Crime Fiction of Arthur W. Upfield* (1988). Yet Stephen Knight is right when he argues that Browne reads the Bony books "as an American".[23] Both Cawelti and Browne were no doubt attracted to the Bony series because of the adaptability of the books in terms of a tradition of American popular culture studies. As a "nomadic" detective who visits outback locations to investigate crimes, Bony functions in some ways like a Western hero, a character caught up in

a moment when the forces of civilization and wilderness life are in balance, the epic moment at which the old life and the new confront each other and individual actions may tip the balance one way or another, thus

---

[22] David Latta, ed., *Sand on the Gumshoe: A Century of Australian Crime Writing* (Hornsby, N.S.W.: Random House Australia, 1989), 166.
[23] Stephen Knight, *Continent of Mystery: A Thematic History of Australian Crime Fiction* (Carlton South, Victoria: Melbourne University Press, 1997), 122.

shaping the future history of the whole settlement.[24]

The critical interest in Upfield's work in America can also be seen as a reflection of the popular acceptance of his novels in that country. A 1989 article in a regional American newspaper identified this acceptance of Upfield's books, noting that for every 8,000 to 10,000 Bony books published in Australia, 300,000 were published in the U.S. The article focuses in particular on a local resident, Louise Mueller, who corresponded with Upfield for over thirty years, and on *The Bony Bulletin*, a newsletter for Upfield fans edited by Phillip Asdell.[25] That the Bony books played out U.S. anxieties concerning the Negro presence is revealed in correspondence between Upfield and an American Doctor, Robert Spicer. Apparently in response to a letter from Upfield complaining that his American publisher had rejected or wanted changes made to the manuscript of *Bony and the Black Virgin* (1959), Spicer outlined the problem of "the interbreeding of races" in America. For Spicer, Bony was "an idealized individual ... uniquely adjusted [and] incorporating the more admirable traits of both races", in contrast to the vicious compensation in other [halfcastes]". Because of a recent public uproar, Spicer wrote, Upfield's publisher would have been more than aware of America's "sensitized attitudes".[26]

Upfield's work has drawn less critical attention in Australia. In his brief survey of Australian crime fiction in "The Case of the Missing Genre: In Search of Australian Crime Fiction" (1988), Stephen Knight makes a connection between British and Australian crime fiction by suggesting that Conan Doyle's development of the Sherlock Holmes series may have been "provoked" by the success of Fergus W. Hume's *The Mystery of a Hansom Cab* (1886). In following this history, Knight writes that there "is more to crime fiction in Australia than Fergus Hume, Arthur Upfield and Peter Corris, those three ... who come to mind in this context."[27] As well as the location of stories by overseas writers in Australia, he finds other crime writing as the occasional production of more mainstream Australian authors such as Jessica Anderson, Judah Waten, Frank Hardy, and Miles Franklin. His work also uncovers the

---

[24] John Cawelti, *Adventure, Mystery, and Romance: Formula Stories as Art and Popular Culture* (Chicago: University of Chicago Press, 1976), 193.
[25] Terry Lorbiecki, "The Bony Bulletin: Shedding Light on Australian Mysteries," *Menomonee Falls News*, 19 January 1989, 1, 5. Asdell and Mueller were generous in providing information for this thesis.
[26] Robert Spicer, Letter to Arthur Upfield, 18 January 1960. Held in private collection.
[27] Stephen Knight, "The Case of the Missing Genre: In Search of Australian Crime Fiction," *Southerly* 48.3 (1988): 236.

production of Australian crime fiction as a series of sub-genres, revealing overall a rich field of the genre which, he writes, "may be a valuable prism through which to refract Australian culture for analysis".[28] The most comprehensive investigation into Upfield's work in Australia has been performed by Joe Kovess, whose research has resulted in a large private collection of material in preparation for a biography. Apart from the journalistic work of Pamela Ruskin and brief biographies and outlines of his work elsewhere, however, academic articles focussing specifically on Upfield are few. In 1974 Heather Paish wrote an article entitled "Bony and the Colour Question" in which she tracked the changes in Upfield's work over time to show how socio-historical context affected his portrayal of Aboriginal people. In 1980 Basil Sansom published an anthropological discussion of Upfield's work in *Anthropology News*. Sansom concluded, "For all the outback that Upfield taught me about ... I think he wrote very horrid immoral books."[29] In an article "Australian Tales of Mystery and Miscegenation" (1991), Tamsin Donaldson read Upfield's *The Barrakee Mystery* and Sally Morgan's *My Place* as an example of "sexual contact" histories to argue that *My Place* is the more authentic. In a more recent survey of the genre in, "The Vanishing Policeman: Patterns of Control in Australian Crime fiction", Stephen Knight is perhaps a little dismissive of Upfield's work, describing the character Bony as "deplorable" and the Bony books as "essentially plodding novels whose underlying meaning is the resolution not of random outback crimes but the concealment of the racial crimes involved in the founding of the new country".[30] The theme of genocide touched on by Knight was taken up with more enthusiasm by Kay Torney Souter in her articles "Babies in the Deathspace: Psychic Identity in Australian Fiction and Autobiography" (1996-7) and "Filling 'Terra Nullius': Bony in the Deathspace" (1995). In the second, Torney Souter suggests that Upfield's Bony series deals with the Australian interior as a "Deathspace", the unspoken/unwritten site of the partial genocide of the Aboriginal people, the theft of Aboriginal children, the rape of Aboriginal women, and the "concealed corpses of Australia". She concludes that, as a mixed-race detective, only Bony is able to decode the Deathspace,

---

[28] Knight, "The Case of the Missing Genre," 247.

[29] Basil Sansom, "Boney: A White Man's Half-Caste Hero," *Anthropology News* 17.7 (1980): 113.

[30] Stephen Knight, "The Vanishing Policeman: Patterns of Control in Australian Crime Fiction," in *Australian Popular Culture*, ed. Ian Craven (Cambridge: Cambridge University Press, 1994), 113.

like the patriarchal father of psychoanalysis [Bony] is both a symptom and a decoder of the illness he comes to read [and] help[s] to return the repressions of the Deathspace to the fullness of completed narrative.[31]

In his more recent *Continent of Mystery*, Knight distinguishes Upfield as the detective fiction writer who was most readily identified with crime writing in Australia.[32] He suggests that it was as a "trusty guide to the outback, not too foreign, but yet an authoritative interpreter of the non-European", that Bony "presented a fictional resolution to the uneasy presence of the Aboriginal in early stories".[33]

Detective Inspector Napoleon Bonaparte, C.I.B.

Upfield (1888-1964)[34] was born in Gosport, England, and by the time he was sixteen he had a "one-hundred-thousand-word novel locked in his desk [and] not one examination passed".[35] Apparently considered inappropriate as an heir to the family's drapery business, Upfield was sent by his father to Australia in "late 1910 or early 1911"[36] with the parting words: "You are going out to Australia to try farming. I have come to look

---

[31] Kay Torney, "Babies in the Deathspace: Psychic Identity in Australian Fiction and Autobiography," *Southerly* 56.4 (1996-97): 28-29. An anthropological precedence for this notion of the interior as the site of a disavowal of outback crimes against the Aboriginal people can be seen in W.E.H. Stanner's use of the term "forgetfulness". For a discussion of this, see Tom Griffiths, *Hunters and Collectors: An Antiquarian Imagination in Australia* (Cambridge: Cambridge University Press, 1996), 108-109.

[32] Knight, *Continent of Mystery*, 2.

[33] Knight, *Continent of Mystery*, 158. Gail Hermanis, a student at Adelaide University, has recently completed an honours thesis focusing on Upfield's use of Pidgin English. She intends to extend this into postgraduate research.

[34] Ed.: It had been generally accepted that Upfield was born on 1 September 1888. A check of the records in England made about 25 years after his death revealed he was born in 1890.

[35] Jessica Hawke, *Follow My Dust: A Biography of Arthur Upfield* (Melbourne: Heinemann, 1957), 31. Hawke was Arthur Upfield's second partner. Although *Follow My Dust* was published under her name, it was a reworked version of an unpublished autobiography given the provisional name "Tale of a Pommy". His correspondence reveals that Upfield wanted to write an autobiography, but did not want its narration to be in the first person. The "voice" in *Follow My Dust* is mainly Upfield's. Upfield discussed this in a letter to Charles Lemon, 2 May 1957, Battye Library (W.A.) Accession 2138A.

[36] Ray Browne, *The Spirit of Australia: The Crime Fiction of Arthur W. Upfield* (Bowling Green, OH: Bowling Green State University Popular Press, 1988), 4.

on Australia as the ideal country for you. It is so far away that you will never save enough money to return."[37] Ray Browne suggests that the attitude of Upfield's parents at this time "must have cut deeply into Arthur's personality and psyche and left permanent scars".[38] Arriving in Australia as a British immigrant while in his early twenties, Upfield travelled the interior before volunteering for military service during World War I and serving with the AIF at Gallipoli. Upon returning to Australia, he again roamed the countryside until, when he was 36, a friend encouraged him to reconsider novel writing.[39] In a letter to Miles Franklin, he wrote:

> I set out in the beginning to write mystery stories, because I like mystery stories, and to cram them with the Australian scene as I saw around [sic] the edge of the swag I happened to be carrying, or from the back of a stockman's horse I happened to be riding to earn a crust.[40]

Upfield initially had difficulty publishing his books in Australia, and in 1929 he turned to England for the publication of the first book featuring Bony.[41] In all, there were 14 Bony titles published either in Britain, the U.S. or Australia during the 1930s and 40s, and 15 published after 1950.[42] As early as 1937 Upfield was able to write to Charles Lemon that "Angus & Robertson ... want more of Bony and say they will make him a national figure". By 1957 he estimated that he had sold 1.8 million novels worldwide.[43]

In asserting his authority as an "outback expert", Upfield called into question Ion Idriess' knowledge of "Central Australia". In a letter to Charles Lemon he wrote that he had just met the travel writer, Robert Croll,[44] who had informed him that Idriess was regarded as "a tourist after

---

[37] Hawke, *Follow My Dust*, 39.

[38] Ray Browne, *The Spirit of Australia*, 5.

[39] Ray Browne, *The Spirit of Australia*, 5,152-153.

[40] Arthur Upfield, Letter to Miles Franklin, 1 February 1949, Mitchell Library, N.S.W., ML MSS 3659/1.

[41] Philip Asdell, *A Provisional Descriptive Bibliography of First Editions of the Works of Arthur W. Upfield: Australian, British, and U.S.* (Frederick, Maryland: P.T. Asdell, 1984), 2. He published *The House of Cain* in 1928, a book that did not include the character Bony.

[42] Asdell, *A Provisional Descriptive Bibliography*, 2-3.

[43] Arthur Upfield, Letter to Charles Lemon, 18 Jul. 1937; 2 May 1957, Battye Library, W.A., Accession 2138A.

[44] Who wrote *Along the Track* (1930), *Wide Horizons: Wanderings in Central Australia* (1937), and *I Recall: Collections and Recollections* (1939).

his Flynn of the Inland". Upfield told Lemon that Idriess' books lacked depth, and that he had noticed in Idriess' "biographical ... yarns [and] Walkabout articles ... that mental state of excitement associated with neurosis".[45] After leading a 1947 Walkabout-sponsored geographical expedition, Upfield later wrote to Walter Cousins of Angus & Robertson that he had to "counter a degree of hostility ... created by the misstatements, absurdities, and the retelling of silly gossips [sic] in the books of Ernestine Hill and Frank Clune".[46] At least a part of Upfield's animosity towards the travel writers, however, may have been caused by his own financial incapacity to explore Australia in search of material for publication. Earlier he had written to Lemon that he had run out of "good pictures" needed to accompany articles submitted to Walkabout, and he expressed disappointment that the Sydney Morning Herald had not taken up his offer to "send [him] touring through Central Australia with a good camera".[47]

Perhaps it was his inability to travel that forced Upfield to concentrate more on the writing of the detective fiction he had begun earlier. In 1938 he wrote to his publisher, Angus & Robertson, requesting Sir Baldwin Spencer's "two volumes on the Australian Aboriginal", which he felt were essential for research for his "next Bony yarns".[48] Angus & Robertson's representative, Walter Cousins, responded by saying that Wanderings in Wild Australia was out of print, and instead sent for Upfield's inspection Herbert Basedow's The Australian Aboriginal (1925) and the two volumes of Spencer's and Gillen's Across Australia (1912).[49] After his perusal of these texts, Upfield returned Basedow's book as "of secondary importance", and decided to "keep those by Spencer and Gillen".[50] In Forty-Two Faces, John Hetherington's description of Upfield's study revealed, among other books, Spencer and Gillen's Across Australia and the Bible.[51] Despite apparently gleaning much of his anthropological knowledge from Across Australia, Upfield was later extremely proud

---

[45] Arthur Upfield, Letter to Charles Lemon, 7 October 1935, Battye Library, W.A., Accession 2138A.

[46] Angus & Robertson Papers, Mitchell Library, N.S.W., ML MSS 3269/82.

[47] Arthur Upfield, Letter to Charles Lemon, 15 April 1935, Battye Library, W.A., Accession 2138A. Upfield was a regular contributor to Walkabout, and his article "Coming Down With Cattle: Droving in Australia," (Walkabout 1.1 (1934) 9-15) was the very first one published in that magazine.

[48] Angus & Robertson Papers, Mitchell Library, N.S.W., ML MSS 3269/82.

[49] Angus & Robertson Papers, Mitchell Library, N.S.W., ML MSS 3269/82.

[50] Angus & Robertson Papers, Mitchell Library, N.S.W., ML MSS 3269/82.

[51] John Hetherington, Forty-Two Faces: Profiles of Living Australian Writers (Melbourne: Cheshire, 1962), 23.

when Ernest Hooten, Professor of Anthropology at Harvard University, urged his class to study the depiction of Aborigines in the Bony series. He gained even more confidence in his authority on all things Aboriginal when Hooten provided words for reproduction on the back cover of many of his books:

> Mr Upfield is a shrewd anthropological observer as well as a skillful novelist. "Bony", his halfcaste aboriginal detective, is a unique figure in this class of literature.[52]

In 1946 Upfield wrote to Cousins:

> If you would have [Hooten's] opinion printed on the jacket and on a page of *Death of a Swagman* it would delight me and show that a man does not receive much reward in his own country.[53]

In his Bony books Upfield also reveals the influence of both the work of the Italian criminologist, Cesare Lombroso (1835-1909), and Freudian psychoanalysis. Lombroso believed that criminals were a physical type, and were therefore recognisable by physical characteristics such as the shape of the head, ideas clearly connected with phrenology.[54] Upfield's use of the psychoanalytic ideas of the time is manifest mainly in an interest in "abnormal psychology",[55] although an acceptance of the distinction between the conscious and the unconscious, the ego and the id, permeates his work.[56]

The three components essential for the development of the popular Bony series came together in the 1920s, when a "halfcaste", Leon Wood,[57] known as Tracker Leon, visited Upfield in the hut of which he was caretaker. Upfield had been working on the draft of a novel later to be published as *The Barrakee Mystery* (1929). Before Leon's arrival, the draft centred on the idea of a white detective who is "brought in to investigate

---

[52] Ernest Hooten, quoted in Hawke, *Follow My Dust*, 235.

[53] Angus & Robertson Papers, Mitchell Library, N.S.W., ML MSS 3269/82.

[54] His major work was *L'uomo delinquente* (1876). Upfield refers to Lombroso occasionally in the Bony books and on other occasions uses his work to have Bony point out such things as the remarkably high percentage of "killers having light blue eyes". See Arthur Upfield, *Death of a Swagman* (Sydney: Hinkler, 1994), 47.

[55] Ray Browne, *The Spirit of Australia*, 78.

[56] In Arthur Upfield, *Wings Above the Diamantina* (London: Pan Books, 1972), 132, Bony tells his "Watson", Sergeant Cox, that "Textbook knowledge of psychology is ever an asset".

[57] Pamel Ruskin, "Arthur Upfield: They Still Follow his Dust," *This Australia* 5.3 (1986): 55.

the death of an Aborigine", with a central motif of the story being the idea that "some halfcaste children are born white and change color years afterwards".[58] Suggesting an exchange of reading material, the autodidact Leon departed from Upfield's hut with issues of the *Wide World Magazine* and *The Times Literary Supplement*, and left Upfield with Bulwer Lytton's *The Last Days of Pompeii* and Abbot's *Life of Napoleon Bonaparte*. Watching him depart, Upfield turned to the inadequate draft of *Barrakee* and decided that he could improve it by remodelling its protagonist on the impressive Leon. Later catching sight of the titles of the books left by the visitor, Upfield melded the final component to invent: "Detective Inspector Napoleon Bonaparte", or "Bony".[59]

Despite moulding the protagonist of the series on an Aboriginal person, Upfield's Bony books approach the question of the indigenous people and the halfcaste problem with an ambivalence that is remarkable. As Knight observes, "Upfield's creation of a part-Aboriginal detective is at once respectful and contemptuous of Aboriginals."[60] There are passages in his books that reveal a relatively enlightened attitude towards Aboriginal people, and others—sometimes only pages away—that draw upon social-Darwinist ideas of their inferiority to represent them as low Others.

As was the case with the travel writers discussed in Chapter 2, religious and romantic notions of the "noble savage" were called upon by Upfield to represent Aborigines as peoples unspoiled and threatened by civilisation. For instance, in *Bushranger of the Skies* (1940) Upfield commingled the noble savage stereotype with American-Western style representations of Indians to ludicrously portray one Aboriginal character as "Chief Burning Water" of the "Wantella nation".[61] The dialogue used in the novel extends this connection further, with Aboriginal people conversing in a strange mixture of pidgin and the type of wooden "Indian talk" used in American "Westerns". For instance: "You are a stranger to the Land of Burning Water",[62] and "You givit that thing, eh?"[63] Sometimes the representations of the Aboriginal people can be more directly related to the sociohistorical context in which they were written. For instance, in the years leading up to World War II, Upfield expressed the concern in his

---

[58] Ray Browne, *The Spirit of Australia*, 155.
[59] Hawke, *Follow My Dust*, 169.
[60] Knight, *Continent of Mystery*, 122.
[61] Arthur Upfield, *Bushranger of the Skies* (Sydney: Pacific Books, 1965), 6.
[62] Upfield, *Bushranger of the Skies*, 8.
[63] Upfield, *Bushranger of the Skies*, 10.

private letters that Hitler was about to initiate another war.[64] This anxiety was manifest as a critique of Western civilisation through a revisiting of the noble savage stereotype. In *The Bone Is Pointed* (1938), a character named John Gordon expresses despair at the decline of an Aboriginal tribe in the area, and tells Bony that the Aboriginal people had "never had the curse of Adam laid on them".[65] Before this, Bony declared pride in

> "... being the son of an aboriginal woman, because in many things it is the aboriginal who is the highly developed civilized being and the white man who is the savage."[66]

In a later discussion with another character, "Old Lacy", Bony continues:

> "That I stand midway between the black man, who makes fire with a stick, and the white man, who kills women and babes with bombs and machine guns, should not be accounted against me."[67]

Naming as the threat to the Aboriginal people "The Shadow of Civilisation",[68] Bony later muses: "It was full time that the Creator of man wiped out altogether this monster called civilisation and began again with the aborigines as a nucleus."[69] In *Murder Must Wait* (1951), this recourse to religious ideologies to locate the Aboriginal people in Pre-Adamic time continues:

> The first white man to set foot in Australia brought with him the Serpent from the Garden of Eden ... [and the ensuing] segregation of [Aboriginal people] into compounds and settlements of an ever dwindling remnants of a race.[70]

Again like many of the travel writers, criticism of the Aborigines was facilitated by recourse to social Darwinist ideas which located the Aboriginal people in a distant past as the remnants of a race about to be

---

[64] Arthur Upfield, Letter to Walter Cousins, Angus & Robertson Paper, Mitchell Library, N.S.W., ML MSS 3269/82.
[65] Arthur Upfield, *The Bone Is Pointed* (Sydney: Hinkler, 1994), 119.
[66] Upfield, *The Bone Is Pointed*, 43.
[67] Upfield, *The Bone Is Pointed*, 52.
[68] The chapter title.
[69] Upfield, *The Bone Is Pointed*, 121.
[70] Arthur Upfield, *Murder Must Wait* (London: Heinemann, 1958), 125. Compare Arthur Upfield, *Death of a Swagman* (Sydney: Hinkler, 1994),18, and a remarkable passage in Upfield, *Bushrangers of the Skies*, 69-70, in which the narrator lambastes white Australia for the genocide of Aboriginal people.

naturally extinguished by the whites. Perhaps the clearest example of this in the series is to be found in *Bushranger of the Skies*, when a halfcaste character seeks to exact revenge for the dispersion of the Aboriginal people. In pointing out the uselessness of his actions, Bony says:

> Where you have failed ... is by not recognizing forces which neither you nor I, nor a million like us, can withstand. I refer to the forces of human evolution ... Why have the Australian blacks become submerged? Why have the Abyssinians been conquered? Because humanity is no different from the animals and the insects in the jungles. There the strong devour the weak. It is the same in the animal world. The weak go to the wall. Those who will not struggle to survive, will not compete with the competitors, must go under. [71]

The acceptance of the Aborigines as inferior to the whites permeates Upfield's work, but it is often ignored by critics in favour of the passages that reveal a more enlightened attitude. In *The Spirit of Australia*, Browne concludes that Upfield's approach toward the Aboriginal people, "with the possible exception of a few stereotypic statements scattered throughout the books, was generally praise and approval".[72] Where Upfield was most revealing, however, was in his portrayal of Bony himself. Without doubt, the values to which Bony ultimately subscribes are almost entirely those of the white culture, and his career as a detective is built upon the idea that only through ambition and success can he outpace his Aboriginal origins. In Browne's words: "Upfield always discussed the Australian situation in terms of the broader concept of primitivism vs. civilisation."[73]

In the end, however, Bony was simply a textual device used to help sell books, and Upfield's correspondence reveals a readiness to transform the character into whatever the reading public might desire. Even Browne notes with surprise and without explanation that "Bony grow[s] lighter in color through the books".[74] Pressure from Upfield's American publisher to tone down Bony's colour was apparent in correspondence to Charles Lemon. In discussing editorial changes to *An Author Bites the Dust* (1948) recommended by a representative of Angus & Robertson, Upfield reveals the whitening of Bony:

---

[71] Upfield, *Bushranger of the Skies*, 164. In an unabridged version of the novel—Large Print Series (Anstey, Leicestershire: FA Thorpe Ltd., 1978)—a final sentence to this passage reads: "If the British hadn't come to Australia another nation would have arrived in due time."
[72] Browne, *The Spirit of Australia*, 25.
[73] Browne, *The Spirit of Australia*, 12.
[74] Browne, *The Spirit of Australia*, 23.

I wrote back pointing out that America has been harping at me to evade as much as possible Bony's mixed race, and that I have done so rigidly with this book because Bony mixed with literary snobs and suchlike who would not accept him too freely.[75]

In 1937 he wrote to Angus & Robertson that he was concerned that the way Bony might be portrayed on the "air and screen" might, through "distortion", ruin the character "in the minds of the book readers". Upfield pointed out that he had "gone to great pains to present him to readers as a cultured, softly spoken man" and that to "present him on the air or on the screen as a half-wit or a guttural speaking nigger would do us a great deal of harm". His suggestion, then, was that a clause be included in any contracts allowing the portrayal of Bony on air stipulating that he be portrayed as

> a cultured man who speaks with reasonable grammar and yet not pedantic, and with a soft and pleasing accent [and not] ... as a character in Dad on our Selection, as a half-wit, or as an Australian aborigine.[76]

On another occasion, however, it suited Upfield to turn to Bony's aboriginal "side" to portray him as the victim of a "boning". When he was writing *The Bone Is Pointed* he sought advice from Baldwin Spencer "for the real method of boning—that is will power"[77] and from "the [aboriginal] Christian parson who stated that the boning was accomplished by willing to death. I refer to David Unaipon".[78] Upfield's reliance on such "authorities" for this portrayal of a white notion of boning was later a part of a defence of criticism by John K. Ewers that it may have been "stretching the long bow to ask the reader to believe that Bony, civilized as

---

[75] Arthur Upfield, Letter to Charles Lemon, 2 January 1948, Battye Library, W.A., Accession 2138A. For a discussion of the portrayal of "Boney" by white actors, compare John Newfong, "'Boney'—a television series based on Arthur Upfield's novel, Fauna Productions, Sydney," *Identity* 1.7 (1973): 39-40.

[76] Arthur Upfield, Letter to Angus & Robertson, 26 April 1937, Angus & Robertson Papers, Mitchell Library, N.S.W., ML MSS 3269/82.

[77] By will power Upfield refers to the power of individual Aboriginal people to "will" someone to death from a distance. In Upfield, *The Bone Is Pointed*, 137, he differentiated between the psychological aspect of boning and "mental willing".

[78] Arthur Upfield, Reply (n.d.) to John Ewers's letter of 18 July 1938, Angus & Robertson Papers, Mitchell Library, Sydney, ML MSS 3269/82. Upfield later wrote to Cousins: "My authority is David Unaipon, the aboriginal parson, writer and poet, and inventor." Compare Adam Shoemaker, *Black Words, White Page: Aboriginal Literature 1928-1988* (St. Lucia: University of Queensland Press, 1988), 42-50.

he was, would be susceptible to black magic". "You may find", Upfield replied to Ewers, "that I have stressed Bony's racial alliance with the aborigines the more easily to convince the reader that he could be a victim".[79]

Bony as Grotesque

The typical formal structure of the Bony series can be seen in *Winds of Evil* (1937). In this book, the outback town of Carie has been plunged into social disorder by the threat posed by two murders and the inability of the "city" police to solve the problem. Bony is represented as a "sort of bush Sherlock Holmes"[80] working under the pseudonym "Joe Fisher", who arrives at the bequest of a local grazier who has a personal connection with the police chief, Colonel Spender. Bony immediately adopts the plodding local constable as his "Watson", confiding in him his outstanding methods and successfully impressing upon the constable his remarkable ability to make progress where the city police have failed. "Remember, Lee," he tells the policeman, "that although some people sneer at me on account of my mid-race, I am superior to the blacks because I can reason, and superior to many white people because I can both reason well and see better than they."[81] For the reader, Bony's presence in Carie's disrupted social space offers an immediate sense of the beginnings of the re-ordering of events. His drawing together of information as part of the investigation into the murders works to unify disparate knowledges from a central position in a way that parallels the ideological unification of the nation. This homogenising of knowledges allows him to identify the murderer—who happens to be the grazier who called upon Bony to solve the crime—and the restoration of order to Carie, closing off and concealing the crime within the book, allowing Bony to move to another site of social disruption in a perpetual and repetitious solving of the nation's crimes.

Nevertheless, the formal structure of Upfield's Bony books fails to close off completely the social disruption epitomised so clearly in the characterisation of Bony as a "halfcaste". The progeny of a black mother and a white father, and found in the shade of a sandalwood tree in Far North Queensland, Bony's name was derived from the fact that he was "eating the pages of Abbott's *Life of Napoleon Bonaparte*".[82] Described as

---

[79] John Ewers, Letter to Arthur Upfield, 18 July 1938; Upfield's reply (n.d.), Angus & Robertson Papers, Mitchell Library, N.S.W., ML MSS 3269/82.
[80] Arthur Upfield, *Winds of Evil* (Sydney: Hinkler, 1994), 49.
[81] Upfield, *Winds of Evil*, 65.
[82] Arthur Upfield, *The Battling Prophet* (Sydney: Hinkler, 1994), 99.

"Of average height and build, [and] ... remarkable for the dark colouring of his skin, which emphasized his blue eyes and white teeth",[83] as a youth Bony was offered the choice "to be an aboriginal or a white man". Choosing to become white, he did so "with distinction in all but blood".[84] His incorporation into white society was effected by his early mission education and the subsequent taking of an M.A. from Brisbane University [sic].[85] With this educational background, Bony returned to the bush to be initiated into an Aboriginal tribe and to learn the culture of his mother's people. After joining the Queensland Police Force as a tracker, he was able, with the combination of his Aboriginal and European knowledges, to rise quickly through the ranks to the position of Detective Inspector.[86]

Bony's incorporation into the teleological time of white society is therefore never complete, since he remains white in "all but blood". The Aboriginal "side" of Bony relegates him to at least a partial identification with the type of "primitive" Others constructed in anthropological discourses. These opposing "sides" are imbricated in Western notions of time, allowing the university educated Bony to apply the historical/scientific knowledge of the Eurocentric culture in the timeless void of the disappearing Aboriginal culture. Throughout the series Bony cites as his "greatest asset" an "unconsciousness of the value of time".[87] "This world of the bush is my background, my natural element." It is:

> like a giant book offering to me plain print and the language I understand. The book is so big, however, that I require sometimes a great deal of time to find in it the passages interesting me at the moment. And finally, as I think I have told you, time is my greatest asset; without it I am as ordinary men.[88]

As a member of the Queensland Police Force, Bony is expected to complete one case then efficiently *progress* to the next. Quite often throughout the series he is threatened with "the sack" for ignoring Colonel Spender's orders to drop a case and attend to another. "Patience", Bony

---

[83] Upfield, *The Bone Is Pointed*, 29.

[84] Upfield, *The Bone Is Pointed*, 164.

[85] Upfield, *Death of a Swagman*, 18. His academic qualifications vary a little, although the differences may have had more to do with country of publication than inconsistency on the part of Upfield. In *The Battling Prophet* (1956) Bony announced that he had received a Master of Science degree from Brisbane University (quoted in *The Spirit of Australia*, 33.)

[86] Browne, *The Spirit of Australia*, 33-34.

[87] Upfield, *The Bone Is Pointed*, 161.

[88] Upfield, *The Bone Is Pointed*, 160.

says in *The Bone Is Pointed,*

> "is a great gift ... Unfortunately neither Colonel Spender nor my immediate
> chief, Superintendent Brown, has that gift. The Colonel ... constantly yells
> for results. I give results, but in my own way and in my own time".[89]

Like Sherlock Holmes, Bony works in conjunction with the police and
yet is disparaging towards them. He is employed by the Queensland Police
Force and yet he feels free to choose the cases that interest him and to
ignore white time to spend many months—"six months" if necessary[90]—
completing them. "Actually, of course," he tells Old Lacy in *The Bone Is
Pointed,* "I am not a real policeman, but ... have no hesitation in accepting
the salary."[91] This distance allows him to criticise city detectives who have
been sent into the outback to solve its crimes. While the local policemen
were acceptable as people who had some knowledge of the interior, city
detectives were more used to "bullying loose women and thieves for
information". In the bush they were unable to obtain information from
"such things as sand and birds and tracks" because they had not Bony's
ability to ignore time and read the bush.[92]

Bony's capacity to vacillate between the primitive and the civilised can
be read through the "oceanic" ideas discussed by Freud in *Civilisation and
Its Discontents.*[93] Journeys into timelessness are also explorations of the
primitive unconscious, where, at least momentarily, the ego accesses the
secrets of its own past, taps into the wealth of undeveloped potential and
brings to the surface the treasures it needs to solve crimes. As Bony says,

> added to my inherited maternal gifts are those inherited from my white
> father. I see with the eyes of a black man and reason with the mind of a
> white man, and in the bush I am supreme.[94]

As Browne points out, Upfield depicted the tracking skills of the Aborigines
as "natural" rather than cultural,[95] and like the travel writers, and especially
Frank Clune, there is a sense in the Bony books of an inextricable

---

[89] Upfield, *The Bone Is Pointed,* 161.
[90] Upfield, *The Bone Is Pointed,* 87.
[91] Upfield, *The Bone Is Pointed,* 45.
[92] Upfield, *Death of a Swagman,* 14.
[93] Sigmund Freud, "Civilization and Its Discontent, 1933," in *The Standard Edition of the Complete Psychological Works of Sigmund Freud: Volume XXII,* trans. and ed. James Strachey (Harmondsworth: Penguin, 1973), 7-158. Compare 64-67.
[94] Upfield, *Winds of Evil,* 65.
[95] Browne, *The Spirit of Australia,* 50.

connection between the primitive landscape and its indigenous inhabitants. This is manifest in the Bony series as a "Spirit of the Land"[96] felt acutely by Aborigines and much less so by whites.[97] Although it permeates the series, this notion of a "Spirit" is perhaps best expressed in a book published outside the time-frame under investigation in this chapter. In *Bony and the Black Virgin* (1959), Bony explains to a white man that all that is needed before the clues to the murder are discovered, is time:

> "Call me a primitive, and I shall not mind. I believe in the Being which rules this Land, who watches from behind every tree and every sandhill ... This Spirit of the Land is subject to many moods. It can be benign, jealous, vengeful, and it has a sense of humour ... Doubtless it has been sniggering at the efforts of every hurrying policeman, and of every white man who is alien to itself, although familiar with the physical contours of the land it rules. It will not snigger at me, but it will try my patience, my human patience, *because I am with it and of it through my maternal forebears.*"[98]

What this passage reveals is that the inability of civilised whites to tune in to this Spirit prevents them from solving outback crimes. In practical terms, this is manifest throughout the books in portrayals of Bony's remarkable ability to transcend the constraints of the ego by slipping into the "unconsciousness of the value of time" discussed above. Only Bony can tap into "secrets many ... in the scientific world would refuse to credit because they have been unable to get under the skin of the Australian Aborigine".[99]

This ability to read the "book of the bush" outside white time is re-enforced in the Bony series by the Western constructions of Aboriginal time as a natural cycle within the static time-frame of a dying people. According to this view, time for the Aborigines is not a linear progress

---

[96] Called the "bunyip" in Upfield, *Winds of Evil*, 142, and the "banshee" in Upfield, *Death of a Swagman*, 18.

[97] It may be useful to recall that in Chapter 3 Upfield was identified as a contributor to *Walkabout* who wrote of the influence of the bush on whites: "It is not strange that many white men who have lived close to the beating heart of Australia also have felt the pressure of a watchful spirit, for they have been exposed to the same conditions as were the aborigines:" See Arthur Upfield, "This Jealous Land," *Walkabout* 14.6 (1 April 1948): 38.

[98] Arthur Upfield, *Bony and the Black Virgin* (Sydney: Hinkler, 1994), 61. Emphasis added. In Upfield, *The Bone Is Pointed*, 42, Bony says: "in bush townships I am a grown man. Out there in the bush I am an emperor. The bush is me: I am the bush: we are one."

[99] Upfield, *Bushranger of the Skies*, 126.

away from the past and towards the future, but a closed circuit of regeneration/degeneration tethered to a timeless present. As Johannes Fabian points out, this differentiation between "Western Linear Time and primitive Cyclical Time" was another distancing device used by anthropologists to "establish 'contrast'" between the time of West and its Others.[100] In his texts, Upfield conflates the "timelessness" of the Aborigines with constructions of their time as cyclical, and opposes this temporality to the progressive time of the whites. From his base within the teleological time of civilisation, then, Bony slips into an unconsciousness of the value of Western time to await the revelation of clues to crimes through their exposure by the "natural" world, to simultaneously read the landscape as both an Aboriginal and a European.[101] He uses his white education to analyse the context of the crime, and is "able when in his beloved bush to tense his senses to the acuteness of the aborigines".[102]

Bony's ability to oscillate between these two positions in the reading of the national space undermines the attempted temporal distinction between the white people and the Aborigines. The difficulty presented by a character such as Bony is that he cannot be excluded fully from the temporal frame of the people of the nation because he is white in "all but blood". As a "bridge spanning the gulf between" the white world and the world of the indigenous peoples,[103] Bony is a symbolic amalgamation of both the people of the nation and the "Low Others" through whom their identity is partially differentiated.

Situated between the present and the past, life and death, the civilised and the primitive, the people and their "Low Others", Bony functions as a simultaneous presence/absence that takes on a character of its own. As he says, "in me, you see neither black nor white, you see a hybrid".[104]

---

[100] Johannes Fabian, *Time and the Other: How Anthropology Makes Its Object* (New York: Columbia University Press, 1983), 41.

[101] Drawing upon the work of Conan Doyle, Basil Sansom distinguishes two traditional methods for the detection of criminals: "synthetic" ("when you put things together and work forwards towards a result"); and "analytical" ("you have a result, and you have to work backward to find out how it happened"). Identifying Holmes' methodology as "analytical", he argues that in his portrayal of "Boney" [sic], Upfield portrayed a detective who used neither method, one who "goes into a community and waits for the murderer to do something foolish." Sansom then bristles with indignation that, in doing so, Bony allowed "a parade of deaths" until the murderer was revealed, and was thereby a "terribly expensive detective." (Sansom, *Boney*, 112-3.)

[102] Upfield, *Bushranger of the Skies*, 138.

[103] Arthur Upfield, *The Widows of Broome* (Sydney: Hinkler, 1994), 17.

[104] Arthur Upfield, *The Barrakee Mystery* (London: Pan Books, 1969), 83.

In his work on popular fiction and national identity, James Donald uses the term "grotesque" to describe "Dr Jekyll and Mr Hyde" characters such as Bony who oscillate between identifications with an idealised national type and their degenerate low Others.[105] Drawing upon the work of Peter Stallybrass and Allon White, he argues that

> cultural "low Others" ... become an eroticized constituent of fantasy life. In the "inner dynamic of the boundary constructions necessary to collective identity" ... the[y] cannot simply be excluded. They remain a troublesome presence for an official culture, returning in the form of the *grotesque*—or rather in its two forms. The first is "the grotesque as the 'other' of the defining group or self". Distinct from this is "the grotesque as a boundary phenomenon of hybridization or inmixing, in which self and other become enmeshed in an inclusive, heterogeneous, dangerously unstable zone ... The point is that the *exclusion* necessary to the formation of social identity at [one] level is simultaneously a *production* at the level of the Imaginary, and a production, what is more, of a complex hybrid fantasy emerging out of the very attempt to demarcate boundaries, to unite and purify the social collectivity."[106]

The social function of these fantasies, Donald argues, is "aggressively centripetal".

> Conjuring up chaos, they drive towards unity, order and wholeness. The textual rendering and widespread circulation of such fantasies ... gives at least some stability to the restlessness of desire, demarcating its familiar boundaries.[107]

One method used by Upfield to re-establish the boundaries between the white people and their "low Others" was to portray Bony as a character internally divided between the pull of the bush and its decivilising influence, and the power of knowledge used to combat it. Although Bony has superior access to the mysterious unconscious world, its power still threatens him, and he is involved in a type of *self-surveillance* against the fear of a

---

[105] It is interesting to note that Upfield made the connection between his work and that of Stevenson: Bony was torn between the influences of his Aboriginal and white ancestry, "influences that had well nigh assumed personalities like those of Dr Jekyll and Mr Hyde" (Arthur Upfield, *The Barrakee Mystery*, 153). In Upfield, "This Jealous Land," 38, this extended to a description of the interior as "not unlike a Jekyll-Hyde combination".

[106] James Donald, "How English is it? Popular Literature and National Culture," *New Formations* 6 (1988): 36-37.

[107] Donald, "How English is it?" 40.

reversion to primitiveness.[108] As the narrator says in *The Bone Is Pointed*:

> Almost all his life this man of two races had sailed a sea over which he had been blown by the wind of ambition towards the Land of Great Achievement. But below the surface of the sea lurked monstrous things, shadowy things that waited, waited always to drag him under and down to a worse existence than that known by his maternal ancestors.[109]

This notion of the potential to revert to primitiveness can be seen in the 1947 writings of Walter Murdoch, who argued that it was

> the survival, in civilized times, of impulses which were useful and indeed indispensable to savage man but which are not compatible with civilization, that causes the trouble in the world today.

Like Donald, Murdoch used Dr Jekyll and Mr Hyde as a fictitious example of the ego and the id, noting especially Stevenson's depiction of the precariousness of the "crust of civilization that keeps our sudden impulses hidden".[110]

While in Stevenson's writing, Dr Jekyll's primitive Other was able to emerge through the temporary annulment of the ego by a "powder", Bony is perpetually threatened because of the precariousness of his position as a halfcaste. In many revealing passages throughout the series, he expresses this fear of "degeneration" to the position of an inferior Other. "You cannot know", he tells Sergeant Blake in *The Bone is Pointed*, "of the eternal battle I fight, to lose which means for me and mine ... degradation."[111] In *The Mystery of Swordfish Reef* Bony's momentary reversion to his Aboriginal "side" is accompanied by a darkening of his skin colour. Driven to attack after being called a "nigger boy",

> Bony actually screamed when he leaped at Malone ... [His] transformed face astonished the Bluenose to the extent of delaying his defensive action for a split second, for Bony's face had become jet-black in colour, his eyes glaring blue orbs set in seas of white, while his teeth reflected the light like the fangs of a young dog ... Never before in his life had his aboriginal instincts so controlled Napoleon Bonaparte to the exclusion of that other

---

[108] I am grateful to Ron Blaber for suggesting the idea of Bony performing a type of "self-surveillance" during discussions after the presentation of an earlier version of this chapter at the 1996 ASAL conference in Brisbane.

[109] Upfield, *The Bone Is Pointed*, 173.

[110] Walter Murdoch, *Walter Murdoch: 72 Essays* (Sydney and London: Angus & Robertson, 1947), 324-325.

[111] Upfield, *The Bone Is Pointed*, 164.

complex part of him inherited from his father and on which was based so magnificent a pride. Reason had fled before the primitive lust to destroy.[112]

As Browne wrote in response to this passage, "It is as if Upfield has been saying all along: the Aboriginal is never far from and is ultimately inseparable from his original state".[113] In effect, Bony is caught perilously between the civilised ego and the primitive id. His years of education and training in the white world have developed his ego, but the influence of his Aboriginal side threatens constantly to overtake it. This idea of Bony's "primitive lust to destroy" resonates strongly with the fear expressed by Baldwin Spencer that it is "risky" to walk in front of Aborigines because "a savage is sometimes seized with an uncontrollable impulse to spear or club a stranger—white or black—walking close in front of him".[114]

Bony's ability to resist the influence of his maternal ancestors depends upon his position in either the bush or civilisation. As the narrator says in *The Bone Is Pointed*:

> Within Bony's soul constantly warred the opposing influences planted therein by his white father and his black mother, and according to external influences of the moment, so did the battle favour one side or the other.[115]

Perhaps the best illustration of this appears in an episode in this same book portraying the "boning" of Bony. In an indication of an acceptance of the type of "psychic powers" of the Aboriginal people spoken of by Elkin in *Aboriginal Men of High Degree*, Upfield depicts Bony as the victim of a "willing to death" by two aboriginal men, Nero and Wandin.[116] In keeping with Elkin's ideas of the "quietness and silence of so much of their life, the absence of rush and of urgent appointments" being conducive to the Aboriginal people's receptivity to psychic powers, Bony is aware that all he need do to "defy the magic" is escape the bush.[117] Deciding to stay, his susceptibility to the powers of the Aborigines is increased, and their boning threatens to succeed. Through his ability to read his own unconscious, however, Bony is able to recognise the signals transmitted

---

[112] Arthur Upfield, *The Mystery of Swordfish Reef* (Sydney: Hinkler, 1994), 204-205.
[113] Browne, *The Spirit of Australia*, 38.
[114] Baldwin Spencer, *Wanderings in Wild Australia* (London: Macmillan, 1928), 168.
[115] Upfield, *The Bone Is Pointed*, 136.
[116] Upfield, *The Bone Is Pointed*, 145-147. Upfield's use of the name "Nero" is interesting, as it transfigures the "contest" between Bony and the Aboriginal "magic man" into a battle between a French and Roman Emperor.
[117] Upfield, *The Bone Is Pointed*, 163.

from the Aboriginals performing the boning. As throughout the rest of the series, Bony's battle to resist the powers of the nearby Aboriginals becomes one of the modern versus the primitive, the ego versus the id, and knowledge versus instinct. This time, "deprived [by the boning] of [his] greatest asset, the unconsciousness of the value of time",[118] Bony turns instead to his "developed ego" for assistance. "Was he a savage?" he asked himself, "an ignorant nomad of the bush ... to be frightened away from this absorbing investigation by the mental power of a people free from the curse laid upon Adam?"[119] He decided that he was not, and sought to regain control over his unconscious by remembering his position in the white world: "We've got to think not of ourselves", he tells the dogs accompanying him, "but of the investigation, of Marie, of the boys, of old Colonel Spender ... who has helped me to become what I am".[120]

It is Bony's exceptional ambition as a detective, then, that prevents him succumbing to what Robert Young calls, the "allegedly decivilizing activity of miscegenation",[121] by tentatively elevating him to the position of a member of white society. "I will not consent to investigate cheap and tawdry crimes of violence, or lesser crimes", Bony says,

> "because my pride would be shamed, and also I have to avoid the fear of failure which might grow in me did I accept any and every assignment given to me by my department. Once I forget that I am a police inspector and a Master of Arts, I become Bony the halfcaste, and the banshee of the bush would lure me back and down into its secret cave, to stand naked before it and to recognize it as my lord and master."[122]

Paradoxically then, at least a part of the fear of the nation symbolised by Bony's hybrid identity is neutralised in Upfield's texts through its displacement as *Bony's* internal dilemma. Like the people of the nation, Bony wishes to be white, to repress the threat to purity posed by his ancestry.

Another method of negating the threat of Bony's hybrid presence is in the traditional function of the detective hero as a type of superhuman character.[123] Bony may be internally divided between the people and their Others, but it is this very combination that provides him with extraordinary

---

[118] Upfield, *The Bone Is Pointed*, 161.
[119] Upfield, *The Bone Is Pointed*, 140.
[120] Upfield, *The Bone Is Pointed*, 175.
[121] Robert Young, *Colonial Desire* (London: Routledge, 1995), 175.
[122] Upfield, Death of a Swagman, 18.
[123] Compare Julian Symons, *The Detective Story in Britain* (Essex: Longmans, Green & Co., 1962), 16-17.

powers as a detective. It is Bony's exceptional ability to make a difference in a society continually threatened with disorder that provides the reader with the vicarious pleasure of the power to effect change. Not only does Bony have at hand the same kind of reasoning power and scientific knowledge that enabled Sherlock Holmes to contest the criminal threat to British society; he also has the ability to slip into timelessness. From within a timeless void he can apply to each crime the knowledge of the modern West, the cultural knowledge of the Australian space provided by the Aboriginal people, and "sharply honed" animal instincts. In this way, Bony is an amalgam of the modern and the primitive.

At least a part of the appeal of Bony as a character, then, can be related to what Donald calls "the ambivalent 'repugnance and fascination' evident in representations of the low-Other".[124] It is this ambivalence of identity that allows readers to accept Bony's prowess as a "halfcaste" detective and yet disavow his black presence. Bony, it seems, is to be accepted into white society, but only on the condition that he does not see himself as white, and that his black ancestry is slowly displaced from the Australian space through assimilation. No better example of this expected displacement can be seen than in the portrayal of Bony's eldest son, Charles. Already "whitened" to an extent through Bony's marriage to another "halfcaste",[125] Charles is following his parent's absorption into the teleological time of the nation by studying at the university Bony himself attended,[126] to "be a medical missionary to his grandmother's people".[127] In this respect, Bony was a halfcaste suspended between those who were to slip back into the past and those who were to be accepted grudgingly into the future, and it was Upfield's ability fictitiously to enact the dilemma of a character caught perilously between these two positions that allowed Bony to be accepted by the white population. Split between "the mind of the white man and the mind of the Australian black man", and yet "a bridge spanning the gulf between them",[128] Bony functions simultaneously as a neutralised hybrid character through his inability to take on a stable identity, and as a symbol of an extraordinary Australian type of the future.

---

[124] Donald, "How English is it?" 37.
[125] Upfield, *Bushranger of the Skies*, 53.
[126] Upfield, *The Bone Is Pointed*, 31.
[127] Upfield, *Death of a Swagman*, 27.
[128] Upfield, *The Widows of Broome*, 17.

Responses

The white response to Bony's presence was often fictitiously enacted in the series in the form of his meetings with white women. Almost invariably, white women were simultaneously captivated and repulsed by the presence of the halfcaste detective. Elizabeth Nettlefold in *Wings Above the Diamantina* "was puzzled by [Bony's] address, and hostile yet to the fact of his admittance to her home as an equal". Her confusion was caused mainly by his appearance when the "light shone directly on his face". Then, she was "held by his blue eyes, by the force of intelligence gazing from them". Noting "the delicate mould of his features, pure Nordic and with no trace of his aboriginal ancestry", she was, however, disturbed by "the colour of his skin".[129] In *Winds of Evil*, Stella "received a queer little shock" when for the first time she gazed into Bony's eyes:

> Not till long afterwards did she recognize just what she was now seeing in the depths of his blue eyes. In that first moment of meeting Napoleon Bonaparte, she recognized a mind superior to that of any halfcaste she had ever met.[130]

In *The Widows of Broome* Mrs. Sayers caught Bony's gaze above a match held to her cigarette, and immediately "felt the impact of his personality". Unlike Stella, she was able instantly to acknowledge the "mental power which subjugated in everyone the consciousness of his mid-race".[131] Nevertheless, Bony's status always remains one of suspension between the people and their others. Recognising by Elizabeth Nettlefold's expression that he faced "the same battle he had during his career so often ... won", he quickly assures her that he has "been married twenty years".[132]

Almost invariably, the critical reception of Upfield's texts in the 1930s and 40s highlighted the fact that Napoleon Bonaparte was a Detective Inspector with exceptional powers derived from his "mixed blood".[133] Bony is "a synthetic figure", a critic wrote in the *Bulletin's* Red Page, "the usual efficient sleuth with endearing habits who baffles his orthodox colleagues."[134] The "unique feature" of Upfield's *The Warrakee* [sic] *Mystery*, wrote a critic in the *Adelaide Observer*, "is an invention: the

---

[129] Upfield, *Wings Above the Diamantina*, 61-62.

[130] Upfield, *Winds of Evil*, 77.

[131] Upfield, *The Widows of Broome*, 164.

[132] Upfield, *Wings Above the Diamantina*, 62.

[133] Many of the reviews used here were taken from Upfield's own collection, and were generously provided by Joe Kovess.

[134] Unsigned review of *An Author Bites the Dust*, *Bulletin*, 26 May 1948, 2.

detective is a brilliant halfcaste ... having all the skilled arts of Sherlock Holmes added to the natural gifts of a black tracker".[135] Other reviews praised Upfield for his portrayal of the Aborigines. A reviewer in the Adelaide *Advertiser* wrote that "Mr Upfield conveys with a sure hand the atmosphere of the burning heart of Australia, and writes some really clever sketches of the aborigines and their customs".[136] Another in the Newcastle *Sun* felt that "Upfield has studied the habits of the blacks and has an affection for and understanding of them that is rare".[137] At the same time, some of the reviews indicate uneasiness with this black intrusion into a White Australia. A reviewer in Melbourne's *The Australasian* argued that

> Mr Upfield evidently wishes to suggest that, in spite of civilisation and education, the Australian black will always at one time or another revert to the life and condition of his forebears,[138]

and one Brisbane reviewer described Bony as "almost too good to be true".[139]

In addition to solving the problem of Bony's mixed race, this criticism of Bony allowed the books to be dismissed as something less than "Literature". A review of *The Widows of Broome* pointed out that

> As a story of the life of Broome and as a detective adventure of Bony, the book has about equal value. Add these two together and you get its true worth—good reading for the ordinary Australian.[140]

Another wrote that *The Barrakee Mystery* was "not an attempt at literature, but it is one of the most exciting, well constructed, and well written tales we have read for a long time".[141] A review in the Hobart *Mercury* suggested that

> Upfield has endeavoured to produce Edgar Wallace-fiction on an Australian background, and why he is not successful is rather hard to say ... undoubtedly [he] knows Australia; undoubtedly he knows the men and women in it.[142]

---

[135] Unsigned review of *The Barrakee Mystery*, *Adelaide Observer*, 29 June 1929.

[136] Unsigned review of *Bushranger of the Skies*, *Advertiser* (Adelaide), 21 September 1940, 10.

[137] *Sun*, Newcastle, 16 August 1940.

[138] *The Australasian*, 29 June 1929.

[139] *Producer's Review*, 15 August 1940.

[140] Unsigned review of *The Widows of Broome*, *Austrovert* 4 (1951): 4.

[141] Unsigned review of *The Barrakee Mystery*, *Herald* (Melbourne), 10 July 1929.

[142] Unsigned review of *The Barrakee Mystery* and *The House of Cain*, *Mercury*

Conclusion

Upfield's work provides an example of the adaptation of the conventions established by earlier crime writers and the invention of a new detective in the form of Bony. The popularity of the Bony series despite its depiction of a halfcaste character was enabled by ideas surrounding the emerging policies of assimilation. For white readers Bony was an ephemeral presence, symbolic of the aboriginal people whose blackness was destined to be absorbed into the white "race". As a character who expressed despair at his own blackness and sought to repel it with white civilisation and knowledge, he reflected white fears of regression caused by the increase in the Aboriginal population. In this way he performed a type of self-surveillance against accepting himself as a white.

Simultaneously, the skills available to him from his access to primitive powers, Aboriginal culture, and white modernity, allowed him extraordinary capability as a detective. These extraordinary powers allowed white readers to enjoy a vicarious identification with Bony as an individual who was able to effect change. Like the female characters who see in Bony that which confuses them, white readers are able momentarily to "forget" Bony's blackness. This ability to forget his colour is at least partially admitted by an imaginary projection into the future to see Bony as the product of assimilation. As a "glimpse" of an extraordinary Australian type of the future, Bony is symbolic of an amalgamation of the modern and the primitive. He alone can be seen as the product of what Marianna Torgovnick called the dialectic through which whites imagine a sense of self, for he is able to "mediate ... between the civilising super-ego and the 'primitive' [id]".[143]

Chapter 7 in "Another Time, Another Place: The Narration of the Australian Nation 1930-1950," 224-252. Ph.D. thesis, University of Southern Queensland, 1998. Some minor changes by the editors.

(Hobart), 21 February 1930, 3.
[143] Marianna Torgovnick, *Gone Primitive: Savage Intellects, Modern Lives* (Chicago and London: University of Chicago Press, 1990), 17.

PULP FICTION:
POPULAR CULTURE
AND LITERARY REPUTATION

RICHARD NILE

On 7 November 1947 Mervyn Blake, novelist and, for more than two decades now, a spokesman on behalf of Australia's national literature, addressed the bi-monthly meeting of the Australian Society of Writers (A.S.W.) at its Collin Street headquarters in Melbourne. According to the only surviving account of the occasion, many of the members of the society had already "arrived in the local world of *belles lettres*". One of Melbourne's most distinguished literary identities, Blake was the A.S.W.'s president. Described as a large man in his mid fifties, "florid of face but not flaccid of muscle", he earned his years with considerable dignity, for "Prosperity riding on one shoulder and Success on the other kept those shoulders well back".

In the mild tones of his distinctive Anglo-Australian voice Blake delivered his lecture: "The Structure of the Novel". In his concluding remarks, he endorsed serious literary effort in Australia upon which the audience responded with a customary "polite clapping of hands". These were well-rehearsed lines for Blake and familiar arguments for the members of the society. Literary democracy, they seemed to concur, required that obligations concerning the making of nationalist traditions of writing be emphatically stated and perpetually reiterated.

Soon after the meeting broke up at 5.00 pm Blake, in the company of Melbourne social pages editor, Nancy Chesterfield, made for the Australia Hotel a few doors down from the society's rented premises. "I want you to give a full report of what I said this afternoon", he said with what she noted was characteristic "candour made charming by the way he smiled". As they walked, he added almost routinely, "Publicity is an author's very breath of life".

The journalist questioned him about the current standing of Australian literature and its future prospects: "Do you think if the modern novelist turned out his wares in similar length and scope and digression to, say, the novels of Walter Scott and Thackeray, that they would be acceptable to modern publishers?" Blake responded with a decisive "No" and went on to explain: "Nowadays [publishers] demand sensationalism slickly put across, for their shareholders must be given their pound of flesh."

Nancy Chesterfield seemed to be interested in probing the matter further when they settled in at the lounge bar of the Australia. In his gentlemanly way, Blake ordered a round of drinks. He gulped his double brandy almost before she had sipped hers and asked for another. He was fatigued, he said, it had been a long day, he had been "on the wagon" since before lunch and was now interested in a quick charge before dinner. Just ahead of the six o'clock curfew on hotel drinking, Blake let slip a comment which the reporter noted: "No sooner do we reach the top than we are old and able to enjoy only—brandy." This may have been an understandable off-the-cuff comment at the fag-end of the day but it was also a somewhat curious admission, she thought, from a man so conscious of his public standing.

At chiming to end the great Australian stupor, kegs of men swilled onto unsteady pavements. The more dignified couple made a polite distance for the procession to pass. They then motored to Blake's residence in the Dandenongs.

Gathering that evening was a select literary group who would wine, dine and bed down for the night. Blake and his wife, Janet, were well known for their stylish literary soirees. Their guests on 7 November included Wilcannia-Smythe, "cold, suave, white haired" but "reputed to have the most musical pen in Australia"; Twyford Arundal, "small, wispy, weak of eye and chin, but a poet at top flight"; and the novelist Ella Montrose also in her fifties who had not published for several years but who kept up her literary associations by "reviewing books and writing pars".

The special guest was Marshall Ellis, "one of London's leading literary critics", whom Mervyn Blake seemed to be keen to impress but whom Nancy Chesterfield thought was little more than a puffed up imitation of G.K. Chesterton. Dinner was served around 8.00 pm and conversation moved almost ineluctably on to literary matters. It stayed there for the remainder of the evening.

As cigars and port were taken, the topic of Blake's speech became the subject of discussion. There was serious comment and good natured banter which quickened on the nicotine and alcohol. Despite the generally congenial atmosphere, Nancy Chesterfield noticed that Blake was becoming agitated: "Our sole interest at the moment is Australian literature, and the influence we may exert upon its development", he said firmly. "We are interested ... in literature with a capital L, not commercial fiction that receives the approval of the common herd."

The exchange followed the party into the drawing room where Australia's bestselling novelist, I.R. Watt, was mentioned—upon which Blake's irritation narrowed into invective. The populariser lacked the sophistication of the dedicated writer of fictions, he tubbed. Positive London reviews were muddle-headed. "There was never yet a best-seller that had any claims to be good literature", he said. Such a proposition, everyone knew, was quite preposterous, but Mervyn Blake was Mervyn Blake and, in any case, late in the evening it was the kind of sneering that might be anticipated.

Arundal, who had difficulty concealing his weakness for alcohol, moved to contradict his host but, in the attempt, fell and cracked his head on the edge of a stool. The sight of blood trickling down his thinning features brought forward a prudent closure to all argument. The guests expressed concern for "poor Twyford" who quite unintentionally had provided a circuit breaker. As soon as Arundal was cleaned up, guests retired to their rooms. As they excused themselves and thanked Janet for a lovely evening, Blake beat a retreat to his study. This had not been one of his better performances. He had been flat from the start. He had failed to impress Marshall Ellis. Janet said as much as she passed him one of her derisory looks that were becoming more commonplace of late. He resented her chiding but the night ended without further incident.

By morning Mervyn Blake was dead. His bulky corpse was pushed up against the study door which took some prising open. The scene looked as if he had "tried to claw" himself out. Images of the struggle paddled in hangovers. Blake's once florid face was drained of significance, the normally pale eyes, which required the assistance of penny weights to close, were expressionless. The scene suggested a heart attack, or perhaps a blood vessel had exploded silently in the brain. During the ensuing investigation into his death Janet Blake was charged with murder which she admitted immediately when accused, as if she had expected to be found out.

The literary world was quite literally stunned. Most had known the Blakes as a model literary couple who had survived the hard times together and who seemed now to be enjoying the fruits of Mervyn's considerable labours. There were vague rumours that he had engaged in extra-marital affairs but nothing too serious, including a sometimes talked about homosexual liaison. Apart from these, however, there was no solid evidence to suggest that he was anything other than a faithful husband. But even if Janet had suspected infidelity, everyone seemed to judge, she simply did not appear to be the jealous type. Professionally, Mervyn Blake tended to be overly opinionated but he was mostly agreeable. Surely no-one would want to kill him—least of all Janet.

At her trial Janet Blake explained without emotion that she had come to detest the man with whom she had shared the better part of her adult life. For many years she had lived in his shadow and had "ghosted" for him in the writing of his "masterpieces". He became insufferable, she said, as his dependence on her grew. The Great Mervyn Blake resented deeply the fact that without his wife's help he was no more than a second-rate writer, a washed-up former talent—no better than the likes of Ella Montrose whom he had patronised and looked down on for years.

Even after the fact, words like "charlatan" and "imposter" seemed improbable when applied to Mervyn Blake, so large had been his presence within Australia's literary communities. Yet it seemed incontrovertibly the case that Blake was a fraud. Years before it was fashionable to say so, he had done a Demidenko and fooled almost everyone. And as with the Demidenko farce, he too had become overly fond of his made up life, perhaps his final undoing.

Maybe Mervyn Blake had started out as an impressionable young man too eager to please and to be noticed. But once established, it seems he could not give up the lie of his double life. Most people had accepted that he was everything he seemed to be simply because he was Mervyn Blake—the most pathetic of his vanities and of theirs: "His novels were acclaimed as fine contributions to the national literature by people whose work he in turn praised with equal fervour."

In proper proportions, self love was tolerated within the community of literary elites because it was accepted that writers are egotists; it could even be an asset, as the occasion warranted, but Janet Blake said she could no longer endure her husband's superior attitude towards her. In the course of describing her motive, she revealed that for many years she had not only secretly written her husband's novels but that she was, in her own right, the hand that signed I.R. Watt. The royalties from Janet Blake's pseudonymous Watt books afforded the couple's literary lifestyle as the commercially successful but critically maligned populariser became Mervyn Blake's deepest secret.

Janet Blake maintained a marriage of convenience by not identifying herself as a writer and by acting out her role as the wife of one of the most respected and powerful literary figures in the country. Her husband accepted the conditions of her compliance and agreed never to discuss Watt in public. This seemed a simple enough compact at the time but in several acts of compensation Mervyn Blake became with time more staunch in his views concerning the national mission to make a serious Australian literature. Janet appeared increasingly stoic as his supportive wife. They complemented one another perfectly but an arrangement so squarely rooted in fabrications sapped even their formidable reserves. On the night of 7 November 1947 Mervyn Blake broke the agreement and his wife killed him.

Australian literature can claim a respectable number of suspicious deaths and suicides, such as Kenneth Mackenzie and poor old war-torn Jim Throssell who was married to Katherine Susannah Prichard, the death of Charmian Cliff is discreetly not mentioned in *The Oxford Companion to Australian Literature*, though George Johnston's tuberculosis is included, Louis Esson died from syphilis while a better than fair share of writers have drunk themselves to death, Joe Lynch is immortalised by poets for having disappeared into Sydney Harbour, Lesbia Harford's heart simply could not sustain her, Deidre Cash also died too young. The death of Mervyn Blake, however, is the first case of homicide. "I'm glad I killed him", Janet Blake confessed:

> "I hope that during those last moments, when he frantically struggled to open the door, that he knew I had poisoned him. I hope that as the light of his life flickered and went out, that as he slipped into the pit of death, he remembered how he had been turning down the light of life for me—turning it down slowly for more than twenty years."

With that statement Arthur Upfield closed his novel, *An Author Bites the Dust* (1948), a story of literary intrigue, theft and double cross.[1]

The events of *An Author Bites the Dust* are an intentional fallacy but the fictional literary scandal casts a revealing light on some of the tensions that exist between the makers of a national literature—writer's with a social conscience—and popularisers such as Upfield who wrote novels as a commercial enterprise. An Upfieldian murder-mystery involving the detective Napoleon Bonaparte (Bony), *An Author Bites the Dust* is also a none-too-subtle tilt at literary pretensions and the character of Mervyn Blake can be readily translated into the national posturing of figures such as Vance Palmer who around the time of publication was powerful within the literature.

Upfield met Melbourne's literary establishment in the 1930s but felt excluded from their cliques on the basis that he was not a proper author. According to his biographer, Jessica Hawke, they quickly rejected him:

---

[1] Arthur Upfield, *An Author Bites the Dust* (Sydney: Angus & Robertson, 1948).

He attended a few of their gatherings, and met personally several whose novels had been reviewed in the Also Ran columns of the *Times Literary Supplement*. He was presented to lofty people who wrote poetry, or who had written paragraphs for the *Bulletin*, and who had produced a short story or two which was awarded something or other by a literary society. They were nice people, but when they came to discuss Australian literature they were intolerable.

These people never wrote for money! Oh No! ... In the press they lauded the work of their fellows and in return were lauded; for this was at the close of a short era when tenth-rate Australian novels had been praised as works of high literary merit, and the swindled public threatened to knock down a bookseller or librarian who offered one.[2]

Bald claims that typified his attitude, such as there are only "two subjects to write about—crime and sex" must have irritated the likes of Palmer who wrote deliberately and slowly in an attempt to convey the Australian experience. The character Bony makes the case that popular fiction is the "backbone" of Australian culture because it possesses "no pretensions".[3] In his own voice Upfield claimed: "Better a good story with plenty of errors than a piece of prose perfectly done and having no story."[4]

Vance Palmer was Australia's man of letters who dressed in invariably brown tonings—usually with a blue shirt and a bow tie. That bow tie which was his literary trade mark for over half a century, signified Palmer as a serious writer and cultural spokesman. It may test credibility to say that Vance Palmer was the actual model for Mervyn Blake—he was a mild-mannered man of medium height—or that Janet (Nettie) Palmer was Janet Blake—she found her husband insensitive but did not want him dead—yet there are certain parallels if only in the Palmers' commanding presence in the politics of Australian literature and their pretensions to speak on behalf of Australian writers and Australian writing. They were, in a sense, ripe for the picking.

Vance Palmer was the sort of Melbourne literary figure that Upfield found absurd: Palmer's books were failures but he commanded considerable influence; he presumed to carry a heavier literary load than many of his contemporaries; he was a representative of literary elites and spokesman on their behalf; but importantly in the days before "academic experts, mass

---

[2] Jessica Hawke, *Follow My Dust: A Biography of Arthur Upfield* (Melbourne: Heinemann, 1957), 166-167.

[3] John Hetherington, quoted in *The Spirit of Australia: The Crime Fiction of Arthur W. Upfield*, Ray B. Browne (Bowling Green, OH: Bowling Green State University Popular Press, 1988), 136.

[4] Hetherington, quoted in *The Spirit of Australia*, 135-137.

media pundits, cultural functionaries", he was an "elderly bookman" as John Gross described the "man of letters" in England.[5] "As a man of letters and a citizen" but not as a writer, David Walker noted in *Dream and Disillusion*, "Vance Palmer has been highly praised".[6] "Man of letters" suited him like the bow ties he wore and yet the label was already by the 1940s an anachronism dating back at least half a century. In his dogged and somewhat old-fashioned way, Palmer sought to "civilise strident nationalism" by making the literature "more worthy of respect", a lifelong commitment which did not diminish with the passing of time.[7] By 1942 he had been appointed to the board of the Commonwealth Literature Fund and between 1947 and 1953 he served as chairman. "In practical terms his occupancy of that position", wrote biographer Harry Heseltine, "represented the pinnacle of Palmer's power to influence Australian culture."[8] Right up until the time of his death in 1959, Palmer was broadcasting nationally through the A.B.C. the fortnightly "Current Books Worth Reading".

Vance and Nettie Palmer were the most influential literary partnership of their generation. Drusilla Modjeska in *Exiles at Home* has observed that Nettle Palmer became in the interwar period the "most influential critic since A.G. Stephens".[9] Exhibiting signs of the determined steadiness which also characterised her husband, she was once delivered one of those fabulous Miles Franklin backhanders: "We have had many brilliant critics but they only did sporadic work—you have been more continuous."[10] If Nettie was persistent but not brilliant, then her reviews were influential among writers and they put bread and butter on the table.

Vance Palmer did not make a living out writing. That task often fell to Nettle who afforded the couple's literary lifestyle until his contributions from regular broadcasting picked up in the 1940s. He compensated for the financial shortfall by his accomplishments as a cultural politician. In 1943 Nettie confided in her daughter Aileen that both she and Vance had acted quite deliberately and with a certain peremptoriness to become arbiters of literary and cultural tastes. "Your two parents happen to be more powerful

---

[5] John Goss, *The Rise and Fall of the Man of Letters: Aspects of English Literary Life Since 100* (London: Weidenfeld & Nicolson, 1969), xiii.

[6] David Walker, *Dream and Disillusion* (Canberra: ANU Press, 1976), 31.

[7] Walker, Dream and Disillusion, 31.

[8] Harry Heseltine, *Vance Palmer* (St Lucia, Qld: University of Queensland Press, 1970), 25.

[9] Drusilla Modjeska, *Exiles at Home: Australia Women Writers 1925-1945* (London; Sydney: Sirius Book, 1981), 50.

[10] Miles Franklin to Nettie Palmer, 31 May 1940, quoted in *Exiles at Home*, 50.

than in years past", Nettie explained, "mostly by the effluxion of time and by the fact that the time has been passed in the city, where reputations are made ..."[11]

Australian literature in the first half of the twentieth century sometimes speaks of the "Palmer standard" but, Walker, among others, has observed that it is "difficult to reconcile" Vance's "frequent allusions to vitality with the often soporific influences of his prose or his celebrations of robust manliness with Nettie's frustrations at his rather distant and patriarchal bearing towards her". Palmer standard or not, Vance was prone to shifting "personal responsibilities for creative failure onto his society" and he was rather inclined to absolve any other shortcomings as a "man trying to cultivate healthy cultural principles in a sick, falsely complex, society".[12] Nettie supported him in this regard. "The plain truth is", she recorded in her diary in 1927, "that our promiscuous reading public is not used to the deepest kind of reality in books about the background it knows".[13]

In addition to their disdain for commercial fictions and Australian reading tastes, the Palmers affected a disliking for what Vance identified as the nation's false bourgeois values. In this he profoundly misunderstood class relations, particularly the values of a highly literate working class whose promiscuous habits he also blamed for his failure; and he failed to appreciate the wider associations of the industrial settler society. He would have preferred an alternative community of artisans and craftsmen, instead of the workers and managers who made up working relations in the cities and the women who stayed at home and organised domestic life around the suburbs where the Australians lived predominantly. He called for a literature that rumbled with crude vigour but in terms of "style, content and morality his novels were more discreetly inoffensive than one might have suspected from a man who declared his opposition to the timid morality of the drawing room society".[14] Palmer drew succour from the drawing room and, as denial is depicted as having consumed the Blakes in *An Author Bites the Dust*, it may help explain the pertinacity with which he spoke on behalf of a literary tradition which, in the terms it was defined, bore very little relation to anything he ever did as a writer.

Under the aegis of a Palmer-style nationalism, derived from the principles of guild socialism, there was little room for commercial writers who, it was widely fancied, compromised the effort to make the literature

---

[11] Modjeska, *Exiles at Home*, 50; refers to Nettie Palmer as the "Arbiter".
[12] Walker, *Dream and Disillusion*, 196-197.
[13] Vivian Smith, ed., *Nettie Palmer: Her "Fourteen Years."* (St. Lucia, Qld: University of Queensland Press, 1988), 25.
[14] Walker, *Dream and Disillusion*, 198.

a serious and socially conscious undertaking. As makers of fictions, socially conscious writers encouraged one another to write in particular ways. As public intellectuals they were expected to maintain a consistent critical line which would add to the store and ultimately build up Australian literary stocks. Those involved in this national-building project understood and accepted their obligation towards the greater good: they supported one another, even to the extent of issuing false praise; they accepted more generally that they should not openly criticise the effort; and they attempted to persuade those who did not observe the requirements to change their ways. Katharine Susannah Prichard, for instance, insisted that she would prefer to fall from "universal standards" than not write about Australia, an extraordinarily self centred and, although not intended, a deeply offensive statement concerning her country and the people who made their lives there.[15]

A middle-class coterie of writers, many of them based in Melbourne or carrying a Melbourne influence—such as Prichard—supported one another in the establishment of an Australian national aesthetic. They sometimes told white lies to get by and issued false praise for work they did not like. In 1930, for instance, Prichard wrote to Nettie Palmer asking her to say something nice about Mollie Skinner's *The Black Swans* (1929) which Prichard thought was a poor book but would not say so openly. Nettie Palmer obliged but a year or so later admonished Dorothy Cottrell not to waste her considerable literary skills writing popular novels which did not fulfil national prescriptions. According to Nettie Palmer, Cottrell had more to offer the literature than *Earth Battle* (1930): "Anxious onlookers can only hope she will some day write a careful sound book. We ask merely of her, something different and better."[16] Those who broke ranks and uttered unkind things about their literary allies, on the other hand, were reprimanded. "You're only pretending", Nettie Palmer told Frank Wilmott who had spoken disparagingly about Katharine Susannah Prichard, "when you criticise K.S.P. on account of sheer themes ... no, and 'cowyard obstetrics' won't dispose of Coonardoo either."[17]

In an insecure environment where there were few financial returns, the impulse to join the nation-building project might have been quite strong.

---

[15]Katharine Susannah Prichard, Letter to H.M. Green, 4 November 1929, H.M. Green papers, NLA, MSS 3926.

[16] Richard Nile, "Literary Democracy and the Politics of Reputation," in *The Oxford Literary History of Australia*, ed. Bruce Bennett and Jennifer Strauss (Melbourne: Oxford University Press, 1980), 143-144.

[17] Nettie Palmer, Letter to Furnley Maurice, 28 October 1928, in *Letters of Vance and Nettie Palmer 1915-1963*, ed. Vivian Smith (Canberra: NLA, 1977), 46.

Kylie Tennant who in an ironic moment had written to critic H. M. Green declaring herself "Kylie Tennant: Writer Incorporated" commented in equally self-deprecating terms in *Ride on Stranger*: "After all, you can't quarrel with free shelter, even if the bread is too lavishly buttered with National Culture."[18]

All traditions, cultural or otherwise, I am trying to suggest, are inherently political and dependent upon key groups for their maintenance and reproduction. In circumstances where it was commonly believed that Australian literature was yet to be made, the degree of authority possessed by a few well-placed individuals—to invent the basis of national expression—was considerable.

In a process of manufacturing consent out of a blend of social conscience and good manners, Katharine Susannah Prichard's *Working Bullocks* (1926) became the commonly accepted literary marker for the writers of the Palmer acquaintance. Louis Esson had read the novel in manuscript and wrote enthusiastically to Vance Palmer that he found it "most unconventional", and "less like an ordinary story than actual life. You feel you are living in the kauri (sic) forests."[19] In a published review in *The Bulletin* Esson commented further that Prichard was Australia's best contemporary novelist who had established a new "high water mark" in the literature:

> Katharine Prichard might be described as the most "modern" of Australia's writers. She has discarded a great deal of useless baggage, preferring to travel freely and make direct contact with life, and we always feel that her best novels are drawn from vital sources. They are always real and intensely alive in every page ... Working Bullocks, Miss Prichard's latest novel, recently published by Jonathan Cape, is her finest work, and probably the best novel written in Australia ... obviously a work of genius of which any country might be proud.[20]

Prichard's friend from school days, Nettie Palmer sealed her approval soon after.[21] *Working Bullocks* achieved high status because of its vigour and narrative sophistication and, in the opinion of Louis Esson, Vance and Nettie Palmer at least, because it took its Australian environment for

---

[18] Kylie Tennant, Letter to H.M. Green, 26 March 1941, H.M. Green Papers, NLA MSS 3925.

[19] Louis Esson, Letter to Vance Palmer, 31 December 1925, quoted in *Louis Esson and the Australian Theatre*, Vance Palmer (Melbourne: Georgian House, 1948), 67.

[20] Louis Esson, "Katharine Susannah Prichard," *Bulletin* 31 March 1927, 2.

[21] Smith, *Nettie Palmer*, 23-24.

granted.

A generation on from its publication, Miles Franklin wrote that *Working Bullocks* ended a long literary drought which set in soon after *Such is Life* was published. Tom Inglis Moore wrote in almost identical terms,

> "the vigour of the 1890s was carried over into the first decade of the century ... The period from 1904 to the late 1920s, say 1926, was marked by ... an interlude between the movement which began in the 1890s and the renaissance that began about 1926."[22]

Not long before his death Vance Palmer reaffirmed the unqualified success of *Working Bullocks* and the tradition sprang from it, which he and a dedicated group of contemporaries had worked hard to invent and maintain.[23] The "long drought" thesis of Australian literature survives through to the present.

Commercially, *Working Bullocks* was a failure and Prichard paid more for the manuscript to be typed for submission to Jonathon Cape, her publisher, than she received back in royalties.[24] It was read by only a few people. Publication statistics also reveal that there was no long drought in Australian literature. No fewer than 1200 Australian novels were published between *Such Is Life* and *Working Bullocks*.[25] The "long drought", so often discussed in critical discourse is a critical position originally invented and subsequently maintained by literary elites who understood the historical significance of the times they so busily occupied. National hegemony was achieved in a very clubby environment which produced and ordered the literature. The temper was rarely democratic, the bias was hardly offensive, the Australia they invented was conventional.

Janet Blake never existed and therefore never killed her self-important husband. Yet there are times when I actively wish she had. What an everyday wonder she would have been. What a difference she might have made. But I am left to my necro-fancy that she will do-in Vance Palmer.

---

[22] Tom Inglis Moore, "Australian Literature: 1901-1951," *Australian Quarterly*, 23.2 (1951), 6.

[23] Vance Palmer, Review of *Working Bullocks*, *Meanjin* 16.1 (Autumn 1957), 90-91.

[24] Katharine Susannah Prichard, Letter to Nettie Palmer, 13 June 1927, Palmer Papers, NLA, MSS 1174/1/2669. In other correspondence Prichard claimed she had made less money from *Working Bullocks* than from any novel she had written: 15 September 1928, Palmer Papers, NLA, MSS 1174/1/2975-8.

[25] Richard Nile, "The Rise of the Australian Novel," Ph.D. thesis: University of New South Wales, 1987, ch. 1.

But he is long dead. Perhaps he had a heart-attack or a blood vessel silently exploded in his head. He is as resolute in death as ever he was in life. Come on Janet ... I trail off. To the study. I indulge further in Upfield's *An Author Bites the Dust*. I fantasise that I am being really subversive ... if only my colleagues in the English department knew.

First Published: in *Journal of Australian Studies* 58 (1998): 66-74.

"The Fleeting Moment and the Ageless Past": Nostalgia in Arthur Upfield's Detective Fiction

Ada Coe

The relationship between detective fiction and psychoanalysis has been explored at length and repeatedly, particularly insofar as a "detective story reorders our perception of the past through language",[1] in the same way that psychoanalysis does, to give it new meaning and coherence. A recent manifestation of this phenomenon is the proliferation of historical detectives, especially Victorian ones. In these contemporary stories, the nineteenth century is portrayed as an acceptable illusion of that time, as the authors feel it should have been: self-aware, uncomfortable about social divisions and gender discrimination, instead of generally smug and self-satisfied, safe in the attitude that "God's in His heaven—All's right with the world", which Browning so powerfully satirizes. It is a process of transference of guilt, and sublimation of atonement, perhaps. In a curious mixture of wish-fulfillment fantasies and Orwellian restructuring of the past, "facts," as they have been handed down in various writings or in the memory of human beings, are cast aside. And yet, as Winston Smith in *Nineteen Eighty-Four*, reflects, "how could you establish even the most obvious fact when there existed no record outside your own memory?"

Facts, objective or subjective or deliberately distorted, and memory, reliable or unreliable, are the very basis of detective fiction, but some authors combine the detective's reconstruction of the events of the crime in the past in order to heal the present, with a nostalgic presentation of a way of life that is dying out, inevitably if regrettably, but still affects the present. In this essay I want to look closely at some works by one such

---

[1] Albert Hutter, "Dreams, Transformations, and Literature: The Implications of Detective Fiction," in *The Poetics of Murder*, ed. Glenn Most and William Stowe (New York: Harcourt Brace Jovanovich, 1983), 230-51.

author, the expatriate Englishman in Australia, Arthur Upfield, to examine his juggling of time past.

Auerbach, in *Mimesis*, bases his distinction between history and legend on the role the past plays in the narrative. Where the narrative leaves gaps, where there is a sense of a shadowy past in the background, according to Auerbach, we are dealing with history, whereas legend brings the past into the foreground, turning it into a local and total present. In what have been called "the golden years of detective fiction", with the major exponents of the cerebral detective story that adhered to the formula set by Conan Doyle in his Sherlock Holmes stories, the genre approximated Auerbach's definition of legend, in its presentation of a uniformly even foreground, balancing past and present in equal weight. However, contemporary detective fiction has more and more blurred the distinction, as defined by Auerbach, between legend and history, creating a new kind of tension in the dialectic of narrative and meaning. The narrative of detection follows the linear, backward-looking structure, whereas the meaning struggles to pull into different directions to expand in range.

Upfield's novel *Man of Two Tribes* opens with a specifically pinpointed moment in time, the ringing of an alarm clock at 3:45 am, which is then followed by a reference to the 4:20 express train from Port Pirie. The town, Chifley, is then mentioned, both present and absent, in the naming of its essential features, invisible in the darkness. Follows a description of the Nullarbor Plain, it too, invisible on this moonless night, 330 miles of

> table-flat, treeless land beneath which the aborigines believe Gamba still lives and emerges at night to hunt for a blackfellow rash enough to leave his own camp fire.[2]

Here in a nutshell, on one page, is summarized the clash of different temporal points that runs through most of Upfield's Bony novels—the contemporary white colonial civilization represented by the alarm clock that is to wake Senior Constable Easter, himself representative of the white system of law and order, the white town contrasted with the aboriginal tribal way of life, the aboriginal mythical "Dream Time" and the timelessness of the Australian natural landscape. *Man of Two Tribes* is one of many novels set in small outback towns, either real or imaginary, while several are set on sheep stations or out in the bush, but the Australian natural landscape always predominates. Even those novels with an urban setting constantly remind the reader of Bony's aboriginal background and closeness with nature. He is always a tracker as much as a detective, either

---

[2] Arthur Upfield, *Man of Two Tribes* (Sydney: Arkon, 1981), 1.

balancing, or torn between, the influences of his aboriginal ancestry and the white upbringing. He is described as a "composite" of the two races, having inherited from his mother "the spirit of nomadism, the eyesight of her race, the passion for hunting",[3] and from his father "calm and comprehensive reasoning"; while to his education must be attributed his Cartesian deductive method of reasoning, his ability to quote Nietzsche and Voltaire.

The very nature of tradition has been examined at length by anthropologists and literary critics. It has been pointed out, among others by Robert M. Torrance, that the aboriginal bond with the mythical past, the ancestral "Dream Time", is in itself a sterile, stunting relationship. Torrance quotes Maddock's description of "a metaphysical discontinuity, a duality between men and powers",[4] and goes on to argue that in such a case "there can be no future that is not an imperfect repetition of a timeless past lying ahead no less than behind".[5] Upfield, however, describes a people in a state of transition, with everything that was of value definitely behind in the past, and with doubtful hopes of the "mirage" of civilization ahead in the future.

Australian recorded history, that is, beginning with the records of the arrival of the white man, was barely a hundred and fifty years old when Upfield was writing the bulk of his novels, and Australia was still searching for, and striving to establish its national identity. There was British colonial tradition on the one hand, and the ancient Aboriginal people on the other, and a vast growing number of immigrants from Europe and Asia. Himself a British expatriate, Upfield was only one among several writers who felt a strong sense of Australianness, which could not be any one of these elements yet should take them all into account. It is this sense of a new Australian identity that Upfield explores in his novels, occasionally with some cutting remarks in passing about the white colonial attitude or the establishment, but mostly by implication.

Historians have written about the "various impulses, ideas, and aspirations" that "sought expression, in one form or another, during the whole period from Eureka to the First World War, helping to turn a mixed and scattered population into a people and bring them into harmony with their background",[6] admitting, however, that the aborigines were among

---

[3] Arthur Upfield, *The Sands of Windee* (Sydney: Pacific Books, 1969), 1.
[4] Kenneth Maddock, quoted in *The Spiritual Quest*, Robert Torrance (Berkeley: University of California Press, 1994), 67.
[5] Kenneth Maddock, quoted in *The Spritual Quest*, 68.
[6] Vance Palmer, *The Legend of the Nineties* (London: Cambridge University Press, 1954), 12-13.

the ethnic groups excluded from the "new democracy". The aborigines' "culture, this imaginative life, had so little concrete form, it was so much a matter of primitive habits and observances, that it had small chance of being taken seriously by people whose minds were preoccupied with a particular kind of progress".[7]

That Upfield speaks the language of his own time should hardly be surprising, although he has been blamed for it repeatedly. He is progressive for those decades in his deep, underlying sympathy for the aborigines, but is, admittedly, occasionally bogged down in the white-colonial vocabulary and attitudes. However, he is one writer who, in his search for "the Spirit of Australia", never ignores the rights of the original inhabitants.

Working within a genre that is essentially concerned with deconstructing the past in order to reconstruct it, Upfield in his novels is also thematically engaged with casting nostalgic glances backwards towards a vanishing way of life. About the search for an Australian identity in the early part of the century, Palmer concludes, somewhat disgustedly perhaps, that "Far from building a new world in isolation, Australia seemed bent on making terms with the old".[8] Upfield is not so much concerned with "making terms" with it as with singing of past ideals and virtues, sometimes in distinctly Homeric terms.

In the early novels, more strongly than in the later ones, we find also a strong flavor of Kipling and of H. Rider Haggard, of the gentlemanly code of honor of the days of the Empire, which was an extension of the public school code. Bony will sometimes conduct an investigation according to this code—on one or two occasions, although he is a Detective Inspector following a case, he refuses to eavesdrop, explaining that he despises that kind of behavior. His attitude to women generally betrays a turn-of-the-century gallant courtesy, and not a little sentimentality. He tends to idealize white women, describing them in nineteenth-century terms, and compares himself to a medieval knight. This sentimentality leads him to a grand *beau geste* at the end of *The Sands of Windee*, when he accepts the public humiliation of failure in order to protect a beautiful young woman and her lover. Torn between his pride in his reputation as never having failed to finalize a case and his admiration for the young woman, complicated perhaps by a sentiment of pride that she appealed to him for help, he seeks advice from one of the other characters, a priest, who tells him "The bigger the sacrifice, the bigger the man. I believe you are a big man, my son."[9] Not only the situation but the language itself—lofty,

---

[7] Palmer, *The Legend of the Nineties*, 17.
[8] Palmer, *The Legend of the Nineties*, 12.
[9] Arthur Upfield, *The Sands of Windee*, 213.

moralistic—is reminiscent of the novels of the turn of the century. Even in the later novels Bony never totally loses his old-world courtesy towards women, but the attitudes and the language become somewhat less dated.

Several of the Bony novels are set on sheep stations in the Outback. The landowners, male or female, represent the ideal of the old country squire under a different guise, laying down the law, administering justice, supervising and controlling the everyday running of these huge properties, and caring for their dependents. The setting is agrarian, with distinct echoes of Jefferson's agrarian democratic philosophy, equating husbandry and virtue; it is semi-feudal, the relationship being symbiotic, relying on mutual trust, respect, and dependence. Everyone knows his or her place in this kind of structure and, on the whole, accepts it. Occasionally this pattern is transposed into a sort of urban setting, as in *Bony and the Mouse*. Daybreak is "a one-pub town", created, owned, and controlled by Melody Sam, and the whole area around it, as far as the eye can see, is known as "the Land of Melody Sam".[10] He came to these parts decades earlier, prospecting for gold, and is now a "tycoon! A dictator! A political boss!",[11] and, though well over eighty, he keeps a sharp eye on his town. But rural or urban, these are rulers who are very close to the land and the people, in small, tight-knit communities, and present an idealized image.

Visiting Australia in the 1880s, Francis W.L. Adams, a young poet and disciple of Matthew Arnold, wrote,

> This is a true republic; the truest, I take it, in the world. In England the average man feels he is an inferior; in America he feels he is a superior; in Australia he feels he is an equal.[12]

It may be a limited definition of equality, but we can recognize it as the same kind of friendly personal relationship juxtaposed with knowing one's role in society that we see in the episode Auerbach quotes in the first chapter of *Mimesis*, between Ulysses and his old nurse. She washes the stranger's feet because that is her task, but there is no spirit of servility or submission in her behavior.

To what extent Upfield admires those English-squire type landowners is a moot point. The tone seems neutral to me, and the more English-squire like they are the more distant they appear. He reserves his unbridled enthusiasm for the country itself and for those who are closest to it. There is no doubt, however, about the author's admiration for Melody Sam, who

---

[10] Arthur Upfield, *Bony and the Mouse* (London: Pan Books, 1970), 5.

[11] Upfield, *Bony and the Mouse*, 8.

[12] Francis Adams, quoted in *The Legend of the Nineties*, 28.

is an unforgettable, utterly delightful character, in his directness, his down-to-earth quality, and his eccentricities. Nor is there any room for doubt about Upfield's admiration for the previous generation, for the men who went out into the Australian bush at the turn of the century, who drove bullocks up and down the Outback along uncharted tracks and who lived according to their own laws and sense of justice. These are the old men, in their seventies and eighties when Upfield was writing in the early decades of the twentieth century, whose rough, tough exterior does not hide their essential simple honesty and goodness. He openly regrets their passing. For all his extended kingdom, Melody Sam can also be said to belong to this category. The description of him as someone who "towered so high above his fellows, who was so much withdrawn in isolation, and yet could stand four square in any company he chose",[13] easily applies to other such characters, in other books. These old men, usually large, with full manes of white hair, are still physically and mentally active and alert despite their years, and despite the regular "benders". One of them, Mr. Luton, in *The Battling Prophet*, is described as having "the eyes of the voyager by land or sea, eyes accustomed to searching beyond horizons, and the years had not come between".[14] The old pioneering days are over in a society where land is allotted and taxed by an anonymous government and the virtues of these drovers in particular, possibly of pioneers generally—surprisingly Homeric virtues of simple courage, physical strength, and resourcefulness, and generosity—may well die out with them.

These characters, described as "giants", take on an aura of legendary heroes, as Upfield, through his detective Bony, wallows in nostalgic regret for the old days. Within the structure of the narrative plot, author and detective sometimes oppose the ready justice of these men to the abstraction of the present-day legal system, despite the fact that as a Detective-Inspector, Bony belongs to the latter. His sympathies, however, often lie with the former. As he himself stresses repeatedly, he is "not a policeman", and, like those old men, he sometimes slithers between the loopholes of the law to serve the cause of ultimate justice. In a conversation with Melody Sam, Bony, half-caste and ostensibly a yardman at the latter's hotel, warning Sam that he cannot exact personal vengeance on the murderer, says "I am a primitive, as you are. I like simplicity in living, and in common justice", but urges that they have to live in the world others have made, which, according to Bony, "is not the world we would have made".[15] Throughout the novels, justice is associated with a "primitive"

---

[13] Upfield, *Bony and the Mouse*, 143.

[14] Arthur Upfield, *The Battling Prophet* (Sydney: Arkon, 1981), 6.

[15] Upfield, *Bony and the Mouse*, 24.

way of life, while "the law"—often ponderous, intricate, clumsy, and possibly unfair—is part of the white man's system of civilization. And "primitive," as the above quotation from *Bony and the Mouse* attests, for Upfield is not a racist slur—Melody Sam is a white man—but a compliment, the evidence of the most basic, perhaps because simplest, that is least complicated, virtues.

Complementing this category of characters are the aborigines of the same generation. Their great virtue is to have known a time when their tribe was independent of the white man. Their tragedy is to find themselves lonely representatives "of a race remarkable for its morality, its justice, its freedom from greed".[16] They are close to the "real Australia," to the land and to its spirit. Chief Wilmot, white-haired, naked except for his pubic tassel, mystic markings painted on his body, is as "venerable" as the centuries-old eucalyptus tree when he stops "to regard this living monument to which he was linked in defiance of Time and Death".[17] He has removed the white man's clothing, that "tragic disguise, the uniform of a tragic civilization," and as he stands before the tree, shoulders squared, the representation of strength and dignity, "for the first time Bony saw deference in the son's attitude".[18] The underlying irony is that these three aborigines, Chief Wilmot, his son, and his son's wife, are going to carry out a traditional aboriginal religious ceremony as part of a scam devised by white people, and will not even share in the takings. Yet at no time does Upfield ever make fun of aboriginal legends or beliefs. On the contrary, he suggests that there may be something behind their "magic". And, as here in this novel, usually the aborigines appear at their best and most dignified when they doff the trappings of the white civilization to return to the earth and to their origins.

Vance Palmer, in his *Legend of the Nineties*, mentions that the aborigines were somehow omitted from the formula in the search for the new Australia. While Upfield is convinced that they have to be an important element in the equation, he seems somewhat uncertain as to how exactly to fit them in. Within the complex temporal framework of the Bony novels, the aborigines occupy both a prominent and an anomalous position. Upfield's attitude towards them is ambivalent. They are the real, original Australians, representing a civilization far older than that of the white man, possessing powers, such as that of telepathy for example, unknown to the whites, yet, regrettably, their culture is in the process of being destroyed by the settlers, and, in Upfield's novels, the worst

---

[16] Arthur Upfield, *Murder Must Wait* (London: Pan Books, 1971), 167.

[17] Upfield, *Murder Must Wait*, 166.

[18] Upfield, *Murder Must Wait*, 169.

aboriginal characters are the ones who have been separated from their tribe, degraded by the white civilization into drunkenness, and left in a no-man's land, between two cultures. Bony, as a university-educated half-caste, occupying a middle-class position in the white man's world but equally at home with the aborigines in the bush, is the reiterated example that the best of the two cultures can merge in an individual, but there are also examples where an individual combines the worst of the two. In merging the two civilizations, Bony himself also merges time-frames. He is the product of the new, emerging Australian legend, the symbol of progress inasmuch as, when Upfield began writing these novels, no half-caste aboriginal had ever, as yet, been awarded an M.A. from any Australian university;[19] but he is also rooted in a tradition as old as time. He is the embodiment of the "timeless land," which dominates Upfield's novels, directly linked to the people who "owned this land with a spiritual passion beyond the understanding of the white man who had dispossessed them".[20]

Upfield has been berated by critics for some of his descriptions of aborigines, yet I want to argue that his attitude is not so much that of the colonial as a throwback to the Enlightenment. It is rather the eighteenth-century view of the Noble Savage, both in its positive aspects and in its limitations, but with a new twist, in that the essential simple goodness is shared by those whites who have discarded at least in part the trappings of civilization and "gone bush", whether these be drovers or landed squatters. Theirs is not a superficial "back to nature" attitude, an equivalent of playing dairy-maid in the palatial Petit Trianon, or a Romantic rhapsodizing over mountains and groves; on the contrary, they have merged into the landscape in a very real way, and have absorbed its essence.

The detective story genre within which Upfield is writing works in a linear time frame, moving forward and backwards simultaneously, as the uncovering of new clues illuminates and explains events in the past; this becomes complicated in Upfield's novels, by the intrusion of a more far-reaching past that dominates the narrative without affecting it directly. The novels do not engage in an exploration of history as a process, as the precondition of the present, in the terms of Lukacs.[21] Upfield is primarily a story-teller, uttering simple statements and developing a plot. He is not interested in making pronouncements or exposing arguments. In the one

---

[19] Tamsin Donaldson, "Australian Tales of Mystery and Miscegenation," *Meanjin* 50.2-3 (Winter-Spring 1991): 345, 352.

[20] Upfield, *Bony and the Mouse*, 75.

[21] Georg Lukacs, *The Theory of the Novel*, trans. Anna Bostock (Cambridge: MIT Press, 1971).

novel, which is something of a personal vendetta, *An Author Bites the Dust*, Upfield waspishly defends "imaginative writing" that tells a story against "writing executed in schoolmasterly fashion and yet so lacking in entertainment value that the general public won't buy it".[22] The argument opposes "Literature with a capital L" to "commercial fiction that receives the approval of the common herd". The coterie of highbrow authors (one of whom becomes the murder victim) defends "good literature ... as understood by the cultured", whereas, in opposition, another character, a critic, points out that the "greatest best-seller of all time ... is the Bible, read by cultured and illiterate all over the world". He insists that the "common herd can and does appreciate literature provided it says something worth hearing with the mind".[23] Upfield, who has a personal axe to grind, of course is on the side of the popular author of fiction who has been rejected by the intellectual elite on the grounds that what he writes is mere "commercial fiction", which is not worth bothering about.

Walter Benjamin, in his discussion of the art of story-telling, suggests that this is dying out as an art because the communication of experience is no longer possible or desirable in our society. The novel, he argues, contains no counsel or wisdom, instead it "gives evidence of the profound perplexity of the living".[24] Upfield's novels are well-constructed detective plots, avoiding discussion of psychological perplexity in life, with artificially neat resolutions at the end when the killer is unmasked, and in that sense indeed they are lacking in wisdom. On the other hand, they do communicate "experience"—the author's passionate love for Australia, his enthusiasm for the country, pour forth in every book. Most novels end with some overwhelming natural phenomenon: a massive rabbit migration, a flash flood, a fierce bushfire, for example. The event is incorporated into the plot, but is not an integral part of it at a psychological level, nor is it explored at great depth, yet the author's awe and excitement rings true as "communicated experience". Just as in his presentation of the past and of the passing generation, Upfield makes it "possible to see a new beauty in what is vanishing".[25] The past, in Upfield's novels, is static; but it is not experienced as a dynamic force by the characters, it simply is, or rather was. In Auerbach's terms, we have in these novels not history but legend, where past and present are juxtaposed as a mechanism of theme, brought into the foreground of the same landscape, like Chief Wilmot and the

---

[22] Arthur Upfield, *An Author Bites the Dust* (Sydney: Arkon, 1980), 73.

[23] Upfield, *An Author Bites the Dust*, 14.

[24] Walter Benjamin, "The Storyteller," in *Illuminations*, trans. Harry Zohn (New York: Harcourt, Brace & World, 1968), 87.

[25] Benjamin, "The Storyteller," 87.

century-old tree, separate and linked, of equal value.

There are constant references to Time, with or without a capital "T," throughout the novels. Bony repeatedly asserts that time is his ally in any investigation, that all he has to do is wait, with the patience of his maternal ancestors, and the clues will inevitably surface to provide him with the solution. He is obviously speaking about the linear, forward-moving temporal concept, which is the essence of the detective narrative. The concern with a Past beyond time, as typified in the repeated references to aboriginal legends, is no intrusion on this. One of the original features of Bony's methods of detection is that so often a large part of his detecting involves doing nothing, communing with nature, becoming part of the landscape, savoring the winds of the great Interior, which bring him "the magically blended perfume of the Fleeting Moment, and the Ageless Past".[26] All the novels include lyrical passages about the "timeless land", in the juxtaposition of primitive and "civilized",[27] nature, and mankind.

Albert D. Hutter argues that detective fiction, like dream interpretation, "involves the transformation of a fragmented and incomplete set of events into a more ordered and complete understanding".[28] While Upfield's detective narrative fits this paradigm, the content simultaneously contradicts it. Aboriginal legends refer to a "dream time" in the distant past, before the creation of the world. In this context, the Past is a totality, clearly defined, unchangeable, "ageless"—the very antithesis of the past in a detective story. It is an established fact, and, above all, it is perfect. Whereas the function of the detective narrative is to heal a past that has been thrown "out of joint" by a crime, the historical past in Upfield has degenerated into the present. Unlike the detective narrative that reconstructs the personal history affected by the crime in question, the collective history is left untouched in its fixed totality.

It has been often pointed out, among others by Todorov,[29] that there are essentially two stories in a detective tale: that of the crime and that of the investigation. At least part of the fascination of Upfield is the way his novels are developed on a series of dualities, which create a basic conflict—man/nature, civilized/primitive, white/aborigine. Bony, at various times and in slightly different words, declares grandiloquently "I am the Bridge built by a white man and a black woman to span the gulf

---

[26] Upfield, *Bony and the Mouse*, 45.

[27] The latter word definitely belongs in quotation marks, as Upfield is often very scathing about alleged civilization.

[28] Hutter, "Dreams, Transformations, & Literature," 231.

[29] Tzvetan Todorov, "Typologie du roman policier," in *Poetique de la prose* (Paris: Editions du Seuil, 1971), 57.

dividing two races."[30] The image is revealing: when Upfield was writing, to begin to attempt to span the gulf was a big step forward; assimilation was still some way in the future. In her criticism of Upfield, Tamsin Donaldson declares that he "might be expected to have little appeal today", but goes on to admit, reluctantly, on a somewhat puzzled note, that, however, "the Bony novels appear to have a firm position in the Australian culture".[31]

The lasting popularity of these works might be explained at least in part by Upfield's undermining of those binary oppositions, and hinting that they no longer work. The simple formulaic detective narrative itself does not suggest any way of overcoming the entrenched polarities, but merely to show up their weaknesses in the decades when Upfield was writing was an achievement. The essential conflict is not only between crime and healing the pattern, but also, paradoxically, in the suggestion that, contrary to the normal structure of the detective story, in the wider context of the collective history, with the passing of the old generation, the present will need to go on searching for a different kind of healing.

First Published in *Antipodes* 13.1 (1999): 31-35. A shorter version of this article was presented at the University of Binghamton, New York, at the 1998 conference on "Re-Covering the Past."

---

[30] Upfield, *Murder Must Wait*, 175.
[31] Donaldson, "Australian Tales of Mystery and Miscegenation," 344.

UPFIELD'S NAPOLEON BONAPARTE: POST-COLONIAL DETECTIVE PROTOTYPE AS CULTURAL MEDIATOR

MARILYN RYE

Like his namesake, Inspector Napoleon Bonaparte conquers all who come before him; criminals, law-abiding white Australians, the official police bureaucracy, Aborigines of the Australian outback and all readers who follow his adventures. Named for a Frenchman, modeled on the fictional English detective Sherlock Holmes as well as a half-caste Aborigine tracker met in the outback, Upfield's detective functions on many levels as an argument for cultural integration. By creating a heroic detective who is a man of two races, half Aboriginal, half English, Upfield acknowledged that both races have much to contribute to Australian culture. But since Upfield himself was not a man of both races, he was not a truly neutral observer. Moreover, because he was writing in the traditional genre of detective fiction, Upfield ultimately placed a greater value on "reason," which becomes associated both with English culture and the detective tradition.

In his Inspector Napoleon Bonaparte series, written between 1929 and 1964, Arthur Upfield created an early prototype of the post-colonial detective. Although not a post-colonial subject, Upfield approached the task that indigenous writers would undertake as their society and literature transformed the cultural inheritance of the colonialist power. Upfield imagined a detective of mixed cultural background—born of an English father and an Aboriginal mother—who would struggle with the reconciliation of two cultures. Upfield's conception of this character came from his imagination, observation, and experience in the Australian outback, but not from a personal connection with the indigenous culture he described. As a white man his cultural inheritance came from England, where he was born. Therefore, his depiction of Aboriginal culture rested upon his observations as an informed outsider. In most cases, the sum of the anthropologically correct details and observations that Upfield wove into his story did not result in either a realistic or complete picture of

Aboriginal culture.[1] As an outsider, Upfield either idealized the Aborigines into a symbol of the superior state of man when unspoiled by a decadent white civilization or turned them into a symbol of the bestiality of man when unchecked by that same civilization. While Upfield's ambivalent attitudes did not recognize the reality of the Aborigine, by strange coincidence his ambivalence did produce a psychologically accurate portrait of the conflict often internalized by indigenous inhabitants coming to terms with the culture of the European colonizer. In his recognition of this conflict, his appreciation of the culture of the Aborigines, his concern for the historical consequences of the process of colonization in Australia, and his insistence that Australia should not define itself as an Anglo-White society, Upfield articulated many of the concerns pursued by post-colonial indigenous writers, including writers of detective fiction.

Unquestionably, the most decisive moment in both Upfield's and his character Napoleon Bonaparte's careers occurred when Upfield decided to rewrite the draft of his first novel *The Barrakee Mystery* (1929), changing the character of his detective from full-blooded white man into a man of Aborigine and English parentage. While it is easy to identify the repositioning of author in relation to his subject at this moment, the cause behind this repositioning is less easy to identify. Ray Browne, in his pioneer study of Upfield, attributes Upfield's decision to a "stroke of inspiration" and a desire to make the novels as Australian as possible.[2] Browne notes that Upfield actually knew a half-caste tracker named Tracker Leon and that after Upfield's second encounter with Tracker Leon, when they exchanged books, including Abbot's *Life of Napoleon Bonaparte,* Upfield radically reshaped his detective hero.[3] The incorporation of Tracker Leon's biography into Upfield's character's history suggests the accuracy of this account, as does Bonaparte's own explanation of his name. For Upfield's detective, familiarly called Bony, explains that he was named by the matron of a mission after she found him gnawing on Abbot's work.[4] Even agreeing with Browne's assessment of this moment as inspired, inspiration and the actual presence of Tracker Leon do not explain Upfield's decision to make this crucial choice. Rather, his decision reflects his own identification with the position of an outsider

---

[1] James Pierson, "Mystery Literature and Ethnography: Fictional Detectives as Anthropologists" in *Literature and Anthropology,* ed. Philip Dennis and Wendell Aycock (Lubbock: Texas University Press, 1989), 24.
[2] Ray Browne, *The Spirit of Australia: The Crime Fiction of Arthur W. Upfield* (Bowling Green, OH: Bowling Green State University Popular Press, 1988), 32.
[3] Browne, *The Spirit of Australia,* 32.
[4] Arthur Upfield. *The Sands of Windee* (New York: Scribner, 1983), 2.

and his realization that an outsider can play an important role as an observer and intermediary. His choice offers the key to understanding his interest in transforming his work from a simple mystery or adventure story into a more complicated discussion of the issues of race and class. A half-caste figure allowed Upfield to work out in terms of his characters' lives the more complex historical process he was interested in examining. Thus, as Browne notes, the novels became as Australian as possible, since they incorporated Australian landscape and characters. Even more importantly, they became Australian because in them Upfield recognized the particular historical meeting of the two races on the Australian continent and the important role this meeting would play in defining the Australian society of the future.

Upfield's radical choice of a figure who was an outsider to two cultures reflected the circumstances of his own life. In his novels, Upfield created a literary construct based on the materials at hand—in this case the tracker Leon—that represented his own sense of being an outsider. He transformed his personal experience into a means of understanding the process of cultural displacement. He was able to empathize with the position of an outcast of both societies because at an early age his English family had thrust this status upon him. While very young Upfield was sent to live with both sets of grandparents, although his brothers remained at home with his parents. He returned home for short visits only to be shipped out again.[5] This process of rejection culminated in Upfield's being sent to Australia at 22[6] because his father thought him nothing but trouble and believed "that [he] would never amount to any good". As Browne notes, this treatment was "an act of expulsion ... [that] must have cut deeply into ... [his] personality and left permanent scars," especially since lack of money would most likely make this a permanent exile.[7] Even in Australia, Upfield assumed the status of an outsider, since he was attracted to the fringes, the outback instead of the cities, and the disappearing older generation of pioneer homesteaders instead of the more "civilized" city dwellers. As a writer, Upfield again experienced the sense of being an outsider, since he never made it into the Australian literary elite. Although his critical reception can't explain his initial choice of an outsider as a

---

[5] Browne, *The Spirit of Australia*, 4.
[6] Ed.: It had been generally accepted that Upfield was born on 1 September 1888. A check of the records in England made about 25 years after his death revealed the year was 1890. Similarly, the record of his first arrival in Australia has also been checked and shows it was 4 November 1911. Upfield would have been about 21 when he left England.
[7] Browne, *The Spirit of Australia*, 5.

main character, his position outside the literary pale confirms the lifelong pattern of his experience. Thus Upfield's own history made him sensitive and aware of the presence of the Aborigines, also outsiders in Anglo-Australia. It helped him imagine the attraction and rejection a half-caste Australian might alternately feel when defining his relationship to both cultures. His detective is post-colonial in his ability to observe white society from the vantage point of a non-white character with indigenous blood and to use both of his cultural backgrounds in his detection.

Even though Upfield could not duplicate the experience of an indigenous subject, he went much further than most of his contemporaries in his recognition and appreciation of Aboriginal culture. In his novels he introduced that culture to his Anglo-Australian readers. Through his character of Bony, Upfield placed a value on Aboriginal culture that suggested Aborigines could no longer be conceived as exotic extensions of the landscape. Upfield placed a human value upon them and recognized the complexity and uniqueness of their culture. The stories he wrote focused attention on the indigenous culture in the same way that Bony's discussion of the culture often presented it to the Anglo-Australian characters in the novels. Upfield inscribed the process of cultural mediation in his text through the character of his detective and repeated this process in the relationship of text to reader. Through his presentation of a heroic man descending from two races, Upfield required that readers adopt the same attitude towards the Aboriginal race that the enlightened white characters in the novels adopted towards Bony. Bony's exploits convince readers as well that he is "[t]he man who had so often proved that aboriginal blood and brains were equal to those of the white man".[8] With this conclusion, Upfield invites a reversal of the assumption that Aborigines are inferior. And in his novels he gives many examples of the way Bony's Aboriginal heritage contributes to his superior talent.

In every novel Bony must explain his dual ancestry to some other character in the book, thus raising the question of the relationship between the two races. His initial impulse, especially when speaking to others, is to place an equal value on both races and to suggest that his background defines his function as a bridge between the races in Australia.

> I see a problem I've often come across ... the gulf between the mind of the white man and the mind of the Australian black man. As the mind of the Occidental differs widely from that of the Oriental, so differs as widely the minds of the Australian black tracker and the Australian white policeman. My birth and training fashion me into a bridge spanning the gulf between

---

[8] Arthur Upfield, *The Bone Is Pointed* (New York: Scribner, 1985), 30.

them.[9]

Bony often describes himself as a bridge between two cultures, although other narrative references sometimes use metaphors suggesting conflict to define the same relationship. When Bony describes himself as a bridge, he is emphasizing the way the superior qualities of each race combine in him to make him a superior detective. The circumstances of his birth allow him to state that "I have the white man's reasoning powers and the black man's eyesight and knowledge of the bush. The bush will give up its secrets to me."[10] Upfield's narrative often suggests that Bony stands midway between the races as a neutral judge who is "able to look dispassionately on the white man and the black ..."[11] While Bony ultimately abandons this neutrality, this position introduces an unusual toleration for non-Anglo culture.

Bony's Aboriginal inheritance gives him tracking skills, knowledge of the bush country, and an understanding of Aboriginal society. The traits inherited from his mother are all geared towards survival in a harsh landscape. Thus, as he turns his indigenous knowledge towards the solution of crime, his non-traditional methods make him a superior detective. As Bonaparte often stresses, his cases are not set in the traditional English library but in the outback where his superior tracking skills give him an advantage over the white policemen assigned to a difficult case.[12] Bony's knowledge of the Australian bush and its inhabitants allows him to read a landscape which would be illegible to a more traditional detective figure. For example, in *Man of Two Tribes* Bony uses a dead bushman's diary to locate the unknown spot where a missing person vanished. The dead man recorded the arrival of an airplane in a remote spot identifiable only through descriptions of the landscape. Bony recreates the man's path of nomadic wanderings, matching descriptive phrases from the diary with features of the actual landscape. As Bony reads both diary and landscape he demonstrates his bilingualism in the texts of both cultures and his superiority in interpreting both. The novels support Bony's contention that he can read the landscape like "a white man reads a newspaper".[13]

Every novel set in the outback demonstrates Bony's tracking skills through original and ingenious examples. Like Sherlock Holmes, Bony

---

[9] Arthur Upfield, *The Widows of Broome* (New York: Scribner), 1985, 93.

[10] Arthur Upfield, *Death of a Swagman* (New York, Scribner, 1984), 26.

[11] Arthur Upfield, *Wings above the Diamantina* (New York: Scribner, 122.

[12] Upfield, *The Sands of Windee*, 57.

[13] Upfield, *Wings above the Diamantina*, 122.

can recreate complete stories from shreds of evidence such as wool fibers or strands of silk. He can distinguish between the tracks of wild or partly civilized Aborigines. The value that Bonaparte attaches to the importance of this skill in his work becomes clear when he compliments a man he considers an equally successful tracker in a different environment. The highest praise Bony can offer for a superior sailor tracking a lost boat at sea is "you're a man after my own heart, for you can track as well at sea as I can track on land".[14] By demonstrating the value of Aboriginal survival skills, Upfield encourages his audiences to accept the fact of the Aborigine's superior talent and accomplishments.

Upfield also suggests that Bonaparte is a sign of Aboriginal presence and cultural duality in another way. Bonaparte does not dismiss the activities of Aborigines as senseless, as do many of the whites. Instead, he reads the Aborigines' messages to each other about events that have passed and considers their observations about white behavior. He shows a cultural logic behind their actions which has its equivalent in white society. As a man between two worlds, Bony must establish a connection to the ritualistic practices and ceremony of both worlds in order to establish relationships with the inhabitants of each. He partakes of tea with the white ranchers and policemen because he moves easily in that world of polite gestures and conversation. But when Bony needs to get information from Aborigines, he establishes his connection to them through the fact of his own Aboriginal blood and inheritance.

The novel *Sinister Stones* provides an excellent example of his ability to obtain and integrate knowledge from Aboriginal sources. First he confirms his connection to Aboriginal culture by removing his shirt, the covering of civilization, to let the Aborigines see the cicatrices and initiation marks that tie him to their culture and rituals. Clothed or unclothed, English or Aborigine, Bony's ability to be accepted in either culture marks his function as an intermediary. At the same time, for the reader, Bony is a sign of the presence of the Aboriginal figure in the Australian landscape and a predictor of the transformation of Australian society. While the Aborigines are busy marking the clan and status occupied by Bony, he reads them in reciprocal fashion: for him they are more than just features of the landscape as they would be for white settlers. Bony credits them with intelligence. Because he takes their actions seriously, Bony pays attention to messages sent in their "smokes," believes in mental telepathy, and in the mental powers possessed by many tribesmen. Upfield weaves these beliefs into his plots, validating them by making the mysteries' solutions rest upon events that cannot always be

---

[14] Arthur Upfield, *The Mystery of Swordfish Reef* (New York: Scribner, 1985), 90.

explained within the logical solutions of western rationalism.

Two novels particularly lend credence to the value of Aborigine beliefs in arriving at knowledge as they educate readers in some approximation of Aboriginal life. In *Sinister Stones*, Bony concludes that a horse is somehow connected with a murdered man's body, even though he can't give a rational explanation to support his conclusion. Instead, his belief rests upon his interpretation of smoke signals he has watched send messages across the landscape. Although no witnesses observed the murder and no one has found the body, the natives have used mental telepathy to establish that murder was committed. Bony accepts the messages as factual. Bony also believes the Aboriginal system of justice equal to the white man's since both indict the same man. Although he can't read the markings made by Aboriginal medicine men, he believes that the Aboriginal ritual will identify the stone with the murderer's name on it. And in fact, the narrative establishes that the supernatural ritual of the Aborigines and Bony's logical reasoning lead to the identification of the same man as murderer. The narrative adds weight to the Aboriginal presence by respecting the Aboriginal belief system and equating the effectiveness of Aboriginal and Australian justice.

In *The Bushman Who Came Back*, Bonaparte also credits the Aborigines with extraordinary telepathic powers and participates in the process of gaining knowledge through telepathy. In this novel, Bony approaches a gathering of local Aborigines to gather information about the "spirit" dolls belonging to a missing child. Bony's knowledge of Aboriginal legends allows him to hear the Aboriginal flute, the didjeridoo, "tell" the legends and gain a description of the scene of a crime. When Bony leaves the camp, he has a clear mental picture of the body of a local woman who has been murdered. No one has described the scene to him, so his vision of this woman with a wound like a question mark on her back has only been conveyed through the music of the old and blind tribal chief, Canute. Bony uses this information, as well as his observation of Aboriginal behavior in the case, to solve the crime.

Furthermore, Upfield invites the reader to reread Australian history from a point of view sympathetic to the Aborigines. By invoking the history of colonization, its effect on the unspoiled earlier civilization, and the unfavorable position of the Aborigine in a modern Australia that devalues and destroys their culture, Bony's speeches again raise the issue of the colonists' treatment of the Aborigines. Upfield's detective, who evaluates the Aboriginal culture in a positive way, blames the destruction of that culture on white civilization. In *The Bone Is Pointed*, for example, a novel which highlights the problem of the destruction of the Aboriginal way of life, Bony's response to a request to identify himself as Aboriginal or Australian indicates his pride in his Aboriginal ancestry. He replies, "I am Australian, at least on my mother's side, It is better to be half Australian than not Australian at all."[15] His words suggest the white Australian is the outsider. In addition to defining Australian in an original way, he expresses his pride in belonging to a race that has achieved a higher state of civilization.

"There is a very great number of people who regard the Australian aboriginal as standing on the lowest rung of the human ladder. Because they have found no traces of a previous aboriginal civilization, no settlement, no building, no industry, they say that he always has been a man of a very low type. Yet, for all that, he has possessed for many centuries that which the white race is constantly trying to obtain ... Contented Happiness ... Yet the blackfellow possessed cultures when the white man ate raw flesh."[16]

In *The Bone Is Pointed*, Bony admires the Gordons, who have tried to protect "their" Aborigines from the devastating effects of western civilization which would disrupt their culture. Like Bony himself, this family acts as a mediator to shield the Aborigines from the outside world, although not the influences of westernization. For Upfield and Bony, the worst effect of the westernization process seems to be the power of money to disrupt the native economy and turn the Aborigines from independent tribesmen living in nature to dependent hangers-on in western settlements. Bony approves of the Gordons because they have managed to keep the Aborigines around them free from state control and help them manage their money. Putting money in the bank for the tribe as a whole keeps the individuals of the tribe from direct contact with currency; thus, their values are not corrupted. They do not develop the meaner traits of whites but can remain proud and generous. Upfield uses Bony's values to criticize capitalism more than contact with western civilization. Mrs Gordon argues that her family helps the tribesmen who continue to practice "the Christian Socialism ... [they] practised centuries before Christ was born".[17] Thus, the Gordons can only understand the Aborigines by viewing them in terms of known European culture; they cannot step outside their culture to appreciate the Aboriginal society. As Bony's reactions frequently reveal the same context of evaluation, his approval of the Gordons' attitudes is not surprising. Through their interventions, the Gordons help the Kalchut

---

[15] Upfield, *The Bone Is Pointed*, 16.
[16] Upfield, *The Sands of Windee*, 99.
[17] Upfield, *The Bone Is Pointed*, 19.

avoid the fate of other tribes. Upfield places a very impassioned defense of the Aborigines and a sharp critique of their conditions into the mouth of Mary Gordon, whom Bony admires. Her address really raises the issue of the Aborigines' place for white readers, although it is addressed to Bony in the novel.

> And now the shadow of civilization falls upon them although they don't know it. Civilization comes to shoot them down, to poison them like old dogs, and then, to excuse itself, to depict the victims of its curse as half-wits in its comic papers, to sneer at them as naked savages, to confine them to reserves and compounds. It has taken away their natural food and feeds them on poison in tins labeled "food".[18]

Obviously, Bony would know all of this history. But explaining it to him serves to validate Mrs Gordon as a character who avoids the prejudice at large in Australian society. In her speech she simultaneously addresses Bonaparte and the white Australian reader, thus suggesting an equation between the two. Like many characters, she ultimately accepts Bony as a member of her class and society. Bony often casts himself in a similar role to Mrs Gordon's because he takes on the responsibility of explaining the Aborigines to white men. Thus he aligns himself with the liberal whites who recognize the fact of Aboriginal culture, who demonstrate positive attitudes towards it, but who can only see it existing within the framework of the Anglo-Australian value structure.

Bonaparte's distance from his Aboriginal heritage and his closer identification with his English heritage appears in the early novels when he credits success to his ability to improve Aboriginal skills by applying his English inheritance of logic to them. At one point he explains that "my aborigine mentors found me a good student because I inherited the white man's ability to reason more clearly and more quickly than they".[19] His use of a framework of western culture appears also in his viewing Aborigine culture through the eyes of the settlers' descendants. As the narrative often makes clear, he distances himself from the Aborigines when discussing them. In the following example, Bonaparte's use of the pronoun "we" suggests he is aligning himself with the white policeman listening to his explanation.

> "They're full of knowledge and helpful in their own country and are nervous and suspicious when away from it. We feed them and clothe them, and we bring them to understand enough of our language to communicate.

---

[18] Upfield, *The Bone Is Pointed*, 119.
[19] Upfield, *The Bone Is Pointed*, 104.

They smoke our tobacco and ride our horses; many of them drive our cars and trucks and are able to repair wind mills and pumps. Nevertheless, they retain their tribal customs."[20]

In *The Bone Is Pointed*, both Bony and the Gordons recognize the power of Aboriginal customs, but they regard some of them in a negative light. The Gordons forbid certain traditional practices, like "pointing the bone". They are afraid of the political ramifications of this practice, which causes death through symbolic magic and mind control. They know the culture can exist only if it does not pose a threat to the Australian sense of law and order with its belief in a rational process of justice. When the bone is pointed at Bony he almost dies because his Aboriginal blood makes him susceptible to Aboriginal ceremonies. Symbolically, when Bonaparte's maternal heritage takes control over his logical western mind, he becomes susceptible to terror and is almost extinguished as a logical thinking human being. Bonaparte sees his destruction in the possibility of the failure of his reason, whether manifested in an inability to solve any case or an inability to exercise his reason against the power of the primitive physical world of Aboriginal power. His reaction to the boning is to resolve that

[h]e would fight it with all the strength of his mind, and again he would triumph over his aboriginal ancestry as he had so often done before. ... Was he a savage? Was he an ignorant nomad of the bush?[21]

Even though the Aborigines in this book are not assimilated, Upfield's novel diffuses any perceived threat caused by their presence. He presents them as loyal to white benefactors. John Gordon and Jimmy Partner, his Aboriginal foster brother, have a strong mutual allegiance; their loyalty in the face of a racist white man precipitates his murder. Jimmy kills the white man who is torturing his foster brother, John, because John stands up for Aborigines. The protection of the Aborigines is repaid by their loyalty, since the tribe points the bone at Bony out of loyalty towards the Gordons.

One of the most interesting features of Upfield's attitude towards Aborigines is his reassuring message that they can accommodate their presence to white Australian society. Upfield's works validate Aboriginal culture, present it to the inspection of Anglo-Australians, and defuse the idea that it could prove threatening to the established order. *The Bone Is Pointed*, like many other novels in this series, helps familiarize white

---

[20] Arthur Upfield, *Sinister Stones* (New York: Scribner, 1983), 84.
[21] Upfield, *The Bone Is Pointed*, 140.

Australians with the culture of the "other," while at the same time reassuring them that the indigenous race will not challenge their basic assumptions about themselves. Partner's loyalty to Gordon is paradigmatic of Bony's relationship to the state he serves. Bony's whole identity is tied up in his service to the white police force, dependent upon its recognition of him as superior, and rests on his belief that his superiority includes an ability to be more civilized than those who accept him. He may praise his Aboriginal heritage, but his psychological identification is clearly with the white society that hires him to protect it from the criminals who violate the tenets of a stable social order. Bony's identification with whites eventually causes him to devalue Aborigines and the part of himself that is Aborigine, an attitude that reflects Upfield's probably ambivalent feelings about Aboriginal culture. Even while admiring it, his identity as a white man may have led him to hold unconscious assumptions about the superiority of white culture. Yet even Upfield's recreation of his own ambivalence in Bony's ambivalent attitude comes across less as racist than an accurate picture of the ambivalence of an educated native who has been raised to accept English culture as superior.

Upfield creates a very credible past for his character that explains Bony's deepest urges to identify with English culture, the culture of his father. Like many post-colonial detectives, Bony has a love-hate relationship with the West. Bony, who resembles other indigenous people educated by colonialists, identifies more closely with the culture that educates him. Upfield writes that after his mother's tribesmen killed her and abandoned him, Bony was rescued and raised at a mission school, where his intelligence and coloring won him a superior status. In *The Sands of Windee*, Bony gives a remarkable insight into his earliest and enduring identification with English culture as he confides his view of his experience:

> He had been born with the white man's blood in him and as is sometimes the case, a skin as white as his father's. From an early age he had felt his superiority over the other little boys at the mission station, most of whom were black, or of that dark putty color there is no mistaking. At eighteen years ... [w]ith the inevitability of fate his long-dead black mother claimed him from the grave, claimed him and held him. He was bathing with several companions ... and one remarked how peculiar it was that his legs were darker in colour than the upper part of his body. The horror, the agony, the knowledge that, after all, when he had been so certain that the black strain would never show, it was at last asserting itself. [22]

Like many post-colonials Bony has been educated into accepting English

---

[22] Upfield, *The Sands of Windee*, 174.

values as superior. He has no understanding of his Aboriginal heritage until later, when an uncontrollable instinct surges in his blood and draws him back to the bush and his mother's tribe. But his Aboriginal blood cannot keep him there because he needs to return to "civilization" to reaffirm that he still remains superior and is accepted as such.

Bony's defining characteristic is his sense of superiority, first over blacks, then over blacks and whites. Yet instead of bolstering the assumption that Bony is ideologically neutral, his sense of superiority betrays the idea that both cultures carry the same weight. His accomplishment of having reached the apex of a hierarchy where Aborigines are on the bottom and whites higher up gives him a sense of superiority. Bony has no illusions about how he holds his place in this society. He dryly comments that "In this country colour is no bar to a keen man's progress, providing that he has twice the ability of his rivals."[23] His dress, his intellect, his attitudes towards his colleagues, and his perfect record of solving crimes (if not handing over the murderer) impress the fact of his superiority on those around him.

In short, Bony provides his white colleagues with a model of accomplishment they can imitate but not achieve. The policemen who work under him idealize him for his accomplishments and for his refusal to pull rank. Repeatedly Bony insists that they call him by his first name, a privilege he grants to his friends. When Bony finds a worthy but unappreciated colleague like Sergeant Telfer in *The Mystery of Swordfish Reef*, he gives him the credit for the arrest and arranges his promotion. Bony's behavior suggests that an Aborigine would not be a threat to the advancement of the white man. Instead, Bony serves his colleagues and the state and makes the system of criminal justice run more efficiently.

> Unlike many of his fellow members of the C.I.B., Bonaparte did not adopt an attitude of lofty superiority towards uniformed men. Consequently, he never failed to get their generous support and cooperation.[24]

Bony thus acquires an unthreatening moral superiority.

The clothes that identify Bony as a member of white Australian society also are a visible mark of his superiority, his membership in an elite class of natural aristocracy. When not disguised as a horsebreaker or derelict, Bony's appearance differs sharply from that of his colleagues, and he is proud that he doesn't look like a police inspector. While on occasion, often a private occasion, Bony dresses with a sartorial splendor that overwhelms

---

[23] Upfield, *The Bone Is Pointed*, 52.
[24] Upfield, *The Mystery of Swordfish Reef*, 68.

his colleagues, his public appearance suggests a more elegant and restrained taste. He is even perceived as princely by one observer in Bermagui where he adopts the cover of a rich man who has come to pursue swordfish. This inhabitant, Blade, "experienc[ed an] awe of this visitor ... who was so immaculate, so easy in his manner, and still so unusual. He was not unlike an Indian Prince."[25] Bony has a wardrobe of light gray tweeds with matching shirts, ties, and hats, white canvas shoes, creased drill pants, and silk shirts. In private he is flamboyant, as if his most private apparel expresses the flair of his inner thought processes. Neither colleague nor reader will forget Bony's elegant yellow and green silk pyjamas or his dressing gown of "pastel blue with yellow collar and cuffs and a large bright red pocket".[26]

Bony is an intellectual dandy as well, whose university education has helped him develop a superior intellect that few whites can match. Indeed, those same settlers' descendants who might consider the Aborigines uneducated and illiterate demonstrate their intellectual poverty when compared to Bony's. In *The Sands of Windee*, when Bonaparte borrows works by Virgil and Marcus Aurelius from a local priest, his Sergeant wants to know "Who the devil are they?" Bony replies, "They are, I think, strangers in Mount Lion."[27]

As Bonaparte's experience demonstrates, the process of adapting to the colonialists' culture, particularly as that adaptation is accomplished through education, makes neutral attitudes towards an inhabitant's indigenous culture almost impossible. Bony is not exposed to his maternal culture until after his university education, and by then, western values are embedded in Bonaparte's mind. Bony recalls that at 22,

> "my body craved for complete freedom from the white man's clothes. I wanted to go ahunting as my mother's father had hunted, and I wanted to eat flesh, raw flesh, and feast on tree grubs ... this is what I wanted to do; but reason, the trained white man's reason, caused me to behave a little less primitively, and in the end, the white and the black blood in me called a truce."[28]

Upfield's melodramatic statement implies that culture is grounded in genetics as well as education. Because Bony's craving for these foods probably causes most readers to shudder, they most likely would applaud the reason that restrains Bonaparte's initial "primitive" responses. But in

---

[25] Upfield, *The Mystery of Swordfish Reef*, 45.
[26] Upfield, *Sinister Stones*, 212, 214.
[27] Upfield, *The Sands of Windee*, 118.
[28] Upfield, *The Sands of Windee*, 65.

reality, as the novels consistently show, because no truce exists, the narratives demonstrate that Bonaparte usually resolves the inner conflict in favor of his white, patriarchal, and logical inheritance. While Bonaparte is willing to learn a great deal from his tribe's medicine man, Illawalli, Bony refuses the conditions attached for learning the secrets of more mysterious powers: acceptance of a leadership position as Illawalli's heir. Instead, Bony prefers his position as a police inspector to leadership and power in the tribe.[29] When forced to choose, he ultimately rejects his maternal, Aboriginal inheritance that so closely connects him to the physical world. This division and preference is clear in the observation about Bonaparte's dual heritage:

> From his white father Bony had inherited the precious gift of reason, and from his mother the equally precious gift of patience. Reason and patience, developed by an undying passion for knowledge, produced in this half-caste a force for good seldom found among the white races and almost never among.[30]

Whenever Bony abandons this "reason" or behavior perceived as reasonable, he feels intense shame at the stripping away of the trappings of civilization and its accompanying forces for good. Two incidents occur in *The Mystery of Swordfish Reef* that demonstrate how lack of reason becomes identified with dangerous and beastly behavior. The imagery in Upfield's description of Bonaparte at these moments suggests his character's "bestial" and "savage" nature. In the first incident, when Bony is attacked and beaten up by two henchmen of the arch-villain, the intense anger which darkens his appearance and distorts his features transforms him from light to dark, from human to animal.

> The heat in his brain had become too fierce for longer control, and abruptly his mother's blood took charge of him, made him one with her and her people. ... Bony's face had become jet-black in color, his eyes glaring blue orbs set in seas of white, while his teeth reflected the light like the fangs of a young dog. ... Never before in his life had his aboriginal instincts so controlled Napoleon Bonaparte to the exclusion of that complex part of him inherited from his father on which was based so magnificent a pride. Reason had fled before the primitive lust to destroy.[31]

A later scene in this novel confirms the extent to which rage transforms

---

[29] Upfield, *The Sands of Windee*, 107.

[30] Arthur Upfield, *Murder Down Under* (New York: Scribner, 1983), 68.

[31] Upfield, *The Mystery of Swordfish Reef*, 204-205.

Bonaparte from reasonable man to animal. In a second scene, he goes berserk. While in some novels, like *The Will of the Tribe*, Upfield invests the shedding of clothes with a positive connotation of reversion to an uncorrupted past, here the shedding of clothing is equated with a complete reversion to a savage state. Surrendering to his anger, Bony becomes unrecognizable, at least as a civilized counterpart to the white citizens and fellow policemen:

> His general appearance was the antithesis of that ... known to his colleagues. The veneer of civilization, so thin in the most gently nurtured of us, was entirely absent. He was wearing nothing ... His hair was matted with blood. ... His lips were widely parted, revealing his teeth like the fangs of a young dog.[32]

In the final analysis, neither Upfield nor Bonaparte successfully reconcile their attitudes towards the hero's position between two different cultures. Although later indigenous detectives might place more value on the native culture of their birth, Bonaparte remains trapped between an ideal of unspoiled Aboriginal culture and the white culture that judges that culture as inferior. His inability to resolve his dilemma, especially in view of the destruction of Aborigine culture due to the process of white settlement, reflects Upfield's inability to imagine how these two cultures could exist harmoniously in a modern Australian state. The detective figure Upfield created is very much an Australian version of the "noble savage," domesticating the terror of the unknown with the criticism of the known. The idea of the unspoiled savage, living in an Edenic and pre-civilized state, has always functioned as a model of noble behavior that "showed civilized men [what] they were not and must not be".[33] Bonaparte is "noble" and "savage" simultaneously. He presents the ideal of the unspoiled Aborigine whose best characteristics should serve as a model for white behavior. Upfield suggests that this most civilized behavior confirms civilized man's ability to extricate himself from the worst aspects of his civilization and from brute nature.

The conventions of detective fiction provide the only possible means of reconciling the opposing halves of Bonaparte's personality. This reconciliation suggests a plan along which the two halves of Australian society can also be reconciled. As a detective, Bonaparte must identify with the highest moral order. Because of his dual heritage, he faces the

---

[32] Upfield, *The Mystery of Swordfish Reef*, 241-242.
[33] Roy Pearce, *Savagism & Civilization: A Study of the Indian & the American Mind* (Berkeley and Los Angeles: University of California Press, 1988), 5.

difficult task of locating the moral order in one of two cultures—in the uncorrupted Aboriginal past which no longer exists or in Anglo-Australian society which is marred by its racism. Less by coincidence than design, in Upfield's novels the worst villains are often racist and the virtuous people arc whites who accept and appreciate Bonaparte's superiority. Significantly, in *Murder Down Under*, Mrs Loftus, who has murdered her husband and hidden his body under a haystack, will not invite a thirsty Bony in for tea, but sends him back to the well. However, both the descendants of heroic white settlers and his white colleagues treat Bony as an equal or their superior, inviting him into their homes and serving him at their tables. His own superior in the police hierarchy, Colonel Spender, values Bony the most and is most important in establishing Bony's sense of his own worth and his self-esteem. Bonaparte both internalizes Spender's voice, mimicking his comments on Bonaparte's behavior, and is ecstatic when Spender personally comes to retrieve him from a death by boning.[34]

Upfield uses his character of Bonaparte to posit an ideal for Australian society. If Bonaparte can win the recognition and respect of the Anglo-Australian society for Aboriginal culture, he can give his allegiance to a progressive Australian society. Upfield obviously hopes to win the reader's acceptance as well. Since Bonaparte identifies closely with the legal and moral order of the Australian state, and less closely with his maternal heritage, he is not in the strictest sense of the word a "mediator". While he often explains Aboriginal culture to white Australians, he does not function in the reverse fashion to explain white society to the Aborigines except in terms of attributing his own superior authority to his position in white society. But in terms of Upfield's narrative construction of character, Bonaparte mediates between white Australian society and Aboriginal culture. He demands that white readers recognize the existence of Aboriginal culture by so presenting it in his text.

In his heroic figure of Napoleon Bonaparte, Upfield has created a character who is a sign of Aboriginal presence, if not an accurate representation of its reality. In every novel Upfield raises the issue of race and the need to consider the relation between the two cultures of the Australian continent. Because Upfield does not deal in realities but poses a primitive and unspoiled state against a modern and imperfect one, he leaves his detective little choice but to throw in with modern westernized society. What detective could choose to live in a condition of harmony which excludes the possibility of an interesting crime? The lack of a good crime to solve drove Sherlock Holmes to cocaine. Offered a similar choice, Bonaparte also prefers a world where the existence of crime

---

[34] Upfield, *The Bone Is Pointed*, 97, 270.

provides an interesting puzzle. As he says in *The Bone Is Pointed*,

> Just think if the world were as pure and life as simple as it was in Australia before ever Dampier saw it. Ah, but then, I should not have been happy. I suppose. There was no crime higher than the elementary crime of stealing your neighbour's wife. No, no! After all, I think I prefer the shadow in which crime and bestiality thrives.[35]

Rather than judge Upfield's work according to his ability to present an accurate and neutral depiction of Aboriginal culture, we can look at it in terms of what Genette describes as "the history of literary function".[36] Upfield's novels function, as they make us aware, is to reshape the society they describe. Upfield's novels foreshadow the work of later indigenous writers because Upfield struggles against the simplistic and naive attitudes the writer Chinua Achebe felt the Europeans always brought with them. In an interview with J.O.J. Nwachukwu-Agbada, Achebe decried the limited vision of the whites. His criticism pointed out that

> the white man comes, claiming to be the way, the light, the truth: nothing works except him. Now this kind of thinking, this kind of simplicity and self-righteousness ... is dangerous because it is one of the basic causes of distress to mankind today.[37]

The inspired creation of Inspector Napoleon Bonaparte proves that Upfield valued the cultures of both the colonizer and the colonized. Upfield wrote to lessen the distress to mankind.

First Published in *The Post-Colonial Detective*, edited by Ed Christian, 55-72. Basingstoke, UK: Palgrave, 2001. Reprinted with permission of Palgrave Macmillan.

---

[35] Upfield, *The Bone Is Pointed*, 120.

[36] Gérard Genette, *Narrator Discourse: An Essay in Method*, trans. Jane E. Lewin (Ithaca, NY: Cornell University Press, 1980), 76.

[37] J.O.J. Nwachukwa-Agbada, "Interview with Chinua Achebe," *Massachusetts Review*, 28.2 (Summer 1987): 282.

UNCOVERING COLLECTIVE CRIMES: SALLY MORGAN'S *MY PLACE* AS AUSTRALIAN INDIGENOUS DETECTIVE NARRATIVE

RUSSELL WEST

Two men are discovered dead, the bodies eighteen miles apart, on a remote sheep station in drought-stricken outback Australia. The murders have no obvious motivation, and no trace is to be found of their perpetrator. Unable to make any headway with their investigations, the police lay the case to rest until, six months later, the part-Aboriginal detective inspector Napoleon Bonaparte, the protagonist of Arthur Upfield's novel *Bony and the Black Virgin*, is called in to reopen the proceedings. Inspector Bony, of course, successfully solves the mystery of the double murder. It is the hero's skill in "reading the Book of the Bush," a motif frequently mentioned in the story, that marks him out from other investigators and makes him the supersleuth that he is. The indigenous people's traditional ability to read the minute details of the land, the marks left by weather, animals, and human beings, constitutes Bony's uncanny powers of detection:

> A small problem unworthy of a white man's attention! ... Meticulous attention to detail, unlimited patience, and unbounded curiosity received their reward from the ancient Spirit of the Land who had tested him. ... History was written on this page of the Book of the Bush.[1]

But we should note that this is a white writer speaking—the English-born detective novelist Upfield drew upon his experience of working on remote cattle stations in Australia to craft his tales. It is instructive to contrast Upfield's ventriloquism of the black speaker with the chiding tones of a contemporary Aboriginal storyteller in a volume significantly entitled *Reading the Country*: "You people try and dig little bit more deep—you bin digging only white soil—try and find the black soil inside

---

[1] Arthur Upfield, *Bony and the Black Virgin* (London: Pan Books, 1984), 76.

..."[2] If Upfield's tale purports to describe a detective who brushes away the layers of outback dust to reveal the traces of a crime, the indigenous storyteller of today would appear to be implying that the white man is not genuinely interested in, nor indeed capable of, uncovering the past and its secrets.

In this essay I would like to examine two antipodean variations of the detective narrative, first taking a brief look at this novel by the white Australian writer Upfield, and then moving on to a more sustained reading of an autobiography by the black Australian Sally Morgan, *My Place*.[3] Common to the two texts is the capacity of the indigenous investigator to read Australian history for traces of crimes hidden by the passage of time. The order in which I will examine these two texts does not indicate an implicit cultural hierarchy, but follows a historical development: for the best part of the two centuries after the white occupation of Australia in 1788, white writers described the indigenous peoples whose land they had seized; in the 1970s, however, Aboriginal literary voices became more strident and replaced those which had previously determined their representation in white Australia.[4] Upfield's text figures here as a foil to highlight the full radicalism, but also the limitations, of Morgan's investigative project.

The West Australian writer and artist Sally Morgan published her family autobiography, *My Place*, in 1987. Since then her text has been hugely successful, selling over half a million copies in Australia, as well as abroad under the London Virago imprint, with seven reprints to date. For a small country with a population of nineteen million, a traditional antipathy toward high cultural forms, and an ongoing tradition of racism, sales of this quantity are quite remarkable, all the more so in that indigenous literature does not usually belong on the best-seller lists. Part of the reason for this success is perhaps that *My Place* speaks about a currently much debated aspect of recent Australian history: that of the "Stolen Generation", a term coined to refer to the Aboriginal children forcibly removed from their parents under white government policy until the mid-1970s.

In 1997, "Bringing Them Home", the Australian government report of a national inquiry into the separation of Aboriginal and Torres Strait Islander children from their families, concluded that between one in three

---

[2] Paddy Roe, in *Reading the Country: Introduction to Nomadology*, ed. Krim Benterrak et al (Fremantle, W.Aust.: Fremantle Arts Centre Press, 1984), 168.

[3] Sally Morgan, *My Place* (Fremantle, W.Aust.: Fremantle Arts Centre Press, 1987).

[4] J. Healy, *Literature and the Aboriginal in Australia* (St. Lucia: University of Queensland Press, 1989), xx–xxi.

and one in ten indigenous children were forcibly removed from their parents and communities in the period from approximately 1910 until 1970. The children were raised in institutions or given to adoptive families, were often subjected to sexual abuse and racial discrimination, and frequently lost contact with their biological parents. Most indigenous families have been affected, in one or more generations, by the forcible removal of one or more children. The long-term psychic trauma and social as well as familial disintegration caused by these government policies are immeasurable, but the report provides hundreds of individual testimonies to the pain and discrimination experienced by indigenous children and their families in the name of "enlightened" state intervention. The aim of this policy was ostensibly to provide better living conditions for children than in a shattered indigenous society, but it effectively drove a wedge, on the one hand, between "full-blood" Aboriginals, segregated out of sight in conditions of poverty on reserves and marginal settlements, and "half-castes" who were to be assimilated into white society; and, on the other hand, between older and younger generations, so that the linguistic heritage and traditional knowledge of the indigenous peoples was rapidly lost. The policy also aimed to break up a potential block of collective Aboriginal protest by vitiating the cohesion of Aboriginal society. The policy of forced removal needs to be seen in the larger context of the European invasion of Australia and the expulsion of the indigenous people from their lands: the later policy effectively perpetuated the process of cultural destruction initiated by the expropriation of land (the land was the basis for—indeed, the embodiment of—the economic, social, cultural, and religious structures of traditional Aboriginal society, and its reappropriation remains central in Aboriginal activism against all forms of white discrimination). I shall refer consistently to these practices as a form of collective crime, for though child removal was ratified by government legislation, this very legislation deprived indigenous Australians of their most basic human rights on the basis of skin color until into the late 1960s—from the right of free movement, to the right of a minimum standard of living; from the right to sexual and marital self-determination and the exercise of parental responsibility, to the right to legal appeal against such legislation.[5] The crime mystery scrutinized in this essay is that of the darker side of white Australia's history and could be placed under the sign of the story-teller Paddy Roe's injunction: "You people try and dig little bit more deep—you bin digging only white soil—try and find

---

[5] C.D. Rowley, *The Destruction of Aboriginal Society* (Ringwood, Victoria: Penguin, 1972), 183-184.

the black soil inside ..."[6]

Upfield draws upon such commonplaces of Aboriginal culture to create a new sort of detective. By appropriating this aspect of the indigenous people's intimate knowledge of their country, he secured a lucrative place on the detective fiction market, of which the frequent reprints and worldwide translations of the Bony novels are a clear indicator. But it is important that Bony is not merely one of the Aboriginal trackers—blacks co-opted by the white police in colonial Australia for their superior bush knowledge and their skill at finding the traces of criminals on the run, of which the novel makes mention during the preliminary episodes.[7] Bony is a "half-caste" Aboriginal and thus differentiated from the "real" Aboriginal whose skills are used by the white police without them being of any interest to the narrative. Rather, it is Bony's partly white identity (accentuated by a markedly English touch betraying the author's compensatory need to justify the choice of his protagonist[8]) that allows him also to belong to the upper echelons of the white Australian police force. He thereby takes on a mediatory role of discoverer in the narrative process that the text is at pains to underline:

> "History was written on this page of the Book of the Bush. ... It was not unlike trying to read a serial story backwards from the instalment one picks up by chance."[9]

This, of course, as Tzvetan Todorov points out, is the narrative role of the detective or the concomitant narrator in the crime narrative. In his work on the detective narrative, Todorov adapts the Russian formalist concepts of "story line" (*fabula*), meaning the chronological sequence of events forming the basis of the narrative, and the "plot" (*sujet*), signifying the reconfiguration of the story line within and through the event of narration.[10] In Todorav's formulation, the initially obscure series of events resulting in the crime corresponds to the "story line" (*fabula*), and the narrative process of their elucidation is coeval with the "plot" (*sujet*).[11] The detective mediates between the reader and the original course of

[6] Paddy Roe, *Reading the Country*, 168.

[7] Upfield, *Bony and the Black Virgin*, 41.

[8] Beryl Langer, "The Real Thing: Cliff Hardy and Cocacola-Nisation," *SPAN* 31 (1991): 41.

[9] Upfield, *Bony and the Black Virgin*, 76.

[10] Viktor, Shklovsky, *Theory of Prose (1925/1929)*, trans. Benjamin Sher (Elmswood Park, Illinois: Dalkey Archive Press, 1990), 176.

[11] Tzvetan Todorov, "Typologie du roman policier," in *Poétique de la prose suivi de Nouvelles recherches sur le récit* (Paris: Editions du Seuil, 1980), 12-13.

events, working back from the crime as a culminating point in what can be compared to the *fabula*-function, so as to reconstruct the prehistory of the crime in *sujet*-process in which the reader is called to participate. Bony as a reader of the bush partakes both in indigenous knowledge of the land and, at the same time, in the fragmentary, accumulating knowledge of the perplexed white reader. He is a mediator between two cultures of reading—one black, one white.

Where Upfield himself stands, as a white with considerable knowledge of black culture, is difficult to say. He makes some gestures toward advocacy for the indigenous people, commenting that "much money is spent on [the Aborigines'] education—and barriers erected to prevent them benefiting from it",[12] or deftly reveals the psychological mechanisms of racism:

> "So many people fail to see the Aborigines for what they are. To regard them as uncouth savages is such a boost for the ego, and yet, search as you might, you won't find a moron among them."[13]

Yet at the same time, the reader is confronted with repeated comments that indicate some sort of deeply ingrained and unreflected prejudice, when, for example, we are repeatedly told that "for an Aborigine, she [Lottee, the main indigenous character] was good-looking"[14]—as if Caucasian criteria of physiognomic beauty are held to be a universally valid norm shared by writer and readers, to the exclusion of the indigenous people. The ambiguities of Upfield's position are perhaps understandable. *Bony and the Black Virgin* was published in 1959, less than a decade before the white Australian people voted in a referendum to grant the indigenous population Australian citizenship in 1967. Yet it is worthwhile also bearing in mind that in 1958, the Western Australian Commissioner of Police could publicly justify the use of neck-chains to restrain indigenous prisoners, and that less than two decades had passed since the last paramilitary punitive expeditions were sent out against Aboriginals.[15]

I would argue that Upfield's detective novel is very much a product of its time, partly expressing outrage at the condition of the indigenous people in an era that would see the first moves toward granting them basic civil rights, and partly a bearer of ongoing attitudes denigrating the original inhabitants of the fifth continent. It is particularly with regard to

---

[12] Upfield, *Bony and the Black Virgin*, 107.
[13] Upfield, *Bony and the Black Virgin*, 124.
[14] Upfield, *Bony and the Black Virgin*, 122.
[15] Rowley, *The Destruction of Aboriginal Society*, 199, 204.

Bony's own cultural status that the novel operates with a strange sort of double vision made up of insight and wilful blindness combined. Bony says he was found as a child beside his dead mother, who had ostensibly been killed for giving birth to him. The boy was raised on a mission, thus excluding him from full knowledge of traditional Aboriginal culture.[16] Here the novel gestures toward a broader practice of removal of "half-caste" children maintained by the Australian government for three-quarters of the twentieth century. This practice was facilitated by the frequent refusal of the white fathers to acknowledge paternity (together with the absence of black mothers' legal rights to half-caste children). Such paternal disavowal is projected by Bony onto the main suspect for the double murder, Eric Downer: Bony hypothesizes that Eric killed the two victims in order to prevent them from publicizing his surreptitious Aboriginal marriage with Lottee, a marriage that his white man's shame does not allow him to admit to friends and family.[17]

Yet it is the spirit of the Aboriginal mother, we are told, who endows Bony with an acute sense of the limits of his intuitive capacity to read the land and unravel the most difficult of conundrums.[18] And it is Bony's nostalgic attentiveness to Lottee's voice, an avatar of "the mother voice he had never known and always longed to hear",[19] as the embodiment of a lost narrative of black-white sexual liaison, which leads him to give epistemological weight to Lottee's alternative account of the murders, thus modifying his original supposition. In the final denouement, we learn that Lottee was raped by a white man after her secret marriage to Eric and killed her rapist and a second white man who subsequently threatened her with rape; Eric was merely instrumental in disposing of the bodies.[20] Moreover, as the title of the novel indicates, the secret marriage does not culminate in sexual union, thus foreclosing the question of "half-caste" children.

In this way, an ostensibly more complex reason than mere racist shame at the sexual entanglement of white man and black woman is given as the motivation for the murders. Both of these issues had literary predecessors, for instance in Xavier Herbert's *Capricornia* (1937).[21] And the massive exploitation of Aboriginal women by white men has a long history, which

---

[16] Upfield, *Bony and the Black Virgin*, 66.
[17] Upfield, *Bony and the Black Virgin*, 149-150.
[18] Upfield, *Bony and the Black Virgin*, 150.
[19] Upfield, *Bony and the Black Virgin*, 154.
[20] Upfield, *Bony and the Black Virgin*, 153-154.
[21] See Bob Hodge and Mishra Vijay, *Dark Side of the Dream: Australian Literature and the Postcolonial Mind* (Sydney: Allen & Unwin, 1991), 56-58.

is hinted at by Lottee's (secondary, reactive) violence. Ironically, however, it is Bony's own origins in a crime associated with a black-white sexual union, and his own removal to an orphanage—the shadowy fictional trace of real state practices illegal by international human rights standards—that works to operate the textual shift away from the domain of state policy regarding half-blood children, and towards individual indigenous criminality. Thus a structural, collective crime against the indigenous people is elided in the very act of the solving of the fictional riddle. Upfield may condone Lottee's crime, but he nonetheless places black violence in the foreground of the narrative, not unlike more recent white novelists such as Keneally and Ireland[22] and in parallel with practices of stereotyping in other European cultures.[23] At the close of the story, Upfield has Lottee commit suicide, thus confirming the criminalization that Upfield's enlightened liberalism does not permit him to utter explicitly, and effectively diverting attention from less visible crimes perpetrated by white society against the indigenous population. It is difficult to know whether this elision, on the part of a well-informed observer, was conscious or not. By way of comparison, Rowley's groundbreaking and devastatingly detailed classic of 1970, *The Destruction of Aboriginal Society*, refers to child removal practices but, significantly, gives no indication of their endurance over the century, nor of the extent of their implementation.[24]

Through its privileging of black over white crimes, Upheld's narrative itself figures an enduring pattern of Australian "cultural amnesia",[25] a cultural amnesia that is addressed in a subsequent text also structured by the detective story narrative, Sally Morgan's *My Place*. In what follows, I wish to read Morgan's autobiographical account against Upfield, as a text that also places an assimilated Aboriginal "detective" at the center of the narrative activity, but that is written by an Aboriginal author rather than a white one. Furthermore, in place of a detective fiction, this text relates the detection of non-fictional crimes, though no less shocking for that. And the perpetrators of the crimes are not black, but rather white, the very suspects initially targeted but then exonerated in Upfield's narrative. In many respects, Morgan's text reverses the structures of Upfield's detective

---

[22] Healy, *Literature and the Aboriginal in Australia*, 241-262.

[23] Paul Gilroy, *There Ain't No Black in the Union Jack: The Cultural Politics of Race and Nation* (London: Routledge, 1993), ch. 3.

[24] Rowley, *The Destruction of Aboriginal Society*, 232, 236, 302, 380.

[25] Benedict Anderson, *Imagined Communities: Reflections on the Origin and Spread of Nationalism*, (London: Verso, 1991), 204; and Hodge and Mishra, *Dark Side of the Dream*, 14.

fiction, signifying a momentous return-of-the-repressed in contemporary Australian society, accompanied by all the difficulties and pitfalls that such a process entails.

Morgan's immensely successful autobiography contains the narratives of the author herself, as well as those of her mother, her grandmother and her great-uncle. In the opening lines of her grandmother's narrative, Nan, as she is known to her family, introduces herself with the words

> My name is Daisy Corunna ... My Aboriginal name is Talahue. I can't tell you when I was born, but feel old. My mother had me on Corunna Downs Station, just out of Marble Bar ... Now, some people say my father wasn't Howden Drake-Brockman [the owner of the cattle station], they say he was this man from Malta. What can I say? ... Aah, you see, that's the trouble with us blackfellas, we don't know who we belong to, no one'll own up.[26]

Here the question of white fathers' denial of paternity and the consequences for "half-caste" offspring opens an elderly Aboriginal woman's account of her life, taking up the very same complex of sexual, social, and interracial relationships that Bony initially surmises to be at the center of the double murders in *Bony and the Black Virgin*. Essentially, the same tragic historical entanglements of black and white society are at stake, both on an individual and a collective level, and there is the same attempt to deny that entanglement, whether by the replacement of one murder narrative by another or through the policies of removal and assimilation. It is the former technique of narrative repression and elision that is decisively reversed in Sally Morgan's *My Place* through its historiographical project so as to reveal the full extent of the removal policy and its cultural bankruptcy.

Sally's mother, exasperated by her daughter's constant interrogations regarding arcane details of family history, accuses her of behaving "like a bloody detective".[27] This epithet is more than a mere passing quip, for it points to the very principles upon which the narrative is constructed. Morgan's text is organized as a type of detective story. As mentioned above, Todorov has suggested that the detective story is made up of two narratives: first, an absent story line culminating in the crime; and second, a process of narration that follows the elucidation of that crime or the narrative (re)construction of the earlier chain of events making up the crime.[28] The opening section of *My Place*, Morgan's narrative of her own childhood and youth, constitutes this second strand of the detective story

---

[26] Morgan, *My Place*, 325.

[27] Morgan, *My Place*, 238.

[28] Todorov, "Typologie du roman policier," 12-13.

structure (put more accurately, it is a *fabula* that recounts the preconditions of its own unfolding *sujet*-process). We are told of her growing up in suburban Perth in the belief that she has some sort of Indian ancestry, but the text is strewn with clues that point to a submerged Aboriginal heritage. These clues are clearly planted by the author, but are ostensibly invisible to the protagonist herself and to the uninitiated reader. Thus Sally feels a strange fascination for dark-skinned visiting relatives of her own age from the country, whose language she cannot understand,[29] a deep sense of symbiosis with the natural life of the wild swamp biotope behind the South Perth housing estate,[30] or, as an artistically gifted youngster, has recourse, when paper and pencils run out, to "small pieces of charcoal from the fire, and ... strips off the paperbark tree in our yard",[31] thus alluding to Aboriginal traditions of bark painting. These clues to Sally Morgan's rootedness in an Aboriginal cultural heritage are inserted in the text without comment and provide the textual dynamic that makes the discovery of Aboriginal identity an inevitable part of the narrative strategy. This process is accelerated as Sally grows older and little by little explicitly reclaims her submerged Aboriginal heritage, a journey that culminates in a visit to the traditional tribal lands, and finally in the project of recording and transcribing the reminiscences of her mother, grandmother, and great-uncle as representative of three generations of indigenous experience, material that formed the basis of the later sections of *My Place* (at this point, the *fabula* of *sujet*-construction arrives at the moment of its own narration, thus fading into pure *sujet*, foregrounding the process by which indigenous history comes to light and is narrated by an older generation to the listening younger generation).

However, other clues planted in the text are commented on explicitly by the narrator but cannot be explained at their points of occurrence in the narrative. The very fact that these clues cannot be decoded is signaled as a disturbing hermeneutic problem for the child:

I was often puzzled by the way Mum and Nan approached anyone in authority; it was as if they were frightened, I knew that couldn't be the reason, why on earth would anyone be frightened of the government?[32]

And when one summer the State Housing Commission painted all the houses in the Morgans' street, the renovation

---

[29] Morgan, *My Place*, 47.
[30] Morgan, *My Place*, 59.
[31] Morgan, *My Place*, 45.
[32] Morgan, *My Place*, 96.

really panicked Nan ... I tried to reason with her, but to no avail. ... For her, they were here to check on us, and the possibility of eviction was always there, hanging in the air.[33]

Likewise, Sally cannot understand Nan's excessive pandering to the rent collector who comes from the State Housing Commission once a month.[34] These explicitly problematized puzzles within the text do not underpin the affirmation of an Aboriginal identity. On the contrary, they are indices of the destruction of Aboriginal identity, of a deeply internalized insecurity. As clues or indices in the etymological sense of the word, they point toward a concrete causal connection. They are mute, as clues inevitably are, for reasons that are intimately linked to the policies maintained by the white government of Australia.

The causal motivation for these textual puzzles is condensed in a clue of the first variety mentioned above, a fear experienced on the part of Sally herself about the time her father died, in 1961:

> I felt very strongly about families sticking together. So strongly, in fact, that I had a secret meeting with my brothers and sisters; for some reason, I was frightened we would be put in an orphanage.[35]

Here the adults' strange silences are elucidated, implicitly, by the small girl's own instinctive fear—for during this period, the policy of forcible removal was still being carried out on a large scale all over Australia. It is precisely this threat which the narrator claims to have instinctively sensed. At this stage in the narrative, however, there has been no explicit mention of these governmental policies, and this childish reaction functions as yet another mute clue buried in the text that neither the reader nor the narrator are yet in a position to interpret.

It is only in the later sections of *My Place*, when Sally's mother, grandmother and the latter's brother take over the narration, that the *fabula*, or chain of historical events taken up and reorganized by Sally's *sujet*-construction, is revealed. The three later narratives represent Sally Morgan's family history, but also furnish the details of a crime committed collectively over generations against the indigenous peoples. What constantly recurs in the narratives of the two preceding generations are accounts of being taken away from parents by the officials of the Native Welfare Department. Sally's grandmother and her brother Arthur record

---

[33] Morgan, *My Place*, 103-104.

[34] Morgan, *My Place*, 104.

[35] Morgan, *My Place*, 50.

being taken away from their mother.[36] In turn, Gladys, Sally's mother, recounts her removal, saying at one point in her account: "Even when I was sick, I belonged to the Native Health Department. I wasn't even allowed to have the comfort of my own mother."[37] Two generations of Aboriginal experience of forcible removal in turn determine the silence that hangs over the third generation, that of the narrator herself. Sally's mother recounts:

> Bill [her white husband] had only been dead a short while when a Welfare lady came out to visit us. I was really frightened because I thought, if she realized we were Aboriginal, she might have taken the children away. ... It was after the visit from the Welfare lady that Mum and I decided we would definitely never tell the children they were Aboriginal.[38]

Even Morgan's disturbed and violent father appears at times to have wielded the threat of forcible removal against his wife, despite his own ostensibly irrational fear that his children might be "stolen" when he is absent at the pub.[39]

The historical fact that thus determines the structure of the narrative from the outset is on occasions also inscribed in the margins of Morgan's text, in the clear register of an objective historical discourse. A footnote draws attention to the "active policy of miscegenation in Western Australia through the 1930s", which entailed "the legal removal of 'half-caste' Aboriginal children from their mothers".[40] The text also mentions curfews and pass laws for black people,[41] the sexual exploitation of black girls and women,[42] brutal beatings of children in homes,[43] and the chaining of Aboriginal laborers or shooting of Aboriginals for sport.[44] However, the central structure of the text is determined by the policy of forcible removal of Aboriginal children from their families and the concomitant suppression of the narrator's Aboriginal identity for fear of the family being broken up. It is the pressure exerted upon Aboriginal people over a century by government policy that motivates the hidden core of a detective story whose mystery is, on the one hand, a hidden indigenous identity, and, on

---

[36] Morgan, *My Place*, 332, 207.
[37] Morgan, *My Place*, 250.
[38] Morgan, *My Place*, 304-305.
[39] Morgan, *My Place*, 301.
[40] Morgan, *My Place*, 211.
[41] Morgan, *My Place*, 250, 334.
[42] Morgan, *My Place*, 266, 336-337.
[43] Morgan, *My Place*, 186.
[44] Morgan, *My Place*, 181.

the other, a silenced history of cultural and social sabotage systematically undertaken by white government, to a great extent out of sight of the public.

One role of these autobiographical writings is therefore to address a fundamental blind spot in Australian national consciousness. Another Aboriginal woman autobiographer, Ruby Langford, has described her undertaking thus:

> My story is about twentieth century Aboriginal Life. About the way we live today. And it's probably the only information a lot of students get that puts the Aboriginal point of view. Because Koori [Aboriginal] history and culture is almost never taught in schools, and if it is, it is usually as it is seen by whites, and not from an Aboriginal perspective.[45]

This point is reinforced by the prominent Aboriginal activist Marcia Langton: "Australians do not know and relate to Aboriginal people. They relate to stories told by former colonists."[46] Morgan's narrative fulfills this educative role, negotiating between two Australias and two versions of Australian history.[47] Morgan recounts being sent as a child to negotiate between her war-traumatized and deranged father and her terrified mother: "'He'll listen to you,' they said. I don't think he ever did ... One night, I told Nan I didn't want to go, but she said, 'You must, there's no one else'."[48] This relationship of mediation between violent white father and Aboriginal mother prefigures the later role of *My Place*, that of constituting an appellative form that bridges the gap between indigenous experience and a white audience. Todorov suggests that the narrator in the detective story is a mediator whose *sujet*-construction work makes the buried crime-*fabula* available not only for himself, but also for the reader.[49] In this respect, Morgan performs the role of detective-as-mediator in a manner similar to that of Upfield's Bony. The go-between status of the part-Aboriginal sleuth, bridging the gap between black and white cultures, is crucial to this mediator role. The salient function of *My Place* is to make Aboriginal history, in particular the history of forcible removal, available for Australians. As Muecke pertinently suggests, the text also occupies a

---

[45] Ruby Langford (Ginibi), "Introductory Notes to 'Koori Dubays,'" in *Heroines*, ed. Dale Spender (Ringwood, Victoria: Penguin, 1991), 129.
[46] Marcia Langton, quoted in *Australian National Cinema*, Tom O'Regan (London: Routledge, 1996), 277.
[47] Anne Brewster, *Reading Aboriginal Women's Autobiography* (Sydney: Sydney University Press, 1996), 125.
[48] Morgan, *My Place*, 41-42.
[49] Todorov, "Typologie du roman policier," 13.

synecdochic position, standing for countless other untold stories of indigenous deprivation.[50] Thus *My Place* prefigured by a decade the massive accumulation of bare facts and figures in the "Bringing Them Home" report and quite possibly paved the way for the public reception of the information transmitted in a more detailed fashion in the later report. The detective story structure underlying Morgan's narrative is thus crucial to *My Place's* status as "a significant act of intercultural brokerage".[51]

The work of mediation undertaken by the book can also be seen in its appropriation of the recent history of Aboriginal politics. Sally's own rediscovery of her past goes hand in hand with the discrete marking of notable political events in the emergent activism of indigenous people in Australia. Thus, the narrative of Morgan's personal discovery of her Aboriginal identity runs parallel to white Australia's progressive awakening to the presence of an indigenous people demanding public and political recognition. Many of the dates Morgan inserts in her text as chronological markers correspond to political milestones outside the narrator's private world, but whose significance is crucial for the public fulfillment of a private quest.

In this regard, Morgan's text is a hybrid form, straddling personal discovery and public emergence. Her text is an example of what Todorov has called a gnoseological or epistemological narrative: a narrative that emphasizes less the question, "What will happen next?" than the question, "How do perceptions change in the course of the story?"[52] Morgan's story, like all detective narratives, is a narration of epistemological transformation both on the individual and the collective planes. The mediating role of the narrator connects these two functions so as to make indigenous history available in a personalized form for the white Australian reader: "Morgan offers ... a knowing and ultimately triumphal relationship with history."[53]

However, if Sally as "detective" fulfills the role of mediator that Todorov ascribes to the sleuth, she as an Aboriginal person also constitutes one of the victims of the crimes—and the public with whom she communicates must find itself on the side of the perpetrators. The task of mediation is thus complicated by the fact that the text's principal readers,

---

[50] Stephen Muecke, *Textual Spaces: Aboriginality and Cultural Studies* (Sydney: University of New South Wales Press, 1992), 133.
[51] Tamsin Donaldson, "Australian Tales of Mystery and Miscegenation," *Meanjin* 50 (1991): 350.
[52] Tzvetan Todorov, "Les deux principes du récit," in *La Notion de littérature et autres essais* (Paris: Editions du Seuil, 1987), 53-54.
[53] Tim Rowse, *After Mabo: Interpreting Indigenous Traditions* (Melbourne: Melbourne University Press, 1993), 102.

white Australians, including myself, inevitably read their own indictment in the revelation of a history of injustice.[54] Thus, inherent to Morgan's project are conflicting components which at once enlighten and alienate. Both aspects are acknowledged in Nan's assessment: "There's been a lot of coverin' up", "Time to tell what it's been like in this country", and "The government and the white man must own up to their mistakes".[55]

This tension between enlightenment and alienation is most clearly evident in Morgan's style. Language is a crucial facet of her undertaking, as is indicated by the narrator's repeated allusions to indigenous languages that remain inaccessible to her as a nontribal Aborigine,[56] which in turn is an implicit judgment on the value of the English language. Something that cannot fail to draw the reader's attention in *My Place* is the resolutely colloquial tone of the narrative, its apparent refusal of sophisticated narrative technique, its artless, indeed naive, register. Stated bluntly, the book is exceptionally easy to read, which, incidentally, makes it a favourite choice of students. The tone of Morgan's autobiographical account is typically suburban and lower middle class, ostentatiously Australian with its references to "chip-heaters" and "kero", to the ubiquitous vegemite sandwich or to goannas in the backyard, and characteristically antipodean in its bland unawareness of, or indifference to, the utter banality of such details. However, it is the contrast with the occasional footnotes that makes one realize that this style is not (only) the narrator's natural "tone of writing", but a careful transposition of a particular Australian social register—all the more so in that the transcribed autobiographical texts of her mother and grandmother assume yet other registers (Nan's narrative is strongly marked as nonstandard English). The everyday Australian register is the central vehicle of the autobiography's communicative function. It allows Morgan to perform two otherwise mutually exclusive functions: on the one hand, to speak explicitly as an indigenous person with the moral authority conveyed by that status, and, on the other hand, to speak implicitly as an average Australian, with another sort of moral authority typical of antipodean working-class reverse snobbery.

The use of conversational Aussie-English is the key to the mediating function served by *My Place*. Morgan's text makes the indigenous tradition, and perspectives upon the historical forces responsible for the destruction of that tradition, available to the white Australian readers in a form that can be readily received. As David Napier comments, a given

---

[54] Rowse, *After Mabo*, ch. 1.
[55] Morgan, *My Place*, 349.
[56] Morgan, *My Place*, 30, 47, 148-49.

culture can only perceive foreignness, be it ethnic or historical, two pertinent forms of alterity made visible in Morgan's autobiography, if it is encoded in a form "enough like us, and only enough unlike us, to be heuristically useful".[57] In their *Dark Side of the Dream*, Hodge and Mishra propound the thesis of a schizophrenic/hebephrenic split in Australian culture, according to which Australian culture oscillates between a paranoid alertness to threatening double meanings in public discourse and a philistine refusal to heed anything but the literal meanings of words. Hodge and Mishra argue that these phenomena are two sides of white Australia's ongoing repression of its colonial past, motivated by a profound but repressed collective guilt regarding the expropriation of Aboriginal land. Thus, a hostile sensitivity to perceived double meanings, and the radical rejection of deeper meanings can be seen as two (only apparently) contradictory symptoms of national repression of a history of illegitimate confiscation of Aboriginal territory.[58] Both these functions can be identified in Morgan's text, and it is not implausible that the acclaim granted to the book is connected to the fact that her style allows these functions to be reconciled. Australian paranoia is given a safe epistemological space in a language that appeals to the featurelessness of Australian discourse; the mystery story allows the admission of a second level of meaning, while couching this discovery in an absolutely flat linguistic code. This dialectic is, of course, central to the detective novel, which alternates between bland surface (whether of persons, events, or things) and a murderous depth. This double function mirrors Morgan's double identity as ordinary Australian and indigenous representative.

In this way, *My Place* can achieve what could only be gestured at by Upfield: the full revelation of a history of white crimes against the original population of the continent. To this extent, Morgan's text touches upon the seldom-asked question of the reader to whom the detective novel is addressed, and of the ways in which the reader is interpellated, manipulated, and guided through the process of discovery of the crime.[59] The principal difference between Morgan's "detective story" and more conventional examples of the genre is that this reader is a collective reader—white Australia as a whole. Thereby, the reader is in some way also identified, albeit never explicitly, and via only one aspect of diverse

---

[57] David A.Napier, *Foreign Bodies: Performance, Art, and Symbolic Anthropology* (Berkeley and Los Angeles: University of California Press, 1992), 140.
[58] Hodge and Mishra, *Dark Side of the Dream*, ch. 10.
[59] Michael Dunker, *Beeinflussung und Steuerung des Lesers in der englischsprachigen Detektiv- und Kriminalliteratur* (Frankfurt: Peter Lang, 1991).

and complex modes of address in indigenous autobiographies,[60] as carrying some sort of responsibility for the crimes revealed. It is also for this reason that the text is so preoccupied with the establishment of a discursive community: in order not to alienate a public that it inevitably places in the dock. The question is, then, to what extent are the conflicting tasks of Morgan's detective narrative, which combines revelation with accusation, at loggerheads?

The very factors making communication with a white reader possible may well militate against the aim of such communication. The construction of a common discursive ground with white readers has drawn deeply hostile responses from indigenous critics. Sally Morgan has been attacked for reaching some sort of "accommodation" with white Australian society.[61] In particular, Morgan's diction would appear to be complicit in this process, as it inevitably panders to the white assumption that a text written by a member of a marginalized ethnic group will lack the sophistication of literary technique and will use an "effortless stream of natural expression from a 'speaking' rather than a 'writing' subject."[62] It has been suggested that the individualized narrative voice of *My Place* speaks directly to a comfortable Australian middle-class sensibility and mode of subjectivity and thereby renounces its own potential for cultural subversion.[63] In comparison, for instance, to Ruby Langford (Ginibi)'s *Don't Take Your Love to Town* (1988), Morgan's text offers a "comfortable positioning of the reader"; it is careful not to unduly disturb the complacency of the reader.[64] In other contemporary indigenous narratives, such as those of the storyteller Paddy Roe, Aboriginal English is used as a cultural bridge between black and white cultures, albeit as one that involves considerably more work for white readers.[65]

Morgan's diction is particularly problematic, because the confessional voice is the primary vehicle of the revelatory function of the detective narrative. This employment of an expressive, individual voice in Morgan's

---

[60] Rowse, *After Mabo*, ch. 4.

[61] Mudrooroo Narogin, *Writing from the Fringe: A Study of Modern Aboriginal Literature* (Melbourne: Hyland House, 1990), 14-15.

[62] Pam Gilbert, *Coming Out from Under: Contemporary Australian Women Writers* (Sydney: Unwin Hyman, 1988), 190; and Muecke, *Textual Spaces*, 130.

[63] Subhash Jaireth, "The I in Sally Morgan's My Place: Writing of a Monologised Self," *Westerly* 40.3 (1995): 69-78.

[64] Rowse, *After Mabo*, 103; and Muecke, *Textual Spaces*, 135.

[65] Stephen Muecke, introduction to *Gularabulu: Stories from the West Kimberley*, Paddy Roe, ed. Stephen Muecke (Fremantle, W.Aust.: Fremantle Arts Centre Press, 1983), vi; and Ross Chambers, *Room for Maneuver: Reading (the) Oppositional (in) Narrative* (Chicago: University of Chicago Press, 1991), 19-20.

narrative may well be at odds with the defense of indigenous culture to which the text aspires. It is significant that against Sally's coercive drive to revelation and confession, which earns her the epithet of "bloody detective", Nan is less ready to reveal her experience, in keeping with traditional indigenous customs of secrecy and more recent habits of judicious silence in the face of police repression and anthropological probing.[66] Sally's triumphant "She's agreed to talk", when Nan finally gives way to the granddaughter's demands for information, acquires chilling associations in this context.[67] Moreover, the major accusatory force of the text resides in Nan's sections of the narrative, and not in those of her granddaughter. This suggests that the detective narrative is not the only strategy apt to lay bare a history of oppression. More disturbingly, it also raises the possibility that the detective metanarrative may not always work in the service of indigenous interests; that on the contrary, it may infringe upon or curtail them.

Thus Morgan's narrative style appears to offer itself to recuperation within white society. The deflection of the message implemented by the text, both in its generic (detective) affiliation and its populist diction, runs the risk of having its accusatory force flattened and blunted. In other words, the discursive strategy employed by the text to enable its unpalatable message to be conveyed to white Australia, a collective subject adept at forgetting the racial crimes of the past, may risk vitiating its own objectives. The detective structure of the text reveals a crime, but in the mode of its revelation to a reading public (a public inevitably compromised by that revelation) it implicitly diverts the force of its indictment.

In this context of textual containment it is worth recalling the stalling of the long-awaited reparation of wrongs done to the indigenous peoples of Australia in the 1990s and early 2000s.[68] Significant in this respect was the Australian government's attempt before the High Court to challenge the historical existence of the Stolen Generation, a revisionist coup that was rejected in decisive terms by the court; the same judge, however, also ruled in 2000 against the first two cases for compensation filed by members of the Stolen Generation. Moreover, as the "Bringing Them Home" report claims, Aboriginal children are still being removed from their families at an unacceptable rate, whether by the child welfare or the juvenile justice systems, or both. This means that a high proportion of the

---

[66] Muecke, Stephen, *Textual Spaces*, 119-30.

[67] Morgan, *My Place*, 320.

[68] For regular updates on current issues, see the ATSIC Web address: [Ed.: Website removed. Try: http://www.fahcsia.gov.au/Pages/default.aspx.]

people affected by the past laws, practices, and policies of forcible removal continue to have their own children taken from them in turn. A process of second (or subsequent) generation removal has been found to have occurred in more than one in three cases.[69] This larger context in which Morgan's project of detection/accusation is to be situated inevitably modifies the ostensibly optimistic stance of the story, giving its enlightenment values of historiographical education, informed dialogue, and discursive community a decidedly ironic edge. The text celebrates the restoration of indigenous community after generations of deliberate dislocation on the part of white policy; and yet, as the text attains canonical status, the crimes it reveals and "overcomes" by laying them bare continue to be perpetrated by a white Australia reluctant to embrace profound structural change in its relationship to its indigenous peoples.

If *My Place* is to be read as an ethnic detective story, it may need to be categorized as a postmodern antidetective narrative, in which the traditional meting out of justice as a result of the detection of the crime can no longer be taken for granted, in keeping with other postmodern narratives that eschew narrative closure and axiological resolution.[70] The dissonance between narrative resolution of crimes against indigenous peoples present in Morgan's text and the real continuation of a historical process of expropriation and discrimination is also a common characteristic of indigenous detective fiction from other parts of the English-speaking world.[71] In a genre once noted either for its indifference to sociopolitical questions or for its ideology of defense of middle-class order against a threat from below,[72] this aspect of indigenous detective fiction represents a radical rupture and demands a rethinking of the very notion of crime narrative. For all its importance as a milestone of contemporary indigenous literature, this profound ambivalence in *My Place*, paradoxically associated with the very terms in which the text endeavors to inform white Australians of their own past, complicates and hampers Morgan's project. Even when Morgan's autobiography confronts and revises earlier

---

[69] See part 12.

[70] Stefano Tani, *The Doomed Detective: The Contribution of the Detective Novel to Postmodern American and Italian Fiction* (Carbondale: Southern Illinois University Press, 1984), 39-40.

[71] Tim Libretti, "Lucha Corpi and the Politics of Detective Fiction," in *Gosselin* (1999): 62; and Michelle Pagni Stewart, "'A Rose by Any Other Name': A Native American Detective Novel by Louis Owens," in *Gosselin* (1999): 170.

[72] Bernard Benstock, "The Education of Martin Beck," in *Essays on Detective Fiction*, ed. Bernard Benstock (London: Macmillan, 1983), 189; and Stephen Knight, *Form and Ideology in Crime Fiction* (London: Macmillan, 1980), 1-7.

representations of crimes against the indigenous peoples, to be found for instance in Upfield's Bony narrative, such an undertaking appears to be trammeled by the broader discursive formations constraining the enunciation of indigenous discourses of activism and protest. Or, alternatively, to reformulate an issue addressed by John Irwin, the ethnic mystery story, once it has been unraveled, does not cease to hold the interest of the reader; it does this through its synecdochic refiguring of a social dilemma whose urgency as a nonfictional task remains insistently in the form of a "mystery to a solution," necessarily beyond the boundaries of the inevitably limited reach of the fictional project.[73]

First Published in *Sleuthing Ethnicity: The Detective in Multiethnic Crime Fiction*, edited by Dorothea Fischer-Hornung and Monika Meuller, 280-296. Madison: Fairleigh-Dickinson University Press, 2003.

---

[73] John T. Irwin, *The Mystery to a Solution: Poe, Borges, and the Analytical Detective Story* (Baltimore: Johns Hopkins University Press, 1994), 2.

INSPECTING WOMEN:
ARTHUR W. UPFIELD
AND NAPOLEON BONAPARTE

WINONA HOWE

As our family drove across Australia last summer, we stopped at a large number of used bookstores searching for copies of Arthur Upfield's books featuring Bony, Upfield's charming and intuitive, half-aboriginal detective Napoleon Bonaparte. The search turned into a longer quest than I had anticipated. "Upfield is very collectible," I was repeatedly assured (or consoled). "They sell out as soon as they come in." Some booksellers had never heard of Upfield. They snapped their bubblegum as they pointed me in the direction of the mystery and Australiana sections and continued to chew as they rang up my purchases. Others, however, were Upfield critics and wanted to talk about the author. "You've got to realize, he was writing in a different era," they said. When I explained to a Perth bookseller that I was examining how Upfield treated women, her answer was succinct: "He didn't."

Before we inspect women in Upfield's work, however, it is necessary to look at the relationship between the author and his central character. Although Upfield is usually identified with Clarence Bagshott (the successful author despised by the literati in *The Devil's Steps* and *An Author Bites the Dust*) and Bony with Tracker Leon (whom Upfield himself designated as the model for his detective), there is also a close connection/identification between Upfield and Bony. A description of the aging Upfield near the end of Jessica Hawke's *Follow My Dust!* (Upfield's biography) states:

> Now in his early sixties, Arthur Upfield is remarkably virile mentally and physically ... Outwardly arrogant, he is inwardly humble [and] welcomes friends generously ...[1]

---

[1] Jessica Hawke, *Follow My Dust! A Biography of Arthur Upfield* (Melbourne: Heinemann, 1957), 237.

Bony hardly ages during the nearly thirty-five years of his career. He both announces and demonstrates arrogance on numerous occasions (although, in actuality, he is willing to learn from anyone), and is unfailingly generous to those he works with. Hawke's description of Upfield could easily double for Upfield's description of Bony (when the detective is working undercover in the outback), except that Upfield's coloring is attributed to the elements rather than genetic heritage:

> His face and arms were varnished by the wind and the sun. His clothes were of dungaree or drill. His boots were elastic-sided and meant for horse-riding. His hips could accept the hardness of ground, and, awake or asleep, his lungs throve on air both dry and pure. His body was thus built to perfection of physical fitness.[2]

The isolated life that Upfield often led was undoubtedly a major factor in his attitude towards women—a strange melange of idealization and contempt, compounded by rebellion against the accepted norm. His father's advice may also have had a bearing on the way Upfield regarded the female gender:

> "If you will remember three wise sayings, you will save us from much worry, and yourself from disaster and sorrow. One: never play around with girls in your home town; do so in a distant place where you aren't known. Two: never make a promise in writing. Three: if you can seduce a girl before marriage, others may seduce her after marriage."[3]

Clearly Mr. Upfield was concerned that his son would bring disgrace to the family name; he prefaced the "wise sayings" with a macabre metaphor (particularly in the context of sex) that dealt with the fear of local scandal: "[S]hould you cut your throat we must not be spattered by the blood."[4]

Upfield's actual relationships with women can perhaps best be described as odd. When he worked in a restaurant, he was annoyed by "a curvy waitress, full-lipped and known to men as a teaser" because of her habit of brushing against them. Upfield tied a large parsnip under his apron; the waitress groped him and allegedly fainted, apparently in shock at the size and condition of this faux penis.[5] Another incident concerned a young woman who repulsed Upfield when he pressured her for sex. While

---

[2] Hawke, *Follow My Dust*, 100.
[3] Hawke, *Follow My Dust*, 36-37.
[4] Hawke, *Follow My Dust*, 36.
[5] Hawke, *Follow My Dust*, 44.

walking together one evening, Upfield arranged for the girl to stand near a nest of green ants and she was bitten repeatedly; he later appeared at her house, offered to help out, and went upstairs to her room without invitation. Upfield "swept back the sheet, pulled up the nightdress, and dabbed the bites with nicotine ... The girl wriggled but was held down with one hand" while he ignored the protestations of the girl's mother at his unorthodox behavior.[6] On another occasion, Upfield was walking home on a moonlit night when he saw a girl in white walking ahead of him. He thought it was his boss's daughter and hurried to catch up with her, but she hastened ahead, apparently to evade him. "'Hoity-toity,' thought Upfield. 'Too high in the social register to be escorted by a common working man. Blast her!'"[7] As he drew nearer, she appeared to be walking on the lagoon and then disappeared. The young woman who would not allow Upfield to walk with her had turned out to be a figment of his imagination.

Upfield's attitudes toward women who tease, women who feel they are too good for the men around them, and women who refuse to be sexually accommodating are reflected in occasional sarcastic or biting comments. For example, in *The White Savage*, when Bony opens a suitcase that may contain clues to his current case, he accompanies the ceremony with a retelling of the Pandora story:

> "All the boys crowded around her, as they do even to this day, and when she opened the box all the terrible afflictions mankind has since suffered escaped ... Thus with the coming of the First Woman universal misery was introduced among men."[8]

In the context of opening a mysterious box, the story is not inappropriate. It is, however, a strange choice in a book that is centered on Bony's search for a rapist and murderer, and where the women portrayed are largely, or even entirely, innocent victims who must seek a way to live with what Marvin Rhudder has done to them or to those they love. In *The Sands of Windee*, when a minor character wonders why the aborigines are fighting, Bony replies, "Woman! Woman undoubtedly is the cause of it. Ninety per cent of murders, riots, and private fights are caused by woman—peace-loving woman."[9]

In spite of these scattered comments, Bony's relations with women are very different than those of Upfield's, almost certainly reflecting wish

---

[6] Hawke, *Follow My Dust*, 230.
[7] Hawke, *Follow My Dust*, 110.
[8] Arthur Upfield, *Bony and the White Savage* (London: Pan, 1964), 86.
[9] Arthur Upfield, *The Sands of Windee* (Sydney: Angus & Robertson, 1958), 100.

fulfillment on the part of the author. The women who rejected Upfield for class reasons (such as his imaginary woman in white) will not be allowed to reject his alter ego. Nearly all women who come into any sort of prolonged contact with Bony are unable to avoid falling under his spell, in spite of the social limitations of his mixed race; the conquest is not sexual, but rather emotional or intellectual in nature. Generally, women make this concession quite readily, a pattern that is set in the first book and continues in subsequent volumes. In her first meeting with Bony, Stella Borradale in *Winds of Evil* is "naturally ... conscious of inherited superiority over this coloured man".[10] Her sentiments have definitely evolved by the time she gushes, "I think you are the most dangerous, the most discerning, the most sympathetic man I've ever known. No one, not even a woman, could hide a secret from you."[11] And in *Murder Down Under*, Lucy Jelly, who will become Bony's ally, obeying his orders and trusting him completely, is initially stand-offish, turning down his invitation to dance supposedly because she is already engaged. The real reason is revealed when another woman asks Bony to dance, defending herself afterwards by telling a friend that he is "a perfectly charming man, you know, in spite of his being unfortunately black, my dear".[12]

Many women appear in Upfield's Bony novels. Inspection reveals that, although some characters are stereotypical, others are multifaceted and carefully layered. For example, Mavis Sayers (*The Widows of Broome*) is initially portrayed as truly unpleasant, snubbing Bony because he is "distinctly dark. Colour in him somewhere," she sneers.[13] Bony, however, believes she can help him apprehend a serial killer. He has decided to set a trap, and who better to serve as bait than Mrs. Sayers—intelligent, discreet, physically fit and fearless. Mrs. Sayers quickly acknowledges Bony's mental acuity, and he admires her egalitarian loyalty to Briggs, the companion who has been with her since she was a girl. Mrs. Sayers remains calm during the sting operation, shamming sleep while the telephone wires are cut and when the murderer enters her room. Then she suddenly attacks him, shrieking, "You dirty beast! You scum! I'll snap your neck like a carrot, you dirty, filthy, murderous swine."[14] Bony is not particularly concerned by the level of violence offered by Mrs. Sayers; he describes her performance as magnificent, although a little rough.[15]

---

[10] Arthur Upfield, *Winds of Evil* (New York: Collier, 1987), 77.

[11] Upfield, *Winds of Evil*, 209.

[12] Arthur Upfield, *Murder Down Under* (New York: Scribner, 1998), 99.

[13] Arthur Upfield, *The Widows of Broome* (Melbourne: Heinemann, 1961), 6.

[14] Upfield, *The Widows of Broome*, 235.

[15] Upfield, *The Widows of Broome*, 237.

Mavis Loftus (*Murder Down Under*), the beautiful spouse of a missing man, is viewed as a faithful wife who works hard to make their little home a place of peace and comfort. Bony admits her beauty, but also detects "a will too strong, a composure too ably controlled, a mind too clever, too calculating".[16] He eventually understands the passionate nature that Mrs. Loftus possesses and realizes that she is completely enslaved by "delirious delight",[17] her soul wrecked by her lover's "unclean beauty".[18] Mrs. Loftus is stunned when Mick Landon bluntly reveals how stupid and cowardly he is; her response is to escape both justice and the bitterness of living with her wrong choices by taking poison. Although murdering her husband was a despicable act, she is both stronger and more idealistic than her lover; she also believed she was truly in love with him while he regarded her as nothing more than a sexual object.

Joan Fowler in *Death of a Lake*, a young and beautiful woman on a remote station and the locus of attention and desire for the men who work there, is among the least admirable of Upfield's female characters. Termed the "Golden Bitch" by one of the men who is obsessed by her, she is greedy, manipulative, and amoral. Even Bony is tempted by this beautiful seductress when she asks him to kiss her: "The danger of being seduced had never been previously encountered by Inspector Bonaparte, but one kiss would be both pleasant and ungallant to refuse."[19] Explanations for Joan's behavior might include the example of her mother (also a golddigger with violent propensities), and the corrupting possibility of the almost unchallenged sexual power that she wields. Bony is incensed by her ego and vanity and is unusually caustic with her; when she condescendingly remarks that it was "damn clever" of him to have her suitcase searched, he responds, "Heavens, no, one hasn't to be clever with you. You know, actually, you are extremely dumb."[20]

Tessa in *The Will of the Tribe* can be a bridge from one culture to another; after attending teacher's college, she plans to teach aboriginal children. Two men compete for Tessa's love: Old Ted, a white stockman, and Captain, an intelligent man from her tribe. The two have wrangled repeatedly and finally engage in a serious, physical battle. The responsibility for this situation is laid at Tessa's door by Young Col, who tells Bony,

"Tessa knows how to ravish a bloke, Bony. You know, looks at you with

---

[16] Upfield, *Murder Down Under*, 98.
[17] Upfield, *Murder Down Under*, 270.
[18] Upfield, *Murder Down Under*, 275.
[19] Arthur Upfield, *Death of a Lake*, 75.
[20] Upfield, *Death of a Lake*, 223.

both eyes wide open and an adoring look in 'em ... She's one of those tabbies who has to work on a man or burst."[21]

Tessa, by her own admission, has "waggled her bottom",[22] although she explains that it was only in fun. Bony counsels her to develop a sense of self and to remember that the only person who owns Tessa is Tessa. In one of Upfield's most riveting scenes, Tessa runs for her life from an enraged Captain who has vowed to kill the "snobbish little bitch".[23] This scene is not only suspenseful but loaded with symbolism, as Tessa, requiring more freedom to literally survive, sheds her western clothing, piece by piece. When he finally catches her, Captain neither kills nor beats her; instead he makes a declaration:

> "You've known for a long time, Tessa, that you belong to me ... You have always been my lubra ... I love you, Tessa ... and Bony, and the tribe, are not going to take you from me ... You're my woman, I am your man."[24]

Tessa finally makes her decision—she belongs with Captain and, by extension, the tribe.

Clearly, the opinion of the Perth bookseller on how Upfield treats women ("He didn't") is inaccurate. Women comprise an important aspect of his Bony books, both as characters who are important to the plot and in relation to the protagonist. Furthermore, Upfield does not limit himself to one class, type, or color when he considers women. The women may be pathetic victims, devious killers, or they may be potential witnesses whose resistance to the law Bony must break down before they will reveal what they know. They may work in the kitchens of station managers or they may manage the stations themselves. They may be female children, old crones, or young and beautiful enough that even Bony feels the pull of their sexuality. They may appear to be totally peripheral to his case until a sudden discovery or turn of events shows that they are pivotal instead. Not all of these depictions are realistic; a few are demonized, while more are idealized to a greater or lesser extent. They are, however, individual and, for the most part, pleasurably unpredictable. Taken as a whole, a complex portrait of Australian womanhood emerges in Upfield's writing, a portrait with many different permutations present that are dependent on race, class, age, etc.; a portrait that was indeed painted by Upfield, whether by accident or design.

---

[21] Arthur Upfield, *The Will of the Tribe* (London: Pan, 1965), 56.

[22] Upfield, *The Will of the Tribe*, 122.

[23] Upfield, *The Will of the Tribe*, 145.

[24] Upfield, *The Will of the Tribe*, 150.

Both Upfield and his fictional detective are continually caught in predicaments that they find confusing. Upfield's personal interactions with women indicate a lack of understanding, while Bony, although much more successful in relating to women, also feels inadequate in this context, saying, "[O]ften I wish I were a woman, with all a woman's knowledge of other women and all a woman's knowledge of men."[25] The two respond to women as they do, at least in part, because they are both outsiders: Upfield because of his class; Bony because of his color. Both men, however, author and creation, sometimes find that their inspections bring reactions and responses that mirror those of the governing class. Upfield is a white male and Bony must seek justice as defined by the governing class (although he occasionally puts his own spin on this concept). The fact that the two men's responses are variable, however, indicates that both are aware of their limitations in dealing with societal issues of gender and race to which there are no easy answers or simple solutions. They may inspect women, but they will never completely understand them.

First Published in *Antipodes* 18.1 (June 2004): 77-79.

---

[25] Upfield, *The Widows of Broome*, 99.

THE GENESIS OF BONY

TRAVIS LINDSEY

According to Hawke, in her biographical work written in collaboration with Arthur Upfield, Upfield was boundary-riding from an outstation for five months around 1924 with one other, a part-Aboriginal, part-European called Tracker Leon, who had spent some years as a tracker with the Queensland police. Leon was supposedly found as a baby with his dead mother in the shade of a sandalwood tree. He had been brought up in a mission school, where he made such progress that he was afforded a high school education.

Hawke's account continues that the even-tempered, pedantic Tracker was brown-skinned, lean, of less than middle height, and possessed of eyes of a piercing blue. Unusually for one not of pure Aboriginal descent, he bore the cicatrices of the fully initiated. Tracker Leon and Upfield got on well together until Upfield drifted away, but they were to meet again.[1] A year or two later, again according to Hawke, Upfield, now a cook at an outstation called Wheeler's Well, was rewriting a manuscript in which the narrative line concerned the emerging part-Aboriginal parentage of a supposedly white-skinned boy and the mysterious death of a tribal Aborigine. A white detective with bush skills is assigned to the case. Part way through the rewriting task Tracker Leon rode up and the two yarned on into the night. Upon leaving the next day, Tracker and Upfield, as was customary, exchanged reading matter, Tracker taking copies of the *Wide World Magazine* and the *Times Literary Supplement* and leaving for Arthur two books—*The Last Days of Pompei* and *The Life of Napoleon Bonaparte*. A few days later, so the account continues, Upfield glanced at the titles and immediately began a rewrite of his mystery novel, this time with an unusually named detective hero whose background, appearance and skills closely resembled those of Tracker Leon.[2] The work, *The Barrakee Mystery*, was supposedly completed in 1926 but was of course

---

[1] Jessica Hawke, *Follow My Dust* (London: Heinemann, 1957), 128-29.
[2] Hawke, *Follow My Dust*, 168-69.

not published until 1929.[3]

Bony's background, personality and appearance is fairly consistently described in the Bony novels thus: Detective-Inspector Napoleon Bonaparte of the Queensland Police, the product of an Aboriginal mother and a white father, was discovered at the age of two weeks beneath a sandalwood tree in the far north of Queensland, his mother dead beside him. A kindly matron at a mission school took Bony under her wing and taught him many things. He did so well at the mission school that he was given a high school education and later won a Master of Arts at the university in Brisbane.[4] He joined the Queensland police service and, although having little respect for the rules, he rose in the ranks because of his ability to reason, his extraordinary patience and his tracking skills. These latter were matched only by those of what were described as "wild Aborigines". Bony never failed to crack a case, and in this, it emerges in the later novels, he was driven by his status of "a man of two races," which in his eyes meant that if he should fail he would be finished. Of medium height and slim build, Bony had dark hair, a dark-hued complexion, the facial construction of a white man and piercing blue eyes. A humane man, Bony's one weakness was his vanity. For example, in *The Barrakee Mystery*, where he was guessed to be aged between forty-five and fifty years, he says "If everyone had heard of me there would be no murders."[5]

Besides the extraordinary resemblance to the Tracker Leon of the 1957 *Follow My Dust!*, Bony shares broad similarities with one who is described as a part-Aboriginal friend of Upfield's, one who is not named, in biographical notes supplied by Upfield to the *San Francisco Chronicle* in late 1950. The notes read in part:

> When I had been in the bush about a year, I met a half-caste aboriginal who, many years later, I named Napoleon Bonaparte. I did, eventually, meet a full-blood by that name. The half-caste became my friend. Why? Because of his dry humour and his profound natural wisdom. He was the son of a station owner, and had received a high school education. Like all his type, the bush had drawn him back and claimed him. Nothing

---

[3] Hawke, *Follow My Dust*, 177.

[4] As a university graduate of Aboriginal descent, Bony was well ahead of his time. According to Tamsin Donaldson, "Australian Tales of Mystery and Miscegenation," *Meanjin* 50:2-3 (1991): 345, the first real-life people of Aboriginal descent to graduate from a university were Margaret Valadian of Queensland and Charles Perkins of New South Wales, both in 1966.

[5] Arthur Upfield, *The Barrakee Mystery* (London: Pan, 1970), 63, 64, 65, 70, 73, 82, 83.

detrimental in that. Were it not for my wife the bush long ago would have claimed me. He had a degree; I hadn't. He had never been accepted by society; I ignore society as such. So what? He taught me how to track ... as far as I could go with him. He read the character, the names, the age, and the gender of any human tracks he came across. He revealed to me the wonder of ants' nests, how to obtain water by tapping the root of a certain tree and setting fire to the foliage. He tried to get me interested in *The Iliad* and failed.

No one ever spoke an ill word of him. No one could. His voice was without accent, modulated, a trifle pedantic. His looks! Whenever I saw Basil Rathbone on the screen I saw Bony. I am unaware if Basil Rathbone has blue eyes capable of looking right through you.[6]

And in a circa 1954 draft article, a copy of which was given to me by Pamela Ruskin, the former journalist and agent of Upfield, Ruskin attributes this to Upfield:

I did not invent Napoleon Bonaparte. I copyrighted him from life, adding very little to his fictional make-up. I adopted him because I sought a bridge to span the aborigines to the white race. I adopted him because of his aboriginal instincts and knowledge and for his intelligence and education gained from his white father.[7]

There is one other, earlier reference to a Tracker Leon-like individual. Upfield's unpublished autobiographical work completed around 1938, "The Tale of a Pommy", and which work, as I have said, may be seen as the well from which Hawke's biography was drawn, refers to a swagman Upfield met around 1925 on the road to Bourke. According to this account, Upfield was engrossed in watching a battle taking place between bull ants and black ants at his feet when he was disturbed:

I heard a voice from behind me, a voice which was soft and liquid and finely modulated. "There is not a great difference between the behaviour of men and that of the ants," remarked the voice. "Neither the Ant nor Man could maintain the social structure without the application of laws and the blind obedience to them ..."

These observations, coupled with the pleasing voice, caused me quickly to twist around to look upward into a dark-brown face having sharp Nordic features and the blue eyes of the Nordic, which at the moment were beaming ...

---

[6] Arthur Upfield, "Bony to his Friends," Biographical notes supplied to the *San Francisco Chronicle* via his publisher Heinemann on 26 November 1950, *Meanjin* Archive, University of Melbourne.

[7] Pamela Ruskin, Draft article, Archive of Pamela Ruskin, circa 1954, 3.

He was wearing clean khaki trousers of drill and a shirt of the same colour and material. On his feet were the usual elastic sided boots. He was hatless and I saw no hat attached to his swag. His hair was short and fine and straight. For a half-caste he was remarkably free of self-consciousness and entirely free of shyness.[8]

Upfield and his new, but never named, companion engaged in an extraordinary conversation, inspired by the ants, concerning ideology, ancient empires and a possible new empire under Lenin's successors. The pair for a time travelled together:

> What a companion was that half-caste! To me, a quite ordinary man, his erudition was delightful and never at any time forced on one. His mind was a storehouse of knowledge of the kind obtained by wide reading as well as through observation. He showed me to what height of efficiency a human being could reach in the art of tracking: and the wiles that could be used to fault the keenest tracker. He opened my eyes—which I had thought were wide open—to gaze at worlds beyond the mundane, the worlds of the insect, the bird, the animal and the reptile. At odd moments he permitted me to see into his heart and regard the picture therein of the eternal warfare between the influences of his black and his white parents.
>
> The companionship endured for a month when he said he would have to end his walkabout and re-join his old mother's tribe. That going back to the tribe was anti-climax; and from the vantage point of today I am convinced that the white man's crime against the black was not, and is not, their wholesale reduction in numbers, but refusal to give them a chance of competing for a civilised livelihood and life's prizes. The crime is all the greater against the half-caste.

The unnamed (1925-positioned) swagman in the circa 1938 "The Tale of a Pommy", the (roughly 1913-positioned) station-owner's son in the 1950 notes for the *San Francisco Chronicle* and the (1924-positioned) Tracker Leon of *Follow My Dust!*, although of different life circumstances, share a tendency towards pedantry, plus a number of physical characteristics. Further, Tracker Leon shares nearly all of Bony's characteristics, including cicatrices, as well as a similar found-beside-dead-mother-beneath-the-shade-of-a-sandalwood-tree-in-north-Queensland - and-adopted-by-a-mission-matron background.[9] The similarities are so complete as to lead me, when considering all the evidence, to conclude that Tracker Leon is a fictional by-product of Bony, created to meet the

---

[8] Arthur Upfield, "The Tale of a Pommy," Manuscript, Archive of William Upfield, Melbourne, c.1938, 130-33.

[9] Hawke, *Follow My Dust*, 129; and Upfield, *The Barrakee Mystery*, 64.

demands of a reading public and the machinery which serves it. This view is, I believe, enhanced by the only very tenuous connection between Tracker Leon and the unnamed, 1913-positioned, "half-caste" swagman encountered in "The Tale of a Pommy". This unnamed creation shares a little more than half of Bony's list of characteristics—missing are descriptions of height, build, colour of hair, educational qualifications and cicatrices, if any—but the publicity-induced need for such a "real-life" inspiration for Bony would have existed, even in the 1930s.

One other, but small, indicator of the probably fictional status of the unnamed swagman is Upfield's use of the phrase already remarked upon in his circa 1938 "The Tale of a Pommy:"

> At odd moments he permitted me to see into his heart and regard the picture therein of *the eternal warfare between the influences of his black and white parents*.[10]

This is similar to two phrases in the sixth Bony novel, the 1938-published *The Bone Is Pointed*: the narrative voice's "Within Bony's soul constantly warred the opposing influences planted therein by his white father and his black mother"[11] and Bony's "You cannot know of the eternal battle I fight".[12] This is the first time in a Bony novel that the "eternal/warfare" phrases have appeared,[13] phrases which suit Upfield's style and which I believe emerged hand in hand with the composite "eternal warfare" phrase (see above) in "The Tale of a Pommy". (I am not suggesting that Upfield originated these phrases, merely noting the context in which he employed them.) Upfield was in fact working on "The Tale of a Pommy" and *The Bone Is Pointed* at the same time.[14] A variant of the

---

[10] The italics are mine.

[11] Arthur Upfield, *The Bone Is Pointed* (Sydney: Arkon, 1984), 136.

[12] Upfield, *The Bone Is Pointed*, 164.

[13] A milder precursor, it should be pointed out, appears at Arthur Upfield, *The Sands of Windee* (Sydney: Angus & Robertson, 1958), 276: "[Bony] explained his upbringing, and attempted to explain the duality of race constantly in turmoil within his soul."

[14] Upfield, Letter to Angus & Robertson, 11 November 1937, Angus & Robertson Collection, Mitchell Library: "I have the next Bony yarn planned, and I have a strong and original background for it. I am so keen about it that I do not wish to hurry in its writing and will complete it about June or July next year ... The job upon which I am now working is my autobiography which I am calling 'The Tale of a Pommy.'" This latter was further edited in May 1938 by Smethurst of the *Barrier Miner* and, according to Upfield, minor changes made—see Arthur Upfield, Letter to Angus & Robertson, 25 May 1938, Angus & Robertson Collection, Mitchell Library.

phrase next occurs in the twelfth Bony novel, *The Mountains Have a Secret* (1948): "[Bony] in whom ever warred the influence of two races."[15] The kernel here is that Upfield seems at a very late date to have either deliberately constructed the 1913-positioned unnamed swagman to better serve as the model for Bony, or, as I believe, the swagman was in the whole a late insert, which manipulation lost its point when his autobiography, "The Tale of a Pommy", was refused by his publishers.

The unnamed, roughly 1913-positioned, "half-caste" model ("... who many years later I named Napoleon Bonaparte") shares a little more than one third of Bony's characteristics and was, I believe, created specifically for the *San Francisco Chronicle*. No mention is made in "The Tale of a Pommy" of such a man even remotely of this time, although *Follow My Dust!* does record an episode of around 1913:

> Upfield learned fast. He was aided much by his early love of maps, and assisted by one or two half-caste stockmen with whom he hunted kangaroos, for they showed him how to read tracks, how to uncover the surface root of a needlewood tree, break a surface root and place a quart pot under the break, and by setting fire to the foliage, force the sap down ...[16]

The reference in the *San Francisco Chronicle* notes to the subject being the son of a station owner is strongly redolent of the character Ralph Thornton, the station owner's son, who learns of his Aboriginal paternity and whom the bush eventually claims, in the first Bony novel, *The Barrakee Mystery*, and of course the Chronicle notes were written about seven years before the emergence of the apparently definitive *Follow My Dust!*

In summary, then, I conclude that the Tracker Leon of *Follow My Dust*, the unnamed station owner's son of the *San Francisco Chronicle* notes and the unnamed swagman of "The Tale of a Pommy" are (like Bony himself) fictional characters created at different times to meet the "origin" demands of the reading public and that which serves it. There is elsewhere, though, a model upon which I believe Bony was based.

I have already referred to Catherine Martin's 1923 novel, *The Incredible Journey*, in which it seems for the first time an Aborigine, a woman called Iliapa, was the prime subject. In the course of the novel, an Aborigine named Nanka tells his story, from which I here quote at length because it is at the very base of my position on the origin of the character Bony. The character Nanka speaks:

---

[15] Arthur Upfield, *The Mountains Have a Secret* (London: Pan Books, 1978), 93.
[16] Hawke, *Follow My Dust*, 63.

"You know I have been long, long away from all my own people, (he said). A police trooper took me to Alice Springs, then away to the Northern Territory. For many years I have been a tracker to the police force. I am now, but not in uniform. I am on what they call the secret service. They gave me the name of being one of the most cunning trackers in Australia. When the inspector of police wants to find things out from the blacks he will sometimes say, "You may as well tell me what really took place, for we have a tracker here, as you know, who can become the very shadow of a guilty man. He may then go to the left or to the right, to the north, south, east or west; he may lie in a cave; or climb a mountain to the sky; he may hide among the rushes round a swamp, or go far by the Great Salt Water that has only one shore; but Jim—that is what they call me—will find him. Jim can track a spider or a bullock, a man or a lizard, even on horseback, running all the time, hardly looking at the ground." After a time they sent me sometimes all alone as far as Queensland and New South Wales to find out about men who were thought to have done some evil thing. I have been sent here in that way. I will tell you why. Some moons ago an inspector of police came on a visit from Adelaide. One day he got a letter from a brother who looks after the men that are in prison all their lives. One of these is a boundary-rider of Roalmah, who was tried some years ago for killing a black man one night at the Wonka Creek ... The boundary-rider paid a very clever man of law to speak for him, so he was not hung, only kept all the time in prison."[17]

In the introductory tale, *The Barrakee Mystery*, Bony appears as the very likeness of Catherine Martin's Nanka. In common with Nanka, Bony was for many years a black tracker in the far west of Queensland[18] and also, like Nanka, escape for his quarry is impossible: "... [Bony] is entitled to admiration for his powers of observation and deduction, as proved by many past successes in the solving of mysteries concerning aboriginals."[19] Further on we read where Bony had solved the case of the kidnapping of the daughter of the Governor of Queensland, which resulted in his being offered senior membership in the police force, and that, now a detective-inspector, he has never failed in a case.[20] In addition, in *The Barrakee Mystery*, Bony, lent by the Queensland police to another jurisdiction (as in nearly all the Bony mysteries), is on Nanka's "secret service," that is to say he is under an assumed name and is here ostensibly painting river boats while living with the workers at the station crime-scene. Bony, who never wears a uniform, even surpasses Nanka's unrepressed sense of

[17] Catherine Martin, *The Incredible Journey* (Sydney: Routledge, 1987), 50-51.
[18] Upfield, *The Barrakee Mystery*, 73: "For many years he was a blacktracker ..."
[19] Upfield, *The Barrakee Mystery*, 63.
[20] Upfield, *The Barrakee Mystery*, 73.

modesty with his, Bony's, already-mentioned "If everyone had heard of me there would be no murders." Because of these similarities in background, skill and character, and because of the convenient time frame—the 1923 publication for Martin and the supposed 1926 completion for Upfield—I think it most probable that Martin's character Nanka was the source of inspiration for Upfield's Napoleon Bonaparte.

There are two significant differences between Martin's Nanka and Upfield's Bony. The first significant difference is that in the absence of information indicating otherwise, it must be presumed that Nanka is a full-blood, whereas Bony, of course, is part-Aboriginal, part-European. And that positioning of Bony is in itself interesting for reasons other than the provision of literary scope. In a time when Aborigines were corralled by legislation and social attitudes Upfield, I believe, placed Bony beyond the pale in a deliberate counter-attitudinal statement. Bony in his very basics is a familiar figure, but Upfield has also, and again I believe deliberately, retained the value of the "in-between" and left Bony as the undecided, the stranger. These attributes, the undecided, the stranger, are emphasised in the Bony novels as a few footnoted references show.[21] I believe, too, that in order to further emphasize the "betweenness" of his fictional character—his black/white ambivalence—Upfield christened him with the slightly absurd name (to Anglo-Celtic ears anyway, even if such appellations in the bush were not all that uncommon) of Napoleon Bonaparte, a name which sets the wearer apart and helps to ensure that he does not quite fit in.

The second significant difference between Martin's Nanka and Upfield's Bony is that Nanka, although very highly skilled, is a mere black-tracker, whereas Bony has been promoted from black-tracker to detective-inspector. It is extremely unlikely that in the 1920s there was in real life a part-Aboriginal commissioned officer in any Australian police force, so Upfield's action, besides aiding his story line, represents another important counter-attitudinal social statement that adds to the risk he took in such a hero in the field of popular literature.

Chapter 9 in "Arthur William Upfield: A Biography," 82-90. Ph.D. thesis, Murdoch University, 2005. Accessed 28 September 2011: http://researchrepository.murdoch.edu.au/160.

---

[21] In most of the novels, Bony initially presents/establishes himself as "stranger" —for example, see *The Barrakee Mystery*, 65; *The Sands of Windee,* 15; *Mr. Jelly's Business*, 11-12. The "undecidable", the "neither/nor",is emphasized early, or fairly early, in each text, except in *An Author Bites the Dust*.

"In Their Different Ways, Classics":[1]
Arthur Upfield's Detective Fiction

Carol Hetherington

Arthur Upfield is arguably the most successful, if not the most prolific, Australian writer of popular detective fiction in the twentieth century, whether the success be measured in financial terms, in terms of local, Australian readership, or in terms of international popularity and recognition.[2] By the time of his death in 1964, noted with sadness in obituaries in most major national and international newspapers, including the *Times* and the *New York Times*, Upfield had published thirty-three novels, numerous articles for newspapers and magazines, and more than twenty short stories.[3] Two novels serialised during his life-time were published after his death and his last unfinished novel, *The Lake Frome Monster*, was completed using "the copious and detailed notes which Arthur Upfield left for this purpose" (verso of title page), and published posthumously. Translations of the novels have been published in more than a dozen countries and new editions continue to appear in French, Japanese, German and even Vietnamese. Upfield's novels were consistently nominated for crime writing awards.[4] Upfield himself was

---

[1] Geoffrey Dutton, *The Australian Collection: Australia's Greatest Books* (Sydney: Angus & Robertson, 1985), 8.

[2] The "pulp" fiction author Alan G. Yates, who wrote as "Peter Carter Brown", is Australia's best-selling author, writing approximately 300 novels and novelettes from the early 1950s to the early 1980s. See Toni Johnson-Woods, "The Mysterious Case of Carter Brown, or, Who Really Killed the Australian Author," *Australian Literary Studies* 21.4 (2004), 74-88.

[3] Ed.: The number of published short stories found has risen to almost 100 since this paper was written. See Arthur Upfield, *Up and Down Australia: Short Stories,* ed. Kees de Hoog ([Raleigh, N.C.:] Lulu.com, 2008); *Up and Down the Real Australia: Autobiographical Articles and the Murchison Murders*, ed. Kees de Hoog (Morrisville, NC: Lulu.com, 2009); and *Up and Down Australia Again: More Short Stories,* ed. Kees de Hoog (Morrisville, NC: Lulu.com, 2009).

[4] For example *Sands of Windee* (1931) was the June Book-of-the-Month choice for the Crime Book Society; A *Chicago Sun* critic put *Winds of Evil* first on her list of

admitted to the exclusive Mystery Writers of America Inc. and in 1962 his American publisher Doubleday Doran, presented him with a pair of gold cuff-links engraved with his initials and the logo of their Crime Club. Upfield's success derives from his series of twenty-nine novels featuring the fictional detective Inspector Napoleon Bonaparte who first appeared in Upfield's second novel, *The Barrakee Mystery*, in 1929. In these novels Upfield gives a uniquely Australian embodiment to several key elements of the classic detective story: the strongly-drawn, larger-than-life sleuth, the detailed and intrinsically interesting setting and atmosphere, and the carefully-plotted "clue-puzzle" mystery of the murder.[5]

Bony, as he is known by his friends ("all my friends call me Bony"[6]), is of mixed race: half Aboriginal, half European, with dark skin and piercing blue eyes. Bony was found as a baby in his dead mother's arms, under a sandalwood tree in the Queensland outback. Raised on a mission by a redoubtable matron ("the finest woman who ever lived"[7]), Bony received a standard, English education and took a Master of Arts degree from "the Brisbane University".[8] After coming to the attention of the police force for his skills as a tracker, Bony eventually becomes a Detective Inspector with the Queensland police and begins a career in which he is regularly dispatched to other parts of Australia to assist in solving the most puzzling and previously unsolvable crimes. This "man of two tribes" has inherited the best qualities of both—gentleness, keen powers of observation and an instinctive knowledge of "The Book of the Bush" from his Aboriginal mother; and the logic and a capacity for deductive reasoning from his white father. He is also cultured, though slightly pedantic, sympathetic, courteous, possessed of a sense of humour and fair play, and amazingly vain: "I never fail",[9] he boasts; "If everyone had heard of me there would be no murders."[10] He admirably fulfills the requirements of American crime writer S.S. Van Dine that a fictional detective should be "a character of high and fascinating attainments—a man at once human and unusual, colourful and gifted".[11]

---

top ten whodunits for 1944 (quoted in "Arthur William Upfield: A Biography", Travis Lindsey (Ph.D. thesis, Murdoch University, 2005), 161, accessed 28 September 2011, http://researchrepository.murdoch.edu.au/160.

[5] Stephen Knight, *Continent of Mystery: A Thematic History of Australian Crime Fiction* (Carlton South, Vic.: Melbourne University Press, 1997), 13.

[6] Arthur Upfield, *Death of Swagman* (Sydney: Pacific Books, 1964), 28.

[7] Arthur Upfield, *Winds of Evil* (Sydney: Pacific Books, 1968), 78.

[8] Upfield, *Death of a Swagman*, 18.

[9] Upfield, *Winds of Evil*, 79.

[10] Arthur Upfield, *The Barrakee Mystery* (London: Pan Books, 1970), 63.

[11] S.S. Van Dine, quoted in *Bloody Murder*, Julian Symons (London: Faber &

Bony was an audacious creation in the context of 1920s and 1930s Australia. Upfield's high regard for the qualities of Aboriginal people was unusual and the social conditions of Aboriginal Australians meant that the existence of a character like Bony, an educated, half-caste, senior policeman, was highly improbable. This might well have been an obstacle to the novels' acceptance but it proved not to be the case.[12] Readers everywhere loved him. For Anthony Boucher, himself a noted crime writer and influential reviewer for the *New York Times*, he was "my favourite fictional detective of the past twenty years"[13] and "one of the rare detective figures with stature as a man".[14] Within the conventions of the genre a character needs to be possible, rather than probable, credible but not necessarily realistic. Elements of flamboyance, eccentricity, even caricature, are there in all the best fictional sleuths—Agatha Christie's Hercule Poirot, Dorothy Sayers's Lord Peter Wimsey, Colin Dexter's Inspector Morse.

The character of Bonaparte also provides Upfield with another key ingredient of the detective fiction genre: the ambivalence and outsider status of the sleuth that allows him to insinuate himself into the crime situation, to draw out its mysteries and clues, and yet possess the authority to restore the disrupted social order, albeit through his own unorthodox brand of justice. Bony, neither white nor black, is not completely accepted by either society but able to move between both worlds in the course of an investigation. He is city-educated, but he has an instinctive affinity with the bush and has lived in the outback long enough to know its ways. He is comfortable in his dealings with urban police officials, but has the bushman's touch when dealing with the outback communities, both black and white, and their people. He has access to the forensic services of the metropolis, but he is an expert in reading the "Book of the Bush" and the clues provided by the land and the seasons. Perhaps more importantly in the Australian context, he has the power and resources of a police inspector, but is outside the ranks of the rule-bound, plodding bureaucrat. One of his favourite and often-repeated lines is "I am not a real

---

Faber, 1972), 102.

[12] Indeed the acceptance of *The Barrakee Mystery* (1929), in which a white woman has a relationship with an Aboriginal man, is itself surprising considering the outrage provoked by the depiction of a mixed-race union between a white man and an Aboriginal woman in Katharine Susannah Prichard's *Coonardoo*, published in the same year, and the responses to Xavier Herbert's *Capricornia* some ten years later.

[13] Anthony Boucher, review of *The Bushman Who Came Back*, *New York Times*, 23 June 1957, section 7: 18.

[14] Anthony Boucher, review of *The Will of the Tribe*, *New York Times*, 29 July 1962, section 7:16.

policeman":[15] in the words of his long-suffering superior Colonel Spender, "My worst policeman ... My best detective."[16] Even so, in the majority of the books, Bony arrives at the scene of the crime incognito—possibly an additional insurance against rejection by the traditionally anti-authoritarian Australian ever reluctant to deal with officialdom in any form. He can easily slip into whatever role or disguise is required—a pastoralist on a solitary holiday (*The New Shoe*, *The Mountains Have a Secret*), a swagman looking for casual work (*Winds of Evil*, *Death of a Swagman*), an itinerant horse-breaker (*Death of a Lake*, *The Sands of Windee*). While the country policemen with whom Bony works—Constable Lee in *Winds of Evil*, Sergeant Marshall in *Death of a Swagman*—are worthy and admirable, if limited, Watsons to this "Bush Sherlock", the "city detectives", wedded to regulations and red tape are totally at a loss out of their urban environment and worthy merely of contempt. Detective Sergeant Redman in *Death of a Swagman* looks only for fingerprints—he does not see that on "the clean page of the Book of the Bush are printed the boot prints of a man";[17] the bullying, bombastic Sergeant Simone is a "mountainous fool", a "gutter-bred Charlie Chaplin detective".[18]

City/country opposition pervades much of Upfield's fiction and the vividness and accuracy of his varied settings, the representation of rural communities, and the all-important role of landscape in his novels, the intense sense of place, are firmly rooted in his own experiences. Arthur Upfield arrived in Australia from England in November 1911. In the period until August 1914, when he enlisted in the AIF, Upfield lived and worked in outback and rural South Australia, Queensland and New South Wales, employed as a labourer on a wheat farm, a rouse-about, a station cook, a fencer on the dingo fence and an itinerant swagman. This period laid the foundation for a relationship with the Australian bush that was to dominate his life. After his discharge from the army in October 1919 and a short time in England, Upfield returned to Australia in 1921 with his Australian wife, an army nurse whom he had married in Egypt in 1915, and an infant son. He was briefly employed in a factory where "a bell issued orders four times a day" but walking though a park one evening he walked "through a wisp of smoke arising from a little heap of smouldering gum-tree leaves". "After that", he says, "the damned bell could ring until it was cracked."[19] Upfield left his job and, temporarily, his family and

---

[15] Upfield, *Winds of Evil*, 158.

[16] Arthur Upfield, *Wings above the Diamantina* (London: Pan, 1972), 224.

[17] Upfield, *Death of a Swagman*, 52.

[18] Upfield, *Winds of Evil*, 155.

[19] Arthur Upfield, "Tale of a Pommy," Manuscript, Archive of William Upfield,

followed "the lure of the Bush"; he worked on the dingo fence, tried opal-mining, trapped foxes and rabbits, and worked as a drover and as a station cook in New South Wales. In 1927 he moved to Western Australia where, until 1931, he was employed patrolling the rabbit-proof fence (designed to prevent the incursion of rabbits into the state) in a camel-drawn dray. It was a solitary existence and it suited Upfield who had continued to write through all this post-war period. Although he left the bush in 1931, and in 1933 took up a short-lived position with the Melbourne *Herald*, Upfield never lived in a city. He lived on the outskirts of Melbourne, in the Dandenong Ranges; on the coast at Airey's Inlet in Victoria and Bermagui in New South Wales; and finally in the small community of Bowral where he died. He had two more expeditions to the outback: in 1947 he was part of an expedition to Birdsville and the Diamantina River, and in 1948 he led an Australian Geographic Society party on a 5000 mile tour of the north-west of Western Australia.

Some critics have accused Upfield of perpetuating the myth of the noble bushman fostered by Lawson and the *Bulletin* writers who glorified an era that had passed even as it was being recognised, but Upfield, unlike Lawson, was not a sentimental "City Bushman".[20] He depicts a world he knew and lived in, small rural communities as well as lonely outposts and large stations. His rendering of their character and language is sure and accurate. The country doctor or priest, the motherly cook or the local policeman's wife are as much a part of the novels as the weather-beaten old loners, like Dogger Smith in *Winds of Evil*, one of the "immortals" "created in the 1860s, hardened by a diet of meat, damper and tea, and an annual 'drunk' at a bush pub".[21] But as Upfield says himself, it was above all the country, the bush, which captured him. He refers to it, in his unpublished autobiography "The Tale of a Pommy", as "Australia Proper" for which he developed "a passionate love ... which will burn until the end, a love stronger than love of family" and which had made him "its slave in the company of many white men as well as all the blacks and members of the mid-races".[22]

"Location", according to Stephen Knight, "is one of the major dynamics in crime fiction",[23] and while Upfield's settings range from New

---

Melbourne, 87.

[20] Henry Lawson, "The City Bushman," in *In the Days When the World Was Wide and Other Verses* (Sydney and London: Angus & Robertson and Australian Book Company, 1900), 147-57.

[21] Upfield, *Winds of Evil*, 179.

[22] Upfield, *Tale of a Pommy*, 88-89.

[23] Knight, *Continent of Mystery*, 143.

South Wales coastal towns, to farms in the Western Australian wheat belt, to the inland deserts, they all have a non-urban, specifically Australian quality. They are as memorable in his novels as the Oxford of Dorothy Sayers, the Paris of Georges Simenon or the Venice of Donna Leon. Place is crucial. Upfield is a fluent and vivid writer and his passion for the landscape and its many moods and variables always comes through powerfully and effectively.[24] The qualities of light and wind, sunsets and sunlight, sounds and silences are what create the strong presences in the novels and they require considerable descriptive powers. The classic Upfield scene might be the quiet noises of settling birds in the trees near a water-hole in the hour before darkness, or the silent activity of a colony of ants moving tiny, sun-heated stones down their holes for warmth, or the gentle hissing whisper of wind moving sand in the moonlight and the regular clanging of a windmill turning. Knight has dubbed Upfield the "classic tourist thriller writer", suggesting, whether deliberately or not, that Upfield exploits the sensational elements of his settings for a "foreign" audience.[25] Dangers there are—floods, fires, heat—for these are ever-present realities of life in Australia, then as now, and "Australian" animals abound but there are no gratuitous snakes, spiders, or crocodiles: indeed the most common animal in the novels might well be the rabbit, an animal not native to Australia, but one which has become part of the Australian psyche since its introduction with British settlement. Place in Upfield's novels is deftly and convincingly evoked, both genuinely felt and explored and exploited in ways traditional to literature and while his settings are all recognizably and pervasively Australian, they are at the same time remarkably varied.

Within the confines of the genre and its formulae, Upfield's novels are surprisingly individual. In all novels the social background, the people of the bush and the small town, are of great importance but each of the other elements of plot, setting and atmosphere is more prominent in some novels than others. It is hard to generalise without distorting but three novels I shall discuss here—*The Sands of Windee*, *Winds of Evil* and *Death of a Lake*—illustrate these different emphases and some interesting and important features of Upfield's writing and career.

The Sands of Windee, the second Bony novel, published in London in 1931, was the June Book-of-the-Month for the Crime Book Society, assuring it good sales in Britain. Despite its excellent reception in Britain,

---

[24] Upfield himself made no claims to be a stylist and some reviewers, even those who praised his books, have noted stiltedness of style, but none have denied his descriptive power.

[25] Knight, *Continent of Mystery*, 159.

the book was dismissed in Australia in patronising terms by one of the most influential of local reviewers, Nettie Palmer.[26] The incident marked the beginning of resentment on Upfield's part towards the literary establishment lasting his whole life.[27] *The Sands of Windee* is a novel in which intricacies of plot are paramount. The mystery is complex and original. There is no body to be found, although it is known that a murder has been committed. In fact, the body has been disposed of by burning it together with animal bodies, any metal bits dissolved in nitric acid, the bones ground up in a gold-miner's dolly pot and the dust scattered. The book became linked with a sensational murder case. During the writing of the novel, Upfield had discussed with George Ritchie, who was in charge of the Camel Station on the rabbit-proof fence, the need to find the perfect method of disposing of a body. Also present on this occasion was an individual who was later charged and convicted of a murder in which this means had been employed. Upfield was called to give evidence at his trial. Set on a sheep station in New South Wales, the novel involves Bony in a mystery where his knowledge of Aboriginal lore, and his ability to interact with local tribal Aboriginals, is crucial to solving the murder—something that is often a factor in the books. As well, his acute powers of observation, his infinite patience and his willingness to make "Time" his ally, allow him to unravel the mystery. Typically, he operates "under cover". Posing as an itinerant and expert horse-breaker, Bony is able to step into the breach when the station cook goes off on a drinking spree (he makes a creditable pastry crust), and still finds time to strike up an intellectual relationship with the region's Catholic priest (with whom he discusses philosophy and the classics). There is a love interest in the novel and characteristically Upfield treats this in a rather stilted, romantic manner. Women, especially "good" women, are usually idealised in the novels. Despite his enormous vanity, Bony resists finalising the case in an official sense, something that happens frequently with the unorthodox inspector. Of course he knows the answer but decides that justice, as he interprets it, has been served and that bringing things to a correct legal conclusion will only cause pain. The verdict from the London reviewer: "well-written, absorbingly interesting in a score of ways, and, above all else, intensely human."[28]

---

[26] See Nettle Palmer, review of *The Sands of Windee*, *All about Books*, 3.9. September 1931, 179.

[27] *An Author Bites the Dust* (1948) is a biting satire, in the guise of a murder mystery, on the literary establishment and literary pretensions.

[28] Bruce Graeme, "The Crime Book Society's Selection for June is *The Sands of Windee* by Arthur W. Upfield," *Crime Book Society Magazine*, June 1931, 3, 7.

If *The Sands of Windee* has the most famous Upfield plot, *Winds of Evil* has a greater focus on atmosphere and symbolism. In the far western New South Wales community of Carie, a killer, a strangler, is at large. He strikes at intervals, always when a fierce sandstorm envelops the town, reducing visibility to nil in a hissing, red-brown fog, unnerving the people of the town and surrounding country with its highly charged atmosphere, and ensuring that all traces of this unseen killer are obliterated by the winds. Itinerant swagman Joe Fisher arrives in the midst of such a storm. Despite the warnings from fellow travellers on the track, he makes camp at Catfish Hole, the scene of two previous murders. Beautiful in the calm windless daylight, and previously a traditional Aboriginal camping ground for generations, the billabong is now shunned by black and white alike. After the death of the first victim, Alice Tindall, a part-Aboriginal girl, her people leave, fearful of the monster, the legendary bunyip whom they blame for this inhuman crime. Confirming local fears, the killer strikes again, although it is not the swagman but a local girl who is the subject of the attack and who narrowly escapes becoming the third corpse.

Clear views of the crime are obscured in a variety of ways. The clouds of dust hide the perpetrator and the winds sweep away traces of his movements. For the arrogant, oafish Sergeant Simone, facts and clues are obscured by clouds of stupidity and racial prejudice; he suspects Joe Fisher, because of his colour, and eventually arrests Elson, an innocent man. As another wind-storm approaches the town waits nervously, particularly the town matriarch, Mrs Nelson, the local hotel proprietor and property owner. Alone on the hotel veranda, "the throne from which she ruled Carie",[29] she waits and watches, apprehensively it seems, for a drama to play out to its end.

Not very much is as it seems in Carie. Who is Joe Fisher? Joe Fisher is Bony and he spreads his net to ensnare the murderer, but other questions and puzzles abound. Who is Dennington, the Englishman with the unknown past who is employed as a fence-rider on Wirragatta station? Is the murderer an outsider, like him, or is he to be found within the community? The strangler appears to wait for his victims in trees near Catfish Hole, swinging from tree to tree like a gorilla and dropping on his unsuspecting victims. Is he the physically deformed, unnaturally strong Hang-Dog Jack, the Wirragatta cook, ugly, snarling, scowling, a "human travesty"?[30] Or is he the bush bunyip, as the Aboriginals believe, "that horrific thing, half-dog, half-human, which, during the daylight hours, lurks invisibly in the heart of the bush, behind a tree, at the foot of the

---

[29] Upfield, *Winds of Evil*, 21.
[30] Upfield, *Winds of Evil*, 60.

mirage, and at night takes material form",[31] to stalk the venturesome lone wanderer? There "was something about this foul Strangler which was almost supernatural"[32] Bony reflects as he struggles to maintain the reasoned logic of the white man's world and fight against the ancient primeval superstition of the black: "Bony's aboriginal blood tingled and Bony's white man's mind fought to still the tingling."[33]

Bony is "Tortured by inherited superstition" about the "monstrous figure slinking through the shrouded world of wind and noise".[34] But just as the whirling sands hide the evil-doer and conceal his tracks, so other records have been concealed and destroyed by human agency. Traces of older crimes have been obliterated just like the tracks of the strangler. Pages that relate to the true identity of station owner Martin Borradale have been torn from the medical record books; and evidence of the profound derangement of his real father, the disfiguring scars on Mrs Nelson's neck, have been kept hidden by the high buttoned necklines of her black silk dresses.

Disguise, concealment, deformity, disfigurement, disruption and distortion are at the heart of the mystery, integral to the crime. The search for the solution to the mystery is a parallel one—Bony seeks the strangler and Martin Borradale seeks the truth about himself. Finally they are one and the same, the monster at large in society is the monster lurking within the depths of Martin Borradale's misshapen psyche, a phenomenon no less mysterious and inexplicable than the existence of the Bunyip. *Winds of Evil* was selected by American crime writer Craig Rice as one of the top ten "whodunits" of 1944 (the year of its U.S. release) because of its outstanding atmosphere, and it is tempting to overplay the extent to which Upfield manages to fuse the realistic and symbolic elements in the novel. But although there are times when the work moves towards the allegorical, when the disturbances in the natural world suggest a mirroring of the social and psychological disruption, it never quite realises its potential in this respect. The imaginative synthesis that would have allowed this to become a very good literary novel is never quite achieved and *Winds of Evil* remains securely within its genre, but a powerful example of it.

In *Death of a Lake* (1954) the focus is different again. The plot is slight and the psychological tension sustained, but centre stage is the countryside that "dwarfs any human activity, superbly observed and described".[35] Here

---

[31] Upfield, *Winds of Evil*, 226.

[32] Upfield, *Winds of Evil*, 142.

[33] Upfield, *Winds of Evil*, 139.

[34] Upfield, *Winds of Evil*, 225.

[35] L.G. Offord, review of *Death of a Lake* by Arthur Upfield, *San Francisco*

is place, location, becoming a key element in the work involving a perennial Australian pre-occupation—drought. The setting is an inland lake, one of several in central Australia that at times, for a year or so, are full of water after floods, attracting abundant and brilliant wild-life, oases of fertility and colour in a desert; and then for years bare, stark, bleached salt pans. This novel describes the slow death by evaporation of a lake and as the water level falls, tension mounts and the expected discovery of a body in the lake draws closer. Unusually for a Bony novel, there is a strong sexual element in the tension. Jealousy and greed are key factors in the crime and women are to blame. For the first time "bad" women make an appearance—two women who are "schemers", "Proper trollops".[36] Suspense is intensified by the reactions of the birds and animals to the atmosphere, the heat, the drought and the receding waters. Publisher Michael Duffy reprinted *Death of a Lake* in 1988. He has called it "probably the best book I've ever read about drought in Australia".[37]

Death of a Lake was published first in America (in February 1954) and somewhat later (June) in Britain. It was the interest of American publishers, beginning with the publication of three novels in 1943, that gave Upfield a secure financial basis for his writing.[38] Locally, Upfield made money from the regular serialisations of his novels in newspapers and magazines and many Bony mysteries were read on local and national radio and adapted as radio serials. But despite accolades in Britain and a wide following for his work in Australia the economics of publishing, typically, made American sales a necessity for commercial success.

Chronicle, 21 March 1954, 23.

[36] Arthur Upfield, *Death of a Lake* (London: Pan, 1967), 44.

[37] Ramona Koval, pres., "The Arthur Upfield Mystery—Bony," *Books and Writing*, Australian Broadcasting Commission, 12 May 2002, accessed 28 September 2011, http://www.abc.net.au/rn/arts/bwriting/stories/s550978.htm.

Upfield lived near one such lake, Meenamurtee Lake, in his first years in Australia, and witnessed the teeming wildlife; he had also seen water in Lake Eyre on his 1947 outback expedition. The early Australian explorers searched, with often fatal consequences, for a great inland sea. On 25 May 1954 when its first serialised instalment appeared in the *Sydney Morning Herald*, the facing page carried an interview with an old bushman recommending the flooding of Lake Eyre as a solution to problems of drought. As I write this, in March 2007, the morning newspaper has a feature on the movement of floodwaters into a drought-stricken Lake Eyre: Richard Sproull and Asa Wahlquist, "Wildlife Follows the Dark Tide towards Lake Eyre," *Australian,* 9 March 2007, 7.

[38] They were *Murder Down Under* (originally titled *Mr Jelly's Business*), *Wings Above the Claypan* (originally titled *Wings Above the Diamantina*) and *The Mystery of Swordfish Reef.*

Upfield was proud of his ability to sell his work and of his status as one of the very few Australian writers who could support themselves by their craft. However, all his life he was conscious that his work was not regarded as "literary". Upfield has not received the prominence within Australian literary history that he deserves. Some of various reasons for this include ostracism by the "literati" in the 1920s and 1930s, a dismissal of popular fiction genres by critics as unworthy of study, and later a reluctance to engage in discussion of Upfield's treatment of Indigenous issues, even of the character of Bony himself. Some of Australia's most respected critics have delivered favourable verdicts on Upfield's work. Geoffrey Dutton chose *Man of Two Tribes* as one of the hundred best Australian books and wrote: "Upfield's novels are frequently dismissed as mere thrillers. Such a book ... is far more and has a secure place as a work of art."[39] Professor Morris Miller saw that even in his early works Upfield "shows a talent that may ultimately find the art of synthesis".[40] Clem Christesen commented that while Upfield was "generally recognised as a competent writer on the 'popular' level, I personally consider him rather more than this".[41] For Professor Colin Roderick, Upfield "raised the Australian standard" in crime fiction, and judged that "We have had no such promising work since Fergus Hume's celebrated *Mystery of a Hansom Cab*".[42] Despite this, very few critical articles on Upfield have appeared and the only full-length study has been published in America.[43] This was certainly not a matter of indifference to Upfield. In a draft letter, probably to Professor Colin Roderick and referring to *Death of a Lake*, he asks a question which still needs to be answered:

> I would much appreciate your opinion on whether this particular type of mystery story ... could take its place in National Literature. If, of course, it be possible for a crime story to be included in National Literature.[44]

---

[39] Geoffrey Dutton, *The Australian Collection: Australia's Greatest Books* (Sydney: Angus & Robertson, 1985), 226.

[40] E. Morris Miller, *Australian Literature from Its Beginnings to 1935* (Melbourne: Melbourne University Press, 1940), 573.

[41] Clem Christesen, quoted in "Arthur William Upfield," 195.

[42] Colin Roderick, *An Introduction to Australian Fiction* (Sydney: Angus & Robertson, 1950), 139.

[43] Ray Browne, *The Spirit of Australia: The Crime Fiction of Arthur W. Upfield* (Bowling Green, OH: Bowling Green State University Popular Press, 1988).

[44] Draft letter to Roderick, probably Colin Roderick, 18 June 1954, Archive of Don Uren, Mansfield, Victoria.

First Published in *Fact and Fiction: Readings in Australian Literature,* edited by Amit Sarwal and Reema Sarwal, 285-298. New Delhi: Authorspress, 2008.

RE-ASSESSING ARTHUR W. UPFIELD'S NAPOLEON BONAPARTE DETECTIVE FICTION

JOHN RAMSLAND AND MARIE RAMSLAND

Although on the margins of Australian literary circles during his lifetime, Arthur William Upfield produced over thirty novels and several articles. Twenty-nine of his novels, published in England, Australia and later in America and Canada, have as their protagonist Detective Inspector Napoleon Bonaparte, an Aborigine of mixed descent, who unravels through his superior sleuthing the most difficult mysteries that others are unable to solve. Most of these crime stories have been re-published (and re-published) and translated into at least fourteen languages, the first being German, and French the most recent. Our aim here is to re-assess Upfield's "Bony" series, and to demonstrate that to dismiss these stories is to lose a valuable, if controversial, contribution to Australian literature. Narrative, dialogue, characterisation and landscape are aspects that will be considered in assessing the (author's) creative process. Moreover, we shall suggest that as a series, they demonstrate the historicity of a disappearing culture. In this way, we hope to determine which of these aspects ensure the series' continued appeal, especially in France.

Jean Renoir, the great French film director, was fond of saying that in order to arrive at the self, you have to begin with the environment.[1] Arthur Upfield, frequently underrated as a writer in the insular Australian literary world, attempted to do what Renoir preached—without perhaps being aware that Renoir had preached it. Such an approach is constantly evident in the creative endeavours in Upfield's *œuvre*: his lengthy and well-

---

[1] "[M]an is shaped by the soil that nourished him, by the living conditions that fashion his body and his mind, by the countryside that parades before his eyes day in and day out." Jean Renoir, quoted in *Jean Renoir: A Conversation with His Films 1894-1979*, ed. Christopher Faulkner and Paul Duncan (Los Angeles: Taschen, 2007), 13. The great and prolific Paris-born film-maker was the son of the renowned Impressionist painter Auguste Renoir. More than anyone else, Jean Renoir, in films such as *Madame Bovary* (1934), *Une partie de campagne* (1936) and the American production *Swamp Water* (1943), created a world where people are as natural as the landscape.

received detective mystery series of novels about "Bony", the part-Aboriginal police Detective Inspector from Queensland. He succeeded in almost filmic terms by poetically and sparsely using visualised combinations of words that evoked landscape, humans working in it and characters reacting to it, while simultaneously maintaining a narrative thrust. The visual characteristic of his work is so important that his books can be read almost as film scenarios. Each chapter has the structure of a single scene sequence. After all, Upfield's prime aim, like most detective-fiction writers, was to tell a suspenseful story.

Arthur William Upfield was born on 1 September 1890 in Gosport, England and came to Australia at the age of twenty-one in late 1911. He went bush almost immediately, eagerly seeking out isolated places, taking up employment on Outback stations and intermittently humping his swag "on the wallaby" until the 1930s. He was fence patroller for nearly three years, checking sections of the famous Rabbit-Proof Fence in Western Australia, camping by himself and living in outstations and in labour camps along the way. Between 1911 and 1931, he lived a nomadic bushman's lifestyle, with the interruption of voluntary service in the AIF during the Great War years.

Rapidly absorbing the prevailing culture and its values, Upfield became more aggressively Australian than most Australians, fuelled by his many and varied experiences in the sparsely populated countryside. From the beginning, he had dreams of being a writer and stored everything he experienced in his mind. He was to become a significant chronicler of Outback life—"the countryside that paraded before his eyes day in and day out"[2]—of a disappearing Australia that held for his readers a particular fascination.

Arthur Upfield died in Bowral, a small, attractive township in the Southern Highlands of New South Wales on 12 February 1964, leaving an unfinished Bony adventure in manuscript form. Using the author's copious notes, J.L. Price and Dorothy Strange completed the text and it was published by Heinemann in London in 1966 as *The Lake Frome Monster*.[3]

---

[2] Faulkner and Duncan, *Jean Renoir*, 13. Tamsin Donaldson describes Upfield as an "enthusiastic participating observer", in "Australian Tales of Mystery and Miscegenation," *Meanjin*, 50.2-3 (1991), 350.

[3] Stephen Knight, "Upfield, Arthur William (1890-1964)," in *Australian Dictionary of Biography* 12 (Melbourne: Melbourne University Press, 1990), 306.

Landscape, Character and Space

Upfield uses the Outback's overwhelming physical and cultural environment—"the soil that nourished"—in shaping characters' natures and motivations in their milieus of work. These are frequently a cattle or sheep station and become a second layer in an investigative plot-line about a mysterious murder or disappearance that the astute Inspector Napoleon Bonaparte sets out to solve. The author generally followed the linear pattern of setting the mystery, plotting the investigation as carried out by his super-sleuth Bony and culminating inevitably in the solution and the end of the story. This was a pattern followed by most detective-fiction writers from Edgar Allan Poe and Arthur Conan Doyle onwards.

Character and space, nevertheless, acquire "a social and historical specificity" in Upfield's work.[4] His stories create a sustained illusion of the everyday reality of the workplace in remote parts of Australia where small towns are slowly decaying and where cattle or sheep stations, alive and active, dominate the social scene. These two contrasting settings provided the template for most of his Outback novels.

He, like Renoir, had a penchant for realism and communicated to the reader a concrete sense of place—a setting that is a vital part of the reader's experience. His writing shows the same mastery in its situation of characters in their environment as that on display in Renoir's famous films *La Bête humaine* (1938) and *La Règle du jeu* (1939).

The map of place in Upfield is deftly developed through a series of short descriptions that stay in the reader's mind. Imagination is drawn into it as though it is the very reality of life. In his narrative universe, Upfield chooses contemporary incidents of his lifespan and stories set in the 1920s and the 1930s drawn from his own experiences in remote South Australia, New South Wales, Queensland and Western Australia. Some are set in coastal villages and a few close to the main cities. Through such means, he was able to develop an illusion of everyday reality from his own observations, both present and those stored from his past. At one level, the Bony novels are a history of the author's own life. They carry with them the dominant attitudes of the time in Australian culture.

His fictional evocation of the sites of outdoor work reveal possible influences of Emile Zola and Israel Zangwill (who wrote about the impoverished East End of London),[5] in their sociological fiction which

---

[4] Falkner and Duncan, *Jean Renoir*, 13.

[5] Israel Zangwill (1864-1926), author and philanthropist. His novels like *Children of the Ghetto (or Jago)* (1842), *Ghetto Tragedies* (1893) and *Dreams of the Ghetto* (1898) had strong sociological and contemporary themes written in a journalistic

Upfield adapted in the detective format. He had read Victor Hugo and Charles Dickens and, in his youth, had become absorbed in the exploits of the fictitious Sexton Blake, a London sleuth who like Sherlock Holmes resided in Baker Street. He was able, partly through such influences and his own observation, to capture the web of small town country life where everyone knows everyone's business, while there are still undisclosed secrets that progressively unravel.

There is a strong interdependence in Upfield's workplace—"the living conditions that ... fashioned mind and body"[6]—usually set on the grazier's property where volatile cooks, itinerant horsebreakers, hard-drinking stockmen, rough rouseabouts, lonely but lively jackaroos and even secretive book-keepers are part of the farming enterprise. Such characters are distinctly Dickensian. They are set against a desolate landscape with a harsh climate—a duality of space. According to Stephen Knight, Upfield created "a worm's eye view of awesome natural grandeur" by deliberately using a dry style and meticulous plotting to achieve "a sense of human inadequacy in a dominating continent".[7]

Knight views Upfield's stories as "the most strongly, perhaps even excessively Australianised of all the local (that is, Australian) mysteries". He finds them rich in "loving detail, weighed with Aboriginal lore and white bush practices". Nevertheless, to him, they are "structured in the European pattern", with "barely indistinguishable characters, mechanical plot action and a thoroughly materialised means of detection". He adds that some readers take a white post-colonial interpretation in that "Bony" allowed Upfield "to elide real problems between blacks and whites", obscuring "both aboriginality [*sic*] and white injustice".[8] In this, Upfield was most certainly a man of his time. However, all evidence supports the view that the author meant to "honour" Aborigines and the environment— radical at the time. In *The Bone Is Pointed* for example, Upfield through one of his protagonists, a sympathetic station owner, argues:

---

style. He had a background as a teacher, then as a journalist.

[6] Faulkner and Duncan, *Jean Renoir,* 57. Renoir also believed that for him observation was his "point of departure".

[7] Knight, *Australian Dictionary of Biography*, 303-304. See also Stephen Knight, *Continent of Mystery* (Melbourne: Melbourne University Press, 1997) and *Form and Ideology in Crime Fiction* (Bloomington: Indiana University Press, 1980).

[8] Stephen Knight, ed., "Introduction," in *Dead Witness: Best Australian Mystery Stories*, (Ringwood: Penguin Books, 1989), xx-xxi. See also Stephen Knight, "The Case of the Missing Genre: In Search of Australian Crime Fiction," *Southerly*, 40.3 (1988): 235-249.

I'm worried about it ... I'm only worried about the possibility of Bonaparte putting in a confidential report that may affect the Kalchut in a roundabout manner. Neither mother nor I want to see official interference with them. That would mean their swift de-tribalization and inevitable extinction. No matter how kindly officialdom might deal with them, once they are interfered with it is the beginning of the end.[9]

With these words, Upfield had made his position clear. He was opposed to intervention either by the New South Wales Protection Board or Christian missionary authorities, or both. A supportive relationship between a compassionate, fair-minded property owner and the local Aboriginal people still inhabiting their homeland seemed better, even though they provided a labour pool for outdoor station work like horse breaking and droving or, in the case of the women, homestead domestic service. Thus, Upfield can be considered a sentimental resister of some aspects of colonial imperialism. His view depended, however, on the real existence of idealistic graziers like his fictitious character, John Gordon, in *The Bone Is Pointed*.

In 1928, Upfield's first novel *The House of Cain* was published. The next year, *The Barrakee Mystery*, the first of the "Bony" books, introduced readers to the Aboriginal and university-educated sleuth, Napoleon Bonaparte. Upfield soon captured the public's imagination. His readers delighted in his unfamiliar remote bush settings and seemingly exotic main character who continued to fascinate throughout the series. Bony took on a life of his own in the minds of the readers, as did Conan Doyle's Sherlock Holmes.

Bony and the Kelly Gang (1960) was set in and around Bowral. In it he demonstrated his honed skill at research and capturing the historicity and grandeur of the landscape:

[t]he autumnal tints; the soft blues of the shadows and the jet black gaping jaws of the surrounding mountain slopes and cliffs. From a rise [Bony] saw the houses of Cork Valley, pure white against the green wall of trees divided by the living silver of a high waterfall.[10]

---

[9] Arthur Upfield, *The Bone Is Pointed* (Sydney: Arkon, 1972), 228; first published in 1938.

[10] Arthur Upfield, *Bony and the Kelly Gang* (London: Heinemann, 1960), 18. Compare the following description from *The Oxford Literary Guide to Australia*, ed. Peter Pierce (Melbourne: Oxford University Press, 1987), 33: "[T]hese valleys were originally settled by Irish rebels, who made their own laws and handed their way of life to their children and their children's children, generation after generation. They even distilled their own liquor in illicit stills, and continue to do so. Even today policemen are an anathema to valley people."

In contrast to this painterly, poetic description, a truck driver in the novel remarks laconically of Bowral itself that it is "Smallish. Four-pub town. Three policemen. Five hundred yapping dogs."[11] Upfield was as laconic as his truck-driver character about his final settling place after wandering all over Australia.

In *The Bachelors of Broken Hill* (1950), the story opens with what we can now view as an acknowledgement to country, indicating Upfield's belief in the prior ownership of the land by the Indigenous people. This is followed by a brief history of the place and description of the town:

> Long, long ago, the aborigines came and called it Wilya-Wilya-Yong. It was a dark, barren hill formed like a scimitar, its back broken, its slopes serrated and pitted and scarred. One day a white man talked with a black man and learned that Wilya-Wilya-Yong meant the Place of Youth.
>
> White men brought their sheep and a poor German named Charles Rasp was employed to herd them. ... he broke off a piece of the Place of Youth ... and experts declared it to be loaded with silver-lead. ... Men came on horseback and on foot, in wagons and Buffalo Bill coaches, and they sank holes and rigged machinery. ... The camp became a shanty town named Broken Hill.[12]

Dualism and Ambivalence

Pamela Ruskin interviewed the ageing author for the July 1962 edition of the popular Melbourne weekly magazine *Everybody's* which was available for many years on newsagents' racks, especially in Victoria. Ruskin was a freelance journalist, close friend of the author and his literary agent.[13] Her portrayal of the seventy-year-old had him living quietly in his mountain home within 100 miles of Sydney:

> The slim whipcord figure has thickened a little, and the crisp, dark, wavy hair has greyed, but he is essentially the same Arthur Upfield who adventured all over Australia learning to read what he calls "The Bible of the Bush".[14]

---

[11] *Upfield, Bony and the Kelly Gang*, 10.

[12] Arthur Upfield, *The Bachelors of Broken Hill* (London: Heinemann, 1958), 1.

[13] Ramona Koval, pres., "The Arthur Upfield Mystery—Bony," *Books and Writing*, Radio National, Australian Broadcasting Commission, 12 May 2002, accessed 28 September 2011,
http://www.abc.net.au/rn/arts/bwriting/stories/s550978.htm.

[14] Pamela Ruskin, "Arthur Upfield Makes Crime Pay," *Everybody's*, 25 July 1962, 44-45.

Ruskin goes on to describe his "puckish deep-set eyes", thin lips and ears like "vase handles". He is blunt, has no patience "with the insincerities of social life", and has never learnt to suffer fools gladly. She recognises that he "loathes pretentiousness of any form" and that he has a "great hatred for literary snobs" who have a "strangling effect on Australian literature". She refers to his satire on the literary world with the playful title *An Author Bites the Dust* (1948), one of the few Bony novels in which he provides a metropolitan setting far from the Outback.

An earlier untitled draft article written by Ruskin includes a statement from Upfield about the central character of his crime fiction:

> "I did not invent Napoleon Bonaparte. I copyrighted him from life. ... I adopted him because I sought a bridge to span the aborigines to the white race. I adopted him because of his aboriginal instincts and knowledge and for his intelligence and education gained from his white father."[15]

Upfield always acknowledged Tracker Leon, a well-educated Aboriginal man he shared a hut with for five months in 1924 when he worked as a New South Wales rabbit-proof fence inspector and a rabbit and fox trapper, as the source for creating his Aboriginal detective. When Leon and Upfield parted company, they exchanged reading matter and Upfield acquired *The Life of Napoleon Bonaparte* by John S.C. Abbott.[16]

In the second novel of the series with a euphonic and relentless title, *The Sands of Windee* (1931) where both sand and wind are powerful natural elements, one of the female characters tells Bony that he is a man for all seasons:

> "You know you are a surprising person ... [I]n the first place you are a university graduate, yet you break-in horses most expertly; secondly you play divinely on an ordinary tree leaf; and now I find you cooking, having been told you that you can really cook. What else can you do?"[17]

And we are then told that "[n]o other men of her acquaintance, and they ranged from an Irish peer down to a horse-boy, possessed as likeable personality as this half-caste".

Bony immediately takes up his own self-portrayal which remains a

---

[15] Pamela Ruskin, untitled draft article ca.1954, quoted in "Arthur William Upfield: A Biography", Travis Lindsey (Ph.D. thesis: Murdoch University, 2005), 84, accessed 28 September 2011, http://researchrepository.murdoch.edu.au/160.

[16] Jessica Hawke, *Follow My Dust: A Biography of Arthur Upfield* (London: Heinemann, 1957), 169.

[17] Arthur Upfield, *The Sands of Windee* (Sydney: Arkon, 1984), 63-64.

consistent template throughout the series. As a part-Aborigine, he recognises that he could not resist "the call of the bush" despite "the mantle of the white man's civilization": "I have never known a half-caste, even with the educational attainments I possess, remain all his life in a city among white people." He then provides a narrative of his formative years:

> "From the mission where I was reared I graduated to a high school and there to the university [of Queensland]. Mastering the arts and sciences came to me with extraordinary ease. Many people who knew me foretold for me a brilliant career. 'Observe the white man's culture in Bony,' they said. For a while I believed them and then one day I began to want something I couldn't define or name."[18]

In *Death of a Swagman* (1945) he adds more detail:

> "No, I have no brothers and sisters", he told her, and related how he had been found, when a small baby, in the shade of a sandalwood-tree in the far north of Queensland, and how he found a mother in a matron of the mission station to which he had been taken.[19]

This was the Dickensian lost child found. He goes on to portray himself as an adult. The successful completion of a Master of Arts degree provided proof that "the Australian half-caste is not a kangaroo". Beyond white prejudice, he sees himself as having to conquer "the almost irresistible power of the Australian bush":

> "But it will not baffle me [Bony asserts], because I am neither wholly black nor white. I have the white man's reasoning powers and the black man's eyesight and knowledge of the bush. The bush will give up its secrets to me."[20]

Upfield's many readers would have concurred. This is what fascinated them primarily.

This dualism and ambivalence in Bony's character—a man apart from both cultures—is Upfield's leitmotiv. It is clearly influenced by Robert Louis Stevenson's exploration of dualism of personality in a number of his novels,[21] and yet, unlike Stevenson, is not "good *versus* bad/evil" but the

---

[18] Upfield, *The Sands of Windee*, 64-65. Upfield refers consistently to the "call" or "lure of the Bush".

[19] Arthur Upfield, *Death of a Swagman* (Sydney: Arkon, 1964), 10.

[20] Upfield, *Death of a Swagman*, 18-19.

[21] For example, *The Strange Case of Dr. Jekyll and Mr. Hyde* (1886) and *The Master of Ballantrae* (1889).

Aboriginal traditional world-view *versus* that of the so-called "mantle of white civilisation". Bony's duality of personality constantly combines the mystical intuitiveness of his Aboriginal mother with the "sophisticated intelligence of his white father".[22] This is paralleled with a duality of space: the decaying small township and the prosperous, enterprising sheep station.

Ambivalence runs deep in Upfield's creation. At one level, there is Bony's relationship with the Queensland police force from which he frequently resigns. He only takes on difficult cases that present an intellectual challenge and freely rejects those that are not of interest: "Copy my example ... Never permit yourself to be concerned with inspectors and chief commissioners and people of that class. They are all right in their places."[23]

In *The Bachelors of Broken Hill*, Bony again elaborates on the dualism of his persona and the uniqueness of his policing and detection methods:

> I obey orders when it suits me ... I am unique because I stand midway between the white and black races, having all the virtues of the white race and very few vices of the black race. I have mastered the art of taking pains, and I was born with the gift of observation. I never hurry in my hunt for the murderer, but I never delay my approach.[24]

Bony's opposition to bureaucracy and authority in the police force is not unlike that of Simenon's Maigret who is a police official of high rank, but opposed to the mindlessness of authority. This has become a great tradition in detective writing and is more recently reflected in Colin Dexter's Inspector Morse, Jack Frost and the like—part of the rules of the game of the crime novel which goes right back to Edgar Allan Poe's Auguste Dupin and Arthur Conan Doyle's Sherlock Holmes.[25]

There is ambivalence at a deeper level though with this Detective Inspector—he keeps his ritually scarred back and chest of the fully initiated warrior hidden under impeccably styled Western clothes, and his

---

[22] William Wilde, Joy Hooton and Barry Andrews, ed., *Oxford Companion to Australian Literature* (Melbourne: Oxford University Press, 2000), 770.

[23] Upfield, *Death of a Swagman*, 86.

[24] Upfield, *The Bachelors of Broken Hill*, 15.

[25] See Helmut Heissenbüttel, "Rules of the Game of the Crime Novel," 78-92; Michael Holquist, "Whodunit and Other Questions: Detective Stories in Postwar Fiction," 150-74; William Stowe, "From Semiotics to Hermeneutics: Modes of Detection in Doyle and Chandler," 366-383; in *The Poetics of Murder: Detective Fiction and Literary Theory*, ed. Glenn Most and William Stowe (New York: Harcourt Brace Jovanovich, 1983).

Aboriginal sensibilities are hidden behind eyes of reassuring blue. As we read:

> [He] was plainly stamped as a city man by his clothes and heavy suitcase. Of average height and build, he was remarkable for the dark colouring of his skin which emphasized his blue eyes and white teeth when he smiled at something said to him by the driver.[26]

And in *The Sands of Windee*:

> Father Ryan surveyed him with interest, noting his grey lounge suit, the dark grey tie beneath a spotless collar, and the black shoes. He wondered at Bony's taste in clothes and the absence of striking colours.[27]

Nevertheless, his forensic skills include those of a tracker, allowing him to follow microscopic clues missed by usually feckless local police. This is best displayed in the fourth chapter of *The Sands of Windee*, "The Ants' Nest", in which Bony, patiently observing the behaviour of ants at the scene of the crime, locates a small cut sapphire: "Up out of the hole an ant carried a piece of blue glass, which reflected the light strongly while it was still deep in the shadow."[28] His interpretive skills in reading footprints were in advance of his time. This aspect of crime detection was highlighted in March 2006 by Professor Nigel Allinson of the University of Sheffield who leads a team of researchers working on a computer system to make "shoeprints at crime scenes as useful as fingerprints and D.N.A."[29]

Occasionally, Bony is disturbed about his mixed background, and the equilibrium between the two cultures he has achieved is shaken:

> He sighed because it was one of those times when within him war was waged between the spirit of his father and the spirit of his mother. During these times of spiritual strife his black ancestry invariably almost won.[30]

---

[26] Upfield, *The Bone Is Pointed*, 29.

[27] Upfield, *The Sands of Windee*, 205.

[28] Upfield, *The Sands of Windee*, 17.

[29] "We all leave footprints, and ... they are good intelligence and can be good evidence." Nigel Allison, "Shoeprint analysis to fight crime," *BBC News* (website), 31 March 2006, quoted in *Australian Natural History: Human Ecological Context for 'Bony' Mysteries by Arthur William Upfield*, N.L. Nicholson, accessed 22 September 2011, http://nicholnl.wcp.muohio.edu/DingosBreakfastClub/Australia/UpfieldMysteries. html, 6.

[30] Upfield, *The Sands of Windee*, 74.

And yet he could present a bold, defiant and almost egotistical portrait of himself, which tended to hide emotional uncertainty, ambivalence and contradiction, and expose vanity:

> "I do not believe I suffer from an inferiority complex. ... I am a proud man, and take pride in my accomplishments and my civilized state. I loathe the dirty, the bestial, the ugly things of human life, and adore the beautiful."[31]

In theoretical terms, Bony is in binary opposition: he is a member of the undecidables, the unclassifiable of strangerhood. Upfield positions his creation as an undefined stranger, a "half-caste" or "hybrid", who nevertheless can cross with ease between black and white classification and retain the values and insights of the in-betweens. Bony's in-between, schizoid world is reflected in the life of the author as the outsider or stranger in many contexts.[32]

The author relished the nickname of "Hampshire" that labelled him an English new arrival to Australia—a "New Chum"—but, on the other hand, he was fiercely loyal to the bush which flows over to his creative work. He wrote in an Australian milieu; his prose is Bush Australian in texture.

There is a great deal of the mystic in the life of both author and his protagonist; they both have carefully chosen friends, yet are not joiners of institutions. We learn that Bony is sceptical of all great world religions, but believes in the fundamental existence of God:

> Of all things spiritually beautiful Bony is a worshipper. A beautiful view, a glorious sunset, and a lovely woman—not necessarily a beautiful featured woman—always won homage from him.[33]

Nevertheless, Upfield was proud of a pair of cufflinks—"plain gold with a pair of manacles engraved on them"[34]—which symbolised his long-standing membership of the American Crime Writers Association. He claimed he was one of the few foreigners admitted to full membership. It was the one institution that Upfield favoured with his suppressed desire to belong.

---

[31] Upfield, *The Sands of Windee*, 211.

[32] Lindsey, "Arthur William Upfield," 17.

[33] Upfield, *The Sands of Windee*, 68. Like Jimmy Little—Mother Earth and Father Time—Bony does not belong to any denomination.

[34] Pamela Ruskin, "Arthur Upfield Makes Crime Pay," 44.

Audacity and Bony as Super-Sleuth

Given the dominant and rigid racist and racial views of 1920s and 1930s Australia, it was an audacious move on Upfield's part to make his "half-caste" detective the central protagonist of his long-lasting series, which he kept alive until his death in 1964. It was not until 1955 that Charles Chauvel released his melodramatic motion film *Jedda* with two central Aboriginal characters, Jedda and Marbuck. In this film, these two people are destroyed in the end by the so-called inevitable consequences of the clash of cultures. While Bony is sometimes in a deadly, dangerous situation, he survives; not only that, he triumphs. Jedda and Coonardoo, in Katharine Susannah Prichard's pioneering novel of the same name, serialised in the *Bulletin* between September and December 1928,[35] are portrayed as tragic figures, reminiscent of the solitary protagonist in Henry Kendall's melancholy colonial poem "The Last of His Tribe" and Truganini, historically the most famous of the Tasmanian Aborigines who became the tragic face of genocide.[36]

Coonardoo is not a fully rounded character but a catalyst influencing others. She is portrayed by a series of vignettes that culminate as "the old gin dying beneath the tree".[37] The symbolism of the last vignette is as doom-laden for Aboriginal culture as that found in the Kendall poem. The vision was one of a sad passing away rather than a coming into being.

In contrast, Bony is a triumphal figure although at times at an emotional cost; he is one of the rare "supermen" of the bush. Through his dualism and his ability to balance the two cultures, he represents the coming into being in contemporary society. There is rich potential in the future and no doom-laden message in his stories.

It is sometimes claimed that Upfield dealt with issues of Aboriginality at a time when this was an under-theorised area of critical knowledge.[38] This may have been so in popular culture in Australia, but most of the relevant material that Upfield used in his novels came from his own personal observations of Aboriginal life and society in different parts of

---

[35] The novel *Coonardoo* by Katharine Susannah Prichard (London: Jonathan Cape, 1929) was published in the same time-frame as the first Bony novels.

[36] See the entry "Trukanini" [*sic*] in Sylvia Kleinert and Margo Neale, ed., *The Oxford Companion to Aboriginal Art and Culture* (Melbourne: Oxford University Press, 2000), 722; also "Aborigines in Australian Literature" in Lindsey, "Arthur William Upfield," 70-81.

[37] J.J. Healy, *Literature and the Aborigine in Australia* (St Lucia: University of Queensland Press, 1989), 150.

[38] Lindsey, "Arthur William Upfield," 1.

remote Australia where he had worked. Like Charles and Elsa Chauvel, the documentary film-makers, sometimes his observations were acutely interpreted, and sometimes they were not; they were at times miscued. They were accurate, in filmic terms, visual evidence of the exotic. Neither Upfield nor Chauvel were professional anthropologists or ethnologists. They were amateurs in the field with their own artistic aspirations and their own documentary mindsets. Upfield deals with Aboriginality as a "singularly polemic subject",[39] but as the recurring statement of Aboriginality in the *œuvre* it is not necessarily "cruelly patronising" at all, although the unfortunate phrases and sentences that creep in from time to time can be used separately to prove otherwise—but only in a polemic sense. His work can indeed be plundered for the politically incorrect.

The claim by Michael Pollak and Margaret MacNabb that Upfield added very little to our understanding of social issues in Australia is a claim that is impossible to sustain. They condemn the author for being an Englishman and for being "cruelly" patronising to Aborigines.[40] They state that a re-reading of the books leads to "grave disappointment".[41] Their assertion demonstrates they have not made a careful reading of the discourse in Upfield's creative writing. And their condemnation is written from a European perspective that is narrowly metropolitan and anti-bush. Upfield tells it like it was for his generation of bushmen. At least, he was an observer-participant in that foreign country of the past and is part of the shaping of national identity. Pollak and MacNabb use "Gothic Matilda" in the title of their published study but fail to recognise the importance of one who spent time "on the wallaby", time that resulted in the creation of a great fictional character—a grave oversight on their part. Another literary critic and cultural historian J.J. Healy completely ignores Upfield in his major study, *Literature and the Aborigine in Australia*, in which he does not even rate a footnote.

Publication and Reception

In an unpublished transcript, Upfield said: "I write because the pleasure it gives me is transcendent."[42] For his part, Lindsey describes Upfield's writing process as follows:

---

[39] Lindsey, "Arthur William Upfield," 7.

[40] Michael Pollak and Margaret MacNabb, *Gothic Matilda: The Amazing Visions of Australian Crime Fiction* (Woollahra, NSW: Unity Press, 2002), 9.

[41] Pollak and MacNabb, *Gothic Matilda*, 35.

[42] Caroline Baum and Janet Bell, prod., "In Search of Bony," DVD, SBS Corporation, 2006. Upfield's voice-over was spoken by actor David Field.

[H]e would paste paper on a board listing the characters and outlining the plot ... Typing away with two fingers and ignoring spelling, he would complete the first draft. This would be put in a drawer for a month.[43]

Time would then be spent on a general reading of the manuscript before a complete re-writing began, uninterrupted, "five hours from one o'clock to six—every day from five to six weeks."[44] The whole process for each book took about seven months. His prolific and consistent output in this genre in Australia has only recently been surpassed by Peter Corris with the publication in 2007 of his thirty-first Cliff Hardy novel, *Appeal Denied*.[45] Recently on National Radio, Corris acknowledged Upfield's contribution to crime fiction decades ago and the lack of interest in the genre itself by Australian publishers. Today, it is the opposite. Crime and crime fiction sell. After all, according to Paul Auster (born 1947), American poet, essayist, translator (French to English) and mystery novelist, crime fiction is one of the oldest and most seductive forms of story writing.[46]

The Bony books were eagerly received by Australian readers.[47] Their lack of a deep knowledge of the land and the Indigenous people made them curious and non-discerning about the portrayal of certain aspects: the clichés, superficial characterisation and misinformation about Aborigines.[48] Nevertheless, the genre is replete with clichés from Conan Doyle to Raymond Chandler. Upfield's literary agent, Pamela Ruskin, admitted that "none of the stuffy old city-dwellers like me had any idea" of the rural life he depicted so colourfully. [49] And realistically, as celebrated on the back cover of the French translation of *Madman's Bend* (*Le méandre du fou*):

---

[43] Lindsey, "Arthur William Upfield," 235-236. This is a method also used by the poet Judith Wright.

[44] Arthur Upfield, letter to Louise Mueller, 17 February 1960, quoted in "Arthur William Upfield," 236.

[45] Ramona Koval, pres., "Australian Crime-Writer Peter Corris," *The Book Show*, Radio National, Australian Broadcasting Commission, 18 June 2007, accessed 28 September 2011, http://www.abc.net.au/rn/bookshow/stories/2007/1954123.htm. It should be noted that our emphasis in this chapter is on detective fiction that showcases an Australian setting. It is for this reason that we are not discussing the prolific output of Carter Brown (pseudonym for Alan Geoffrey Yates), whose novels are, with a few exceptions, set outside Australia.

[46] Paul Auster, quoted in "Des polars des quatre coins du monde," *La Presse*, 26 April 1992.

[47] This is explained by the control that English publishers had (and still have) of book distribution in Australia.

[48] Koval, "The Arthur Upfield Mystery."

[49] Baum and Bell, "In Search of Bony."

"De mince filet paresseux, le [Darling] va gonfler en un énorme torrent dévastateur. Arthur Upfield nous donne là une description tout à la fois fidèle et exaltée d'une nature fantasque et redoutable."[50] Towards the end of her documentary, *In Search of Bony*, Lisa Matthews shows a young, enthusiastic French couple undertaking a long journey in the Outback in a four-wheel drive. They have three Bony adventures close at hand, which they are using as reference books. The cover, with its distinctive emu design, allows the viewer to make out the French translation of *Madman's Bend*. The scene is used as an example of the phenomenal reception of the series by European readers.

No one can deny the authenticity of Upfield's landscapes. Add details about Australia at the time, Aboriginal culture and a singular protagonist, and the allure of the exotic is powerful, almost inevitable. The most popular of the series are those novels that concentrate on these aspects. All twenty-nine novels were published in London, the United States between 1943 and 1983 to favourable reviews on the main, and Germany—all but one in Australia and France, *The Barrakee Mystery*, the first Bony novel. The rights to this novel were not available for French publication as it was "feared that it would be judged racist".[51] Upfield had revised the manuscript several times before publication and for the American publishing house. By the 1950s, eighteen of the novels had been published in eight languages, and by 1996 they were in fourteen languages. Reception of Upfield's work was, and still is, mixed. There is general consensus about evocative landscapes, originality of character and captivating dialogue/voice. For Indigenous historian, Gary Foley, reading Bony in the 1960s made him think more positively about himself as an Aborigine.[52] There was uproar amongst political activists in Australia when *Boney*, the televised series, produced by John McCallum and featuring New Zealand actor James Laurenson, was released in 1972,[53] and indifference when two Bony novels were republished in 1998 by Duffy and Snellgrove.[54] The power of the series had dissipated in modern Australia after a long and successful

---

[50] Arthur Upfield, *Le méandre du fou* (Paris: 10/18, 1999).

[51] Email from translator 8 June 2007.

[52] Baum and Bell, "In Search of Bony."

[53] The series was nonetheless popular in Australia. It was popular, too, in Asia and Europe, especially Scotland, but not in America.

[54] *Death of a Lake*, described as "a story of sexual tension and murder ... probably the best book ever written about drought in Australia"; and *Man of Two Tribes*, with "descriptions of Aboriginal culture and landscape are outstanding": accessed 28 September 2011, http://www.duffyandsnellgrove.com.au. Both have striking covers depicting a dark profile against a colourful outback scene.

innings with readers of popular literature.

The notion has been widely promulgated that the Bony series provided Upfield with a handsome income, allowing him to write full-time. Whether this is true or somewhat exaggerated, prestigious recognition came from the Mystery Writers of America but very little from Australia. In 1947, the *Daily Telegraph* reported that *Death of a Swagman* was the year's "best detective story", featuring "the most important Sherlock".[55] However, Upfield dealt with the lack of recognition from local literati by writing a rather bitter novel, *An Author Bites the Dust*. In it, he satirises not only the literary "giants" in contrast to "popular" authors but publishers and literary journalists as well. In a chapter entitled "The Cosmic Blonde", an undercover Bony listens to some journalistic rhetoric:

> "[Australian] literature is fast growing up, and it is vitally important that the work of our authors should be judged with extreme care, that the grain should be winnowed from the chaff, so that the authors of the future will be influenced by the masters of the present."[56]

The "Bony" books sold in their thousands in America and Europe and relatively well in Australia at the time. Several were re-printed more than once, and E.T.T. Imprint intends to publish them again. In the Angus and Robertson Australian editions of the 1990s, the editorial note reads as follows:

> Part of the appeal of Arthur Upfield's stories lies in their authentic portrayal of many aspects of outback Australian life in the 1930s through to the 1950s. The dialogue, especially, is a faithful evocation of how people spoke. Hence, these books reflect and depict the attitudes and ways of speech, particularly with regard to Aborigines and to women, which were then commonplace. In reprinting these books the publisher does not endorse the attitudes or opinions they express.

When considering Upfield's crime stories, Andrew Milnor, Professor of Social Theory at the State University of New York, poses the question: "Is a writer to write in his time and for his time, or outside of time?"[57] Since the novels are based on the author's vast experiences and acute observations, they have socio-historical value for the twenty-first century and can be

---

[55] *Daily Telegraph*, 27 December 1947, 15.
[56] Arthur Upfield, *An Author Bites the Dust* (Sydney: Pacific Books, 1969), 97. See also 73-75.
[57] Milnor, Andrew, "The Historical Context of Arthur W. Upfield's Bony Novels," accessed 28 September 2011,
http://www.postcolonialweb.org/australia/upfield/milner1.html.

read and re-read today in that light.

Several novels were reprinted several times (including, for example, seven editions of *The Bone Is Pointed*). In 1961, the German publisher, Goldmann, listed Upfield as the second highest seller of the sixty-five crime authors they published, selling about 663,000 copies. 1955 saw the first German publication, *Death of a Lake* (*Der sterbende See* translated by Arno Dohm). The following year, four were translated and published; in 1960, there were six, and between one and three each subsequent year until 1968.[58] The reception heightened each year.

With the first French versions in 1991, *La Mort d'un lac* (*Death of a Lake*) and *L'Homme des deux tribus* (*Man of Two Tribes*), began the exacting task for the translator, Michèle Valencia, of completing at least two books every year.[59] To date, *La Mort* has sold 43,136 copies and *L'Homme* 51,067. Critical comments were positive. All novels sold from 26,000 to 49,000 copies.[60] They were labelled *"fétiches"*; Bony is *"sûr de lui, d'une parfaite politesse et d'un remarquable instinct"*;[61] he is *"affable, patient [et] énigmatique"*,[62] *"un detective 'ethnique'"*,[63] and, according to Patrice Gagnant, he is "a breath of fresh air in crime fiction, a cool oasis in the dry Australian continent and an example of tolerance and generosity".[64] Through him, the reader gets to know and respect the Australian Aborigine. Philippe Meyer claims in his regular literary column that Bony is one of those characters whom the reader anxiously looks forward to meeting again in his next adventure,[65] and *L'Express* points out

---

[58] Pt One: "Published Writings," Arthur Upfield Papers, Melbourne University Archives: 1961: three; 1962: three; 1963: two; 1964: two; 1965: three; and one in 1966, 1967, 1990, 1991 and 1992.

[59] Three books were published in French in 1994; four in 1995; three in 1996, 1997 and 2000; *Pas de traces dans le bush* (*Bushranger of the Skies*), published in 1994, was republished in 2001 and 2002. The series was published in Paris by Éditions 10/18 with Jean-Claude Zylberstein as editor. The only other Upfield book, also translated by Valencia, *The Melbourne Cup Mystery* (1998) / *Le Pari fou de la Melbourne Cup* (2004), was published in Paris by Éditions de l'Aube.

[60] Email from translator 8 June 2007).

[61] "Review of *Le Récif aux espadons*," *Le Soir*, 12 July 2000.

[62] "Des polars des quatre coins du monde," *La Presse*, 26 April 1992.

[63] Jacques Baudou, "Un détective 'ethnique'"; *Le Monde*, 20 February 1995.

[64] Patrice Gagnant, "Napoléon part à la pêche," *Le Progès – Lyon*, 17 September 2000. "Bony, c'est une bouffée d'air pur dans l'univers noir, une oasis de fraîcheur dans l'aridité du continent australien en même temps qu'un témoignage de tolérance et de générosité."

[65] Philippe Meyer, "Le Point de ...," *Le Point*, 29 June 1996.

that each Bony novel has the same *"charme sauvage"*.[66] *Le Retour du broussard* (*Bony Buys a Woman*) was among its choice of thrillers for 1996—*"frissons et insomnie garantie"*.[67] Other aspects and comments by French critics included: *"le rythme lent et prenant"*, poetic description of the *"etrange beauté"* of the country/continent"[68] and *"une superbe leçon d'écologie!"*.[69]

The editor wisely chose Aboriginal dot-point artworks for each book cover,[70] published them in *livre de poche* format, and cited Tony Hillerman as having been influenced by Upfield in presenting each story well-grounded in an authentic landscape and locality.[71] As Indigenous Americans, Hillerman's protagonists use their inherent skills and knowledge to solve each mystery. Hillerman labelled Upfield as "the pioneer of ethnological crime fiction" (*"le pionnier du polar ethnologique"*).[72] With France's long history of respect for the genre, sales of the Bony series were incredible: according to *Libération*, they sell like hot cakes.[73]

In the German editions, there appear lists of characters for each novel—name and what they do or who they are—which are followed by stating the location. Striking black and red covers with white tides bear stylised images, and for the later editions more realistic ones. For the American reader, Andrew Milnor published a list of "local additions to standard English" used by Upfield in two of his novels. Milnor states that this is a "standard postcolonial technique" that forces the outsider/reader to learn about the culture presented.[74]

Not only is the choice of the cover design significant but also the title given to each work and chapters. Both are imbued with linguistic and cultural connotations. For example, *The Barrakee Mystery* was changed to

---

[66] Michel Grisolia, "Sept noirs pour nuits blanches; *L'Express* (16 May 1996) 122.

[67] Culture/Livres, *L'Express* (16 May 1996), 112.

[68] "Des polars", *La Presse*; Gagnant, "Napoléon part à la pêche."

[69] "En d'étranges contrées", *Le Progrès – Lyon*, 13 November 1998 (*Du crime au bourreau*).

[70] Arnhem Land artist, George Milpurrurru, *Blackheaded Python* (*Le Monstre du lac Frome*); Terry Pollard Tjampitjinpa, *Dream of the Serpent at Lampintja* (*Bony et le sauvage blanc*); Western Desert artist, Daisy Napanangka Nelson, *The Dream of the Rainbow Serpent* (*La Loi de la tribu*)—details only.

[71] Joe Leaphorn and Jim Chee are his two Navajo cops first introduced in 1970.

[72] Arthur Upfield, *Le Monstre du lac Frome* (Paris: 10/18, 1995), 6.

[73] *Libération*, 17 May 2007, "Les enquêtes ... d'Arthur Upfield se vendent comme des petits pains," accessed 24 June 2007, http://www.liberation.fr.

[74] Andrew Milnor and George P. Landow, "Undefined Australian Vocabulary in Arthur W. Upfield's Detective Fiction," July 2003, accessed 28 September 2011, http://www.postcolonialweb.org/australia/upfield/1.html.

The Lure of the Bush in America, and *Bony and der Bumerang* (Bony and the Boomerang); *Mr Jelly's Business* as *Murder Down Under* (US); *Bony Buys a Woman* as *The Bushman who Came Back* (US); *Journey to the Hangman* was re-titled *Bony and the Mouse*; *The Mountains Have a Secret* as *Crime au sommet* (Crime at the Top) and *Tödlicher Kult* (Deadly Cult); *The Lake Frome Monster* as *Gefahr für Bony* (Risk for Bony). Several editions, after the televised series went to air, carried the word "Boney" in the title, along with an image from the series.

The serialisation of the stories in newspapers before their publication in book form and readings on the radio also contributed to healthy sales. These included among others *Mr Jelly's Business*, *Wings above the Diamantina*, *Venom House*, *Death of a Lake*, *The Battling Prophet*, and the *Toronto Star Weekly* of 14 February 1948 published a complete novel, *The Bone Is Pointed*.[75]

Language and Referends

Arthur Upfield's writing style was variously described as being "somewhat antiquated",[76] "vividly" descriptive, stilted, gauche, coarse, fast, slow, full of vitality, fluid, competent, economic, "crisp and simple".[77] No matter how differing these reactions to his style, his forte lies in his evocative and enduring images, and his conscious depiction of contemporary spoken language, resulting in strong portrayals of individual characters. Indigenous author Philip McLaren, however, found that the dialogues were far too verbose and therefore somewhat unrealistic.[78]

There is a "geographical determinism" in the stories, both in dialogue and description.[79] And from each story, the reader retains an unforgettable image or character. Such as the discovery of the sapphire brought to the earth's surface by ants (*The Sands of Windee*); the frenzied rabbit migration (*The Bone Is Pointed*); the frantic crossing on horseback of the

---

[75] The complete novel was published across pages 1-15, four columns per page, and divided into chapters I—XXIII.

[76] *New York Times Book Review*, 20 June 1965, 25.

[77] Geoffrey Dutton, "Arthur W. Upfield: Man of Two Tribes," *The Australian Collection: Australia's Greatest Books* (London: Angus & Robertson, 1966), 223-6. In this highly praising review, Dutton likens the novel, because of its symbolic dimensions, to Patrick White's *Voss*.

[78] Koval, "The Arthur Upfield Mystery."

[79] George Landow, "Confusions of Racial Identity in Arthur W. Upfield's Detective Fiction," accessed 28 September 2011, http://www.postcolonialweb.org/australia/upfield/2.html.

rising flood waters of the Paroo River (*The Barrakee Mystery*); the difficult track across the mudflats of the dry inland sea-bed: "A something rose and subsided erratically ... Great mud blisters rose and sank without bursting ... as though the skin was stretched taut with pus";[80] the piles of seaweed and the unpredictable giant waves of the Western coast (*Bony and the White Savage*); the process of pointing and un-pointing the bone; the unrelenting, scorching heat of the arid interior; mission influences on Aborigines and legends (*Bony Buys a Woman*); and the sensual ritual in honour of a lost lover (*Bony and the White Savage*).

In authentic crime-fiction style, there is a certain intratexuality, where reference is made to other crime mysteries in other novels of the series that Bony has managed to solve with the help of Time. Some have even brought him near to death. The works are rich with allusions to Biblical, Greco-Roman and Indigenous mythologies, to figures in English and American literature (especially the works of Shakespeare)[81] and cinema, and to historical places and events. Humour is also a marked characteristic of the stories, together with typical colourful bush colloquialisms, the slow drawl of rural folk, the ungrammatical sentence structure of the migrant and the Pidgin-English of the Aborigines. Small of stature, bullock-driver Blair explains his supposed part in the murder of an Aborigine:

> "I grabbed the maids' step-ladder, took it down to the black, made him stand ... I told you, I murdered the nig by 'itting 'im on the 'ead with a rotten cucumber. I own to it."[82]

Later the policeman retorts: "What beats me is all this hullabaloo about a bloke who knocks a nig."[83]

Dialogue between white and black is depicted in several ways. At times it involves a tribal elder:

> "Jimmy Partner he say you [Old Nero] tellum big fellerblack p'liceman come to Opaltown."
> "Too right, Johnny Boss [Gordon]. Wandin he bin tell it me mulga wire."[84]

At other times, it is the language of a part-Aborigine or a part-anglicised

---

[80] Arthur Upfield, *Bony Buys a Woman* (London: Heinemann, 1967), 191.
[81] For example, the title of chapter eight in *Bony Buys a Woman* is "Much Ado About a Bloodstain".
[82] Upfield, *The Barrakee Mystery*, 40.
[83] Upfield, *The Barrakee Mystery*, 270.
[84] Upfield, *The Bone Is Pointed*, 72.

(civilised) character: "Stay still Misther Ralph ... Bime-by your strength come, and we get out."[85] Bony also speaks this way when addressing other Aborigines: "What for you catch ...? What for you all fight?"[86]

In *The Bachelors of Broken Hill*, the ubiquitous Italian country café owner vividly describes the murder incident: "A customair! In my cafee! He stand, he bend back ovair one of my tables. He fall and breakit da table—smashup."[87] And a proud Australian Swede challenges Bony:

> "Me, I real Australia. All yous New Australians. Not sports. You too soon in Australia to be sports. ... I been in country forty-one year. I real Australia. How long you been in Australia?"
>
> "Forty-one minutes." ...
>
> "Ya! I tink now why you spik like Bob Menzies. What place you born, eh? London?"[88]

Australia and Australians of all types figure large.

A fine thread of French referential language runs through the series in keeping with the protagonist's name, Napoleon Bonaparte; references such as: Waterloo, Javert, Sisyphus, a man murdered in France with coffin dust",[89] Xavier, one of Bony's pseudonyms, that gains the response: "Hell! Bony will do me",[90] Madame Lafarge, Maeterlinck, gargoyles. And the occasional French word appears: *au revoir*; *à la* the detective,[91] "Soup *à la* Bovril. Salted *Boeuf*. Dried vegies *à la* Mildura", *Table d'hôte*;[92] "toot sweet" for *tout de suite*,[93] *en déshabillé* and le mot d'énigma.[94] This Frenchified language contributes to the humour, common in Australian writing, which runs throughout the series.

"As a translator, you have to be bold, because there is always something you [don't know]."[95] This statement by French translator, Michele Valencia, modified her assertion that she had not found Upfield's novels difficult on the whole. Naturally, the major difficulties at first were Australianisms and slang. Since these occur often, she needed to resolve

---

[85] Upfield, *The Barrakee Mystery*, 167.
[86] Upfield, *Bony Buys a Woman*, 142.
[87] Upfield, *The Bachelors of Broken Hill*, 8.
[88] Ed.: Arthur Upfield, *Death of a Lake* (London: Heinemann, 1954), 69.
[89] Upfield, *An Author Bites the Dust*, 173-4.
[90] Arthur Upfield, *Mr Jelly's Business* (Sydney: Angus & Robertson, 1964), 19.
[91] Arthur, *The Mountains Have a Secret* (Sydney: Hinkler, 1991), 130.
[92] Arthur Upfield, *The Lake Frome Monster* (Sydney: Hinkler, 1994), 50.
[93] Upfield, *The Bachelors of Broken Hill*, 131.
[94] Upfield, *Mr Jelly's Business*, 157, 205.
[95] Email correspondence with translator, 8 June 2007.

them quickly. Accuracy in re-creating language register was her primary aim. Understandably this was not always achieved. With the specific readership in mind, she usually adapted images to ensure a naturally fluid text. Each translation had to be completed for publication in a short time, on demand by eager readers, two, three or four months. Since the books were "not meant for specialists", Valencia chose to reproduce in the translations only a few terms, such as "lubra" and some flora and fauna. Explanations were added as footnotes. And how do you translate the game of cricket for a French readership?

Michele Valencia has a doctorate in English and a diploma in translation from the *École Supérieure d'Interprètes et de Traducteurs* in Paris. Her preferred novels are the ones rich in Australian culture, especially Aboriginal mythology, the intricate relationship between land and people, the desert and the bush. She names: *The Bone Is Pointed*, *The Torn Branch*, *Death of a Lake*, *The Man of Two Tribes*, *The Will of the Tribe* and *The Sands of Windee* as those that impressed her most. For her part, Sylviane Soulard chooses *Wings above the Diamantina* (*Les Ailes au-dessus du Diamantina*) as the novel to introduce a reader to Upfield's world. Soulard then lists what she calls *les incontournables*—the books that cannot be ignored. These include five of Valencia's preferred novels (omitting *La Loi de la tribu* (*The Will of the Tribe*)), as well as *Le Retour du broussard* (*The Bushman Who Came Back*) and *La Mort d'un trimardeur* (*Death of a Swagman*).[96] Valencia's understanding was that Upfield's choice of plot, characters and settings was not only based on his personal experiences and intimate knowledge but was influenced by his socio-political stance on issues he considered important in Australia at the time. When the Indigenous people were being depicted by the media as "half-wits", Upfield tried to make his readers understand that "the reverse is the truth".[97]

Conclusion

Over the years, especially since his death, Upfield's portrayal of Bony has become controversial in the political arena for many Aboriginal activists and spokespersons.[98] Unpleasant, derogatory phrases and sentences

---

[96] Sylviane Soulard, "Expression et dissimulation dans le bush," *Correspondances Océaniennes*, 6.1 (2007), 21-24.

[97] Michele Valencia, quoted in "Arthur William Upfield," 147.

[98] Baum and Bell, "In Search of Bony" debates these issues. Some prominent Aboriginal identities interviewed admire Upfield's work as providing a positive image of an Aboriginal superhero at a time when most Aboriginal characters in

from the texts can be justly condemned, but the positive nature of the author's accomplishment in the twenty-nine novels can be unjustly overlooked. Upfield is the first author to place an Aboriginal hero in the centre of his fiction rather than on the periphery as had other Australian writers (like Rolf Boldrewood). Not only that, from the very outset, Bony is presented as a hero, a kind of superman—a man of outstanding physical courage, of superior intellect, an outstanding bushman.

Was Upfield a racist? Such a question needs a separate in-depth study to provide a convincing answer. Our quick answer here is categorically not. However, Upfield carried a number of prejudices about Aborigines that were typical of his day. Even so he never dwells on these, as other contemporary fiction writers did. His strength lay in his ability, through his economic and painterly prose, to evoke the specific Outback landscape that accorded with his particular murder-mystery plotline. He is a deft interpreter of small-town and country-station life, which he maps, textures and patterns in its workaday world. He provides the reader with a pleasing array of eccentric characters who are not merely added, but are an integral part of his imagined landscape and his vision of the world in sparsely populated spaces. Upfield's stance in the Bony series is clearly dependent, as Roland Barthes defined it, as subject to the personal choices he made. And he somehow was just able to avoid the pendulum swing between the Rousseauian "Noble Savage" and the savage representation.[99]

As the French film director Jean Renoir did in his films, Arthur Upfield created in his novels an ordinary, everyday world of characters absorbed with their environment and as seemingly naturalistic as the landscape itself. Upfield, like Renoir, watches his characters in deep focus, giving them space to live and breathe, and in those terms he explores the "rapport between characters and environments" while locating them in the genre of detective fiction.[100] However, like Renoir, he "enlarges the significance of a setting, a countryside or a face",[101] thereby creating his

---

fiction were mercilessly lampooned. Others feel strongly that his depiction of Aboriginal culture is misleading, romanticised and that it does not reflect reality (Lydia Miller, Arts Unit, Australia Council). Some of the discussion centred on the 1970s "Boney" television series, rather than the novels. There was some confusion between the two, with the most telling negative comments relating to the TV series.

[99] Frances Peters-Little, "'Nobles and Savages' on the television," *Aboriginal History*, 2.7 (2003) 17

[100] Ginette Vincendeau, "Noir is also a French Word," in *The Book of Film Noir*, ed. Ian Cameron (New York: Continuum, 1992.), 56.

[101] Claude Beylie, "The Artistry of Jean Renoir," in *Movies of the Thirties*, ed. Ann Lloyd (London: Orbis Publishing, 1983), 184.

main protagonist, Bony, in heroic, larger-than-life proportions.

Like every other writer of merit, Arthur Upfield displays banalities, mundanities and prejudices that make him, as a literary figure, and his books real, yet complex, ambiguous and flawed. In his novels, the treatment of Aborigines and Aboriginality cannot just be explained away by his being a man of his time. His close relationship with the educated part-Aborigine Leon may not have been part of his general experience. As a farm worker, he may have only observed groups of Aborigines from a social and psychological distance, and across the cultural divide of the Outback. However, his work has to be addressed as literary criticism and not only through the polemics of racial politics and political correctness. These, of course, have to be taken into account and the flaws in his writing have to be acknowledged.

Upfield's reception in Europe, especially France and Germany, has revived a strong international interest in his work established earlier in North America. While many of the locations and landscapes in the novels have become progressively familiar to Australians through colourful, popular television documentaries and holiday excursions in four-wheel drives to the most remote parts of the Outback, to the American and European all of this is still at a vast distance and thus remains an exotic fascination to them, fuelled further by the outstanding marketing and distribution of the Bony crime stories.

First Published in *Mostly French: French (in) Detective Fiction*, edited by Alistair Rolls, 93-120. Oxford: Peter Lang, 2009.

Bibliographic reference: *Investigating Arthur Upfield: A Centenary Collection of Critical Essays*: John and Marie Ramsland. "Re-assessing Arthur W. Upfield's Napoleon Bonaparte Detective Fiction." In Alistair Rolls, ed. *Mostly French: French (in) Detective Fiction*. Oxford: Peter Lang, 2009.

BONY AT HOME AND ABROAD:
THE ARTHUR UPFIELD PHENOMENON

CAROL HETHERINGTON

Arthur Upfield (1890-1964) is a unique phenomenon in the literary history of early-to-mid twentieth century Australia. He is the first example in our literary history of a home-grown author with international status: the young twenty-one-year-old from England soon "developed a passionate love for the Australian bush which ... burn[t] until the end"[1] and pervades all his work. Others have been equally popular in Australia —Ion Idriess (1889-1979), Frank Clune (1893-1971), E.V. Timms (1895-1950) and F.J. Thwaites (1908-1979) can all make this claim.[2] But none of these writers featured significantly in the American or European markets. Another Upfield contemporary, Nevil Shute (1899-1960), had and still has a considerable international reputation but this was established well before he came to Australia in 1950, and only a small number of his total output, six of thirty-five novels, have Australian themes or settings. Best-selling author Morris West (1916-1999) belongs to a marginally later period. His first novel was published in 1945 but his major success did not come until the mid 1950s. The incredibly prolific Carter Brown (1923-1985) undoubtedly surpasses Upfield in terms of sheer volume of output and market penetration. But his slick, hard-boiled thrillers are American in plot and setting. There is nothing "Australian" about them. While he is undeniably one of Australia's greatest literary exports, as Toni Johnson-Woods says, "few readers realised that the Americanesque stories were

---

[1] Arthur Upfield, "The Tale of a Pommy", quoted in "Arthur William Upfield: A Biography", Travis Lindsey (Ph.D. thesis, Murdoch University, 2005), accessed 28 September 2011, http://researchrepository.murdoch.edu.au/160, 28.

[2] Thwaites's romance *The Broken Melody* (1930) was immensely popular and was made into a feature film in 1938. Idriess and Thwaites were both published in England; several of Thwaites's romances (three, possibly four, were translated into French and one, possibly two, into Spanish); Timms's 12 novel series The Great South Land Saga was published in the United States (but only in 1975 after Timms's death).

written by an Australian author".[3] Upfield is the only author of his generation to have produced an exclusively and distinctively Australian product which was marketed world-wide, attracting a readership and maintaining a reputation that has lasted from the 1930s up to the present day. However, the nature and extent of Upfield's success both at home and overseas have not been properly explored and fully understood. What was the extent of his success? What sort of people read his books and why? What made him different from other authors of his generation who tried and failed to gain international recognition? Did his novels sell because they are good crime or because they are Australian crime? Is genre or geography the key factor in his success?

Answers to these questions can shed some interesting light on the marketing and reception of Australian literature in a global context. In addressing them I would like to borrow an idea from Professor Jill Roe. At the February 2007 *Association for the Study of Australian Literature* mini-conference in Sydney she gave a paper titled "Six Silly Things People Say about Miles Franklin". One can similarly list three fallacious arguments about Arthur Upfield: that he was virtually ignored in Australia; that he gained entrée to the American market because Australia had become interesting to Americans due to their troop presence here during World War II; that his sensational "tourist thrillers" were produced by the cheap and nasty paperback industry, part of an American cultural imperialism that penetrated markets worldwide.

Fallacy One: Ignored at home

Upfield was as guilty as anyone of perpetuating half-truths and myths about himself. He liked to play up the claim that he was ignored at home and celebrated overseas. Indeed it is a quintessentially Australian complaint, whether in reference to writers, inventors or businessmen. Certainly he was given scant recognition by the "literary establishment". The details of this, although fascinating, are outside my scope here, but it means that an acquaintance with Upfield and his work in Australia is a generational thing. Many younger Australians, including those in the field of literary studies, have either not heard of Upfield or remember him dimly because of a television series broadcast in the 1970s, or even the 1990s, or because of paperback editions of his work on bookshelves in the

---

[3] Toni Johnson-Woods, "The Promiscuous Carter Brown," *Journal of the Association for the Study of Australian Literature* Special Issue (2008):168-183, accessed 28 September 2011,
http://www.nla.gov.au/openpublish/index.php/jasal/article/view/741/983.

homes of their parents or grandparents.

Upfield arrived in Australia in 1911 and wrote thirty-four novels between 1928 and 1964, all with Australian themes and settings, twenty-nine of them in a crime fiction series featuring the part-Aboriginal Detective Inspector Napoleon Bonaparte, "Bony" as he prefers to be called—"all my friends call me Bony".[4] In 1936, Upfield gave up his life in the outback to become a full-time writer. As well as his crime fiction, he wrote feature articles, short stories and anecdotes about outback life, landscape and culture. His work appeared frequently in the pages of newspapers, particularly the *West Australian* and the Melbourne *Herald*, and in a range of popular publications such as *Walkabout*, the *Australian Journal*, the *Wide World Magazine* and the *Bulletin*. Upfield books sold well and in Australia most were also serialised in newspapers or magazines and read as serials on radio. In 1953 a 30-part radio series "Man of Two Tribes" based on Bony novels was produced by Australasian Radio Productions and was broadcast nationally; a selection of episodes was repeated in 1958 and future film and TV productions were contemplated.[5] At one stage (between 1954 and 1955) Upfield and illustrator Robert Sperring explored the possibility of developing a comic strip series of Bony. When the first television series featuring Bony was made in 1972 there were still plenty of people around who could remember the detective. W.G. Cousins, managing director of Angus and Robertson between 1932 and 1950, had aimed to make Bony a "national figure"[6] and one would have to acknowledge that by the end of the 1930s Bony was acquiring that status.

Despite Upfield's sense of injustice at his meagre income and his annoyance with publishers, it does seem that even before his move into the American market he was making a modest living, although shortcomings and inadequacies in local publishing and distribution, and the inherent smallness of the market, were limiting factors. Granted, he had needed to supplement the income from his books with articles for newspapers and magazines but by 1937 he had bought a comfortable house in the Dandenong Ranges, outside Melbourne. To J.K. Ewers he wrote:

---

[4] Arthur Upfield, *Death of a Swagman* (Sydney: Pacific, 1969), 28.
[5] See Arthur Upfield, Letter to Morris West, 13 June 1952, Arthur Upfield Collection, Baillieu Library, University of Melbourne.
[6] Arthur Upfield, Letter to J.K. Ewers, 20 December 1936, quoted in *The Collected Bony Bulletins, Original and Complete*, ed. Philip Asdell, comp. Claudia Stone (Tucson, Arizona: Corgi Publishing, 2007), 190.

The house you visited here I bought last May with an acre of land adjoining and, having thrown the properties into one I have had three additional rooms, a hall and passage added to the house. One of my dreams has come true in this my study, a room 12x12 with double windows and glass doors off the hall, carpets on the floor and a desk and book cases.[7]

Upfield had already travelled a considerable distance from the camel-drawn dray on Western Australia's Number One Rabbit-Proof Fence where he wrote his early novels by hurricane lamp after long days as a patrolman.[8]

By 1942 Angus and Robertson's New York agent had managed to place five novels with Doubleday and the next year three Napoleon Bonaparte mysteries appeared in America—*Mr Jelly's Business* (as *Murder Down Under*), *Wings Above the Diamantina* (as *Wings Above the Claypan*) and *The Mystery of Swordfish Reef*—and Upfield's international reputation began to take shape. Other titles quickly followed at a regular rate. The financial rewards were immediate. In a statement from Doubleday for May 1943, and referring only to royalties for one novel (*Mr Jelly's Business* (*Murder Down Under*)), Upfield received £370 which was almost as much as his annual war-time salary at military headquarters in Melbourne.[9] The trade-mark black Daimler was already in Upfield's mind if not quite yet in his garage.

Fallacy Two: A war-time love affair with Australia

Attributing Upfield's success in the United States to a war-time fascination with Australia has become common. It occurs regularly in the press—for example in recent articles[10] and a television documentary[11] in 2007—and in scholarly commentary. Ray Browne asserts that "American GIs who served in Australia and the Pacific theatre during World War II read Upfield, brought him back with them, and introduced a new author to the United States."[12] Stephen Knight has gone as far as claiming that

---

[7] Upfield to J.K. Ewers, 6 August (completed 14 September) 1937, *The Collected Bony Bulletins*, 191.

[8] Jessica Hawke, *Follow My Dust* (London; Melbourne: Heinemann, 1957), 189-191.

[9] Lindsey, "Arthur William Upfield," 158 -159.

[10] Caroline Baum, "The Case of the Disappearing Detective," *Good Weekend,* 20 January 2007, 26- 29.

[11] Caroline Baum and Janet Bell, prod., "In Search of Bony", DVD, SBS Corporation, 2006.

[12] Ray Browne, "The Ethnic Detective: Arthur W. Upfield, Tony Hillerman and

Upfield's success was "boomed on an aura of American militarism".[13] Another example of a half-truth promulgated by Upfield himself, it originates most probably in some rather vague and fanciful passages in Jessica Hawke's (Upfield's partner's) biography of Upfield[14], written with a good deal of input from Upfield, if indeed not written mostly by him, and in some biographical notes supplied by Heinemann to the *San Franciso Chronicle* in 1950. The latter, which refer to an American serviceman buying every Bony book in the Sydney Angus and Robertson bookshop, are promotional rather than reliable.[15]

An examination of correspondence between Upfield and his publishers would seem to discredit this view. At best the connection between American publication and a burgeoning interest in Australia due to war-time American troop presence is exaggerated. W.G. Cousins had been testing the American market for Upfield since 1937 with no success: Cousins both visited New York himself and worked through agents. He repeatedly notes individuals' interest in Australia and publishers' indifference.[16] Publishers he approached included Simon & Schuster, who turned down *The Bone Is Pointed* in 1939, and Dorrance who had published Upfield's first novel, *The House of Cain*, in 1929. When Cousins sent them *Wings Above the Diamantina* in 1937 they rejected it, saying it had "something of greater Australian than American reading interest".[17] There is no evidence in the files that his efforts were increased as a result of the war. The only reference in the Angus and Robertson records to increased North American interest in Australian writing refers to Canada, not the United States, and comes in a letter from Upfield to Cousins:

Beyond," in *Mystery & Suspense Writers: The Literature of Crime, Detection & Espionage,* ed. Robin Winks & Maureen Corrigan (New York: Scribner, 1998), 1029-46, 1044.

[13] Stephen Knight, *Continent of Mystery: A Thematic History of Australian Crime Fiction* (Carlton South, Vic.: Melbourne University Press, 1997), 191, see also 159.

[14] Hawke, *Follow My Dust*, 234.

[15] Lindsey, "Arthur William Upfield," 156.

[16] See W.G. Cousins, Letters Arthur Upfield, 21 October 1937; 23 January 1938; 24 January 1938; and 14 April 1939, Angus & Robertson Archive, MLMSS3269, Mitchell Library, State Library of N.S.W., Arthur Upfield Folders 1932-1939. Upfield himself on the one hand thanks Cousins for placing the books in America and on the other takes the credit for the idea himself (see Lindsey, "Arthur William Upfield," 156).

[17] Lindsey, "Arthur William Upfield," 137.

A couple of weeks ago I received confidentially a report that the Toronto Star Syndicate ... needed urgently Australian fiction suitable for newspapers, and copies of magazines and papers publishing Australian fiction, for offer over North America. As this indicated to me a sudden wide interest in Australia, I sent them per airmail samples of my short stories and by ordinary mail a copy of Diamantina offering serial rights ... this interest in Australia may have been aroused by the work of our boys in Egypt as well as by the growing number of air trainees in Canada.[18]

It is interesting to compare this passage with its counterpart in Hawke's biography. She writes that

[a]fter the American boys arrived in Australia, another man said: "Look! America is cabling for special articles and stories from Australia, as the people over there are keen to know all about us now their lads are here. Why don't you push some of your books across?"[19]

In any event, nothing seems to have come of this overture on Upfield's part. *Wings Above the Diamantina* appears not to have been serialised by the *Toronto Star* and other, later serialisations of Bony novels by Canadian newspapers were negotiated by Upfield's American agents. Likewise, if increased interest in Australia was a factor in Doubleday's decision to publish Upfield's fiction, I have been unable to find mention of it. The archive in the Baillieu Library contains correspondence both with MCA Management, Upfield's first agents in the United States, and with Doubleday, from the early 1940s to the 1950s. The letters do express personal interest in Australia on the part of the writers but nowhere is there anything to suggest that this is of paramount importance to potential readers. Discussion of characterisation, or the accuracy of small details of plot, is more common than discussion of Australian themes or setting.

Display advertisements in the *New York Times* for the first two titles published in America place no emphasis on the "Australian connection" even when other house titles are advertised in terms of war-time issues—such as their suitability as presents for GIs overseas. A full-page advertisement for *Murder Down Under* in *Publishers Weekly*[20] introduces "Australia's Leading Mystery Story Writer" but this is dwarfed by the large font advertisement for the fact that it is one of two Crime Club selections for the month. In even smaller font towards the bottom of the page is the comment that the book is "Particularly timely right now in

---

[18] Upfield letter to W.G. Cousins 3 Feb. 1941, Angus & Robertson Archive.
[19] Hawke, *Follow My Dust*, 234.
[20] Advertisement for *Murder Down Under*, *Publishers Weekly*, December 1942.

view of Australia's sudden prominence." One would also expect reviewers, at least at first, to make some reference to the issue if it was important as a selling point but this is not the case. The *New York Herald Tribune* reviewer wrote in January 1943:

> "Mr Upfield makes a successful debut in our midst, with promise of more to come ... Not to dwell on the pleasing novelty of the Antipodean setting, *Murder Down Under* is a solid, meaty affair worthy of any fan's attention").[21]

A reviewer of *Wings Above the Diamantina* finds only that "the descriptions of strange flora, fauna and weather phenomena [are] nicely handled [and] will make you grateful for not being rushed",[22] and the influential Isaac Anderson in the *New York Times* complains "the author might have spared us some of the scenic background".[23] Only one reviewer, columnist Dorothy Quick, linked the Australian setting and American troops, commenting that "Australia is very much in the news now and everyone is intensely interested in the country down under. Our boys are there and so we want to know what it's like."[24] And in discussions of marketing the books, there is only one mention of promoting the "cultural tourism" aspect. In August 1948, four titles were advertised "as the Crime Club offer of a vicarious vacation in Brazil, Australia, Paris and New York".[25] It was a departure from usual practice and in this display advertisement the location of Upfield's book is of no greater or lesser interest than the locations in the other three. So though location is undoubtedly important in Upfield's novels, indeed his treatment of place is his strongest claim to

---

[21] Will Cuppy, Review of *Murder Down Under* (*Mr Jelly's Business* in Australia), *New York Herald Tribune*, 10 Jan. 1943, 13.

[22] Elizabeth Bullock, Review of *Wings Above the Claypan* (*Wings Above the Diamantina* in Australia), *Book Week*, 9 May 1943, 8.

[23] Isaac Anderson, Review of *Wings Above the Claypan* (*Wings Above the Diamantina in Australia*), *New York Times*, 16 May 1943, 8.

[24] Dorothy Quick, Newspaper clipping, undated but possibly 1943, Box 1, Arthur Upfield Collection, Baillieu Library, University of Melbourne.

[25] Isabelle Taylor, Letter to Arthur Upfield, 22 June 1948, Arthur Upfield Collection, Baillieu Library, University of Melbourne: "You may be interested to hear that in scheduling MOUNTAINS for August we have in mind a departure from our usual scheduling custom. Heretofore we have endeavoured to spread our books with foreign backgrounds through the whole list but in August we are concentrating them in that one month so that they will be advertised as the Crime Club offer of a vicarious vacation in Brazil, Australia, Paris and New York. Our salesmen seem to be amused by this and think it will stimulate interest in all four books." The display advertisement appeared on 22 August 1948.

"literary status", it does appear to have been relevant to his American success only in so far as it is an important component of the crime fiction genre.

Doubleday's perceived audience were not American servicemen and their families, or a public newly aware of a distant and previously unfamiliar country. They were dedicated crime fiction buffs always eager to meet new fictional sleuths from different backgrounds, whether cultural or geographic. They were not captivated by new locations *per se*: for these readers, Paris was of interest only in the mysteries of Georges Simenon, Oxford only in the work of Dorothy Sayers, Australia only in the adventures of Bony. Crime fiction was big business. The Doubleday Crime Club began in 1928 and operated until 1991. It published a wide range of crime and detective literature and had a huge following. It was part of a crime fiction industry, a close-knit network of crime devotees, publishers, magazines and reviewers, involving Dorothy Gardiner from the Mystery Writers of America, Howard Haycroft from the Detective Book Club, and reviewers like Anthony Boucher, Will Cuppy and Elizabeth Bullock.

Upfield's success was orchestrated by a thoroughly professional organisation. From 1950, after a rift with Angus and Robertson, Doubleday became his main publisher. From 1952 they acted as both his agent and publisher and co-ordinated publications and rights negotiations with their contact in London, Richard Steele, who liaised with Heinemann and handled at least some of the translation rights. Upfield was not a passive partner in all this: the correspondence shows him constantly querying issues of rights and royalties, and he was active in joining professional bodies like the Mystery Writers of America and contributing to their "trade" journal *The Third Degree*. It is clear, though, that commercial success of international proportions was only possible with such a supporting apparatus—comprising editing, publishing, marketing, distribution and reviewing.

Fallacy Three: Fame through "American Paperbacking"[26]

The view that Upfield's American, and therefore worldwide, success derived from sensational "tourist thrillers" mass-produced in cheap American paperback format[27] betrays lack of attention to the publishing history and to the details of literary production in the crime fiction genre.

---

[26] Stephen Knight, "The Case of the Missing Genre: In Search of Australian Crime Fiction," *Southerly* 40.3 (1988), 240.
[27] See Knight, *Continent of Mystery*," 159.

Quite frankly, one also suspects a certain prejudice: all of these terms— "tourist", "thriller", "paperback", "American"—are used pejoratively, not least the term "American", even in scholarly articles. And when the Australian memory of Upfield may be coloured by the crude, and often salacious paperback covers of the 1970s,[28] it is not surprising that one often hears people mistakenly categorise Upfield as a pulp-fiction writer. This blurs the telling distinctions between pulp fiction and popular fiction and obscures differences in the cultural and commercial circumstances of their production. It is important to separate Upfield from a pulp fiction writer such as Carter Brown and from the pulp fiction industry where titles were often completed in a matter of weeks and rushed through production at breathtaking rate.

Wherever they were first published—in Australia, England or America —Upfield's novels were all published first in hardcover editions. The Doubleday Crime Club editions were handsome, well-designed hardbacks. The books also appeared in omnibus editions marketed by subscription book clubs such as the Unicorn Mystery Book Club and the Detective Book Club; these contained works by other notable crime writers like Ellery Queen, Georges Simenon (creator of Maigret) and Sax Rohmer (creator of Fu Manchu). In fact, relatively few English language paperback editions were released in Upfield's life-time—five in the prestigious green and white English Penguin editions between 1949 and 1962 (Upfield was the first living Australian author to be published in Penguin)[29], one in a New American Library edition in 1948 and eight in the US Berkley Medallion Books series in 1963 and 1964, shortly before or just after Upfield's death in 1964. The real proliferation of paperback editions did not begin until the 1970s.[30]

Crime fiction was taken extremely seriously in the United States,

---

[28] The dust-jackets of the English language hard-back editions of Upfield novels are well-designed, attractive and tasteful. Similarly, the American paperback editions have appealing, discreet, unsensational covers. Perhaps contrary to commonly held views, it is the English paperbacks published by Pan (an imprint of Heinemann) from the 1970s onwards that are lurid and often quite crudely and misleadingly suggestive. A good selection can be seen on these websites: accessed 27 September 2011, http://homepage.mac.com/klock/upfield/widows.html; and accessed 27 September 2011, http://www.ouble.com/upfield/bony].

[29] When Penguin's founder, Sir Allan Lane visited Australia in 1953 he made a special trip to Upfield's home at Airey's Inlet near Geelong. See "A Visit to Bony," *Argus* 21 February 1953, 8.

[30] English language paperback editions include Pan editions published in Australia and the UK; Pacific Books, Arkon, Eden and Hinkler editions in Australia; Scribner and Collier editions in the USA.

regarded as a reputable craft. Nowhere is this clearer than in the correspondence between Upfield and his American editor, the head of Doubleday's mystery department, the highly respected and long-serving Isabelle Taylor. She took great pains with Upfield's manuscripts. It is clear that her experience, her careful attention to detail and her thorough knowledge of the craft of crime fiction did a great deal to improve the quality of the finished product. Upfield appears to have taken her criticism well, happily acceding to her requests to make cuts or changes. He responded to her obviously sympathetic reaction to his work and recognised her respect for him as a writer, as well as for his potential readers. The changes and corrections made by Taylor range through details of every kind—the age of a dog in *The New Shoe*, the hair-do of a female character in *Sinister Stones*, the use of Texan slang words by an American character in *The Mountains Have a Secret*, the exact figures for a wool clip in *Venom House*. Choice of titles was one point on which Taylor and Upfield often disagreed. When working on a new book in 1959, he commented: "Doubleday have a habit of calling my books what they like."[31] Sometimes this was simply because a title would mean nothing to an American audience: *Bushranger of the Skies* became *No Footprints in the Bush* because the term "bushranger" was unfamiliar to American readers; similarly *Wings Above the Diamantina* was published as *Wings Above the Clay Pan*. In most cases, however, changes were made for sound literary or commercial reasons, not to accommodate any particular American prejudices. One would have to agree with Taylor's reasoning: she found the title "The Fourth Ring" "unimpressive ... its significance in the story is minor and comes just at the end. What [she asks] do you think of 'The New Shoe' which, by its matter-of-factness as a mystery title, becomes provocative?"[32] *The Mountains Have a Secret* was submitted with the title "Can That Man Be Dead?" Taylor changed the title because "its significance is only apparent after one has finished reading the book. It is very much better selling policy to have a title which is provocative and, at the same time, applicable to the initial problem or mystery with which the book begins."[33]

In 1953 *The Devil's Steps* appeared in Italian and a steady stream of translations followed in more than a dozen languages.[34] As in the United

---

[31] Arthur Upfield, quoted in *The Collected Bony Bulletins*, 29.

[32] Isabelle Taylor, Letter to Arthur Upfield, 21 November 1950.

[33] Taylor to Upfield, 7 April 1948.

[34] The first Upfield novel to be translated was the early, "non-Bony" novel *The House of Cain* which was published, possibly as a supplement, by the Oslo newspaper *Aftenposten* in 1929, but this appears to have been something of an

States, they were all published by houses with a special interest in crime fiction—by Garzanti Libri in Milan and most enthusiastically by Wilhelm Goldmann in Munich. All the Bony novels were translated into German, although not in publication order, and like the Crime Club editions they were initially hardback books on quality paper, only later issued in pocketbook editions. Various anniversary and omnibus editions appeared, including four titles in the Meisterwerke der Kriminalliteratur (Masterpieces of Crime Fiction) series. By 1967 a total of 25 Bony books had been published in German editions. In the 1990s, through the initiative of the German author Gisbert Haefs,[35] the final four titles were issued. Upfield titles were marketed under licence to Goldmann in Switzerland and also in the former German Democratic Republic and even exported back to Australia.[36] The serial rights for *The Widows of Broome* were sold to *Quick* magazine, a popular illustrated weekly, for 11,000 Deutschmarks in 1956. In a 1962 Goldmann publicity leaflet showing the figures for the previous decade, Upfield is placed second in a list of 65 foreign authors. Sales of his books were by then 663,000.[37] Dr Lothar Pützstück, a German scholar and Upfield fan, estimates that even by the 1970s sales would have been well over the one million mark with individual titles selling 100,000 copies and many going through nine editions.[38] Today three German titles are still in print.

French translations came much later, beginning in the 1990s. Of 24 translated titles, 18 are currently in print from Editions 10/18. They are quality paperbacks with attractive covers featuring authentic Aboriginal artwork. Given French interest in Indigenous Australian culture it would be natural to assume that this prompted the publisher to commission the translations. However, Editions 10/18 is also a crime fiction specialist. The impetus for publishing the Bony books came as a result of the firm's success with translations of the work of American mystery writer Tony

---

aberration.

[35] Gisbert Haefs is well known in Germany for a series of non-historical mysteries and several voluminous historical novels. He also writes science fiction and works as a translator (notably of the works of Arthur Conan Doyle) and editor.

[36] In Wilhelm Goldmann, Letter to Arthur Upfield, 2 September 1955, Arthur Upfield Collection. Baillieu Library, University of Melbourne, Goldmann comments that "[m]y firm makes regular shipments to Australian booksellers. Since many Germans have migrated into Australia, the demand for German books is steadily increasing and thus you will find German editions of your novels, too, in Australian bookshops."

[37] Goldmann publicity leaflet, 1962, Arthur Upfield Collection, Baillieu Library, University of Melbourne.

[38] Lothar Pützstück, Email to author, May 2008.

Hillerman, whose work has similarities with Upfield's.[39]

Genre not Geography—Marketing Bony

So what does this tell us about Upfield in the global market? There is compelling evidence to suggest that Upfield's ability to break into the international market and to establish a global reputation was entirely due to the fact that he was first and foremost a crime writer. Without this key qualification it is doubtful that an American publisher would have been interested in more than one or two novels, if that. Indeed, what was needed was to gain the attention of a dedicated crime fiction publisher: as noted earlier Simon & Schuster and Dorrance were not interested in Upfield. But his books were not sensational thrillers like the pulp fiction sold in news-stands; they were carefully crafted and edited products for an essentially middle-brow crime fiction audience. Their "tourist" value, their Australian interest, was subordinate to their detective aspect. Genre not geography was the central factor.

The last Bony mystery was published in 1966 but his story continues. It is no accident that Bony soon became as frequently mentioned as Upfield himself. Even before Upfield's death, Bony took on a life of his own—the detective sent his friends Christmas cards and bookmarks with seasonal greetings and even wrote an introduction to Jessica Hawke's biography of Upfield. Since then his fans have been accommodated by numerous paperback editions in English in Australia, England and the United States and in numerous other languages, the most recent being Vietnamese. Some editions had specially commissioned introductions by critics or well-known crime writers. As well, braille, sound recording and large print publications have appeared right into the twenty-first century. As mentioned earlier, the tales inspired two television series—broadcast in Australia, UK and Germany. In the 1980s a small independent American publisher, Dennis McMillan, republished four early, and virtually unobtainable, works: three non-Bony novels—*A Royal Abduction*, *The House of Cain* and *Gripped by Drought*—and the non-fiction *The Murchison Murders*. The first two had specially commissioned introductions by leading popular fiction writers, crime writer Tony Hillerman and science-fiction writer, Philip Jose Farmer respectively. These were attractive limited editions, designed to be the collector's items they have become.

There were more than enough aficionados and collectors ready to buy

---

[39] I would like to thank Dr Susan Barrett of the University of Bordeaux for sharing information obtained from the translator Michelle Valencia, and for her discussion about French interest in Australian Indigenous culture.

them. From 1981 to 1990 Philip T. Asdell, an American enthusiast, published an occasional newsletter entitled *The Bony Bulletin*. In 1981 the subscription rate was $3.30 for three issues, surface mail world-wide. In all, 33 issues were published. This type of fan publication, while acting as an information exchange for readers and collectors, also attracts contributions ranging from the whimsical to the scholarly, responding to the material, "sometimes amateuristically, but usually with a surprising amount of knowledge and skill".[40] *The Bony Bulletins* include several series of articles such as "Bony Was There" (linking the novels to their physical locations), "Women in the Bony Novels", "Australian Words and Expressions", "Flora and Fauna in the Bony Novels". There are bibliographic lists of various kinds—first editions, paperback editions, translations and a listing, by novel, of the animals most commonly mentioned. There is textual criticism—an analysis of variations between the 1928 edition of *The Barrakee Mystery* and its American edition, *The Lure of the Bush* (1965). One also finds archival correspondence, reprints of critical articles and interviews, and reproductions of newspaper clippings, photographs and book covers. Contributors include crime professionals such as American Betty Donaldson, Australian Upfield fans and collectors, and Swedish fan Klas Lithner, himself a public prosecutor, who recounts his conversion to Bony "fandom" when he bought a copy of *Death of a Lake* displayed in the window of a London tobacconist in 1957.

Not long after the demise of *The Bony Bulletin*, another occasional publication appeared, *Marsupial Mutterings* published between 1994 and 2007 by another American, Jan Finder. Finder himself, although a self-deprecating amateur, convinced the American Association of Australian Literary Studies to include him in their program for its ninth annual conference in 1994 and he presented a paper on Upfield's disputed date of birth. The *Mutterings* contain an item by anthropologist Dr Lothar Pützstück, who has published on Upfield in German, detailing the German editions of Bony novels, an article by Australian post-graduate Travis Lindsey on Upfield and academe, contributions from Australian writers Stuart Mayne and Lucy Sussex, and a discussion about the possibility of a Bony cookbook. *Marsupial Mutterings* is not necessarily finished yet but in the meantime internet sites have stepped in to fulfill the role of the printed newsletter. There are several sites, some interactive, devoted to Upfield and the interest shows no sign of abating. They continue to enhance and enrich the reading experience for their fellow enthusiasts.[41]

---

[40] Ken Gelder, *Popular Fiction: The Logics and Practices of a Literary Field* (London; New York: Routledge), 2004, 6.

[41] One of the most useful is maintained by Australian enthusiast Kees de Hoog and

Since 2007 there have been more comforting signs for Upfield fans. In 2007 Claudia Stone, an exploration geologist from Tucson Arizona, published *The Collected Bony Bulletins*—all 33 issues of *The Bony Bulletin* scanned, bound and with a contents listing, index and introduction. In 2007 Jan Finder, editor of *Marsupial Mutterings*, republished an extremely rare early non-Bony novel, *Beach of Atonement*. Also in this year Kees de Hoog, who maintains the main Upfield website, published the first collection of Upfield short stories, *Up and Down Australia*, with an informative introduction. He followed this in 2009 with *Up and Down the Real Australia*, a collection of autobiographical articles. In April 2008 filming commenced on a new ABC tele-movie initially titled *Blood on the Sand*, later changed to *Three Acts of Murder*, based on the events surrounding the Murchison murders of 1932 when Snowy Rowles, an acquaintance of Upfield's, committed a real-life murder, using the method of disposing of a victim's body featured in Upfield's novel *The Sands of Windee*. The film was released in June 2009. A new biography by American academic Andre Milnor was published in mid 2008.

How then do we categorise the Arthur Upfield phenomenon? I submit that in global terms Upfield is, like Carter Brown, essentially significant as an Australian export rather than an exporter of Australia. Of course there were and will be readers interested in the novels solely for their Australian focus; and for many their total knowledge of Australia stems from these books. But I believe that the reason for their initial success internationally lay overwhelmingly in their very nature as crime fiction. They fitted perfectly into an industry that was well-equipped to deliver them to a ready audience. They were a product eminently suitable for an established market. Ken Gelder in his *Popular Culture* has described the "processing" of popular fiction—the "entire apparatus of production, distribution (including promotion and advertising) and consumption."[42] The Upfield "phenomenon" has all the characteristics Gelder identifies as central to "the logics and practices" of this literary field, including the prime importance of the investigator, the serialisation of this figure through a number of works regularly produced, the "generic endorsement" of the product by other practitioners in the field, and the generation of "cultural capital" through the growth of a "para-academic" apparatus of magazines and sites devoted to the author or genre. The continuing growth of the Upfield phenomenon is a distinguishing feature of the self-perpetuating

---

is archived regularly by the National Library of Australia's PANDORA archive. It has links to a number of other sites: accessed 28 September 2011: https://sites.google.com/site/upfieldbony/.
[42] Ken Gelder, *Popular Fiction*, 75.

literary field of popular genre fiction, exemplified in the tribute titled "Arthur Upfield: The Man Who Started It" made by American mystery writer Tony Hillerman, who read Bony books as a boy in Oklahoma in the 1950s: "When my own Jim Chee of the Navajo Tribal Police unravels a mystery ... when he reads the signs left in the sandy bottom of a reservation arroyo, he is walking in the tracks made by Bony 50 years ago."[43]

First Published in *Journal of the Association for the Study of Australian Literature*, Special Edition 2009. Accessed 25 September 2011, http://www.nla.gov.au/openpublish/index.php/jasal/article/view/869. Reprinted with permission of the Association. Minor revisions made by the author.

The research for this article was supported through Professor David Carter's 2006 ARC grant "America Publishes Australia: Australian Books and American Publishers, 1890-2005".

---

[43] Tony Hillerman, "Arthur Upfield: The Man Who Started It," in *A Royal Abduction*, by Arthur Upfield (San Francisco: Dennis McMillan, 1984), vi.

APPENDIX 1

THE PUBLISHED WORKS OF ARTHUR UPFIELD

Novels - First Editions

1. *The House of Cain*. London: Hutchinson & Co., 1928.*
2. *The Barrakee Mystery*. London: Hutchinson & Co., 1929.
3. *The Beach of Atonement*. London: Hutchinson & Co., 1930.*
4. *The Sands of Windee*. London: Hutchinson & Co., 1931.
5. *A Royal Abduction*. London: Hutchinson & Co., 1932.*
6. *Gripped by Drought*. London: Hutchinson & Co., 1932.*
7. *Wings Above the Diamentina*. Sydney: Angus & Robertson, 1936.
8. *Mr Jelly's Business*. Sydney: Angus & Robertson, 1937.
9. *Winds of Evil*. Sydney: Angus & Robertson, 1937.
10. *The Bone is Pointed*. Sydney: Angus & Robertson, 1938.
11. *The Mystery of Swordfish Reef*. Sydney: Angus & Robertson, 1939.
12. *Bushranger of the Skies*. Sydney: Angus & Robertson, 1940.
13. *Death of a Swagman*. New York: Doubleday & Co., 1945.
14. *The Devil's Steps*. New York: Doubleday & Co., 1946.
15. *An Author Bites the Dust*. New York: Doubleday & Co., 1948.
16. *The Mountains Have a Secret*. New York: Doubleday & Co., 1948.
17. *The Widows of Broome*. New York: Doubleday & Co., 1950.
18. *The Bachelors of Broken Hill*. New York: Doubleday & Co., 1950.
19. *The New Shoe*. New York: Doubleday & Co., 1951.
20. *Venom House*. New York: Doubleday & Co., 1952.
21. *Murder Must Wait*. New York: Doubleday & Co., 1953.
22. *Death of a Lake*. New York: Doubleday & Co., 1954.
23. *Sinister Stones*. New York: Doubleday & Co., 1954.
24. *The Battling Prophet*. London: Heinemann, 1956.
25. *The Man of Two Tribes*. New York: Doubleday & Co., 1956.
26. *The Bushman Who Came Back*. New York: Doubleday & Co., 1957.
27. *Bony and the Black Virgin*. London: Heinemann, 1959.
28. *Journey to the Hangman*. New York: Doubleday & Co., 1959.
29. *Valley of Smugglers*. New York: Doubleday & Co., 1960.

30.   *The White Savage.* New York: Doubleday & Co., 1961.
31.   *The Will of the Tribe.* New York: Doubleday & Co., 1962.
32.   *The Body at Madman's Bend.* New York: Doubleday & Co., 1963.
33.   *The Lake Frome Monster.* London: Heinemann, 1966. Completed posthumously by J.L. Price.
34.   *Breakaway House.* Sydney and London: Angus & Robertson, 1987.*
35.   *The Great Melbourne Cup Mystery.* Sydney: Imprint, 1996.*

Note: Asterisks identify novels without Bony.

Other Works

36.   *The Murchison Murders.* Sydney: Midget Masterpiece Publishing Co., c.1934.
37.   *Up and Down Australia: Short Stories.* Edited by Kees de Hoog. [Morrisville, North Carolina:] Lulu.com, 2008.
38.   *The Gifts of Frank Cobbold.* Edited by Sandra Berry. New Malden, Surrey: Number 11 Publishing, 2008.
39.   *Up and Down the Real Australia: Autobiographical Articles and the Murchison Murders.* Edited by Kees de Hoog. Morrisville, North Carolina: Lulu.com, 2009.
40.   *Up and Down Australia Again: More Short Stories.* Edited by Kees de Hoog. Morrisville, North Carolina: Lulu.com, 2009.

APPENDIX 2

ALTERNATIVE TITLES FOR SOME NOVELS

The Barrakee Mystery	The Lure of the Bush
The Body at Madman's Bend	Madman's Bend
Bony and the Black Virgin	The Torn Branch
Bony and the Kelly Gang	Valley of Smugglers
Bony and the Mouse	Journey to the Hangman
Bony and the White Savage	The White Savage
Bony Buys a Woman	The Bushman Who Came Back
The Bushman Who Came Back	Bony Buys a Woman
Bushranger of the Skies	No Footprints in the Bush.
Cake in the Hatbox	Sinister Stones
The Clue of the New Shoe	The New Shoe
Journey to the Hangman	Bony and the Mouse
The Lure of the Bush	The Barrakee Mystery
Madman's Bend	The Body at Madman's Bend
Mr Jelly's Business	Murder Down Under
Murder Down Under	Mr Jelly's Business
The New Shoe	The Clue of the New Shoe
No Footprints in the Bush	Bushranger of the Skies
Sinister Stones	Cake in the Hatbox
The Torn Branch	Bony and the Black Virgin
Valley of Smugglers	Bony and the Kelly Gang
The White Savage	Bony and the White Savage
Winged Mystery	Wings Above the Claypan Wings Above the Diamantina
Wings Above the Claypan	Wings Above the Diamantina Winged Mystery
Wings Above the Diamantina	Wings Above the Claypan Winged Mystery

SELECT BIBLIOGRAPHY

Books and Essays

Acheson, Carole. "Cultural Ambivalence: Ngaio Marsh's New Zealand Detective Fiction." *Journal of Popular Culture* 19.2 (Fall 1985): 159-174.

Albert, Walter. *Detective and Mystery Fiction: An International Bibliography of Secondary Sources.* Madison, Indiana: Brownstone, 1985.

Asdell, Philip. *A Provisional Descriptive Bibliography of First Editions of the Works of Arthur W. Upfield: Australian, British, and U.S.* Frederick, Maryland: P.T. Asdell, 1984.

Anderson, Benedict. 1991. *Imagined Communities: Reflections on the Origin and Spread of Nationalism.* London: Verso, 1991.

Auerbach, Erich. *Mimesis.* Translated by Willard R. Trask. Princeton: Princeton University Press, 1974.

"Australian Geographical Society Tour to the North-West (Division) of Western Australia," *Walkabout* 30.5 (October 1948): 29.

Barzun, Jacques, and Wendell H. Taylor. Preface to *The Bone is Pointed*, by Arthur W. Upfield. New York: Garland, 1976.

—. Introduction to *The Fly on the Wall*, by Tony Hillerman. New York: Garland, 1983.

Baum, Caroline. "The Case of the Disappearing Detective." *Good Weekend* 20 January 2007, 26- 29.

—, and Janet Bell, pres. "In Search of Bony." DVD, SBS Corporation, 2006.

Bennett, Tony. "Marxism and Popular Fiction: Problems and Prospects." *Southern Review* 15.2 (1982): 218-233.

—, ed. *Popular Fiction: Technology, Ideology, Production, Reading.* London; New York: Routledge, 1990.

Benjamin, Walter. "The Storyteller", in *Illuminations.* Translated by Harry Zohn. New York: Harcourt, Brace & World, 1968.

Benstock, Bernard. "The Education of Martin Beck." In *Essays on Detective Fiction*, edited by Bernard Benstock, 189-209. London: Macmillan, 1983.

Benterrak, Krim, Stephen Muecke and Paddy Roe. *Reading the Country:*

Introduction to Nomadology. Fremantle, W.Aust.: Fremantle Arts Centre Press, 1984.

Beylie, Claude. "The Artistry of Jean Renoir." In *Movies of the Thirties*, edited by Ann Lloyd. London: Orbis Publishing, 1983.

Brewster, Anne. *Reading Aboriginal Women's Autobiography*. Sydney: Sydney University Press, 1996.

Bringing Them Home: Report of the National Inquiry into the Separation of Aboriginal and Torres Strait Islander Children from Their Families. Accessed 23 September 2011: http://www.hreoc.gov.au/pdf/social_justice/bringing_them_home_repo rt.pdf.

Browne, Ray B. *Heroes and Humanities: Detective Fiction and Culture*. Bowling Green, OH: Bowling Green State University Popular Press, 1986.

—. *The Spirit of Australia: The Crime Fiction of Arthur W. Upfield*. Bowling Green, OH: Bowling Green State University Popular Press, 1988.

—. "The Ethnic Detective; Arthur W. Upfield, Tony Hillerman, and Beyond." In *Mystery and Suspense Writers: The Literature of Crime, Detection and Espionage*, edited by Robin W. Winks and Maureen Corrigan, 1029-1046. Scribner Writers Series. New York: Scribners, 1998.

Budd, Elaine. "P.D. James: Ordinary Lives, Extraordinary Deaths." In *Thirteen Mistresses of Murder*, 65-74. New York: Ungar, 1986.

"Bush Whodunits Were Winners." *Parade* March 1970: 4-5, 28.

Cawelti, John G. *Adventure, Mystery, and Romance: Formula Stories as Art and Popular Culture*. Chicago: University of Chicago Press, 1976.

Chambers, Ross. *Room for Maneuver: Reading (the) Oppositional (in) Narrative*. Chicago: University of Chicago Press, 1991.

de Hoog, Kees. *When Bony Was There*. Raleigh, NC: Lulu.com, 2010.

—. "Arthur W. Upfield: Creator of Bony," Accessed 23 September 2011: https://sites.google.com/site/upfieldbony.

Donald, James. "How English is it? Popular Literature and National Culture," *New Formations* 6 (1988): 36-37.

Donaldson, Betty. "Another William Upfield: September 1, 1888— February 13, 1964." *Armchair Detective* 8.1 (November 1974): 1-11.

Duke, Michael. *Detective Inspector Napoleon Bonaparte: His Life and Times*. Newcastle upon Tyne, U.K.: Cambridge Scholars Publishing, 2010.

Dunker, Michael. *Beeinflussung und Steuerung des Lesers in der englischsprachigen Detektiv- und Kriminalliteratur*. Frankfurt: Peter

Lang, 1991.

Dutton, Geoffrey. "Arthur W. Upfield: Man of Two Tribes." In *The Australian Collection: Australia's Greatest Books*, 223-226. London: Angus & Robertson, 1985.

Essen, Louis. "Katharine Susannah Prichard", *Bulletin* 31 March 1927, 2.

Ewers, J.K. "Arthur W. Upfield." *Walkabout* 18 (1 August 1952): 8-9.

Fabian, Johannes. *Time and the Other: How Anthropology Makes Its Object*. New York: Columbia University Press, 1983.

Farmer, Philip Jose. "Upfield's Pre-Osteomantic Novel." In *The House of Cain*, by Arthur Upfield, 1-4. San Francisco: Dennis McMillan, 1983.

Fischer, Katrin. "Arthur W. Upfield's Detective Inspector Napoleon Bonaparte." *Mystery Reader's Journal* 20.4 (Winter 2004-2005): 8-11.

Freud, Sigmund. "Civilization and Its Discontent, 1933." *In The Standard Edition of the Complete Psychological Works of Sigmund Freud*: Volume XXII, translated and edited by James Strachey, 7-158. Harmondsworth: Penguin, 1973.

Gelder, Ken. *Popular Fiction: The Logics and Practices of a Literary Field*. London; New York.: Routledge, 2004.

Gettette, Gérard. Jane E. Lewin, trans. *Narrative Discourse: An Essay in Method*. Ithaca, NY: Cornell University Press, 1980.

Gilbert, Pam. *Coming Out from Under: Contemporary Australian Women Writers*. Sydney: Unwin Hyman, 1988.

Gilroy, Paul. *There Ain't No Black in the Union Jack: The Cultural Politics of Race and Nation*. London: Routledge, 1993.

Gross, John. *The Rise and Fall of the Man of Letters: Aspects of English Literary Life since 1800*. London: Weidenfeld and Nicolson, 1969.

Harpman, Geoffrey. *On the Grotesque: Strategies of Contradiction in Art and Literature*. Princeton, NJ: Princeton University Press, 1982.

Harcourt, David. "The Racism of Arthur Upfield." *Nation Review* 1-7 June 1973, 1009.

Hawke, Jessica. *Follow My Dust! A Biography of Arthur Upfield*. Melbourne: Heinemann, 1957.

Haydon, Tom, "The Last Tasmanian", Sydney: Artis Films, 1978.

"He Followed Fergus Home." *Austrovert* 1 (December 1950): 8.

"He Won't Be a Literary Man." *Readers Review* 10.12 (October 1963): 1, 3, 6.

Healy, J.J. *Literature and the Aboriginal in Australia*. St. Lucia: University of Queensland Press, 1989.

Heseltine, Harry. *Vance Palmer*. St. Lucia: University of Queensland Press, 1970.

Hetherington, John. *Forty-Two Faces: Profiles of Living Australian*

Writers. Melbourne: Cheshire, 1962.

Hillerman, Tony. "Mystery, Country Boys, and the Big Reservation." In *Colloquium on Crime: Eleven Renowned Mystery Writers Discuss Their Work*, edited by Robin W. Winks, 124-147. New York: Scribner, 1986.

Hodge, Bob, and Vijay Mishra. *Dark Side of the Dream: Australian Literature and the Postcolonial Mind.* Sydney: Allen & Unwin, 1991.

Hulme, Peter. *Colonial Encounters: Europe and the Native Caribbean, 1492-1797.* London; New York: Routledge, 1986.

Hutter, Albert D. "Dreams, Transformations, and Literature: The Implications of Detective Fiction." In *The Poetics of Murder*, edited by Glenn W. Most and William W. Stowe, 230-251. New York: Harcourt Brace Jovanovich, 1983.

"In Passing", *Australian Journal* 1 January 1935, 100; 2 December 1935, 1701; 1 February 1937, 238; 1 March 1937, 380; 1 April 1937, 532; 1 November 1937.

Irwin, John T. *The Mystery to a Solution: Poe, Borges, and the Analytical Detective Story.* Baltimore: Johns Hopkins University Press, 1994.

Jaireth, Subhash. "The I in Sally Morgan's *My Place*: Writing of a Monologised Self," *Westerly* 40.3 (1995): 69-78.

Johnson-Woods, Toni. "The Mysterious Case of Carter Brown, or, Who Really Killed the Australian Author," *Australian Literary Studies* 21.4 (2004), 74-88.

—. "The Promiscuous Carter Brown." *Journal of the Association for the Study of Australian Literature* Special Issue (2008), 168-183.

Keating, H.R.F. *Writing Crime Fiction.* London: Black, 1986.

King, Margaret J. "Binocular Eyes: Cross-Cultural Detectives." *Armchair Detective* 13 (1980): 253-260.

Knight, Stephen. "Crime Runs Rampant." *Australian Society* 6.7 (July 1977): 61-62.

—. *Form and Ideology in Crime Fiction.* London: Macmillan, 1980.

—. "The Case of the Missing Genre: In Search of Australian Crime Fiction." *Southerly* 48.3 (1988), 235-49.

—. "Upfield, Arthur William (1890-1964)." *Australian Dictionary of Biography*, 12 (1990) 305-306.

—. Introduction to *Dead Witness: Best Australian Mystery Stories*, edited by Stephen Knight. Ringwood: Penguin, 1989, xx-xxi.

—. "The Vanishing Policeman: Patterns of Control in Australian Crime Fiction." In *Australian Popular Culture*, edited by Ian Craven. Cambridge: Cambridge University Press, 1994.

—. *Continent of Mystery: A Thematic History of Australian Crime Fiction.*

Carlton South, Vic.: Melbourne University Press, 1997.

Koval, Ramona, pres. "The Arthur Upfield Mystery—Bony." *Books and Writing*. Radio National, Australian Broadcasting Commission, 12 May 2002. Accessed 24 September 2011: http://www.abc.net.au/rn/arts/bwriting/stories/s550978.htm.

—. "Australian Crime-Writer Peter Corris." *The Book Show*, Radio National, Australian Broadcasting Commission, 18 June 2007. Accessed 24 September 2011: http://www.abc.net.au/rn/bookshow/stories/2007/1954123.htm.

Kramer, Leonie, ed. *Oxford History of Australian Literature*. Melbourne New York: Oxford University Press, 1981.

Landow, George. "Confusions of Racial Identity in Arthur W. Upfield's Detective Fiction." Accessed 25 September 2011: http://www.postcolonialweb.org/australia/upfield/2.html.

Langer, Beryl. "The Real Thing: Cliff Hardy and Cocacola/Nisation." *South Pacific Association for Commonwealth Literature and Language Studies* 31 (1991): 29-44.

Langford, Ruby (Ginibi). "Introductory Notes to 'Koori Dubays'." In *Heroines*, edited by Dale Spender. Ringwood, Vic.: Penguin, 1991.

Latta, David, ed. *Sand on the Gumshoe: A Century of Australian Crime Writing*. Hornsby, N.S.W.: Random House Australia, 1989.

Lawson, Henry. "The City Bushman." In *In the Days When the World Was Wide and Other Verses*. Sydney; London: Angus & Robertson and Australian Book Company, 1900, 147-57. Accessed 24 September 2011: http://freeread.com.au/ebooks/e00024.txt

Lee, Christopher. *Popular Literature: Study Book*. Toowoomba, Qld.: University of Southern Queensland, 1995.

Lewis, Margaret. *Ngaio Marsh: A Life*. London: Chatto & Windus; New Zealand: Bridget Williams Books, 1991.

Libretti, Tim. "Lucha Corpi and the Politics of Detective Fiction," In *Multicultural Detective Fiction: Murder from the "Other" Side*, edited by Adrienne Johnson Gosselin; 61-82. New York: Garland, 1999.

Lindsey, Travis Barton. "Arthur William Upfield: A Biography.: Ph.D. thesis, Murdoch University, 2005. Accessed 24 September 2011: http://researchrepository.murdoch.edu.au/160/

Terry Lorbiecki, "The Bony Bulletin: Shedding Light on Australian Mysteries," *Menomonee Falls News*, 19 January 1989, 1, 5.

Lukacs, Georg. *The Theory of the Novel*. Translated by Anna Bostock. Cambridge: MIT Press, 1971.

Martin, Murray S. "The New Frontier in Australian Detective Fiction." In *Antipodes* 9.2 (December 1995): 113-117.

McClure, James. *Spike Island: Portrait of a British Police Division*. New York: Laurel, 1980.

—. *Cop World: Inside an American Police Force*. New York: Laurel, 1984.

—. "A Bright Grey." In *Colloquium on Crime: Eleven Renowned Mystery Writers Discuss Their Work*, edited by Robin W. Winks, 167-88. New York: Scribner, 1986.

Michaels, Eric Michaels. "Para-Ethnography." *Art and Text* 30 (September-November 1988): 42-51.

Miller, Morris E. *Australian Literature from Its Beginnings to 1935*. Melbourne: Melbourne University Press, 1940.

Milnor, Andrew J. *Arthur W. Upfield: The Life and Times of Bony's Man*. Newcastle upon Tyne, U.K.: Cambridge Scholars Publishing, 2008.

—. "The Historical Context of Arthur W. Upfield's Bony Novels." Accessed 25 September 2011: http://www.postcolonialweb.org/australia/upfield/milner1.html.

—, and George P. Landow, "Undefined Australian Vocabulary in Arthur W. Upfield's Detective Fiction", July 2003. Accessed 25 September 2011: http://www.postcolonialweb.org/australia/upfield/1.html.

Modjeska, Drusilla. *Exiles at Home: Australian Women Writers 1925-1945*. Sydney: Sirius Books, 1981.

Moore, Tom Inglis. "Australian Literature: 1901-1951." *Australian Quarterly* 23:2 (1951) 57-66.

Morgan, Sally Morgan. *My Place*. Fremantle, W.Aust.: Fremantle Arts Centre Press, 1987).

Muecke, Stephen. *Textual Spaces: Aboriginality and Cultural Studies*. Sydney: University of New South Wales Press, 1992.

Murdoch, Walter. *Walter Murdoch: 72 Essays*. Sydney and London: Angus & Robertson, 1947.

Napier, A. David. *Foreign Bodies: Performance, Art, and Symbolic Anthropology*. Berkeley and Los Angeles: University of California Press, 1992.

Narogin, Mudrooroo. *Writing from the Fringe: A Study of Modern Aboriginal Literature*. Melbourne: Hyland House, 1990.

—. "Westralian Lead." In *Crimes for a Summer Christmas*, edited by Stephen Knight, 25-47. Sydney: Allen & Unwin, 1990.

Nile, Richard. "The Rise of the Australian Novel." Ph.D. thesis, University of New South Wales, 1987.

—. "Literary Democracy and the Politics of Reputation." In *The Oxford Literary History of Australia*, edited by Bruce Bennett and Jennifer

Strauss, 130-146. Melbourne: Oxford University Press, 1998.

Nwachukwa-Agbada, J.O.J. "Interview with Chinua Achebe", *Massachusetts Review*, 28.2 (Summer 1987) 273-285.

O'Regan, Tom. *Australian National Cinema*. London: Routledge, 1996.

Palmer, Vance. *The Legend of the Nineties*. London: Cambridge University Press, 1954.

—. ed. *Louis Esson and the Australian Theatre*. Melbourne: Georgian House, 1948.

Pearce, Roy Harvey. *Savagism and Civilization: A Study of the Indian and the American Mind*. Berkeley and Los Angeles: University of California Press, 1988.

Peters-Little, Frances. "'Nobles and Savages' on the Television." *Aboriginal History* 2.7 (2003).

Pierce, Hazel. "From Poe to the Scientific Detective," in *A Literary Symbiosis: Science Fiction/Fantasy Mystery*. Westport, CT: Greenwood Press, 1983.

Pierson, James C. "Anthropologists as Detectives and Detectives as Anthropologists." In *Murder 101: Essays on the Teaching of Detective Fiction* edited by Edward J Rielly, 166-177. Jefferson, NC: McFarland, 2009.

Pollak, Michael, and Margaret MacNabb, *Gothic Matilda: The Amazing Visions of Australian Crime Fiction*. Woollahra, N.S.W.: Unity Press, 2002.

Pützstück, Lothar. *Das Bild des Fremden im Detektivroman mit völkerkundlichem Inhalt : ein Beitrag zur Diskussion "Anthropology in Fiction" anhand ozeanischer Beispiele*. Bonn: Holos, 1988. 31-52.

Roderick, Colin. *An Introduction to Australian Fiction*. Sydney: Angus & Robertson, 1950.

Roe, Paddy. *Gularabulu: Stories from the West Kimberley*. Edited by Stephen Muecke. Fremantle, W.Aust: Fremantle Arts Centre Press, 1983.

Rolf, Patricia. "With Fame—Some 'Bloody Money'." *Bulletin* 1 December 1962: 16, 18.

Rose, Deborah Bird. *Hidden Histories: Black Stories from Victoria River Downs, Humbert River and Wave Hill Stations*. Canberra: Aboriginal Studies Press, 1991.

Rowley, C.D. *The Destruction of Aboriginal Society*. Ringwood, Vic.: Penguin, 1972.

Rowse, Tim. *After Mabo: Interpreting Indigenous Traditions*. Melbourne: Melbourne University Press, 1993.

Ruskin, Pamela. "Mystery Man of the Outback." *People* 27 August 1952,

12-14.

—. "He Made Australian Crime Pay," *Australian Journal* 1 April 1958: 18-21

—. "Arthur Upfield Makes Crime Pay," *Everybody's* 25 July 1962, 44-45.

—. "Arthur Upfield: "They Still Follow his Dust," *This Australia* 5.3 (1986): 53-58.

—. "Arthur Upfield Made Crime Pay", *Mean Streets* 5 February 1992, 24-30.

Sanders. William B. *The Sociologist as Detective: An Introduction to Research Methods.* New York: Praeger, 1974.

Sarjeant, William A.J. "The Great Australian Detective." *Armchair Detective* 12.2 (Spring 1979): 99-105; 12 (Fall 1979): 358-359.

Shearer, Derek. "Books Offer Clues to Solving the Mystery of a City." *Los Angeles Times*, Travel Section, 5 October 1986.

Shklovsky, Viktor. *Theory of Prose (1925/1929).* Translated by Benjamin Sher. Elmswood Park, Ill.: Dalkey Archive Press, 1990.

Soulard, Sylviane. "Expression et dissimulation dans le bush", *Correspondances Océaniennes*, 6.1 (2007), 21-24.

Squier, Susan. *Babies in Bottles.* New Jersey: Rutgers University Press, 1994.

Spencer, Baldwin. *Wanderings in Wild Australia.* London: Macmillan, 1928.

Smith, Vivian. ed. *Letters of Vance and Nettie Palmer, 1915-1963.* Canberra: National Library of Australia, 1977.

—. ed. *Nettie Palmer: Her Private Journal "Fourteen Years", Poems, Reviews and Literary Essays.* St. Lucia, Qld: University of Queensland Press, 1988.

Stewart, Michelle Pagni. "'A Rose by Any Other Name': A Native American Detective Novel by Louis Owens." In *Multicultural Detective Fiction: Murder From the Other Side*, edited by Adrienne Gosselin, 167-83. New York: Garland, 1999.

Stone, Claudia, comp. *The Collected Bony Bulletins, Original and Complete.* Tucson, Arizona: Corgi Publishing, 2007.

Symons, Julian. *The Detective Story in Britain.* Essex: Longmans, 1962.

—. *Bloody Murder.* London: Faber, 1972.

Tani, Stefano. *The Doomed Detective: The Contribution of the Detective Novel to Postmodern American and Italian Fiction.* Carbondale: Southern Illinois University Press, 1984.

Todorov, Tzvetan. "Typologie du roman policier." In *Poetique de la prose.* Paris: Editions du Seuil, 1971. Reprinted in *Poétique de la prose suivi de Nouvelles recherches sur le récit.* Paris: Editions du Seuil,

1980.

— ."Les deux principes du récit." In *La Notion de litérature et autres essais*. Paris: Editions du Seuil, 1987: 47-65.

Torgovnick, Marianna. *Gone Primitive: Savage Intellects, Modern Lives*. Chicago London: University of Chicago Press, 1990.

Torney (Souter), Kay. "Babies in the Deathspace: Psychic Identity in Australian Fiction and Autobiography," *Southerly* 56.4 (1996-97): 19-36.

Torrance, Robert M. *The Spiritual Quest*. Berkeley: University of California Press, 1994.

Vincendeau, Ginette. "Noir Is Also a French Word." In *The Book of Film Noir*, edited by Ian Cameron, 49-58. New York: Continuum, 1992.

Walker, David. *Dream and Disillusion*. Canberra: Australian National University Press, 1976.

Walker, Terry. *Murder on the Rabbit Proof Fence: The Strange Case of Arthur Upfield and Snowy Rowles*. Victoria Park, W. Aust.: Hesperian Press, 1993.

Wilde, William H., Joy Hooton and Barry Andrews. *Oxford Companion to Australian Literature*. Melbourne: Oxford University Press, 1985-2011.

Winks, Robin W., ed. *Colloquium on Crime: Eleven Renowned Mystery Writers Discuss Their Work, 1-6*. New York: Scribner, 1986.

Wright, Eric. *Death in the Old Country*. New York: Signet, 1985.

Young, Robert. *Colonial Desire*. London: Routledge, 1995.

Archives

The major archives of manuscripts, letters and other documents by and about Arthur Upfield are held in the following libraries in Australia.

1. National Library of Australia, Canberra, A.C.T.
2. Baillieu Library, University of Melbourne, Victoria.
3. Mitchell Library, State Library of New South Wales, Sydney.
4. Battye Library, State Library of Western Australia, Perth.

CONTRIBUTORS

Ray B. Browne (1922-2002) was born in Millport, Alabama. In World War II he served in Europe with an Army artillery unit. He received a doctorate in English and folklore from the University of California, Los Angeles in 1956, and then taught at Nebraska, Maryland and Purdue universities. In 1967, Professor Browne arrived at Bowling Green State University where he founded the Center for the Study of Popular Culture, the *Journal of Popular Culture* and The Popular Press. He later founded the Popular Culture Association and the American Culture Association. He wrote nearly a dozen books and edited more than 40 others. With his wife, Pat, Professor Browne started a major archive at Bowling Green now called the Browne Popular Culture Library. He died in 2002. Ed.

John G. Cawelti taught at the University of Chicago and the University of Kentucky. He has published ten books, among which are *Apostles of the Self-Made Man* (1965), *Adventure, Mystery and Romance* (1976), *The Spy Story* (1987), and *The Six-Gun Mystique Sequel* (1999). He has published many essays and has made oral presentations at more than one hundred universities and scholarly conferences in the United States and abroad. Cawelti's scholarly work has been mainly in the new field of studies in popular culture, where he has been particularly concerned with the analysis of popular genres or formulas.

Ada Coe is a retired professor of Comparative Literature. She is Australian of Italian descent, has lived for many years in the U.S., and likes to travel. She has published on modern playwrights, detective fiction, and has recently turned her attention to her third lifelong passion, opera, taking up the cudgels in defense of that ignored art form: the libretto. Her latest article (unpublished) examines the literary merits of Illica's *Andrea Chénier* (music by Giordano). She recently gave the introductory talk prior to performances of the Sacramento Opera of Handel's *Orlando*.

Tamsin Donaldson (1939-) moved to Australia in 1969 from Britain with a degree in modern languages and ambition to learn an Australian language. Her Australian National University Ph.D. thesis was published as "Ngiyambaa the language of Wangaaybuwan." Liza Kennedy, the main person who winangaybuwan dhii bunmiyi (made me understand), used to say "why did it have to be you, come from overseas, to take a hinterest?" Now I can easily answer "because I needed to feel at home in Australia."

Kees de Hoog (1950-) migrated from Holland to Australia with his family in 1955. He joined what is now the Australian Department of Human Services in 1972, and retired from it in 2011. During that time he completed B.Sc. and M.B.A degrees at the University of Western Australia, and for short periods worked in the Department of Veterans Affairs and the Social Security Appeals Tribunal. As an interest outside of work he has authored the "Arthur Upfield: Creator of Bony" internet pages since 2004, and has published with Lulu.com three anthologies of Upfield's short works, two of Upfield's non-Bony novels, and two related books.

Carol Hetherington is currently employed as Manager of the Bibliographic Information Service within the database *AustLit: The Australian Literature Resource*, and as an editorial assistant for *Australian Literary Studies*. She has worked for many years at The University of Queensland, as a research assistant and bibliographer with the English Department, and as a librarian in the Fryer Library of Australian Literature. Her research interests include bibliography, book history and the American publication of Australian literature. Her most recent publication is "American Friends: Clinton Hartley Grattan and W.W. Norton," in *Reading Across the Pacific*, ed. Robert Dixon and Nicholas Birns, (Sydney: Sydney University Press, 2010), 81-90.

Tony Hillerman (1925-2008) was born in Sacred Heart, Oklahoma and received his early schooling there. He served in World War II and was awarded the Silver Star, the Bronze Star and the Purple Heart. He then attended the University of Oklahoma, and after graduating in 1948, he worked on newspapers and wire service in Oklahoma, Texas and New Mexico. Moving to New Mexico in 1953, he received an M.A. in journalism from the University of New Mexico where he taught for 20 years. His first mystery novel, *The Blessing Way*, published in 1970, was followed by more than 30 books featuring the Navajo culture and Navajo tribal policemen. He received numerous mystery writer awards, the Navajo Tribes Special Friend Award, and the Public Service Award from the U.S. Department of Interior.

Winona Howe received a Ph.D. in English from the University of California, Riverside in 1991. She is Professor of English at La Sierra University in Riverside, California, where she teaches courses in nineteenth-century British literature, children's literature and young adult literature. Howe has published articles on film studies, modern revisions of folk tales, and Victorian authors Wilkie Collins, Charles Dickens, George Eliot, and Elizabeth Gaskell. On a lengthy trip to Australia in 2003, she particularly enjoyed reading some of Upfield's novels in the specific locations that he described so vividly.

Margaret Lewis has a keen interest in the literary study of crime fiction. She published the authorised biography of classic crime writer Ngaio Marsh in 1991, followed in 1994 by a study of Ellis Peters, creator of the Brother Cadfael mysteries. Her career as a teacher and writer took place in the north of England, where, with her husband Peter, she still runs a small independent publishing company, Flambard Press.

Travis Lindsey, married with three adult children, worked for a bank for 38 years in Australia, London and New Zealand. His career was interrupted by national service in the Air Force and for a number of years he also played rugby badly. Upon retirement from the workforce he enrolled at Murdoch University in Perth, completing degrees in literature, including a doctorate.

Murray S. Martin was born and educated in New Zealand where he worked in the National Library Service until emigrating to Canada in 1963. In 1967 he moved to the United States, holding several positions at the Pennsylvania State University and becoming Associate Dean of University Libraries. While there he was a member of the Comparative Literature Faculty and was active in the American Association of Australian Literary Studies. In 1981 he became University Librarian at Tufts University, retiring in 1990 with emeritus status. His publications after retirement included numerous reviews and essays on library subjects and on Pacific Literature. He died in 1998.

Mudrooroo (1938-) Born in Narrogin, Western Australia, he was known as Colin Johnson and published the black bodgie novel *Wild Cat Falling* in 1965. He spent seven years in India, returning to Australia in 1975, and published several novels including *Long Live Sandewarra* (1980), *Dr Woodreddy's Prescription* (1983), *Doin' Wildcat* (1988), *Master of the Ghost Dreaming* (1991), *Wildcat Screaming* (1992), *The Kwinkan* (1993),

The Undying (1998) and *Underground* (1999); a play; and poetry. His works on Aboriginal mythology and literature include *Writing from the Fringe* (1990), *Aboriginal Mythology* (1994), *Us Mob* (1995) and *Indigenous Literature of Australia* (1997). He lived in Nepal for ten years completing an autobiographical cycle.

Richard Nile Ph.D. is Professor of Australian Studies and Director of the Humanities Research Institute at Murdoch University in Western Australia.

James C. Pierson is Professor Emeritus of Anthropology at California State University, San Bernardino, where he taught from 1971 to 2010. He conducted research with Indigenous Australians in the Adelaide area, beginning in 1969, and continues to research and write about these experiences. His later teaching focused on comparisons between the Stolen Generations in Australia and American Indian boarding school students. He also used selected mystery novels in his classes and continues to enjoy reading and writing about crime and mystery novels that emphasize cultural groups and information.

John Ramsland, Emeritus Professor of History (Newcastle), has published sixteen books and over 100 articles on colonial and post-colonial Australia including crime and punishment, sport, war, Aboriginal and children's history. In addition to other recognition, internationally and nationally, he was awarded a Medal of the Order of Australia for his contributions to historical research. He was the longest-serving Dean of the Faculty of Arts at Newcastle University. His latest book, *In the Wake of the Erebus* (Melbourne: Brolga Publishing, 2011), is about the James Clark Ross Antarctic Expedition 1839-1843.

Marie Ramsland (BA, MLitt, PhD) is a conjoint lecturer in French (Newcastle). Her main research interests are French/Australian literary and cultural connections, regional writings by French and Australian authors, and translation (French to English). She was awarded the Chevalier des Palmes Académiques by the French Government in 2003 for contributions to teaching the French language and establishing relationships between France, New Caledonia and Australia. Her translations include *The Culverin* by Michel Tournier, *Hanoi Blues* by Jeanne Cordelier and *The Great Australian Novel: A Panorama* by Jean-François Vernay.

Glen Ross worked in a range of occupations in various industries until, in his early thirties, he enrolled in a Bachelor of Arts degree at the University of Southern Queensland. Seven years later he had successfully completed a Ph.D. in English Literature. He has now left academia and is running his own business.

Pamela Ruskin arrived in Australia with her family in 1926. She graduated with an arts degree from the University of Melbourne, served in the decoding section of the Royal Australian Navy during World War II, and worked as a freelance journalist with a special interest in the arts. She interviewed many famous people and wrote two books, *The Life of Karl Duldig*, the sculptor, and *Invitation to the Dance*, a history of the Australian Ballet School. She contributed regularly to *Australian Jewish News*, and in 1970 won a Walkley Award for an article on Barry Humphries. She died aged 89 in 2010. Ed.

Marilyn Rye is an Associate Professor of Literature, Honors Director, and Associate Campus Provost at Fairleigh Dickinson University in Madison, NJ. She has published on pedagogy, literature by women, and detective fiction. Her essays on detective fiction have focused on authors such as Conan Doyle, Eugene Sue, Ngaio March, P.D. James, Anne Perry, and J.A. Jance. Her most recent essay is on opera in Donna Leon's fiction and is included in a collection to be published in 2012.

Basil Sansom is an anthropologist who has done fieldwork in Sekhukhuneland (South Africa), Libya, Lebanon and Aboriginal Australia. He is Emeritus Professor in the University of Western Australia and an Honorary Research Fellow in the University of Tasmania. Currently he works as a consultant anthropologist in land rights matters. His major publication is *Camp at Wallaby Cross: Aboriginal in Darwin*, AIAS, Canberra, 1980. He won the annual Australian Anthropological Society prize for best anthropological essay in an Australian journal for 2011.

Kay Soutar (Torney) is Associate Dean (Education) and Associate Professor of English in the faculty of Humanities and Social Sciences, La Trobe University, Bundoora. She has published widely in the area of post-Kleinian literary criticism and studies of the family, and has a special interest in the work of W.R. Bion. Her current work concerns social and blended learning, and learning space design.

Russell West(-Pavlov) is Professor of English at the University of Pretoria, South Africa. He has most recently published *Spaces of Fiction / Fictions of Space* (Palgrave Macmilllan, 2010) and *Imaginary Antipodes* (Winter, 2011), and has a book on "Temporalities" forthcoming from Routledge.